CONTENTS

Designing and Teaching Composition Courses *1*

Teaching Writing as a Process *2*
Using *The Little, Brown Handbook* *10*
Working with Student Writing *30*
Using Collaborative Learning with the Handbook *52*
Using Computers to Teach Writing *66*
Teaching Writing to ESL Students *101*

1 The Writing Process *115*

1 Assessing the Writing Situation *116*
2 Developing and Shaping Ideas *127*
3 Drafting and Revising *140*
4 Writing and Revising Paragraphs *153*
5 Designing Documents *171*

2 Reading and Writing in College *177*

6 Writing in Academic Situations *178*
7 Studying Effectively and Taking Exams *181*
8 Forming a Critical Perspective *185*
9 Reading Arguments Critically *199*
10 Writing an Argument *209*
11 Reading and Using Visual Arguments *219*

3 Grammatical Sentences *225*

12 Understanding Sentence Grammar *226*
13 Case of Nouns and Pronouns *247*
14 Verbs *252*
15 Agreement *263*
16 Adjectives and Adverbs *269*

4 Clear Sentences *275*

17 Sentence Fragments *276*
18 Comma Splices and Fused Sentences *281*
19 Pronoun Reference *286*
20 Shifts *290*
21 Misplaced and Dangling Modifiers *294*
22 Mixed and Incomplete Sentences *300*

5 Effective Sentences *305*

23 Emphasizing Ideas *306*

24 Using Coordination and Subordination *312*
25 Using Parallelism *320*
26 Achieving Variety *324*

6 Punctuation *331*

27 End Punctuation *332*
28 The Comma *335*
29 The Semicolon *347*
30 The Apostrophe *352*
31 Quotation Marks *356*
32 Other Punctuation Marks *360*

7 Mechanics *367*

33 Capitals *368*
34 Underlining or Italics *371*
35 Abbreviations *374*
36 Numbers *376*

8 Effective Words *379*

37 Using Appropriate Language *380*
38 Using Exact Language *386*
39 Writing Concisely *393*
40 Using Dictionaries *398*
41 Spelling and the Hyphen *403*

9 Research Writing *409*

42 Planning a Research Project *410*
43 Finding Sources *418*
44 Working with Sources *426*
45 Avoiding Plagiarism and Documenting Sources *435*
46 Writing the Paper *439*
47 Using MLA Documentation and Format *443*
48 Two Research Papers in MLA Style *447*

10 Writing in the Academic Disciplines *451*

49 Working with the Goals and Requirements of the Disciplines *452*
50 Reading and Writing About Literature *455*
51 Writing in Other Humanities *462*
52 Writing in the Social Sciences *465*
53 Writing in the Natural and Applied Sciences *470*

11 Special Writing Situations *475*

54 Writing Online *476*
55 Public Writing *482*
56 Oral Presentations *488*

Designing and Teaching Composition Courses

CHAPTER 1
Teaching Writing as a Process

CHAPTER 2
Using *The Little, Brown Handbook*

CHAPTER 3
Working with Student Writing

CHAPTER 4
Using Collaborative Learning with the Handbook

CHAPTER 5
Using Computers to Teach Writing

CHAPTER 6
Teaching Writing to ESL Students

*These chapters appear only in this Instructor's Resource Manual
and the Instructor's Annotated Edition*

Teaching Writing as a Process

WRITING AS A *HOW*

Drawing on the results of three decades of research into the composing processes of writers, most writing instructors now emphasize the *how* of writing. While theorists such as Lester Faigley and Susan Miller have pointed out the limitations of trying to define systematically what happens when a writer sits down to compose a work, most writing teachers and their students have effectively adapted a focus on the processes through which students generate and revise their writing, rather than focusing solely on a final product. This book is designed to support that focus on the *hows* of writing.

Most writers agree that at least three components contribute to the processes they use most of the time: *prewriting*, the finding and exploring of ideas and the construction of plans for expressing them (in classical terminology, *invention*); *drafting*, getting the ideas down on paper and generating sentences about them; and *revising*, reconsidering the ideas, the treatment they receive, the plans for expressing them, and the ways they are expressed (in classical terminology, *arrangement*, *style*, and to some extent, *delivery*).

Theories about the writing process have focused on the ways in which writers do the following:

- perceive and explore themselves and their worlds through the medium of language;
- consider their subject matter as the occasion for interpretive analysis and as the testing ground for ideas and hypotheses;
- respond to, understand, and to some degree, invent their audiences; and
- position themselves in relation to writerly conventions, to institutional restraints, and to communities within and outside of the classroom.

These assumptions are based on the theories outlined below.

WRITING AS AN EXPRESSIVE PROCESS

Many theories of the writing process from the 1960s and 1970s focused on its expressive content, the attempts of writers to use language to capture and articulate the unique vision of the writer. For instance, D. Gordon Rohman and Albert O. Wlecke argue that techniques such as meditative exercises, journal keeping, and the composition of analogies (called "existential sentences") help writers find a personal truth in even the most abstract of subjects. They argue that such "prewriting" techniques lead in a smooth and linear fashion to drafting and revision as writers refine the expression of the truth they tell. This privileging of self-discovery, what is sometimes called the *expressionistic* or *romantic* view of composing, is also held by Peter Elbow, Ken Macrorie, William Coles, and Donald Murray, to name a few of its most influential proponents. Elbow argues for the efficacy of freewriting and drafting in helping writers explore ideas before worrying about structure and presentation. Macrorie encourages students to use "case histories" of past experiences and to work from direct observation in order to go beyond the obvious clichés, which he calls "Engfish" (because they stink of insincerity). Coles values prewriting because it allows students to explore multiple relationships to readers and subjects (what he calls "plural I's"). Murray emphasizes aspects of prewriting that cultivate surprise, originality, and new combinations of ideas that lead to personal discovery.

The expressionistic theory gives discovery of ideas primacy in the writing process and sees the writer's personal vision as more important than conventions and codes; its emphasis on pre- and freewriting is an attempt to give writers the power to control or even exploit conventions and expectations in the interests of conveying an original vision. These beliefs have thus attracted criticism from those who believe that the teacher's responsibility is to show writers how to become part of a community, not how to put themselves outside it. However, the expressionists' contributions to our understanding of the formative stages of prewriting and drafting and their respect for students as writing colleagues have benefited many teachers and theorists. Ann Berthoff's work is an interesting example of that influence; she draws on the expressionistic emphasis by stressing the power of the imagination to create relationships between ideas, but in "Recognition, Representation and Revision" she also develops an understanding of revision as a nonlinear part of the composing process, an ongoing reconsideration of those relationships. Where many expressionists might insist that pre-writing generates the ideas, that revision is the process of getting them right, and that editing is the radically separate task of adjusting the etiquette of presentation (spelling, punctuation, and the like), Berthoff and others view revision as a recursive process, as the meaningful reconsideration and development of ideas articulated through the grammar of the paragraph and the sentence.

WRITING AS A COGNITIVE PROCESS

A second school of theories about the writing process is deeply rooted in psychology, particularly in studies of cognition. For such *cognitive* theorists, "protocols" (detailed descriptions of how a document is produced) and draft analyses play a key role. One of the earliest such cognitive studies is Janet Emig's. In *The Composing Process of Twelfth Graders* (1971), she studies writing behaviors: how student writers find and develop their ideas. Drawing on James Britton's terminology, she finds that these processes differ with the audience: if students write for themselves (expressively), they are concerned with the presentation of ideas, but if students write for teachers (transactionally), they are concerned (even obsessed) with mechanical correctness. Emig's technique of asking writers to compose out loud has also been used by Sondra Perl in her studies of unskilled writers and by Carol Berkenkotter in her study of a professional writer's composing processes. Nancy Sommers's comparisons of student and experienced adult writers show that experienced writers come to value the development of ideas far more than mechanical correctness, whereas student writers' concern with correctness and with the demands of the writing situation often impedes the development of ideas.

Richard Young, Alton Becker, and Kenneth Pike also developed a cognitive theory of the writing process; however, theirs depends on the writer's knowledge not of the audience but of the subject. Their "tagmemics" theory models cognitive efforts to know a subject; it focuses on how writers perceive a subject's individuality, variability, and place in a larger system. These cognitive efforts should help writers find and develop new combinations of ideas. Like the romantic theories, tagmemics emphasizes prewriting and only discusses drafting or revision as it manifests writers' developing understanding of their subject matter.

The cognitivist position has been most fully expanded by Linda Flower, John Hayes, and their graduate students and colleagues at Carnegie-Mellon University. They view the composing process as a series of decision-making strategies: planning texts, translating those plans into sentences, and revising the texts produced to bring them in line with the original (or reshaped) plans. Although Emig first suggested it, Flower and Hayes and their collaborators have done most to demonstrate the recursive and hierarchical levels of writing processes, especially in the planning and revising stages of writing activities.

Cognitivists find linear expressionist models too simplistic; they argue that writers continually move back and forth between stages to adjust their plans. Like the expressionists, the cognitivists value personal expression highly, claiming it represents most validly an individual's way of thinking. Cognitivists spend little time discussing the finished forms writing may take; it's rare to see an entire piece of discourse reproduced in their discussions. More recently, they have been giving slightly more emphasis to the audience's role in the cognitive workings of writers. But for cognitivists, the writer's "brain work" and reflections on it remain paramount. This position has been challenged as an attempt to systematize the complex cognitive processes of writers and their varying situations. However, cognitive studies have arguably helped teachers to become more attentive to the varied composing processes of individuals and better able to respond to the particular challenges faced by student writers.

WRITING AS A SOCIAL PROCESS

Most recently, as theorists have focused on the social functions of, and constraints on, writing, studies of the writing process have broadened to examine the contexts in which writing occurs, to define the discourse communities in which particular writing processes participate. This broadening has also been influenced by the changing demographics of college populations. As more and more nontraditional students—older or returning, working class, of non-European origin, international—have entered the academy, teachers have been forced to change their expectations about the kinds of knowledge students bring with them. No longer can a teacher take for granted that students know what an essay looks like, or what "thesis and support" are, or how academics think. (Indeed, research conducted by Robert Connors and Andrea Lunsford suggests that an unfamiliarity with the look of the printed page may be responsible for many student "errors.")

Because of the traditional link between writing programs and English departments, one response to this situation has been to teach students the kinds of discourse that scholars trained in literature and its criticism value: journals, poetry, fiction, and literary analysis. But the "social-epistemic" theorists, as James Berlin called them, have argued that the role of writing programs is to prepare students to read and respond to the various specialized languages—academic, legal, governmental—that they might encounter.

Such social theories of the writing process have two current focuses. According to the political focus, represented by David Bartholomae and Anthony Petrosky, Patricia Bizzell, and others influenced to some extent by the Brazilian theorist Paolo Freire, awareness of the constraints of a discourse community is politically liberating, potentially enabling, and revolutionary. If students can understand the constraints of that community and master them, they can come to control and change the community through their own discourse. For theorists who believe this, discovery of the contexts in which students write and the constraints that govern those contexts comes before any other part of the writing process. In terms of classroom practice such theories emphasize a problem-solving format in which students often work with discursive academic prose in peer-group settings and use revision and rereading to establish articulate positions within and against those discourses. A number of contemporary writing texts now employ this multicultural and overtly political approach to collegiate writing.

Another socially focused theory sees writing as a fundamental tool for learning in all communities and at all curricular levels and attempts to foster the teaching of writing beyond the limits of traditional writing programs. In particular, this focus is apparent in "writing-across-the-curriculum" and "writing-across-the-disciplines" movements, which have achieved increasing success in the colleges where they have been implemented. Toby Fulwiler and Barbara Walvoord, two noted proponents of the movement, have both argued convincingly for the benefits of writing instruction beyond the first-year courses. Related "social construction" theories make the case that knowledge is achieved as a consensus among communities rather than as a hierarchical transfer of information from teacher to student. In *Collaborative Learning: Higher Education, Interdependence, and the Authority of Knowledge,* Kenneth Bruffee argues for collaborative student learning as the process through which students become members in their college communities and in communities of knowledge. While social constructionism has been critiqued for its goal of consensus on the grounds that it erases vital differences and competing discourses within communities, collaborative work has become an invaluable part of most classrooms (see for instance the criticisms of Stewart and the recent review by Sullivan).

Ultimately, most teachers adapt the theories and methods that make the most sense given the needs of their students and the shape of their institutional setting. The key effort of this book is to support a range of pedagogical emphases on the composing processes of writers and to help students understand rhetorical forms as flexible frameworks rather than as rigid formulas—as essential parts of a creative composing process.

RESOURCES FOR TEACHING WRITING

Bartholomae, David. "A Conversation with Peter Elbow." *College Composition and Communication* 46 (1995): 62–71.

———. "Inventing the University." *When a Writer Can't Write: Studies in Writer's Block and Other Composing Process Problems.* Ed. Mike Rose. New York: Guilford, 1985. 134–65.

Beach, Richard, and Lillian S. Bridwell, eds. *New Directions in Composition Research.* New York: Guilford, 1984.

Berkenkotter, Carol. "Decisions and Revisions: The Planning Strategies of a Publishing Writer." *College Composition and Communication,* 34 (1983), 156–69.

Berlin, James. "Rhetoric and Ideology in the Writing Class." *College English* 50 (1988): 477–94.

Berthoff, Ann. *The Making of Meaning: Metaphors, Models, and Maxims for Writing Teachers.* Upper Montclair: Boynton/Cook, 1981.

———. *Reclaiming the Imagination: Philosophical Perspectives for Writers and Teachers of Writing.* Upper Montclair: Boynton/Cook, 1984.

———. "Recognition, Representation and Revision." *Rhetoric and Composition.* Ed. Richard L. Graves. Upper Montclair: Boynton/Cook, 1984.

Bizzell, Patricia. *Academic Discourse and Critical Consciousness.* Pittsburgh: U of Pittsburgh P, 1992.

Bloom, Lynn Z., Donald A. Daiker, and Edward M. White, eds. *Composition in the Twenty-First Century: Crisis and Change.* Carbondale: Southern Illinois UP, 1996.

Britton, James. "Theories of the Disciplines and a Learning Theory." *Writing, Teaching, and Learning in the Disciplines*. Ed. Anne Herrington and Charles Moran. New York: MLA, 1992. 47–60.

Bruffee, Kenneth. *Collaborative Learning: Higher Education, Interdependence, and the Authority of Knowledge*. Baltimore: Johns Hopkins UP, 1993.

Clifford, John, and John Schilb, eds. *Writing Theory and Critical Theory: Research and Scholarship in Composition*. New York: MLA, 1994.

Coles, William E., Jr. *The Plural I: The Teaching of Writing*. New York: Holt, 1978.

Connors, Robert J., and Andrea A. Lunsford. "Frequency of Formal Errors in Current College Writing, or Ma and Pa Kettle Do Research." *College Composition and Communication* 39 (1988): 395–409.

Corbett, Edward P. J., et al., eds. *The Writing Teacher's Sourcebook*, 4th ed. New York: Oxford UP, 2000.

Elbow, Peter. "Reflections on Academic Discourse: How It Relates to Freshmen and Colleagues." *College English* 53 (1991): 135–55.

Emig, Janet. *The Composing Processes of Twelfth Graders*. Urbana: NCTE, 1971.

———. *The Web of Meaning*. Upper Montclair: Boynton/ Cook, 1983.

Faigley, Lester. *Fragments of Rationality: Postmodernity and the Subject of Composition*. Pittsburgh: U of Pittsburgh P, 1992.

Flower, Linda. *The Construction of Negotiated Meaning: A Social Cognitive Theory of Writing*. Carbondale: Southern Illinois UP, 1994.

Flower, Linda, and John R. Hayes. "A Cognitive Process Theory of Writing." *College Composition and Communication* 32 (1981): 365–87.

———. "The Construction of Purpose in Writing and Reading." *College English* 50 (1988): 528–50.

Fulwiler, Toby, and Art Young, eds. *Language Connections: Writing and Reading Across the Curriculum*. Urbana: NCTE, 1978.

———. *Programs That Work: Models and Methods for Writing Across the Curriculum*. Portsmouth: Boynton/Cook (Heineman), 1990.

Hairston, Maxine. "Different Products, Different Processes: A Theory About Writing." *College Composition and Communication* 37 (1986): 442–52.

———. "The Winds of Change: Thomas Kuhn and the Revolution in the Teaching of Writing." *College Composition and Communication* 33 (1982): 76–88.

Hayes, John R., and Linda S. Flower. "Writing Research and the Writer." *American Psychologist* 41:10 (1986): 1106–13.

Jarratt, Susan C., and Lynn Worsham, eds. *Feminism and Composition Studies: In Other Words*. New York: MLA, 1998.

Lindquist, Julie. "Class Ethos and the Politics of Inquiry: What the Barroom Can Teach Us about the Classroom." *College Composition and Communication* 51 (1999): 225–47.

Macrorie, Ken. *Searching Writing.* Upper Montclair: Boynton/Cook, 1980.

Miller, Susan. *Textual Carnivals: The Politics of Composition.* Carbondale: Southern Illinois UP, 1991.

———. "Writing Theory: Theory Writing." *Methods and Methodology in Composition Research.* Ed. Gesa Kirsch and Patrick A. Sullivan. Carbondale: Southern Illinois UP, 1992: 62–83.

Moffett, James. *Teaching the Universe of Discourse.* Boston: Houghton, 1968.

Murray, Donald M. *The Craft of Revision.* New York: Harcourt Brace, 1991.

———. *Expecting the Unexpected: Teaching Myself—and Others—to Read and Write.* Portsmouth: Heinemann, 1989.

Newkirk, Thomas. *The Performance of Self in Student Writing.* Portsmouth: Boynton/Cook (Heinemann), 1997.

North, Steven. *The Making of Knowing in Composition: Portrayal of an Emerging Field.* Portsmouth: Heineman, 1987.

Odell, Lee, ed. *Theory and Practice in the Teaching of Writing: Rethinking the Discipline.* Carbondale: Southern Illinois UP, 1993.

Pemberton, Michael A. "Modeling Theory and Composing Process Models." *College Composition and Communication* 44:1 (1993): 40–58.

Perl, Sondra. "The Composing Process of Unskilled College Writers." *College Composition and Communication* 31 (1980): 389–401.

Perelman, Les. "The Context of Classroom Writing." *College English* 48 (1986): 471–79.

Reither, James A. "Writing and Knowing: Toward Redefining the Writing Process." *College English* 47 (1985): 620–28.

Robinson, Jay L. "Literacy in the Department of English." *College English* 47 (1985): 482–98.

Rohman, D. Gordon, and Alberto O. Wlecke. *Pre-Writing: The Construction and Application of Models for Concept-Formation in Writing.* USOE Cooperative Research Project No. 2174. East Lansing: Michigan State UP, 1964.

Rose, Mike. "Rigid Rules, Inflexible Plans, and the Stifling of Language: A Cognitivist Analysis of Writer's Block." *College Composition and Communication* 31 (1980): 389–401.

Russell, David P. *Writing in the Academic Disciplines: A Curricular History.* Carbondale: Southern Illinois UP, 1991.

Sommers, Nancy. "Revision Strategies of Student Writers and Experienced Adult Writers." *College Composition and Communication* 31 (1980): 378–88.

Sternglass, Marilyn. *Time to Know Them: A Longitudinal Study of Writing and Learning at the College Level.* Mahwah: Lawrence Erlbaum Associates, 1997.

Stewart, Donald. "Collaborative Learning and Composition: Boon or Bane?" *Rhetoric Review* 7 (1988): 58–85.

Sullivan, Patricia A. "Social Constructionism and Literacy Studies." *College English* 57 (1995): 950–59.

Walvoord, Barbara E. "The Future of WAC." *College English* 58:1 (1996): 58–79.

Yagelski, Robert P. "The Ambivalence of Reflection: Critical Pedagogies, Identity, and the Writing Teacher." *College Composition and Communication* 51 (1999): 32–50.

Yancey, Kathleen Blake. *Reflection in the Writing Classroom.* Logan: Utah State UP, 1998.

Young, Richard E., Alton L. Becker and Kenneth L. Pike. *Rhetoric: Discovery and Change.* New York: Harcourt, 1970.

CHAPTER 2

Using *The Little, Brown Handbook*

In many writing courses, the writing done by the students in that class serves as the core. The text or texts the instructor chooses should serve as resources to encourage and improve that writing. And the instructor's choice should be based on a clear understanding of the assumptions on which each text is founded.

ASSUMPTIONS SHAPING *THE LITTLE, BROWN HANDBOOK*

It would be foolish to suggest that all composition instructors who emphasize the composing process are in agreement over specific teaching strategies—or that they ought to be. Two teachers who share a belief in the importance of revision or who encourage students to discover ideas and information through freewriting may also disagree strongly about the purposes for writing. Yet it is possible to identify some generally agreed-upon elements of a process paradigm.

The process paradigm of *The Little, Brown Handbook* is based on the following assumptions:

- Writing consists of a variety of activities including *developing* (exploring, gathering, focusing, organizing); *drafting* (finding and expressing meaning, establishing relationships); and *revising* (rethinking, rewriting, editing, proofreading).
- The activities that make up the writing process are recursive, not fixed in order. For example, revising often includes the discovery of fresh insights, and the drafting of one part of a paper may occur at the same time the writer is gathering materials for another part.
- Writing often is a process of discovering ideas, arriving at knowledge of the self, and selecting effective ways to present concepts and information.
- Knowledge of the conventions of expression and of stylistic options is an important part of the writer's repertoire, but a premature striving for correctness and for grace and clarity often can impede the free flow of ideas and the discovery of appropriate form. Thus, activities

such as editing and proofreading, which pay considerable attention to style, grammar, and mechanics, are generally best left until relatively late in the composing of an essay.

- Skilled writers (in contrast to unskilled writers) are characterized by the range of strategies they know and employ in developing, drafting, and revising—strategies that can be both taught and learned.
- Effective writing is the product of interaction among the four elements of the writing situation: author, subject, language, and audience.

These assumptions shape the advice offered throughout *The Little, Brown Handbook*, not only in the discussions of the writing process (Part 1) and of reading and writing in college (Part 2), but also in treatments of research writing (Part 9), writing in the academic disciplines (Part 10), special writing situations (Part 11), strategies for clear and effective sentences (Parts 4 and 5), and diction (Part 8). Even the discussions of grammatical sentences (Part 3), punctuation (Part 6), and mechanics (Part 7) mix firm and relatively conservative advice with an awareness of the demands of various audiences and of the difference between an early draft and a final, carefully edited draft.

At the same time, discussions in the handbook point out that different writing situations may call for different composing processes and that the knowledge of forms for expression—the *what* of writing—is an important companion to an awareness of the *how*. In this the handbook agrees with the work of theorists and teachers such as Maxine Hairston, James Reither, Patricia Bizzell, and Arthur Applebee. These writers share a belief that the process paradigm needs to be augmented by:

- an awareness of the ways the writing process varies according to the writer's purpose and the social context;
- a recognition of the important roles knowledge of form and convention can play in guiding the composing process; and
- an acknowledgment of the extent to which communities of readers and writers are bound together by specific expectations governing the form and content of discourse.

The handbook recognizes that the processes of composing are "strategies that writers employ for particular purposes" (Applebee 106) and emphasizes this perspective in:

- the writing process (Chapters 1–5)
- reading and writing in college (Chapters 6–11)
- discussions of specialized forms of writing:

  research writing (Chapters 42–48)
  writing in the academic disciplines (Chapters 49–53)
  public writing (Chapter 55)
  oral presentations (Chapter 56)

The emphasis throughout is on seeing the forms as the shared expectations of readers and writers and using these expectations to guide the discovery and expression of ideas so as not to constrain creativity.

NEW FEATURES OF THE TENTH EDITION

The tenth edition of *The Little, Brown Handbook* has been revised to meet the needs of today's students, providing a solid foundation in the goals and requirements of college writing and research. Listed below are highlights of the new edition.

- A new Part 2, "Reading and Writing in College," offers coverage of academic writing; study skills and essay exams; critical thinking, reading, and writing about texts and images; reading arguments critically; writing arguments; and reading and using visual arguments.

- Part 9, "Research Writing," continues to emphasize using the library as Web gateway while keeping pace with the methods and challenges of research in an electronic environment. New coverage includes preparing an annotated bibliography, searching library subscription services (with annotated examples), using Web logs as possible sources requiring careful evaluation and documentation, and using images as research sources.

- Chapter 47, on MLA documentation, includes new annotated sample pages from key source types. Other documentation chapters reflect each style's latest version.

- Key computer material is more fully integrated into the text. Managing files, using a spelling checker, and other computer skills are discussed in the context of editing in Chapter 3. Document design, now Chapter 5, concludes the chapters on the writing process and includes more help with using illustrations and a section on designing for readers with disabilities. Other forms of electronic writing—e-mail, Web compositions, and online colaboration—are gathered in Chapter 54, "Writing Online."

- The handbook has a fresh design, with annotations on visual and verbal examples that connect principles and illustrations directly.

- The handbook's many exercises are available in Word format at *www.ablongman.com/littlebrown*.

FAMILIARIZING STUDENTS WITH THE HANDBOOK

Many students have little experience with a comprehensive handbook like *The Little, Brown Handbook,* so it is well worth your time and theirs to review where they can find material, how the book is organized, and how they might use it. Encourage students to personalize the book by marking sections that are particularly useful to them and by keeping an ongoing list of the sections they find themselves returning to for reference or that correspond to their identified patterns of error. The Editing Checklist (pp. 58–59) is a useful place to begin discussions about recognizing common errors, and it also provides a touchstone for your responses to student papers. It is equally important to make handbook usage part of the continuing conversation of the classroom, with frequent, in-class index and content searches, so that the handbook becomes a familiar resource. Such exercises can be a useful accompaniment to group or class-wide revision work on student papers.

Several users of previous editions of this handbook have successfully used a quiz as a means of orienting students to the material it contains. We offer this one with thanks to George Meese of Eckerd College, Florida.

QUIZ FOR HANDBOOK USERS

Your goal is to show me that you can find answers to common writing questions by using your handbook. For instance, if the question is how to paraphrase material from a book in your research paper, you would need to turn to 44d (pp. 617–23). For each question below, list the page or section you would consult to answer this question. For extra credit, answer the question itself.

1. You need to cite an article in the *New York Times* using the MLA system of citations.
2. You can't decide whether to use *that* or *which* in a sentence.
3. You need pointers for writing the introduction for your essay.
4. You can't decide whether to use *rise* or *raise* as the verb in your sentence.
5. You need to know how to type a business letter.
6. You're confused about the difference between *affect* and *effect*.
7. You need to know whether to put a comma before *and* in the phrase *environment, politics and society*.
8. You need to know if the period goes before or after the quotation marks at the end of a direct quote.
9. You have trouble narrowing the topic for your essay.
10. You need to know how to fix a comma splice in your essay.

ORGANIZING A COMPOSITION COURSE

Organizing a composition course means choosing to emphasize those aspects of writing or kinds of texts that the instructor or the department considers most important and that meet the students' needs. Each institution will set its own goals and standards for what students are expected to achieve in a required writing course, and your class must help students meet those goals. This discussion may be particularly useful for inexperienced teachers who are planning a course for the first time.

In recent years, composition teaching has followed several general patterns for organizing a course, including emphasis on:

- patterns of expression and thought,
- the writing process,
- content and ideas, and
- academic writing (writing across the curriculum).

Each approach can be successful if it meets the needs of a particular group of students and if the instructor pays some attention to all aspects of composing.

EMPHASIS ON PATTERNS OF EXPRESSION AND THOUGHT

Many instructors believe that a composition course ought to give students a chance to understand and practice basic patterns of expression and thought. Such courses may vary widely in the patterns they emphasize:

- rhetorical and logical patterns, such as classification, comparison-contrast, and deduction;
- general essay structures, such as thesis and support or general to specific;
- types of essays, such as informative and argumentative;
- patterns of paragraph development;
- sentence patterns.

Courses designed in this fashion are often used as basic writing courses, designed to meet the needs of students who enter college with limited experience in reading and writing. These courses emphasize the writing skills and patterns of thought essential to success in college courses. Although courses of this kind have their roots in "current-traditional rhetoric," an approach that tended to emphasize product over process, they can be adapted to take students' composing processes into consideration. The course might begin with sentence and paragraph construction, moving to longer essay forms as students become more comfortable with different kinds of paragraphs. A process approach would vary the focus from sentence-level constructions to considerations of the student's overall project in the paragraph and in the essay in order to emphasize their interrelated functions.

Organizing the course

In organizing a skills course, you might begin with a unit on sentence structure, drawing on Chapters 12–16 of the handbook ("Grammatical Sentences"), and you might stress an understanding of phrases, clauses, basic sentence types, and verb forms and tenses. Along with this, you might require paragraph-length writing that helps students to understand the functions of those sentence structures, and make use of the extensive discussion in Chapter 4 ("Writing and Revising Paragraphs"). Paragraph- and essay-length writing can continue through the semester, accompanied by work in Chapters 17–22 ("Clear Sentences") and 23–26 ("Effective Sentences"). Chapters on punctuation, mechanics, diction, and usage can be assigned whenever they meet the needs of the class or of individual students. Students might also use the Editing Checklist to keep track of the patterns of error that recur in their writing. In-class sessions can reinforce this practice by focusing on identifying errors in order to create meaningful revisions.

Teaching suggestions

Start paragraphs as early in the semester as possible to give students a sense of accomplishment and a chance to put into practice what they are learning in the sentence units. Also early on, you can incorporate essay-length writings into the course by requiring students to keep a writing journal with a specific number of pages to be devoted to a single topic at least once a week. You can integrate the journals into the class work by having them serve as topics for the students' paragraph and sentence constructions. This helps students to understand the relationship between the function of individual sentences and paragraphs and the overall purpose of an essay.

Other considerations

Although an effective basic course, often planned for developmental students, can focus on sentence, paragraph, and essay patterns, it also needs to pay attention to the writing process and to audience (see Chapters 1, 2, and 3 in the handbook). Students who have trouble mastering the basic forms of expression are also likely to underestimate the importance of planning and revising and to have difficulty shaping their writing to the needs of an audience. Collaborative revision work can help by providing students with immediate feedback from an identified audience of their peers. These matters can also be reinforced throughout the course with assignments that require planning, drafting, and revising and also create realistic audiences and situations for students to address in their writing. For example, the exercises in sections 1d and 1e on audience and purpose can be developed into group projects on which students work collaboratively to create directed appeals to the campus newspaper, to local government, or to a defined public organization.

EMPHASIS ON PATTERNS OF DEVELOPMENT

Rhetorically oriented courses use standard essay types or patterns of development (for instance, comparison-contrast or process analysis) as a means of probing subjects and developing and organizing essays. Instructors who use such approaches share the belief that helping students understand these patterns and practice them in their writing will enable them to use the patterns in a variety of writing tasks. Most of these instructors would also agree that each pattern of development directs attention to a different aspect of a subject and thus the patterns can be seen as shaping the way we think about a subject and as affecting a reader's attitudes. Instructors of rhetorically oriented courses often rely on a reader or rhetoric to provide examples of essay types and patterns of development.

Organizing the course

If you wish to give your course a rhetorical orientation, you may want to begin with Parts 1 and 2 ("The Writing Process" and "Reading and Writing in College") as a way of showing students how to develop, write, revise, and edit an essay and to adapt it to an audience. Later in the course, you may want to return to this material to remind students how important the stages of the writing process are, particularly planning and revising. You can also point out that Chapters 2 and 4 treat the rhetorical patterns as answers to questions about aspects of a topic as well as ways of organizing and developing essays and paragraphs. You might include a unit on essay types or patterns of essay and paragraph development (Chapters 1–4) with assignments that give students a chance to use the forms. The chapters on sentence emphasis, coordination and subordination, parallelism, and variety (Chapters 23–26, "Effective Sentences") can be introduced later in the course to add variety and style to students' writing. The Editing Checklist and the chapters on common sentence errors, punctuation, mechanics, diction, and usage can be assigned according to the needs of individuals or of the class and may also be used for reference. The course might culminate in a research paper (Chapters 42–48) or oral presentations (Chapter 56) or business and community-based writing projects (Chapter 55).

Teaching suggestions

The risk in a rhetorically oriented course is that students will come to regard the various forms as ends in themselves and ignore the role they play in viewing experience and in shaping communication to an audience or situation. For this reason, many instructors emphasize throughout the course the process of exploring subjects and revising the plan for an essay, and they encourage students to create specific audiences and situations to address in their writing. Collaborative work in which students debate topics in class and/or through a Web site can be enormously useful in helping students to work toward particular audiences and purposes. Students also become aware that the forum of the computer link, the face-to-face discussion, and the revised results (which can be "published" for the class) powerfully affects the choices they make as writers.

EMPHASIS ON THE WRITING PROCESS

Some instructors choose to orient their courses around an exploration of the writing process, so that students become aware of the range of strategies and choices available to them as writers and become confident in their ability to respond to future writing tasks. In such courses,

- students are taught to respond to writing situations with a full awareness of the importance of discovering, focusing, planning, drafting, revising, and editing;
- students are given the opportunity to adapt the process to the demands of different kinds of writing;

- forms of expression are presented as strategies best learned in the context of a particular writing task; and
- grammar, punctuation, and mechanics are introduced when necessary for effective communication in an essay.

Organizing the course

In organizing a course that emphasizes the writing process, you might begin by having students look over the discussion of the process in the handbook (Chapter 1, "Assessing the Writing Situation," Chapter 2, "Developing and Shaping Ideas," Chapter 3, "Drafting and Revising," Chapter 6, "Writing in Academic Situations," and Chapter 8, "Forming a Critical Perspective"). You will have to review briefly the writing process as part of each assignment, both to remind students that each of the elements of composing is important and to show how the kinds of planning and revising a writer must do will vary slightly depending on the subject, the aim of the writing task, and the audience for the essay. You may wish to include personal writing as a way to enhance students' awareness of the range of approaches and personas available to them as writers. When you move to more public kinds of writing, however, section 10f ("Reaching Your Readers") will help alert students to the need to take their readers into account as they shape what they have to say and decide how to say it.

Teaching suggestions

Assignments in a process-oriented course should stress planning and revising in all writing tasks and also suggest a range of writing strategies that students can use to deal with a subject and meet the needs of a reader.

If the assigned essay requires particular attention to paragraphing—a persuasive paper, for example—then students might be required to look at Chapter 4 ("Writing and Revising Paragraphs"). Chapters 23–26 ("Effective Sentences") will also help introduce students to useful strategies, and Chapters 42–48 ("Research Writing") and Chapters 54–56 ("Special Writing Situations") can be good resources when students are asked to write for a business or professional audience or to prepare oral presentations. Coverage of matters of grammar, punctuation, diction, and usage will depend on the needs of the class and of individual students.

Since many problems in student writing stem from a lack of effective planning or revising, a composition course that emphasizes process can have a significant effect on student writing. But students need to be aware that word choice, sentence structure, paragraph development, and essay organization also contribute to the effectiveness of writing. Therefore a course that emphasizes the writing process needs to introduce students to the options made possible by formal proficiency (the flexibility that semicolon usage can add to a writer's repertoire, for example—see Chapter 29). Collaborative peer-group revision work supported by the handbook can help student writers to understand the usefulness of formal strategies in communicating the purpose of an essay to an audience.

EMPHASIS ON CONTENT AND IDEAS (THEMATIC COURSES)

In some writing courses, the writing grows out of the students' strong need to communicate about significant ideas and issues. Such courses focus on ideas and issues, whether personal (family life, education, social relationships) or public policy (pornography, the American legal system). The source for content may be an anthology, a lecture series, films, or the students' own research and experience. Although the handbook uses many examples that are thematically organized around the subject of the environment, students working with this or any other thematic content could be encouraged to draw examples from their own writing to consider in conjunction with those offered by the handbook. Instructors looking for a theme around which to organize their own courses may wish to add to the environment-oriented examples in the handbook with a supplemental collection of readings on the environment, or with other locally available material, so that students get more exposure to extended pieces of discourse on this topic. Because students may be unused to working interpretively with discursive prose, exercises that encourage them to practice responding to quotations, individually and in groups, will be particularly useful. See Exercises 44.5 and 44.10 in Chapter 44, especially sections c and d, for exercises that help students to position themselves in relation to the other authors they are using. Depending on the kinds of material that students are reading, the chapters in Part 10 ("Writing in the Academic Disciplines") encourage students to recognize relationships between formal, discipline-based strategies and thematic content. The chapters in Part 2 ("Reading and Writing in College") help students to read and write in academic situations.

Organizing the course

Since instructors who teach such courses generally value the content of a piece of writing most, they cover the forms of writing and the writing process primarily to help students communicate ideas and feelings clearly and effectively. If you choose to emphasize the content of essays in your composition course, you may wish to begin by introducing students to the writing process and the basic forms of the essay with Chapters 1–5 ("The Writing Process"). These chapters suggest ways students can develop their ideas and organize them into paragraphs and whole essays. Chapters 6–11 on academic writing; study skills; critical thinking, reading, and writing; and reading and writing text-based and visual arguments can also help students to analyze the strategies of the writers they are reading and to respond effectively.

Teaching suggestions

As students struggle to express their ideas, you may wish to assign Chapters 37–41 ("Effective Words") to help them communicate more precisely and Chapters 23–26 ("Effective Sentences") to help them add variety, clarity, and style to their writing. The Editing Checklist can be a useful touchstone in helping students to identify patterns of error that recur in their work; students can often use the recognized error (such as comma splices, fused sentences, ambiguous pronoun references) as the occasion for substantive revision. Chapters on punctuation, mechanics, grammar, and usage can be assigned to the class or to individual students according to need. Whether or not students are required to use research in their writing, the discussion of differences among summary, paraphrase, and analysis in Chapter 44 ("Working with Sources") can help students to work effectively with their quoted sources.

EMPHASIS ON WRITING ABOUT LITERATURE

Writing about literature in a writing course

In a writing class that includes literature, many sections of *The Little, Brown Handbook* will be relevant. Students can begin by reviewing the chapters in Part 2 on academic writing; critical thinking, reading, and writing; and argument, as well as the material in Part 1 about beginning a writing project, and then move on to Chapter 50, "Reading and Writing About Literature," which shows how those general skills translate into questions and strategies for reading and writing about fiction, poetry, and drama. Thorough coverage of MLA documentation in Chapter 47 will also be useful, as will the strategies for conducting research in Chapters 42–45. And the high standards of editing usually found in literary texts can profitably be tied to the discussions of sentence-construction problems in Chapters 17–22 and to matters of punctuation in Chapters 27–32.

Writing about literature in literature courses

Many college and university literature courses now stress writing as well as reading, and *The Little, Brown Handbook* can play a vital role in such courses. The guide to writing about literature in Chapter 50 stresses the interplay of critical thinking, reading, and writing as discussed in Part 2, and it shows students how to transfer those skills to the literature classroom. The thorough coverage of style (Chapters 23–26 on fluid and effective sentences, Chapters 37–40 on diction) can be used not only to help students analyze the works of literature they read but also to help them write more effectively about those works. And the material in Chapter 50 on drafting, writing, and revising a literary analysis, along with the sample student paper and thorough coverage of MLA documentation, will prove invaluable to students and teachers in any literature course.

Teaching suggestions

Because of the pressure to cover content issues, many literature classes underemphasize the role of drafting and revision. Assignments that foreground these processes, such as prewriting in response to quotes, in-class work with student drafts, and group revisions of selected paragraphs and single sentences by student writers, will help students to develop and gain confidence in their writing skills.

EMPHASIS ON ACADEMIC WRITING

Writing across the curriculum in a writing course

Chapters 49–53 (Part 10: "Writing in the Academic Disciplines") cover much of the territory appropriate for a course emphasizing writing across the curriculum. Such a course may ask students to write papers in each of the areas covered by these chapters—literature, the humanities, the social sciences, and the natural and applied sciences—and may ask students to become acquainted with the research tools in each area (also discussed in detail in the chapters). The treatment of the writing process in Chapters 1–3; of paragraphing in Chapter 4; of academic writing, essay exams, critical thinking, and argument in Chapters 6–11; and of the functions of sentence structure in Chapters 23–26 can also be important elements of a course built around the varieties of academic writing.

Writing across the curriculum in the disciplines

In many writing-across-the-curriculum programs, writing instruction is part of content courses, employed both as a tool for learning and as a way of sharing knowledge in forms appropriate to a discipline. Because it is designed as a reference tool and therefore does not impose a particular design on a course, the handbook can be a useful resource for content courses emphasizing writing. It provides discussions of the writing process and of research and documentation in specific disciplines as well as resources for editing style, grammar, and mechanics. Whatever the particular uses of writing in a course, the handbook's advice about the process of writing (Chapters 1–3) is likely to prove valuable.

USING THE HANDBOOK WITH OTHER TEXTS

Although the handbook can be used as the only text in a course, many instructors also adopt a reader, a rhetoric, or a workbook such as *The Little, Brown Workbook*. Each kind of text enables you to emphasize different elements of the course and also provides activities to help students develop their writing.

READERS

Readers are generally of three kinds: rhetorical, thematic, or cross-curricular.

Rhetorical readers

Rhetorical readers illustrate different aims and patterns of writing with selections by professional authors and sometimes by students. Readers of this type frequently begin with writing patterns that students find most accessible—narration, description, exemplification—and move on to patterns that students find more difficult to use—classification, comparison-contrast, inductive and deductive argument. Many readers provide extensive introductions to the rhetorical patterns, discussing their uses in writing and the aspects of a subject that they focus on. Some recent rhetorical readers go beyond the basic rhetorical patterns to discuss common forms of nonfiction writing—such as the problem-solution report, the personal essay, the evaluation, and the proposal—that combine the basic patterns in a number of ways. The questions accompanying the essays in most rhetorical readers direct students' attention to the most important features of the models and suggest ways students can incorporate such features in their own writing.

Thematic readers

Thematic readers illustrate and explore a number of themes, such as the stages of personal growth or family relationships, or topics of general interest, such as capital punishment or the impact of technology. The readings may include fiction or poetry as well as essays. If the main purpose for using the reader is to provide subject matter for essays, a thematic reader may be preferable because, as a rule, readers of this type provide several perspectives on a subject and more background information to get class discussion started and give students material to use in their writing.

Some readers are both rhetorical and thematic in organization and coverage, providing a table of contents for each emphasis. Both types of readers can be used to generate class discussion and topics for student writing. Some readers even provide questions to stimulate discussion and include lists of possible topics for papers, as well as bibliographies for further reading and research.

Cross-curricular readers

Cross-curricular readers typically provide examples of writing in a variety of disciplines and cover a range of topics. Some include essays directed to general readers as well as specialists. Others focus on the kinds of writing expected from students or professionals in a discipline. Readers of this kind often emphasize writing as a social process and are designed to help students participate actively within specialized discourse communities. While the primary aim of readers of this type is to provide models of academic and professional prose, some also arrange readings in thematic clusters designed to encourage discussion and suggest subjects for students to pursue in their own writing. Instructors often choose a problem-posing approach to the readings by encouraging students to work on an essay individually and in groups, identifying difficult passages and terms and creating interpretive responses. Classroom practice focuses on student responses to texts, and particularly on the revision process as the means to create meaningful positions in relation to those readings.

Integrating *The Little, Brown Handbook* with a reader

Instructors who adopt a reader typically make discussion of its essays a major activity in the course, yet they also tend to make significant use of a handbook. If the reader chosen for a course does not provide a rhetorical framework for students' essays or a thorough coverage of writing and reasoning processes, instructors using *The Little, Brown Handbook* may wish to direct students to the coverage of these matters in Chapters 1–3 and 6–11. As students begin working with quotation and citation, Chapter 44 on working with sources can become a useful resource, even outside of the research context. The handbook provides explanations and examples of other matters frequently not covered in readers, such as the revision and editing checklists (Chapter 3); paragraphing (Chapter 4); sentence structure, grammar, and style (Chapters 12–26); diction and usage (Chapters 37–40 and the Glossary of Usage); research writing (Chapters 42–48); and writing in the disciplines (Chapters 49–53). In addition, the handbook can be used as a reference guide for punctuation and mechanics, as an aid in marking student papers, and as a guide for revision. Some instructors who use a reader like to devote one period each week to subjects covered in the handbook; others like to set aside part of each day.

RHETORICS

Rhetorics and handbooks

Rhetorics cover many of the same topics as handbooks—discovering, planning, drafting, revising, rhetorical patterns, and paragraphing—but do so in greater depth, at the same time giving less coverage to grammar, punctuation, mechanics, and usage. A rhetoric usually embodies a particular perspective toward writing and the teaching of writing—a theoretical bias, perhaps, or an emphasis on thesis-and-support essays, personal writing, academic writing, argumentation, critical thinking, or tone and style. Since a rhetoric helps determine the emphasis within a course, it provides less flexibility for the teacher than the handbook does, especially if the rhetoric has been chosen by a department rather than by the instructor.

Integrating *The Little, Brown Handbook* with a rhetoric

Because rhetorics provide full coverage in some areas at the expense of others, instructors frequently adopt a handbook as a supplement. Used in this way, *The Little, Brown Handbook* can provide treatment of sentence style (Chapters 23–26), research writing (Chapters 42–46), and writing in the disciplines (Chapters 49–53) for rhetorics that give only brief attention to these matters. It can also provide discussion and exercises for sentence structure and grammar (Chapters 12–22), punctuation and mechanics (Chapters 27–36), and diction and usage (Chapters 37–40 and the Glossary of Usage). The discussions of the writing process, paragraphs, academic writing study skills and essay exams, critical thinking, and argument (Chapters 1–11) can supplement the material in a rhetoric and provide useful exercises.

When the handbook is used with a rhetoric, instructors often assign its chapters and exercises along with those in the rhetoric, and they devote class time to discussing both texts and reviewing the exercises. They also use the handbook as a reference for students, as an aid to grading papers, and as a guide for revision.

THE HANDBOOK'S ANCILLARY PUBLICATIONS

In addition to its companion Web site (see page 73 of this manual), the handbook comes with an instructional package that will meet the needs of many classes.

For students

- *MyCompLab Plus Interactive E-Book for The Little, Brown Handbook* offers a complete, searchable version of the handbook, video and audio clips on key topics, interactive exercises, writing-related Web links, and links through an access code to the *MyCompLab* Web site.

- *MyCompLab* Web site offers one convenient portal to several of Longman's most popular multimedia resources for composition (described below). An access card comes with the interactive e-book CD featuring the entire contents of the handbook.

  Longman Writer's Warehouse for Composition provides guided assistance through the writing process, access to Web-based journals and writing portfolios, diagnostic tests, exercises, and video-based writing assignments.

  Avoiding Plagiarism Tutorial consists of interactive modules on plagiarism, common knowledge, paraphrase, and summary. The tutorial also covers both MLA and APA documentation.

  Research Navigator provides access to a database of thousands of academic journals and general-interest periodicals, the *New York Times* online archives, and several online research tools.

  Longman ExerciseZone offers diagnostic tests to help students identify where they need help along with more than 2500 exercises on grammar, style, usage, and punctuation.

  The Student Bookshelf is an online library of brief e-books in PDF format, including *Public Literacy, Academic Literacy, Workplace Literacy, Visual Communication, Analyzing Literature,* and *Reading Critically.*

- *The Little, Brown Workbook* parallels the handbook's organization but provides briefer instructional text and many more exercises.

- *ESL Worksheets* provide nonnative speakers with extra practice in especially troublesome areas.

- *Research Navigator Guide for English* teaches students how to conduct high-quality online research and to document it properly, provides discipline-specific academic resources and helpful tips on the writing process, and links through an access code to the *Research Navigator* on *MyCompLab.*

- *Take Note!* is a cross-platform **CD-ROM** that integrates note taking, outlining, and bibliography management in one easy-to use package.

- A separate answer key provides answers to all the exercises in the handbook. It is available both in print and online (password-protected).

- *Course Compass* is a proprietary version of *Blackboard,* the course-management resource, augmented with Longman's *MyCompLab.* For instructors already using *Blackboard* or *WebCT*, the *MyCompLab* resources are available as content cartridges for either platform.

For instructors

- On the handbook's companion Web site, instructors can download the password-protected instructor's manual and answer key as well as more than a hundred transparency masters and *PowerPoint* slides that reproduce key boxes and lists from the text.

- *Teaching Online: Internet Research, Conversation, and Composition* is an accessible introduction to Internet resources for teaching writing.

- *Diagnostic Editing Tests and Exercises* helps instructors assess students' standard American English for placement or to gauge progress. The package is available on reproducible sheets or on TestGen EQ, Longman's online testing program.

- An extensive assessment package includes TASP and CLAST exams. All items are keyed to the handbook. The tests are available on reproducible sheets or on TestGen EQ, Longman's online testing program.

- The Longman resources for instructors include six valuable works: *Teaching in Progress: Theories, Practices, and Scenarios*; *Using Portfolios*; *Comp Tales*, writing teachers' reports on their teaching experiences; and the videos *Writing, Teaching, and Learning* and *Writing Across the Curriculum: Making It Work*

SENTENCE COMBINING WITH THE HANDBOOK

During the past decade, extensive research has shown that having students work with the elements of sentences—manipulating, combining, and altering—leads not only to a greater understanding of sentence structure but also to a greater willingness to experiment stylistically, leading to more flexible, expressive syntax characteristic of mature writing. However, teachers and students can get carried away with sentence combining. Doing exercises with someone else's prose can be fun; students seem to enjoy the activities, but they are no substitute for the students' writing their own sentences and applying the techniques to their own sentences as part of a larger writing assignment.

What sentence combining is

Sentence combining arose from applications of transformational-generative grammar principles to classroom practices. Researchers such as Kellogg Hunt and Frank O'Hare determined that encouraging students to expand sentences by coordinating (adding on), deleting (eliminating repeated words), and embedding (inserting new information into a main clause) enables them to write complex, fluent sentences without having to master elaborate grammatical terminology. The practice they recommend is to give students a base sentence and several other sentences of information to incorporate in the base sentence then have students experiment with various ways to combine the information.

In most sentence-combining instruction, students learn various kinds of combinations, starting with relatively simple coordination and subordination using conjunctions. Then they progress to removing repeated elements and embedding information such as adjectives and phrases, culminating in "advanced" structures such as adverbials and absolutes. After they control the structures, they are introduced to the punctuation conventions the new sentences require. Students are encouraged to practice not only on the words of other writers but on their own sentences in their drafts as they master new stylistic patterns.

A sequence for sentence combining

Chapter 12 introduces students to basic sentence structures, and Chapters 21 and 28 introduce modifying clauses and phrases along with their primary focus on grammar and punctuation. Chapters 28 and 29 present strategies of coordination as well as of punctuation, and Chapters 24 and 25 introduce progressively more sophisticated sentence strategies. In Chapters 23 and 26 students encounter sentence patterns characteristic of mature writing, and in Chapter 4 they get a chance to combine all the strategies in paragraphs.

The handbook exercises you might stress in teaching sentence combining are these:

Chapter 4, Exercises 4.4, 4.11
Chapter 12, Exercises 12.8, 12.10, 12.12, 12.13, 12.15, 12.16, 12.17, 12.21
Chapter 13, Exercise 13.4
Chapter 18, Exercise 18.3
Chapter 21, Exercise 21.7
Chapter 23, Exercises 23.2, 23.6
Chapter 24, Exercises 24.1, 24.3, 24.6
Chapter 25, Exercises 25.3, 25.4
Chapter 26, Exercises 26.1, 26.2, 26.3, 26.6
Chapter 28, Exercises 28.2, 28.4, 28.6
Chapter 29, Exercises 29.2, 29.4

TUTORING WITH THE HANDBOOK

Writing centers and tutoring programs can make good use of the handbook to set common goals and to develop a common language that will sustain the diverse relationships among students, tutors, and teachers. For example, the handbook provides a reference point for teachers' responses to student papers, which can then become the basis for tutoring sessions on the identified points of difficulty in student work: paragraphing, interpretive work with quotes, particular patterns of error. Students are also able to refer to explanations and exercises in the tutor's absence, to keep a journal of their error patterns and sample revisions, and to refer back to the handbook to reinforce what they have learned in tutoring sessions. The handbook can also become a primary reference for the tutoring center or lab by providing advice and practice exercises for targeted areas. Tutors should encourage students to bring the handbook along with their work-in-progress. Once tutor and student together have identified revision areas or targeted patterns of error, they might review the relevant sections of the handbook together; the tutor might then give the student a chance to revise a targeted area on his or her own. As a resource tool for the lab or tutoring center, the handbook can help resolve conflicts over points of grammar and usage, becoming a primary reference or arbiter in debates. It can be a training manual for new tutors, providing simple and clear explanations of problems they will encounter every day. In particular, the revision worksheets included in the chapter on collaborative learning (pp. 56–62 of this manual) can be used as the basis for tutorial sessions. And the handbook can be a reference for students who are working on a paper in the writing center without direct supervision by a tutor.

The Little, Brown Workbook and the *ESL Worksheets* can provide the "raw material" of tutoring—sample sentences, exercises, and brief explanations—to be used in discussion with the student or for independent work. The workbook can be particularly effective for tutoring if students are taking a composition course that uses the handbook, because the language, rules, and exercises encountered in tutoring will be consistent with those encountered in the classroom.

SAMPLE SYLLABI

Syllabus for a ten-week course with four graded papers:

Week	Goals
1	Introduction and course description; diagnostic writing sample. Begin discussion of essay development (Chapter 1); assign first essay. Academic writing (Chapter 6) and critical thinking, reading, and writing (Chapter 8).
2	Developing ideas (Chapter 2), drafting and revising essays (Chapter 3); first peer-response workshop. Preparing a manuscript (Chapter 5).
3	Writing and revising paragraphs (Chapter 4); conferences with students to discuss drafts and journals. Review common errors seen in drafts (Parts 4–6).
4	First essay due. Assign second essay. Repeat emphasis on prewriting (Chapters 1 and 2); discuss correction symbols and grading.
5	Return first essay; discuss clear sentences (Part 4). Peer-response workshop for second paper.
6	Effective words (Part 8); conferences to discuss drafts and journals. If needed, discuss with the class common errors or problems.
7	Second essay due; assign third essay. Work on invention strategies in small groups.
8	Return second essay; peer-group workshop in class; work on effective sentences (Part 5). Introduce basics of argument (Chapters 9–11).

9   Third essay due; assign last essay, which may be a revision of an earlier piece of writing, an essay from another course, or an essay exam. Peer-group activities. If students are keeping portfolios (pp. 45–47 of this manual), final copies of first two papers are due this week. Journals due.

10   Return third essay. Final essay due; individual conferences and course evaluations; last two papers for portfolio due.

Syllabus for a fifteen-week course with five graded papers, including a research paper:

Week	Goals
1	Course introduction and requirements; writing sample. Discuss Chapters 1 and 2. Introduce journals.
2	Assign first paper. Begin draft work. Peer-response session for first paper. Review Chapter 54 if appropriate. Discuss Chapter 3 and Part 4.
3	Conferences about drafts. Discuss Chapter 4.
4	Take up journals. Second peer-response session for first paper. Review Chapter 5. Discuss Chapters 28 and 29.
5	First paper due. Assign second paper. Discuss Chapter 3 again; discuss Chapters 24 and 25.
6	Return first paper. Discuss evaluation criteria and correction symbols. If appropriate, discuss Chapter 55. Draft work on second paper. Peer-response session for second paper.
7	Discuss Chapter 37. Discuss Chapters 23 and 26. Second peer-response session for second paper.
8	Second paper due. Assign third paper. Take up journals. Reemphasize developing the essay (Chapter 2) and conduct microclinics on problem areas with small groups of students. Conferences to discuss drafts and journals.
9	Return second paper. Assign fourth paper (research paper). Discuss Chapter 42. Peer-response session for third paper. Assign each student an appropriate chapter from Part 10.
10	Research week. Library tour (if available). Chapter 43.
11	Return third paper. Documentation week. Chapters 47–50, and appropriate sections of the chapters in Part 10. Miniconferences to address specific research problems.
12	Fourth paper due. Discuss Chapter 48 and appropriate sections of the chapters in Part 10. Discuss Chapter 5.
13	Return fourth paper. Assign fifth paper. Discuss Chapters 9–11. Journals due.
14	Draft work for fifth paper. If students are keeping portfolios (pp. 45–47 of this manual), edited copies of first four papers are submitted this week.
15	Finished copy of fifth paper due. Individual conferences and course evaluations.

RESOURCES FOR DESIGNING A WRITING COURSE

Applebee, Arthur N. "Problems in Process Approaches: Toward a Reconceptualization of Process Instruction." *The Teaching of Writing.* Chicago: National Society for the Study of Education, 1986. 95–113.

Bartholomae, David, and Anthony Petrosky. *Facts, Counterfacts, Artifacts: Theory and Method for a Reading and Writing Course.* Upper Montclair: Boynton/Cook, 1986.

Dawkins, John. "Teaching Punctuation as a Rhetorical Tool." *College Composition and Communication* 46:4 (1995): 533–48.

Eble, Kenneth E. *The Craft of Teaching: A Guide to Mastering the Professor's Art.* 2nd ed. San Francisco: Jossey-Bass, 1988.

Enos, Theresa, ed. *A Sourcebook for Basic Writing Teachers.* New York: Random, 1987.

Farber, Jerry. "Learning to Teach: A Progress Report." *College English* 52 (1990): 135–41.

Fishman, Stephen M., and Lucille McCarthy. *John Dewey and the Challenge of Classroom Practice.* New York: Teachers College P, 1998.

Foster, David. *A Primer for Writing Teachers: Theories, Theorists, Issues, Problems.* Upper Montclair: Boynton/ Cook, 1983.

Gebhardt, Richard C. "Unifying Diversity in the Training of Writing Teachers." *Training the New Teacher of College Composition.* Ed. Charles W. Bridges. Urbana: NCTE, 1986. 1–12.

George, Diana. "Who Teaches the Teacher? A Note on the Craft of Teaching College Composition." *College English* 51 (1989): 418–23.

Graves, Richard L., ed. *Rhetoric and Composition: A Sourcebook for Teachers and Writers.* Upper Montclair: Boynton/Cook, 1st ed. 1976; 2nd ed. 1983; 3rd ed. 1990.

Hashimoto, Irvin Y. *Thirteen Weeks: A Guide to Teaching College Writing.* Portsmouth: Boynton/Cook, 1991.

Herzberg, Bruce. "Composition and the Politics of the Curriculum." *The Politics of Writing Instruction: Postsecondary.* Ed. Richard Bullock and John Trimbur. Portsmouth: Boynton/Cook (Heineman), 1991.

Hoffman, Eleanor M., and John P. Schifsky. "Designing Writing Assignments." *English Journal* 66 (1977): 41–45.

Hunt, Kellogg. *Grammatical Structures Written at Three Grade Levels.* Urbana: NCTE, 1965.

Irmscher, William. *Teaching Expository Writing.* New York: Holt, 1979.

Lindemann, Erika. *A Rhetoric for Writing Teachers,* 2nd ed. New York: Oxford UP, 1987.

———. "Teaching as a Rhetorical Art," *CEA Forum* 15:2 (1985): 9–12.

Lindemann, Erika, and Gary Tate, eds. *An Introduction to Composition Studies.* New York: Oxford UP, 1991.

O'Hare, Frank. *Sentence Combining: Improving Student Writing Without Formal Grammar Instruction.* Urbana: NCTE, 1973.

Passmore, John. *The Philosophy of Teaching.* London: Duckworth, 1980.

Ponsot, Marie, and Rosemary Deen. *Beat Not the Poor Desk! Writing: What to Teach, How to Teach It, and Why.* Upper Montclair: Boynton/Cook, 1982.

Rankin, Elizabeth. "From Simple to Complex: Ideas of Order in Assignment Sequences." *Journal of Advanced Composition* 10:1 (1990): 126–35.

Ronald, Kate, and Hephzibah Roskelly. *Reason to Believe: Romanticism, Pragmatism, and the Possibility of Teaching.* Albany: State U of New York P, 1998.

Scott, Patrick, and Bruce Castner. "Reference Sources for Composition Research: A Practical Survey." *College English* 45 (1983): 756–68.

Shaughnessy, Mina. *Errors and Expectations: A Guide for the Teacher of Basic Writing.* New York: Oxford UP, 1977.

Tarvers, Josephine Koster. *Teaching Writing: Theories and Practices.* 4th ed. New York: HarperCollins, 1993.

Tobin, Lad. "Reading Students, Reading Ourselves: Revising the Teacher's Role in the Writing Class." *College English* 53 (1991): 333–48.

CHAPTER 3

Working with Student Writing

Nothing we do as composition teachers—not lecturing, setting up peer critique groups, leading discussions, or preparing activities—has as much potential for helping students improve their writing as do our efforts to respond as sensitive and thorough readers. Moreover, as readers we can play several roles, some of them simultaneously. We can respond to a work in progress, acting as editors and critics with suggestions for revision or as ordinary readers whose reactions students can take into account as they shape the final product. Or we can be judges of a finished work, justifying a grade (as evaluators) or pointing out strengths and weaknesses (as teachers), encouraging students to build on one and avoid the other.

At some time, of course, all the work that you and students put into the course has to be judged—and in the final analysis, you'll be the one who has to make the judgments and assign the grade. This is one of the hardest parts of your job as a writing teacher, yet it's also one of the most essential. But you needn't go it alone; students can collaboratively do a good deal of the preliminary work for you and set standards that enable you and your students to agree upon grades.

THE ROLES OF RESPONSE

It takes more than an efficient correction system to bring about improvement in writing. How we respond and when are most important. In addition, the correction system we choose needs to be consistent with our purposes for responding and the roles we play as readers.

RESPONSES TO PAPERS IN PROGRESS

Responses directed toward a paper in progress often need to focus as much on the way the writer approaches the task as on the evolving text. On the one hand, it makes little sense to comment on detailed matters of punctuation in a draft full of helter-skelter ideas, thereby drawing attention away from advice about strategies the writer can employ to develop focus and discover purpose. On the other hand, helpful comments on agreement or mechanics coming at later stages in the writing of an essay can enable students to understand the importance of editing and can provide knowledge for later use.

Responses to a paper in progress ought to focus to a considerable extent on the writer's behaviors. Novice writers generally need to pay as much attention to learning how to discover ideas or draft an entire paper as to using topic sentences and effective patterns of paragraph development. Much of the advice in the handbook, especially in Chapters 1, 2, and 3, is directed toward strategies for writing. Other discussions, such as the treatment of paragraphs in Chapter 4, pay more attention to the specific features of essays, though they do not ignore the process of composition.

In commenting on drafts of an essay, we can assume the role of a general reader, noting points of interest or confusion, expressing an interest in more information or requesting stronger support, sharing feelings of pleasure and surprise—but always recognizing that at this point a paper belongs primarily to the writer, not yet to the reader. When a draft of an essay has a clear purpose and structure, however, we can read as editors or critics, identifying particular options for paragraphing or expression the writer might consider during revision or suggesting areas of grammar and style that need attention.

RESPONSES TO FINAL DRAFTS

Response to a final draft ought to provide a clear evaluation and the justification for it yet at the same time look toward future efforts. Student writers need to recognize and consolidate their successes; they need as well to understand what steps they can take in later essays. The essentially supportive tone of explanations in the handbook can help create this kind of understanding even when comments or the number-and-letter codes are used to identify outright errors.

When as evaluators we comment on a graded final draft, we need to provide a clear justification for the judgment on one or more of the following grounds:

- the paper's success in achieving its goals
- the requirements set by the assignment
- the standards established for the course

Comments that refer students to a particular section of the handbook, perhaps to specific sets of exercises, can provide a bridge to future writing efforts.

COMPOSING COMMENTS: PRAISE

Most students will give you an honest effort. They will use the strategies they know to complete an assignment well and to win your approval in the form of a high grade. But effort notwithstanding, students will have differing degrees of success with an assignment. And your reactions will have to differ accordingly.

Any writing effort will have strengths, even if they are few and sometimes hard to find. It's essential to identify them; not only do they show what goals have been attained, but they also help the students see which competencies they can apply to different situations. Even when you praise a very minor feature or an insight that could be developed more, the student has something to start from in a revision or in the next paper. It is also important to remember that critique can be either ego-crushing or empowering for the writer. Encouragement through praise can help keep your students, especially those with the weakest skills, from despairing about their capacity for improving their writing. Of course, the strengths sometimes outweigh the weaknesses; then the only problem is deciding what to praise. No matter what the level of skill in the paper, however, your goal is to help each student recognize and learn to capitalize on her strengths in future papers. The role of encouragement is often underestimated, seen as the "positive spin" tacked onto the "real" message of critique. Instead, it should be seen as an integral part of critique and a powerful tool for improvement. Students need to know when they have revised even one paragraph effectively, when they have gained control over a single pattern of error, when they have successfully used a quotation, even if their overall argument fell apart in the process. You may want to review your comments on a set of papers before handing them back to your students, in order to make sure that you have included some positive commentary on each paper.

COMPOSING COMMENTS: CRITIQUE

What about the weaknesses? The weaknesses are what most of us first see when we read a student paper. We feel compelled to alert our students to these problems so that their writing can improve. But the method of identifying such weaknesses must be constructive and goal-oriented. Ideally, students will be able to read our responses and focus on the one substantive issue or skill that will move their writing forward. As Nancy Sommers discovered in her research on teachers' responses, many teachers try to mark every error (often idiosyncratically and elliptically), leaving students with the confused sense that the paper is "all wrong" but with no sense of revision priorities. The effect of such comments is to superimpose the grid of an "ideal" paper against the actual project that the student writer was trying to accomplish. Sommers proposes instead a carefully selected and focused comment that enters into the student's own project and suggests a way to move it forward. The teacher might also identify a single pattern of error, mark several instances, ask the student to find several more instances and then to hand in revised versions of all those sentences. In some cases, the pattern of error and the substantive comment are linked, as for example a pattern of fused sentences manifesting the writer's tendency to rush cryptically through ideas rather than slowing down to think them through. In those cases, recognition of the error can lead the student to the points in the paper that are most rushed and become the basis for an effective revision (see Richard Straub's useful review article for a discussion of Sommers, Brannon/Knoblauch, and styles of teacher response).

Mina Shaughnessy, in her book *Errors and Expectations*, did all of us a great service by reminding us that the intentionality of student texts is quite different from that of literary works. In a literary work the writer is in control; he or she adheres to or violates conventions based on deliberate decisions. But when students violate the etiquette of syntax or spelling or punctuation, Shaughnessy reminds us, we assume that they did so with the same kind of artistic control experience that writers wield (or with a studied carelessness). And this is not the case. Students rarely if ever make deliberate errors; they are trying to succeed. Often, however, they attempt syntactic structures or make linguistic choices over which they have imperfect control. And so we must not regard their errors and weaknesses as intentions to fail; rather, we must determine at what they were trying to succeed. We must not just identify and criticize their errors; we must analyze them and try to help students fulfill their true intentions.

David Bartholomae, applying some of Shaughnessy's observations to basic writers, argues that such error analysis can be a valuable diagnostic technique for instructors. "By investigating and interpreting the patterns of error in [students'] writing, we can help them begin to see those errors as evidence of hypotheses or strategies they have formed and, as a consequence, put them in a position to change, experiment, imagine other strategies. Studying their own writing puts students in a position to see themselves as language users, rather than as victims of a language that uses them" (258).

Many times, in fact, errors and weaknesses signal growth. Often student papers submitted after sentence-combining practices are plagued with comma splices, as students struggle to master new syntactic patterns. The students are courageously trying new techniques; penalizing them for failing on the first try to master the punctuation etiquette required may defeat your attempts to help them grow. Sometimes, of course, there will be careless errors: a word transposed or omitted in copying, the phonetic mishearing of a term (such as Freud's "edible complex"), an embarrassing or amusing typo (such as "Shakespeare's play of love and punishment, *Romeo and Joliet*"). These represent failures of editing skills, language performance rather than language competence, and can be treated as such.

Finally, remember that exposing their work to the critique of others can make writers feel intensely vulnerable. It is essential to be delicate in your tone when you identify weaknesses so as not to arouse feelings of shame in your students. Especially when you are trying to move through a stack of papers efficiently, you may find yourself falling into a kind of terseness in your comments that may seem harsh to your students. Try drafting your comments in pencil and then reviewing them before handing the papers back to your students; in this way you can fine-tune any comments whose tone is too negative.

COMMENTING ON PAPERS

Composition instructors have developed innovative and useful ways of evaluating student writing, including conferences, tape-recorded commentary, and peer evaluation. The handbook can be a useful aid for all these approaches, particularly peer evaluation (see "Using Collaborative Learning with the Handbook," pp. 52–65 of this manual). Many teachers, however, still prefer to respond to student essays through marginal and summary comments. These responses take three general forms: a correction code, correction symbols, and written comments. Each method has advantages and disadvantages; some teachers choose to combine them to draw on the strengths of each while others feel that correction codes and symbols undercut students' individualized projects. Some teachers use a correction code method accompanied by student conferences in which they give more personalized feedback; other teachers use written comments and establish feedback sessions, during which students respond to those comments and outline a revision plan or a goal for the next paper. The important thing is that your students understand your method and are able to work productively from your comments.

USING THE CORRECTION CODE

To use the correction code, an instructor simply writes in the margin of a paper the number and letter of the section of the handbook a student should consult for help with a particular problem or error, for example, 15b (pronoun and antecedent agreement), 18a (comma splice), or 2b (problem with thesis). The code for each section of the handbook is listed inside the front cover; after a short time, most instructors find they have memorized the codes for common problems and seldom have to consult the list. Here is a section of a student paper marked using the correction code:

17   Parents have become more lenient with regard to television watching. For example, allowing their children to
28b   watch cartoons in the early morning before school. As soon
41a   as they come home from school they sit before the set   39c
again, completely ingrossed with a soap opera or a talk   38c
show. Some parents actually allow their children to watch
19a   television while they are at the supper table. Of course,
the latter part of the evening, the prime time, is solely   21b
set aside for the purpose of watching a special show or a
favorite series. In some ways, parents are using the television as a substitute for personal communication with the
41d   child. The days then, remain a never ending chain of program after program.   28c

When students get their graded papers back, they need only turn to the front of the handbook to understand what the instructor's notations mean and then refer to the appropriate section of the text for a full explanation (the code for each section appears in colored boxes at the sides of the pages). Students, too, quickly learn to recognize the notations for common errors and problems. An important follow-up to this method is to ask students to identify several more instances of one kind of error and to revise those sentences using the handbook. The goal is to help students identify the kinds of errors that commonly occur in their writing so that they can look for those errors on the next draft. As a helpful accompaniment to this method you might ask students to keep a list or journal of the errors that you have marked and that they have revised as a resource for future revisions. That journal can also become the basis for an individual conference, in which you and the student discuss a pattern of error and its significance for revision (a pattern of vague pronoun references that manifests the student's difficulty in defining and working with key terms, for instance).

USING THE CORRECTION SYMBOLS

Correction symbols work in much the same way as the number-and-letter code. An instructor locates the appropriate symbol in the list inside the back cover of the handbook (e.g., *dev, log, agr, coh*) and writes it in the margin of the essay, often drawing a line to indicate the location and extent of the problem. Students reverse the procedure, looking up symbols on the list, which also gives the name of the problem and a reference to the appropriate section of the text: for example, *dm*—Dangling modifier, 21h. Here is the passage from the facing page marked in this way:

Parents have become more lenient with regard to television

watching. <u>For example, allowing their children to watch car-</u> *frag*

toons in the early morning before school. As soon as they come *rep*

home from school, they sit before the set again, completely

<u>ingrossed</u> <u>with</u> a soap opera or a talk show. Some parents actu- *sp* *ww*

ally allow their children to watch television while <u>they</u> are *ref*

at the supper table. Of course, the latter part of the

evening, the prime time, is <u>solely</u> set aside for the purpose *mm*

of watching a special show or a favorite series. In some

ways, parents are using the television as a substitute for

personal communication with the child. The days⌒then, remain *p*

a never⌒ending chain of program after program. *hyph*

Because correction symbols are easier to remember than the number-and-letter code, both students and teachers can spend less time turning away from a paper to consult the list of symbols than they might do with the code. Yet symbols are less specific than the code; *shift,* for instance, covers a variety of problems—20a (person and number), 20b (tense and mood), and 20c (subject and voice). Moreover, instead of being able to turn directly from the paper to a discussion in the handbook, students may need to consult the list of symbols to find the appropriate section of the text. Most of the symbols, however, also appear in the colored boxes in the margins of the pages. It becomes increasingly important, then, to augment the symbol method with comments or conferences that help students create revision priorities. For instance, you might write a marginal comment next to the first instance of a sentence fragment, then put the symbol (*frag*) next to three other occasions of the same error. An end comment or conference would direct the student to Chapter 17 of the handbook, would ask the student to locate several more instances of the error in the paper, and would ask for revisions. Once students understand that the fragment is often an undeveloped thought, they are able to use their recognition of the error to create substantive revisions, not only of sentences but of paragraphs and papers as well.

USING WRITTEN COMMENTS

Written comments can appear in two places: in the margins and at the paper's end. Each does a different job, and students need to learn what those jobs are. Marginal comments generally note specific areas of strength or weakness in student papers. As Nancy Sommers reminds us, marginal comments focus a student's attention on a particular draft, often causing the student to ignore the possibilities of revision and moving on in new drafts. Students sometimes become so overwhelmed by marginal comments that they want only to "fix" what's "wrong" with a particular draft. Sparing use of marginal comments may make students look to the end comments for your directions. Carefully phrased marginal comments can also direct students to revise. Often in such a system, the marginal comments that identify weaknesses are questions or statements that lead students to examine the text more carefully: "Can you give a more precise description of the hotel than 'nice' and 'rad'?" "What's your evidence for this claim?" "Does your reader know what a 'buydown mortgage' is?" Or they can describe your reaction as a reader ("I can't see the connection between these two ideas. Did you leave a step out?"). Occasionally you may want to refer the student to a particular reference source ("Your citations should be in MLA form; see Chapter 47").

Checks in the margin can direct a student's attention to mechanical, grammatical, or stylistic weaknesses. Such individual problems should be summed up as part of your end comment: "Often you provide a quotation to support your assertions, but you rarely analyze the quotations to show how they fit into your argument. Where you do this, as on p. 3, it really strengthens your argument. Where you leave it out, your argument is less persuasive—you make your readers guess the connections you see." "A lot of the check marks have to do with where commas go in complex sentences. Review Chapter 28 to correct these problems."

The second kind of comment, usually at the end of the paper, should direct students to new writing goals. Whether you rely on a single method or a combination of methods to mark students' papers, it is usually important to provide students with a comment at the end of their papers to explain the grade and to tie together the marginal commentary, emphasizing the key points. This is also a good place to assign exercises in the handbook and to remind students what they need to do in future essays. The discussion "Evaluating Essays for a Grade" later in this chapter contains several examples of summary comments. Your end comments need to give clear rhetorical response and guidance to your students: "Your careful examination of King's religious language gives your paper a great deal of credibility. In your subsequent papers you can use this sensitivity to language to support your own assertions." Every writer likes to know he or she has succeeded; tell your students what competencies they show, and give them goals to strive for. Your end comment needs a context just like the student papers do; don't neglect it.

ESTABLISHING PRIORITIES FOR THE STUDENTS

When commenting on students' papers, try to be selective about the issues you address. Two, or at most three, weaknesses are enough for a student to focus on for the next paper. Focus on the largest issues first; if the writer can't address an audience or formulate a thesis, spelling and colon placement are trivial problems. And often, as in the cases discussed above, the weaknesses are signs of growth. Even if a student has not yet learned to analyze evidence, he's learned to provide it; even if a student continues to make comma splices, she's learning to write more complex sentences. Your comments can be phrased to reflect these tentative steps of growth: "I'm glad you tried some of the sentence combining we practiced. Now that you've learned the patterns, take a close look at where the punctuation goes so that you can use those elaborate sentences to their best effect." "You've picked really sharp quotations to back up your points. Next time follow up each of those quotes with a sentence or two of comment to help your audience see how they fit into your argument."

Finally, your response should help the writer set and reach new goals. These will usually involve mastering skills that were not used effectively in the current text or moving on to apply those skills in new contexts. Here is where the critical teaching in comments takes place: you want the student to move to a new level of achievement. The goals should be clearly expressed: "Now that you've mastered simple and compound sentences, it's time to move to complex ones." "It's clear you can persuade an audience that basically agrees with you. Next time why don't you aim to persuade a mildly hostile audience?" And your comments should suggest clear strategies for achieving those goals: "Try brainstorming and using the journalist's questions to generate more details about your subject. Then you can choose which ones you want to use." "Write down all the arguments opposed to your position that you can think of, and try to find reasonable answers to those objections." You may even need to offer a small reward to encourage timorous students to take risks: "Try to write some different kinds of sentence patterns; I won't 'mark off' if you don't quite master the punctuation next time." Your response can also encourage students to reconsider their writing processes: "The drafts of this paper show you just changed a few words; you didn't revise much. Next time, once you've got your ideas down, allow yourself to move paragraphs around, change sentences, scratch out! Revision is the chance to improve the problems mentioned above; make your organization clearer, smooth sentences, add details. Let your drafts be messy."

In sum, your end comments should encourage the student not only to go back into this paper but to move forward to the next. If you keep the tripartite structure in mind—praise strengths, identify weaknesses, set goals—you'll find it relatively easy to write a coherent, goal-oriented end comment. Encourage students to discuss those comments with you before they submit their next paper; often a word or two of reinforcement or clarification can lead to quantum leaps in writing performance.

MAKING SURE STUDENTS UNDERSTAND YOUR COMMENTS
DEALING WITH CODES AND SYMBOLS

Perhaps the most common reason students fail to understand our comments is that they do not understand the symbols or terms we use. If you were to ask a class what a fused sentence is, some students might answer in this vein: "a sentence where everything seems to run together and gets confused or awkward." Such terms as *reference, development,* and *parallelism* are also likely to draw puzzled or incorrect responses, though a few students might be able to give general explanations. Asking students the meaning of such common symbols as *pass, cs, dm,* and *[agr]* will produce similar results.

Telling students to look up correction marks on the front or back endpapers of the handbook can help, as can alerting them to the Glossary of Grammatical Terms or handing out a list of terms you plan to use in written comments. A lot of students, however, are likely to put off learning the symbols or terms until they absolutely have to, perhaps several papers into the semester, when they realize how much help they need to improve their writing. One technique that can speed the process is to foreground student papers in group work and in revision exercises with the entire class. For example, you might hand out a paper that has two sentence fragments and a comma splice in a key paragraph. After asking students to use the Editing Checklist and the relevant sections from the handbook to identify and "correct" the errors, have them work in groups to revise the errors substantively and in doing so to develop the content of the paragraph. In a follow-up class you might hand out the revised paragraphs created in the groups and ask students to compare the different analytical and grammatical choices that were made. Such exercises help students to understand the reasons for seemingly arbitrary codes.

DISCUSSING A GRADED PAPER

Another good way to help students understand your comments is to discuss a graded paper with them. Chapter 3 of the handbook (pp. 55–57 and 63–65) contains two student papers that you may wish to "grade" and then use as the basis of class discussion. In addition, the paragraphs presented earlier in this chapter contain many errors of the kind likely to turn up on student papers. The paragraphs can be distributed in class with either or both of the marking systems or with some other system you prefer. If you choose to distribute the paragraphs without markings, you can ask the students to work with you in identifying errors and choosing appropriate symbols or comments.

EVALUATING ESSAYS FOR A GRADE

A grade can carry several messages: it can describe the overall quality of a paper; it can indicate how close the essay comes to achieving the goals for writing set forth in the course; and it can help tell a student writer what elements to work on in the next assignment. But unless grading standards are clear, the grades we assign will have little value for teaching beyond establishing a final grade for the course.

To help establish clear evaluation standards, many instructors discuss grading criteria with students and distribute sample papers, either already graded or to be graded in class. Another method is to attach to each paper a comment sheet reflecting the goals for the assignment. Preparing a comment sheet for each assignment can be taxing, however, so many instructors prepare a sheet that can be used for all assignments. Here is a sample:

These are the areas in which your paper is

strong		weak
	thesis	
	development	
	paragraphs	
	sentences	
	word choice	
	punctuation	
	style	

Comment/grade:

If you do not like to use comment sheets, you may prefer to hand out grading criteria at the beginning of the course. Sometimes a department or program provides its own set of criteria for grading papers; if yours does not, you may wish to adapt for your own use the following set that reflects the major areas of emphasis in the handbook:

> Thesis:
>
> Organization:
>
> Development:
>
> Grammar and
>
>   punctuation:
>
> Style:
>
> Comment/grade:

- *A* (superior). An A paper meets the standards in all these areas and excels in one or more of them:

  The *paper as a whole* presents a fresh subject or main idea or treats it in an interesting or original manner, displaying unusual insight and taking appropriate account of the audience. The *paragraphs* are fully developed with detail that supports the main idea; sentences within the paragraphs are clearly linked, forming an appropriate pattern; transitions are effective. *Sentences* are varied and imaginative in style, concise and creative in wording. The paper contains few errors in *grammar and punctuation* or errors only in sophisticated matters, and few *spelling* errors.

- *B* (strong). A B paper meets the standards in all these areas:

  The *paper as a whole* presents an interesting subject or main idea and approaches it in a consistent and careful manner, displaying good insight, though without the freshness or originality characteristic of the A paper. The writing makes use of consistent rhetorical strategies and a tone appropriate to the audience. *Paragraphs* are, with only a few exceptions, adequately developed and generally successful in supporting the main idea; transitions are clear, and sentences within the paragraphs are, for the most part, clearly related. *Sentences* are generally clear and correct in structure and style and are not excessively wordy. Word choice is usually appropriate. *Grammar, punctuation,* and *spelling* follow accepted conventions, except for a few minor errors.

- *C* (adequate). A *C* paper is seriously deficient in one of these areas:

  The *paper as a whole* presents a clearly defined subject or main idea, but the treatment may be trivial, uninteresting, or too general and the insight adequate but not marked by independent thought. The plan and purpose are clear but inconsistently or incompletely carried out; tone may be inconsistent. Some paragraphs may lack adequate supporting detail or may be only loosely linked to the main idea. Sentences within paragraphs may be only loosely related, and some transitions may be missing. *Sentences* are generally correct in structure but may be excessively wordy, vague, or, at times, even incorrect. Style and word choice may be flat, inconsistent, or not entirely appropriate to the audience. The paper may display isolated serious errors in *grammar and punctuation* or frequent minor errors that do not interfere substantially with meaning or that do not greatly distract the reader; the paper may contain occasional *misspellings*.

- *D (weak).* A D paper is seriously deficient in any one of these areas:

    The *paper as a whole* presents a poorly defined or inconsistently treated subject or central idea and displays little insight or development. The tone is inappropriate to the audience. *Paragraphs* contain little supporting detail. Sentences within paragraphs are often unrelated to the main idea and transitions are lacking. *Sentences* are frequently incorrect in structure, vague, wordy, and distracting. Style and word choice are inappropriate, incorrect, or inconsistent. The paper may contain serious and distracting errors in *grammar and punctuation* as well as numerous irritating minor errors and frequent *misspellings*.

- *F (unacceptable/no credit).* An F paper is unacceptable in any one of these areas:

    The *paper as a whole* does not have a clear subject or main idea and has no apparent purpose or plan; or the subject and main idea are defined and treated in a way that clearly does not meet the requirements of the assignment. *Paragraphs* are not related to the main idea; sentences within paragraphs are unrelated, and transitions are missing. *Sentences* are so faulty in structure and style that the essay is not readable. Frequent serious errors in *grammar, punctuation,* and *spelling* indicate an inability to handle the written conventions; there are excessive minor errors or misspellings.

These criteria need to be adapted to the level of students in a particular course or institution and to the goals set for the course. For example, admirable organization or style may differ markedly for a student in a two-year technical program and a student in a four-year school that stresses the arts and humanities.

EVALUATING FOR REVISION

REVISION IN COMPOSITION TEACHING

In recent years the process of revision has come to be viewed as increasingly important in composition instruction. Instructors who make revision a regular part of their composition classes argue that writers should be judged not (or not only) on the early version of an essay but on what they are able to make of the essay after they have had a chance to revise it and, perhaps, to take into account the comments of readers.

Composition instructors have long viewed revision as an important process for student writers to learn. What is new is the extent to which revision is being made a regular part of instruction, an emphasis reflected in the extensive treatment of both revision and editing in Chapter 3 of the handbook. In addition, many instructors have begun structuring their classes around collaborative learning groups that provide audiences for papers in progress and advice for revision. This method is reinforced in Chapter 3, which contains checklists for students' giving and receiving criticism. The chapter "Using Collaborative Learning with the Handbook," which follows this discussion, contains suggestions for handouts to help students analyze their peers' work. Furthermore, students' increasing access to computers and the availability of computer classrooms have made possible a range of new approaches to the revision process (see Daniel Anderson's chapter on pp. 66–100 of this manual).

COMMENTING ON DRAFTS FOR REVISION

The distinction made in Chapter 3 of the handbook between revision and editing is important for instructors to keep in mind when responding to a student paper in progress. For essays whose perspective, form, and content are well enough developed to require only editing, your role may be simply to call attention to errors or to suggest ways to polish sentences and paragraphs. Many of the techniques already discussed for commenting on papers can be used to aid editing, particularly those that refer students to sections of the handbook for advice on improving a passage or correcting a problem. In addition, you may wish to refer students to the editing checklist in Chapter 3 (pp. 58–59).

Evaluation for revision, however, is more likely to suggest extensive changes in a paper, often encouraging the writer to adopt a different perspective on a topic. Since revision may and often should involve substantial changes in the direction of an essay, however, you should be wary of comments that impose your view of what a paper should do or how it should be accomplished. Instead, try to identify a problem clearly and offer some possible solutions but at the same time leave the student writers free to make their own choices. Such comments as "Your thesis statement needs to focus more sharply on the specific government toxic-waste regulations to which you object" may be helpful in cases where the student's intentions and the direction of a paper are quite clear. But when a writer is still struggling with subject and intention, such statements may limit the process of revision rather than encourage it. A comment like the following, however, leaves the eventual direction of the essay up to the student:

> I'm not sure which specific regulations you object to most. Is this a place in the essay where you want to focus your concerns sharply for readers? From the

detailed evidence you present later about the struggles of small businesses to pay for state-of-the-art pollution equipment, I suspect that one of your main purposes is to have readers understand the hard times these ordinary people are facing. What do you care most about in this subject, and what do you most want your audience to understand and feel?

In commenting on papers for revision, you should call attention to any serious errors. At the same time, however, keep in mind this maxim: "Don't spend time improving a sentence that ought to be dropped from the paper." Remember, too, that awkward and confused sentences are often signs of confusion about the overall direction of an essay, and problems at the sentence level may disappear as the writer resolves the larger problems.

> You shift pronouns often in this passage, sometimes addressing the reader as "you," sometimes using "one" or "we." I think the root of the problem is that you are not sure of your relation to your readers. Since you are talking about a situation that you face along with most readers, you might choose "we" and stick to it.

In addition, most students need more than advice about what sections of a paper need to be revised; they need advice about the process of revision itself. By focusing your comments on how to go about revising rather than solely on the direction of possible changes, you can avoid doing the students' work for them and can instead help them develop an effective writing/revising process.

COPING WITH THE PAPER LOAD

At this point you may well be asking, "How am I supposed to do all these things—run groups, intervene in processes, hold conferences, analyze errors, write long comments—and remain sane?" That's a good question, probably the most vexing one writing teachers face. You can't avoid it: grading papers takes time, lots of it, time that you'd often rather spend reading or working on your own scholarship or having a personal life or just enjoying fresh air and natural light. The best way to speed up the grading process, then, is to reduce the amount of grading you have to do. Several techniques will help you achieve this goal.

GRADING THE PAPER

Evaluating student papers can be time-consuming: instructors often report spending fifteen to twenty minutes on each paper, making marginal notes, writing summary comments, and deciding on a grade. Many set aside hours of office time for individual conferences. To help make the job of marking papers somewhat easier and quicker, *The Little, Brown Handbook* provides a number of aids:

- a list of correction symbols keyed to discussions in the text;
- a number-and-letter correction code that refers students to appropriate sections of the handbook; and

- a thorough index and glossary of terms directing students to explanations of grammatical and rhetorical terms used in an instructor's written comments.

Some practical tips will help you speed the grading process:

1. Start with carefully designed assignments and give students enough time to complete the assignment successfully. The clearer the assignment, the fewer variables will be left for you to cope with; the more adequate the time, the fewer hasty or careless errors you should have to contend with.

2. Be realistic when telling students when they'll get papers back. Many authorities insist that teachers return papers at the first class meeting after the assignments are submitted. Two class meetings—or a week— is more realistic. The students also need at least one class meeting to review your comments and suggestions on one paper before submitting their next effort—and more time is helpful if they need a conference to discuss those comments with you. Schedule papers far enough apart to let you grade them carefully, and don't make promises you can't keep.

3. Not all papers must be new assignments. Students often profit from revising and reshaping an earlier paper, either one of their own choosing or one that you suggest they revise. Such assignments teach students the crucial importance of revising while giving you time to hold conferences, attend to individual problems, and design subsequent assignments.

4. Set a schedule for your grading and keep it. If you must grade fifty papers in five days, that's ten a day. At half an hour for each paper (a good beginner's rate), that's five hours of grading a day (you'll need a break or two to maintain your concentration).

5. Set reasonable time limits. Buy a timer and be ruthless about paying attention to it. Allow yourself a maximum time per paper—as a beginner, twenty-five or thirty minutes for an average (500–700 word) paper; as you get more experienced, fifteen to twenty minutes. Read the paper through once in its entirety before you mark anything, even minor mechanical errors. This allows you to assess the biggest strengths and weaknesses, to target your attention. Reread the paper, making your minimal marks and marginal comments. Then skim it one more time and compose your end comments. Sometimes the end comments written by beginning teachers are a page or longer; you'll learn to control this with experience. Again, using the three-part formula—strengths, a few weaknesses, and goals and strategies—can help you compose a response quickly.

Although you may find yourself calling on stock phrases to compose your end comments, it will help to refer back to specific marginal comments and moments in the paper as well. For example, you might say, "One of the strongest things about this paper is your use of quotations to support your opinions. On p. 2, for example, I've noted a particularly well-chosen quote and suggested ways that you might further develop your response to it." The relationship that you develop between your marginal comments and your end comment can be particularly helpful in guiding students from their global priorities for revision to local examples of where they might begin (or may already have begun) to develop the paper further.

6. Write a good end comment. If you have clear grading standards, put a letter grade on the paper after you've written your end comment; if not, sort all the papers into roughly defined piles—the good ones, the okay ones, the problem ones—and go back to assign grades later. If your time runs out, finish your note immediately and move on; you're probably asking the student to address too many issues. If you finish early, take a quick stretch and keep going; you'll want that time later. If a paper is very weak, set it aside; you'll want time to write a thoughtful note later. Don't turn the end comment into a justification or apology for a low grade; use it as a chance to teach the student ways to improve. If you think that assigning a very low grade would be detrimental to the student's progress, you can always mark the paper "No grade pending conference," discuss the paper with the student, and grade it after the student has revised it further. This solution works best when used sparingly and privately; otherwise you'll have B+ students clamoring for a chance to rewrite papers to get an A. (You can choose to allow such students to do so, of course, but be prepared to fight accusations of grade inflation.)

7. Keep good records. Don't just put the grade on the paper; record it in your grade book or progress folder immediately. If you're keeping a progress chart in the student's folder, make a few sketchy notes now; you can go back and elaborate later if necessary. If you forget to record grades now, you'll eventually find yourself in the position of returning a set of papers without having recorded the grades; then you have to go through all sorts of contortions to get the papers back to record the grades. Such a time-consuming annoyance can be avoided by keeping records carefully from the beginning.

PORTFOLIOS

You can reduce the number of assignments you actually give letter grades by allowing students to select some of their papers to submit as a portfolio for the class. Usually students submit drafts at an early point in the semester for your comments, then revise them and choose which ones to submit for their final grade in the course. Such an approach grants them more autonomy and may heighten their desire to achieve. Portfolios also encourage students to see writing as a process, enabling their growth as writers; for this reason, many colleges and universities are using portfolios not only in first-year writing but throughout a student's academic career; these portfolios become substantially more than just an evaluation method.

Portfolio grading, at its best, empowers students and spurs revision; thus it has drawn a great deal of attention in recent years as programs struggle with the whole question of evaluation. Several fine collections of perspectives on the portfolio question have appeared in recent years, including *Portfolios: Process and Product,* edited by Pat Belanoff and Marcia Dickson; *Portfolios and Beyond: Collaborative Assessments in Reading and Writing* by Susan Mandel Glazer and Carol Smullen Brown; *Process and Portfolios in Writing Instruction,* edited by Ken Gill and the Committee on Classroom Practices; and *Portfolio Resource Guide: Creating and Using Portfolios in the Classroom* by Judith C. Gilbert. However, some studies (particularly in Vermont) have questioned how well portfolios function in measuring students' writing ability over time. Others have pointed to the fact that while many people claim portfolios' virtues, very few studies have demonstrated either the practical use of handling them in the classroom or their effectiveness in helping students become better writers over the course of their college careers. Portfolio theory is still in its infancy, and much research remains to be done to understand how portfolios can best be used. Thus, this method will certainly continue to draw critical scrutiny.

If you choose to use portfolios in your classes, you'll need to make choices about scheduling them, grading them, and about the process of selecting what should go in them. You may want to experiment with the following options before settling on the arrangements you think work best for you and your students:

- Structuring portfolio assignments over the course of the semester takes some logistical planning. One issue is the pace of your own workload. Consider: if you have four classes of 25 students each, and each student turns in a portfolio of four papers at the end of the term, you'll have 400 papers to grade all at once. Students too may have difficulty managing an unbalanced workload. Moreover, students benefit most from getting feedback throughout the semester—your comments on one paper may help them not only with the revision of that paper but with the first draft of their next paper. To balance the workload for yourself and your students, you may want to require that some of the portfolio revisions be turned in for comments midway through the semester. Alternatively, you can make sure to give back first drafts well enough in advance of the portfolio due date that students will have ample time to work on revisions. Another option is to give very thorough critique on first drafts and minimal comments on the revisions in the portfolio. If you choose the latter option, you may want to have your students write you a memo about each revised paper, or even annotate the paper, to show what changes they made from the first draft, so that you will have a focus for your comments. Or you could have them resubmit the first draft of each paper along with the revised version; in this way you can review your comments on the draft and more quickly evaluate the success of the revision.

- You'll need to give some thought to developing a grading system for portfolios in your courses. You may want to give only comments (no grades) on first drafts, and then give a grade for each revised paper and another for the portfolio as a whole. Alternatively, you can give grades on individual first drafts and then one overall grade for the portfolio. You can give all papers equal weight in determining the overall grade or allow students to choose which papers they'd like to have weighed more heavily. You may want to give credit for degree of improvement, but if you do so you'll need to take care not to end up with inflated grades.

- Students should decide for themselves what to include in the portfolio, but it can be very productive for them to discuss their decisions with you and/or their classmates. You can meet with students to discuss which papers they think they'd like to revise and why. You may want to ask your students to prepare for these conferences by filling out self-assessment forms identifying the strengths and weaknesses of each paper and setting goals for revision. Or have students work in small groups to help one another select which papers should be revised. If you have all your students bring their portfolios to class and pass them around, so that each student looks at fifteen or more, they will quickly get a feeling for what makes a good portfolio.

CONFERENCE

You can also work individually with students on the development of their papers, looking at rough drafts of either portions or complete versions of their texts. You could "evaluate" some papers in one-to-one conferences, assigning verbal grades of "excellent," "very good," "fair," and the like. Since these grades will likely be high, reflecting your evaluation of the project at many stages, you might then assign letter grades only to papers students produce independently, alternating conference and independent papers. This strategy reduces by half the number of written comments you must produce; its drawback is the amount of time such conference teaching requires. Some teachers address the time issue by meeting with selected groups of students for intensive revision discussions focused on those students' particular needs. An additional advantage of conferences is that you can work through relevant sections of the handbook with students, so that they have specific places to look for information as they revise their papers. A good rule of thumb in planning conferences is to set a defined agenda in advance so that students come to the conference with a particular piece of writing, a list of questions, or a revision plan, and with a mutually understood goal for the session.

COLLABORATING

A different kind of workload reduction can be achieved by letting your students do some of the work for you collaboratively. When students work effectively in small and large groups, they can identify writing problems at the draft stage and help their fellow students remedy weaknesses. Group proofreading sessions likewise can find and solve many mechanical problems before they reach your desk. If you train the groups to look for the kinds of problems students are having, they can do a great deal of the diagnostic work for each other. You'll occasionally have to correct a faulty diagnosis, but you will save yourself a little time while promoting students' independent revision and editing skills. If all students have access to computer facilities, you can encourage them to use spelling checker programs, and perhaps to create networked revision groups or e-mail chat groups to support each other's editing processes. See the chapter on "Collaborative Learning" (pp. 52–65 of this manual).

STUDENT-SET STANDARDS

You can also encourage students to set the standard for achievement in the class, perhaps using a model such as the description of letter grades given above. Or, using that model as a general criterion, you might ask students to derive a more specific set of criteria from a particular assignment. Such an exercise might ask: "What kinds of things does this assignment ask for? What might be a minimal (C-level) response to this assignment? What kinds of strategies might an excellent (B- to A-level paper) adopt in responding to this assignment?" Or, early in the semester, you can have students develop sets of criteria that characterize above-average, average, and below-average writing; then hold them to these criteria in assigning grades. Duplicate the criteria and distribute them to the class members; use them to develop goals in assignments, to develop heuristics for group work, and to support your comments.

EVALUATION CANS AND CAN'TS

Some teachers, particularly beginning ones, have an extremely idealistic view of evaluation: they see it as a cure-all for all the writer's problems. To gain these results, they write comments that may approach (or exceed) the original paper in length. The overwhelmed student may try to respond but is usually daunted by all the advice and suggestions—and subsequent papers sometimes are disasters. It's particularly crucial to remember that students can rarely learn a new skill or learn to recognize and correct even a single pattern of error overnight. It takes an enormous amount of practice and consideration for a student to locate sentence fragments in his or her own writing—about as much time as it takes to create well-developed paragraphs. Although it can be frustrating to see recurring errors of exactly the same type that you have carefully marked in previous papers, those errors are rarely a sign of carelessness; more often they suggest that the student needs more personalized support (a conference, a tutoring session, an assigned task using the handbook).

Evaluating individual written products is a matter of seeing how well students have reached intermediate goals in the course. It can't be done on the bell curve; writing progress is too individual a process for that. While you'll want to apply the same standards to all students, you'll probably have to allow some leeway in measuring achievement. Students who quickly master narrow competencies (such as mechanics or syntactic variety) should receive credit for these successes but should probably be judged more on how well they master more open matters—audience manipulation, voice, development, and so on. Students who have a great deal of difficulty mastering the narrow skills—those who come from particularly weak backgrounds or who have dialect interference problems, for example—may have excellent ideas but difficulty in presenting them. They should be rewarded for the content of their papers but encouraged to master the conventions of academic discourse as well. Make it clear to students that you're not evaluating how well they compete against other students—or against your ideals—but how much progress they're making in achieving the goals set for all students.

Likewise, you may be tempted to reward a student's effort on a paper rather than the product he or she actually produces ("This just doesn't hold together, but he worked so hard; look at all these drafts!"); such sympathy may be human, but it's not going to help the student. Giving good grades for effort rather than for results provides students with false assessments of their achievements. It's dishonest. Better in such cases to withhold a grade pending a conference and revision than to inflate students' expectations artificially.

RESOURCES FOR RESPONSE AND EVALUATION

Bartholomae, David. "Released into Error: Errors, Expectations and the Legacy of Mina Shaughnessy." *The Territory of Language*. Ed. Donald A. McQuade. Carbondale: Southern Illinois UP, 1986.

———. "The Study of Error." *College Composition and Communication* 31 (1980): 253–69.

Belanoff, Pat, and Marcia Dickson, eds. *Portfolios: Process and Product*. Portsmouth: Boynton/Cook, 1991.

———. "Toward an Ethics of Grading." *Foregrounding Ethical Awareness in Composition and English Studies*. Ed. Sheryl I. Fontaine and Susan M. Hunter. Portsmouth: Boynton/Cook, 1998. 174–96.

Black, Laurel Johnson. *Between Talk and Teaching: Reconsidering the Writing Conference*. Logan: Utah State UP, 1998.

Boynton, Victoria. "Collaborative Power Sharing." *Composition Chronicle* 6:1 (February 1993): 6–8.

Brannon, Lil, and C. H. Knoblauch. "On Students' Rights to Their Own Texts: A Model of Teacher Response." *College Composition and Communication* 33 (1982): 157–66.

Conners, Robert J., and Andrea Lunsford. "Teachers' Rhetorical Comments on Student Papers." *College Composition and Communication* 44:2 (May 1993): 200–33.

Cooper, Charles R., and Lee Odell, eds. *Evaluating Writing: Describing, Measuring, Judging*. Urbana: NCTE, 1977.

Faigley, Lester. "Judging Writing, Judging Selves." *College Composition and Communication* 40 (1989): 395–412.

Ford, James E., and Gregory Larkin. "The Portfolio System: An End to Backsliding Writing Standards." *College English* 39 (1978): 950–55.

Freedman, Sarah Warshauer. *Responses to Student Writing*. Urbana: NCTE, 1987.

Freedman, Sarah Warshauer, and Melanie Sperling. "Teacher–Student Interaction in the Writing Conference: Response and Teaching." *The Acquisition of Written Language: Response and Revision*. Ed. Sarah Warshauer Freedman. Norwood: Ablex, 1985.

Garrison, Roger. *One-to-One: Making Writing Instruction Effective*. Instructor's Manual to Accompany Garrison's *How a Writer Works*. New York: Harper & Row, 1981.

———. "One-to-One: Tutorial Instruction in Freshman Composition." *New Directions for Community Colleges* 2 (Spring 1974): 55–84.

Gere, Ann Ruggles, and Robert Stevens. "The Language of Writing Groups: How Oral Response Shapes Revision." *The Acquisition of Written Language: Response and Revision*. Ed. Sarah Warshauer Freedman. Norwood: Ablex, 1985. 85–105.

Gilbert, Judith C. *Portfolio Resource Guide: Creating and Using Portfolios in the Classroom*. Ottawa, KS: The Writing Conference, 1993.

Gill, Ken, and the Committee on Classroom Practices, eds. *Process and Portfolios in Writing Instruction*. Urbana: NCTE, 1993.

Glazer, Susan Mandel, and Carol Smullen Brown. *Portfolios and Beyond: Collaborative Assessments in Reading and Writing*. Norwood: Christopher-Gordon, 1993.

Hamp-Lyons, Liz. "Uncovering Possibilities for a Constructivist Paradigm for Writing Assessment." Review in *College Composition and Communication* 46:3 (Oct. 1995): 446–55.

Hillocks, George. "The Interaction of Instruction, Teacher Comment, and Revision in Teaching the Composing Process." *Research in the Teaching of English* 16 (1982): 261–78.

Hunter, Susan, and Ray Wallace. *The Place of Grammar in Writing Instruction, Past, Present, Future*. Portsmouth: Boynton/Cook, 1995.

Larson, Bruce, Susan Stern Ryan, and Ross Winterowd, eds. *Encountering Student Texts: Interpretive Issues in Reading Student Writing*. Urbana: NCTE, 1990.

McDonald, W. U., Jr. "The Revising Process and the Marking of Student Papers." *College Composition and Communication* 29 (1978): 167–70.

Miller, Linda P. "A Conference Methodology for Freshman Composition." *Teaching English in the Two-Year College* 7 (1980): 23–26.

Noguchi, Rei R. *Grammar and the Teaching of Writing: Limits and Possibilities.* Urbana: NCTE, 1991.

Olsen, Gary A. "Beyond Evaluation: The Recorded Response to Essays." *Teaching English in the Two-Year College* 8 (1982): 121–23.

Prendergast, Catherine. "Race: The Absent Presence in Composition Studies." *College Composition and Communication* 50 (1998): 36–53.

Purves, Alan. "The Teacher as Reader: An Anatomy." *College English* 46 (1984): 259–65.

Schiff, Peter. "Responding to Writing: Peer Critiques, Teacher-Student Conferences, and Essay Evaluations." *Language Connections: Writing and Reading Across the Curriculum.* Urbana: NCTE, 1982. 153–65.

Shaughnessy, Mina. *Errors and Expectations: A Guide for the Teacher of Basic Writing.* New York: Oxford UP, 1977.

Shaw, Margaret L. "What Students Don't Say: An Approach to the Student Text." *College Composition and Communication* 42 (1991): 45–54.

Sommers, Nancy. "Responding to Student Writing." *College Composition and Communication* 33 (1982): 148–56.

Speck, Bruce. *Grading Student Writing: An Annotated Bibliography.* Westport, CT: Greenwood, 1998.

Stanford, Gene, ed. *How to Handle the Paper Load.* Urbana: NCTE, 1978.

Straub, Richard. "The Concept of Control in Teacher Response: Defining the Varieties of 'Directive' and 'Facilitative' Commentary." *College Composition and Communication* 47:2 (May 1996): 223–51.

Tarvers, Josephine Koster. *Teaching Writing: Theories and Practices.* 4th ed. New York: HarperCollins, 1993.

Yancey, Katherine Blake, ed. *Portfolios in the Writing Classroom: An Introduction.* Urbana: NCTE, 1992.

Zak, Frances, and Christopher C. Weaver, eds. *The Theory and Practice of Grading Writing.* Albany: State U of New York P, 1998.

CHAPTER 4

Using Collaborative Learning with the Handbook

Collaborative learning activities provide effective ways to get students to write to a tangible audience of their peers, to practice their revision skills in a supportive, nonintimidating environment, and to experience the reality of alternative perspectives and approaches to writing and to the course readings. Group work also shifts classroom learning to an ongoing conversation between students rather than as a constant deferral to the teacher's greater authority. Kenneth Bruffee, a key proponent of collaborative learning, argues that because knowledge itself is the result of consensus among members of a community, and is produced by collaborative activity, "interdependent" student groups offer the ideal learning tool (3). They become "transition communities or support groups that students can rely on as they go through the risky process of becoming new members of the knowledge communities" (4). While Bruffee argues for a long history of informal cooperation and support systems among students as the natural basis for collaborative classroom assignments, others have pointed to the difficulty of grafting collaborative procedures into institutions that base their standards on individual performance and reward individual excellence (Gergits and Schramer). Still others have countered Bruffee's model of consensus as one that overlooks or erases the powerful differences between groups and individuals, differences that are the basis for continual collaborative negotiation (Trimbur and Spellmeyer, for example).

As these theoretical models suggest, it is important to be aware of potentially contradictory messages when setting up collaborative activities. For instance, students may not readily embrace a collaborative revision exercise if the grading system for the class, the teacher's responses on papers, and other classroom practices are all focused on individual performance. Conversely, the more collaborative work that students do, and the more that work is supported by surrounding classroom practices, the more students will understand the goals of group activities and feel confident in negotiating group dynamics. It also helps to remember that collaborative groups are part of a complex social process; as students work to overcome the social awkwardness of organizing and starting the task, they are also finding some common ground, finding ways to communicate across (sometimes) enormous ideological and conceptual differences (see *Singular Texts/Plural Authors*, Andrea Lunsford and Lisa Ede).

FORMING GROUPS FOR COLLABORATION

Inexperienced teachers who are considering collaborative activities may find the following suggestions useful. Collaborative groups can vary in size and configuration depending on the activity—from pairs to groups of four or five. For example, if the task is to choose a passage from the reading and come up with an interpretive response to present to the class, a larger group is useful in producing energetic debates (especially if each student is responsible for presenting some of the material). If you are having students work with the handbook to identify and revise particular problems, groups of three allow for both a range of skills and attention to individual difficulties. Students might begin with the revision checklist (p. 51) or the editing checklist (pp. 58–59) to identify recurrent problem patterns in each other's work, then revise using the relevant sections from the handbook. If your revision groups of three or four are becoming careless in their suggestions for each other's papers, you might pair students in groups of two and ask them to respond in writing and at length to another student's paper.

Some teachers always allow students to choose their own groups; the advantage here is that students generally establish a working dynamic and continue to choose the same group throughout the course. Other teachers select groups in order to mix or isolate skill levels or to create productive environments for silent or outspoken students. Again, you might make this decision based on the particular task and on group dynamics. If the task you have assigned is to revise a sentence or a paragraph in a student essay, you might streamline the process by asking students to work with the person next to them. If you notice a larger revision group veering into discussions of movies or a sociology exam, you might sit in with them for that session to listen to the group dynamic, then make an effort to reorganize groups for the next session (see Brook, Mirtz, and Evans for further discussion of small group dynamics).

One way to reinforce collaborative goals in a course in which grades depend upon individual performance is to incorporate peer-review suggestions into your final graded comments on each student's paper. After reading the student's paper and scanning the peer-review worksheets or marked drafts, you might say, for example, "You have effectively made use of Jeffrey D's suggestion about developing paragraphs 5–8. Audrey F's question about your transitions on pages 4 and 5 might have led you to strengthen your argument—look out for those transitional movements next time!" Another way to reinforce those goals is to assign one or two collaboratively written and graded projects.

Many instructors assign students in pairs or small teams to collaborate on papers; for certain kinds of writing, especially research writing, such strategies can be very effective and will prepare students well for the kinds of writing they may do in their careers. Many of the exercises in Chapters 42–45 can be adapted for collaborative projects. Such projects can be combined with individually produced and evaluated papers as well. For example, you might have students work in pairs to write out the different sides of a debate, then ask each student to produce an individually written paper that takes the other student's perspective into account. "Collaborative Learning" exercises in Chapters 9, 10, and 11 suggest various ways for students to produce arguments and to analyze each other's claims.

DEVELOPING SKILLS IN COLLABORATION

As with any other process, collaborative work is a slowly developed skill. New teachers will sometimes report that they tried it once and it "didn't work" so they're hesitant to try it again. Remember that groups might not seem highly productive at first; students can be unsure of their revision skills, hesitant about showing their work, and dependent on the teacher's greater authority. One way to make group work more productive from the start is to give students shorter, highly directed tasks at first; for example, each group might read and discuss Chapter 4, section c, on developing paragraphs, then work together to revise a student writer's paragraph. It also helps to model the assigned activity within the class as a whole before moving to smaller groups. For example, you might bring in a sample student paper, have each student come up with a revision suggestion or practice revising a sample sentence, then share the results with the class. Then, when students undertake a similar activity in smaller groups, you can refer back to the previous class-wide activity. Also, in many cases in which group work appears to "fail," students are simply confused about the assigned activity. It helps to be extremely clear about what you want each group to accomplish—even to provide a written handout or worksheet (sample worksheets follow this discussion). It's also important that students recognize the relationship between the group activity and their personal goals as writers; many teachers preface group work with a discussion of those goals in relation to the group task.

The crucial thing to remember is that working in revision or writing groups is as much a skill to be demonstrated and learned as any other. In working with a sample paper, for example, you might start with basic questions that help students to look globally at pieces of discourse as a teacher (evaluator) looks at it. "What's the point of this paper? Who are the readers supposed to be? What are some things this writer does well?" Then you might ask students to look more specifically at the construction of the paper: the places where assertions are backed up by evidence and the places where more evidence is needed; the indications of strong organizational control and the places where the text seems choppy and disorganized; the clear definition with supporting examples and the terms of the essay that need further clarification and development. The sample worksheets that accompany this chapter can be modified to guide students through particular tasks. For example, you might ask each student writer to create a self-evaluation of the paper (Form G), then compare it to her or his group's suggestions (Form A, B, or C). If students seem to be supplying vague responses to larger questions about audience and argument, Forms D, E, and F suggest ways to focus the groups on specific areas of the essay.

In addition to identifying strengths and problem areas, collaborative groups can go on to help each writer begin the work of revision. If, for instance, the text seems choppy or disorganized, they can experiment with organizational tools (using Exercise 2.9 in 2c, for example) or look for transition problems (using Exercise 4.9, 4b). If the thesis is underdeveloped, they might apply the questions in 10i, Exercise 10.11, to suggest places where new examples or analysis would help. Or, if the essay seems to lack a directed purpose, Exercises 1.6 and 1.9 in 1d and 1e offer specific and effective practice in thinking about audience and purpose. Many of the other exercises in *The Little, Brown Handbook* are well suited to such collaborative work.

CUSTOMIZING COLLABORATIVE MATERIALS

Many teachers like to modify the worksheets and exercises for the uses of a particular class. For instance, worksheet questions can be adapted to focus on a particular reading or essay assignment. Some teachers begin the course with detailed revision worksheets, then gradually taper off as group members become familiar with each other and confident about their revision skills. Teachers working in a computer classroom can supplement these exercises by creating networked revision groups, e-mail chat groups, and virtual-reality publications that help students experience various audience responses to their work (see Barrett, for example, and Daniel Anderson's chapter on pp. 66–100 of this manual).

While some teachers are active participants in group activities, other teachers try not to intervene directly in groups unless students have questions or have ceased to address the task (for more on this topic see "A Conversation About Small Groups" in Brook et al.). The teacher's primary role in a collaborative classroom is to plan group tasks that are effectively designed and that take the varying needs of students into account. For example, highly skilled students may not always trust their peers to give them revision advice. For those students it is important to emphasize that in learning to critique another writer's work in a way that encourages a productive revision they are honing their own revision skills as well. Conversely, less skilled writers occasionally feel overwhelmed by the group's advice and may seek to deflect attention from the paper by protesting that it's not a real draft or that it's not ready to be read. Here it helps to emphasize that active revision can begin from a sketchy paragraph or from notes. In some cases, the most effective task for a group might be to help the writer pinpoint useful passages in the readings, or to ask the writer to describe verbally where he or she intends to go with the project. In this sense, collaborative work can be flexibly attuned to the needs of various writers at different stages of a project. In a process-oriented class, this emphasis on the way different writers work can be a useful focus for class-wide discussions—and a way to encourage students to take themselves and each other seriously as writers.

Since students may profit from having specific guidelines for collaboration, we've prepared the following worksheets that will help you guide collaborative activities in your classroom.

WORKSHEETS FOR COLLABORATIVE ACTIVITIES

FORM A

General guidelines for peer readers commenting directly on a writer's work

Author: Reader:

As a reader, you are going to comment directly on a photocopy of a classmate's paper. Read the paper through carefully before making any comments. Then follow the guidelines below. If the writer has submitted a self-evaluation sheet, read it after answering question 1.

1. Consider the thesis, purpose, and audience for the paper. Are they indicated clearly? Are they consistent? If not, ask the writer questions to help clarify these essential elements of writing.

2. Skim the paper to see how it is organized. Are there any breaks in the organization? If so, try to explain why you feel that a gap exists. Whenever possible, phrase your comments as questions, not judgments. If you think that the organization needs to be revised significantly, skip to question 7 after answering this question.

3. Now go back and look at each paragraph. Is it unified, coherent, and developed? If not, ask the writer a question to help focus or complete the paragraph.

4. Are the paragraphs connected to one another smoothly and logically? If there are any logical gaps between the paragraphs, ask the writer how one paragraph is linked to the next. If you think that most of the paragraphs need to be revised significantly, skip to question 7 after answering this question.

5. Now look at sentences. Do any sentences confuse you? If so, try to describe your confusion or ask the writer a question about the sentence.

6. Are there any mechanical or grammatical problems in the paper? If so, point them out to the writer, but do not correct them.

7. Decide what the paper's two most important strengths are. Point them out to the writer.

FORM B

Reader response sheet for a descriptive critique

Author: Reader:

Answer the questions below, being as specific as possible.

1. Read the first paragraph and then pause. Write down what you expect will be the topic, purpose, and audience of the paper.

2. Now finish reading the paper. Were your expectations for the paper's topic, purpose, and audience fulfilled? If not, what do you now think the topic, purpose, and audience are?

3. What do you think the main idea, or thesis, of the paper is?

4. What sort of evidence is used to develop or support this main idea?

5. Summarize the paper, devoting one sentence to each paragraph.

FORM C

Reader response sheet for an evaluative critique

Author: Reader:

Answer the questions below, being as specific as possible. If the author has included a self-evaluation sheet, do not read it until you have answered questions 1 through 6.

1. Read the first paragraph and then pause. Write down what you expect will be the topic, purpose, and audience of the paper.

2. Now finish reading the paper. Were your expectations for the paper's topic, purpose, and audience fulfilled? If not, what do you now think the topic, purpose, and audience are?

3. What do you think the main idea, or thesis, of the paper is?

4. What sort of evidence is used to develop or support this main idea?

5. Summarize the paper, devoting one sentence to each paragraph.

6. What did you like best about the paper?

7. Did anything in the paper surprise you?

8. What two features of the paper most need improvement?

9. Please respond to the author's questions on the back of this sheet.

FORM D

Reader response sheet for a thorough critique

Author: Reader:

Answer the questions below, being as specific as possible. If the author has included a self-evaluation sheet, do not read it until you have answered questions 1 through 3.

1. Read the first paragraph and then pause. Write down what you expect will be the topic, purpose, and audience of the paper.

2. Now finish reading the paper. Were your expectations for the paper's topic, purpose, and audience fulfilled? If not, what do you now think the topic, purpose, and audience are?

3. Summarize the paper, devoting one sentence to each paragraph.

4. What do you think the main idea, or thesis, of the paper is? Do you agree with this thesis? Why or why not? What is your position on this topic?

5. What sort of evidence is used to develop or support this main idea? Is this evidence appropriate? Is there sufficient evidence? If not, what sort of evidence should the writer consider?

6. Does the author take into account different points of view about the thesis of the paper? Does the author consider counterarguments?

7. Are there counterarguments that the author does not consider, but should?

8. What did you like best about this paper?

9. What two features of the paper most need improvement?

10. Please respond to the author's questions on the back of this sheet.

FORM E

**Author's and reader's responses in the second round
of a thorough critique**

Author: Reader:

Author's section. Please attach a revision of your original paper to
this form and answer the following questions.

1. What do you think is your reader's point of view on this subject?
   Do you share that point of view?

2. What assumptions does your reader make about the topic? Do
   you agree with these assumptions? Why or why not?

3. What two comments by the reader were the most useful? Why
   were they helpful?

4. What are the two most important changes that you have made
   in this revision?

5. What do you like best about the essay?

6. What two questions would you like your reader to answer about
   this revision?

Reader's section. Please respond to the questions below.

1. Please summarize the author's revision, devoting one sentence
   to each paragraph.

2. How do you think that the author has improved the essay?

3. Has the author changed your feeling about the topic?

4. What is the strongest argument against the revised essay?

5. What two features most need improvement?

6. Respond to the author's questions.

FORM F

**Reader response sheet for an essay assignment
stressing paragraphing
(handbook Chapter 4)**

Author: Reader:

Answer the questions below, being as specific as possible. If the author has included a self-evaluation sheet, do not read it until you have answered questions 1 through 6.

1. Read the first paragraph and then pause. Write down what you expect will be the topic, purpose, and audience of the paper.

2. Now finish reading the paper. Were your expectations for the paper's topic, purpose, and audience fulfilled? If not, what do you now think the topic, purpose, and audience are?

3. What do you think the main idea, or thesis, of the paper is?

4. What sort of evidence is used to develop or support this main idea?

5. Number the paragraphs. Are the author's paragraphs unified, coherent, and developed? If so, note them. Also indicate any that confuse you, and explain why.

6. Do the paragraphs follow a logical order? Describe how the argument does or does not flow from the first to the second, from the second to the third, and so on.

7. What did you like best about the paper?

8. What two features of the paper most need improvement?

FORM G

Self-evaluation sheet to accompany an essay for peer response or instructor's evaluation

Author: In order to help your instructor or peer reader evaluate this essay, you should explain where you are in the writing process. Be as specific as possible in answering the following questions.

1. What are you trying to say in this paper? What is your main idea?

2. Who might be interested in reading this paper?

3. What do you like best in the paper?

4. What do you like least in the paper?

5. What would you work on if you had twenty-four hours more to spend on the project?

6. What three questions would you like to ask your reader? How can your reader help you develop the paper further?

RESOURCES FOR COLLABORATIVE LEARNING AND PEER CRITICISM

Arkin, Marian, and Barbara Shollar. *The Writing Tutor.* New York: Longman, 1982.

Barrett, Edward. "Collaboration in the Electronic Classroom." *Technology Review* 96:2 (Feb./March 1993): 51–55.

Bishop, Wendy. "Helping Peer Writing Groups Succeed." *Teaching English in the Two-Year College* 15 (1988): 120–25.

Bizzaro, Patrick, and Stuart Werner. "Collaboration of Teacher and Counselor in Basic Writing." *College Composition and Communication* 38 (1987): 397–425.

Bormann, Ernest. *Small-Group Communication: Theory and Practice.* New York: Harper, 1990.

Brook, Robert, Ruth Mirtz, and Rick Evans, eds. *Small Groups in Writing Workshops.* Urbana: NCTE, 1994.

Bruffee, Kenneth. *Collaborative Learning: Higher Education, Interdependence, and the Authority of Knowledge.* Baltimore: Johns Hopkins UP, 1993.

Clark, Beverly Lyon. *Talking About Writing: A Guide for Tutor and Teacher Conferences.* Ann Arbor: U of Michigan P, 1985.

Clarke, Irene L. "Portfolio Evaluations, Collaboration, and Writing Centers." *College Composition and Communication* 44 (1993): 515–24.

Corder, Jim W. "Tribes and Displaced Persons: Some Observations on Collaboration." *Theory and Practice in the Teaching of Writing: Rethinking the Discipline.* Ed. Lee Odell. Carbondale: Southern Illinois UP, 1993. 271–88.

Elbow, Peter. "Reflecting on Academic Discourse: How It Relates to Freshmen and Colleagues." *College English* 53 (Feb. 1991): 135–55.

Fontaine, Sheryl L. "The Unfinished Story of the Interpretative Community." *Rhetoric Review* 7 (1988): 86–96.

Forman, Janis, ed. *New Visions of Collaborative Writing.* Portsmouth, NH: Cook/Boynton, 1992.

Fraser, Scott C., et al. "Two, Three, or Four Heads Are Better Than One: Modification of College Performance by Peer Monitoring." *Journal of Educational Psychology* 69 (1977–78): 101–08.

Gebhardt, Richard. "Team Work and Feedback: Broadening the Base of Collaborative Writing." *College English* 42 (1980): 69–74.

Gergits, Julia M., and James J. Schramer. "The Collaborative Classroom as the Site of Difference." *Journal of Advanced Composition* 14:1 (Winter 1994): 187–202.

George, Diana. "Working with Peer Groups in the Composition Classroom." *College Composition and Communication* 35 (1984): 320–26.

Gere, Anne Ruggles. *Writing Groups: History, Theory, and Implications.* Carbondale: Southern Illinois UP, 1987.

————, and Robert D. Abbott. "Talking About Writing: The Language of Writing Groups." *Research in the Teaching of English* 19 (1985): 362–86.

————, and Ralph Stevens. "The Language of Writing Groups: How Oral Response Shapes Revision." *The Acquisition of Written Language: Response and Revision.* Ed. Sarah Warshauer Freedman. Norwood: Ablex, 1985. 85–105.

Golub, Jeff, and the Committee on Classroom Practices, eds. *Focus on Collaborative Learning.* Urbana: NCTE, 1988.

Haring-Smith, Tori. *Writing Together: Collaborative Learning in the Classroom.* New York: HarperCollins, 1994.

Harris, Joseph. "The Idea of Community in the Study of Writing." *College Composition and Communication* 40 (1989): 11–22.

Harris, Muriel. "Peer Tutoring: How Tutors Learn." *Teaching English in the Two-Year College* 15 (1988): 28–33.

Hillocks, George. "Environments for Active Learning." *Theory and Practice in the Teaching of Writing: Rethinking the Discipline.* Ed. Lee Odell. Carbondale: Southern Illinois UP, 1993. 244–70.

Kail, Harvey. "Collaborative Learning in Context: The Problem with Peer Tutoring." *College English* 45 (1983): 817–23.

Knox-Zuinn, Carolyn. "Collaboration in the Writing Classroom: An Interview with Ken Kesey." *College Composition and Communication* 41 (1990): 309–17.

Lunsford, Andrea, and Lisa Ede. "Rhetoric in a New Key: Women and Collaboration." *Rhetoric Review* 8 (1990): 234–41.

————. *Singular Texts/Plural Authors: Perspectives on Collaborative Writing.* Carbondale: Southern Illinois UP, 1992.

Lyon, Arabella. "Re-presenting Communities: Teaching Turbulence." *Rhetoric Review* 10 (1992): 279–90.

Madden-Simpson, Janet. "A Collaborative Approach to the Research Paper." *Teaching English in the Two-Year College* 16 (1989): 113–15.

Reither, James A., and Douglas Vipond. "Writing as Collaboration." *College English* 51 (1989): 855–67.

Roskelly, Hephzibah. "The Risky Business of Group Work." *The Writing Teacher's Sourcebook,* 4th ed. Ed. Edward P. J. Corbett et al. New York: Oxford UP, 2000. 123–28.

Smit, David W. "Some Difficulties with Collaborative Learning." *Journal of Advanced Composition* 9 (1989): 45–58.

Spear, Karen. *Sharing Writing: Peer Response Groups in English Classes.* Portsmouth: Heinemann, 1988.

Speck, Bruce, et al., eds. *Collaborative Writing: An Annotated Bibliography.* Westport: Greenwood, 1999.

Spellmeyer, Kurt. "On Conventions and Collaboration: The Open Road and the Iron Cage." *Writing Theory and Critical Theory*. Ed. John Clifford and John Schilb. New York: MLA, 1994.

Spigelman, Candace. "Habits of Mind: Historical Configurations of Textual Ownership in Peer Writing Groups." *College Composition and Communication* 49 (1998): 234–55.

Stewart, Donald. "Collaborative Learning and Composition: Boon or Bane?" *Rhetoric Review* 7 (1988): 58–85.

Stygall, Gail. "Women and Language in the Collaborative Writing Classroom." *Feminism and Composition Studies: In Other Words*. Ed. Susan C. Jarratt and Lynn Worsham. New York: MLA, 1998.

Teich, Nathaniel, ed. *Rogerian Perspectives: Collaborative Rhetoric for Oral and Written Communication*. Norwood: Ablex, 1992.

Trimbur, John. "Collaborative Learning and Teaching Writing." *Perspectives on Research and Scholarship in Composition*. Ed. Ben W. McClelland and Timothy R. Donovan. New York: MLA, 1985. 87–109.

———. "Consensus and Difference in Collaborative Learning." *College English* 51 (1989): 602–16.

Tobin, Lad. *Writing Relationships: What Really Happens in the Composition Class*. Portsmouth: Boynton/Cook, 1993.

Wiener, Harvey S. "Collaborative Learning in the Classroom: A Guide to Evaluation." *College English* 48 (1986): 52–61.

Yancey, Kathleen Blake, and Michael Spooner. "A Single Good Mind: Collaboration, Cooperation, and the Writing Self." *College Composition and Communication* 49 (1998): 45–62.

Using Computers to Teach Writing

By Daniel Anderson

Information technologies continue to make dramatic alterations in the educational landscape, and many writing teachers are finding themselves called upon to use technological tools in their teaching. Administrators may be asking that curricula adapt to serve the changing demands of constituents. Students may arrive at school either already equipped with information skills or insistent that these skills be included as part of their learning. This chapter helps instructors meet the challenges of this transformational moment in education. The chapter provides an overview of some of the opportunities made possible by information technology, discusses concerns likely to arise as teachers adapt information technologies to teaching, and offers practical advice for using instructional technologies critically. (*The Little, Brown Handbook* also serves to illuminate the use of information technologies. Chapter 3 offers advice on managing files, using spelling and grammar checkers, and other computer skills in the context of revising and editing; Chapter 5 treats document design; Chapters 43 and 44 offer specific information about electronic research; and Chapter 54 focuses on the rhetorical issues of writing online, including e-mail, collaboration, and Web composition; and computer tips appear throughout the text.)

IMAGINING THE POSSIBILITIES FOR TEACHING WITH TECHNOLOGY

Information technologies offer new modes of learning and avenues for research and collaboration. Word processors and basic computing skills help students enhance and strengthen their writing process. Electronic discussions enable them to converse with one another as they explore issues and ideas about writing. File-sharing functions and collaboration programs allow students to work together on projects. Electronic library resources provide students with extended opportunities for research. And students who compose Web pages and other electronic documents can develop and sharpen their writing skills as they participate in emergent forms of communication and literacy.

What makes this range of possibilities exciting for writing instructors is the way all of these activities build upon what we know to be useful methodologies for helping students to become better writers. Here are some ideas about the pedagogical uses of computers:

- You can use computers to foreground the process-oriented nature of successful writing. The fluid nature of electronic text and the capacity to write multiple drafts and revisions can help convey an understanding of the ongoing and evolving nature of successful writing. You can teach your students the difference between surface-level revision and deep or structural revision by having them use advanced word-processing features to track the changes they make to documents. You can also help them master the elements of format and document design.

- Electronic discussion tools can stimulate thinking and provide a space in which students can practice writing. You can create opportunities for students to express their ideas freely in writing using e-mail, blogs, or chat, and you can coordinate discussion activities with class readings or projects. You can further authorize student ideas by making public the transcripts of conversations or encouraging the citation of peer comments in formal class documents. If you appoint discussion moderators or provide credit for productive participation in any of these conversations, you will be enabling your students to take charge of their learning. These activities can also help your students evaluate the ways that conventions and media affect communication, and they can promote writing within a social context by showing students how to interact conversationally with groups outside of the classroom.

- Computers can promote collaboration and student-centered learning in numerous ways. You might employ file-sharing to simplify the logistics of group projects and peer review. You can teach students to use the comment and change-tracking functions of word processors to amplify their ability to conduct peer reviews. Web-based collaboration options can be used to create work spaces for small groups and to conduct peer-to-peer activities. You can even capitalize upon the different levels of computer literacy among your students, allowing the more skilled to mentor their peers about information technologies.

- Students can develop their research skills and information literacy by using computers. When you give research assignments to your students, you have an opportunity to help them learn to think and use resources critically. You can emphasize the ways that library and Internet research complement one another. At the same time, you can ask students to consider the relative advantages and disadvantages of print and electronic resources, and to evaluate electronic resources for credibility. You can show students how to find, manage, and document electronic research. You can learn to supplement your own courses by finding and providing appropriate learning resources for students (the most exciting of which may be related to ways of conducting primary research using Internet communications).

- One of the greatest advantages of information technologies is that they promote new forms of literacy. You'll need to teach your students to read electronic compositions critically and to look at elements of interactivity and design in terms of purpose and audience. You might conduct some comparisons between print and electronic compositions to explore the larger rhetorical issues addressed by each. You might also assign Web or other multimedia compositions to allow students to practice working with visual and hypertextual rhetoric, or you could craft Web composition assignments that ask students to manage and tap into selected Web resources. If you assign some Web projects, you can highlight the importance of audience and issues of publication as they relate to writing.

COMPUTER TECHNOLOGY IN AND OUT OF THE CLASSROOM

For many years the only practical way of integrating technology-related activities into your classes was through full or part-time use of a computer-assisted classroom. Today you may have a number of options when it comes to integrating technology into teaching, including the use of supplemental Internet resources, the use of a companion course Web site or blog, or the use of a computer-assisted classroom or lab.

The key to choosing the best option for integrating computer technology into your teaching is to take time to investigate the resources already available at your institution and to identify others which it might be feasible to develop. Begin by talking with your colleagues in technology support. Ideally, your institution will offer support in the form of technical infrastructure and instructional planning and design. Once you have established a good working relationship with people knowledgeable about the resources at your school, you can consider and choose among the numerous opportunities to adapt information technologies to the teaching of writing. Before leaping into the breach, however, you should acquaint yourself with some of the challenges associated with using instructional technologies and develop strategies that can make your efforts more successful.

The list below details some of those challenges and offers suggestions for how to address them.

ACCESS

You may find that your school has no computer-assisted lab or classroom facilities—or that the equipment in these facilities is outdated. Students may also have inadequate access to technology outside of class. Some students may own the latest computers, others may have three-year-old machines, and still others will have to use the computers in a lab or library. You may not be able to improve or equalize your students' access, but you can work to adapt to whatever level of access they have. If you will be working in a computer-assisted classroom, investigate the capabilities of the environment. If you will be asking students to do Internet work or to interact with a course Web site outside of class, check to make sure your students will have adequate access and make clear to your students what your expectations for participation are. It can be difficult to anticipate every contingency, but you should try to find out ahead of time what access problems are likely to arise and plan accordingly.

SKILLS AND TRAINING

Once you've made sure that your students have access to adequate technological resources, the next step is to make sure that they have the skills necessary to accomplish technology-related work. Again, you'll need to investigate the options available to you and your students. Many institutions offer workshop training courses in computer basics and other aspects of technology. There are also many resources available online which can provide advice for learning about computer technologies (see the handbook's companion Web site). You could even make learning about technology a central focus of your course, something that you and your students do together. Allow knowledgeable students to take the lead in helping one another learn computer-related tasks: by "deputizing" them, you will not only relieve yourself of the burden of having to solve every technical problem, but you'll also foster collaborative work in your classroom.

TIME DEMANDS

It is a cruel misconception that technology makes teaching and learning more efficient. If anything, you will find that using information technologies places heavy demands on your time. Not only must you devote yourself to learning new skills, but you must also invest energy into reconceiving the ways that you teach. The best strategy for protecting your time as you integrate new technologies into your teaching is to take small bites. Don't try to implement every option available to you for every class. In fact, you can build a highly successful semester around exploring a single computer-assisted activity. Additionally, rather than conducting or monitoring all computer-related work yourself, you can allow students to take charge of some of the class activities, appointing them to moderate class e-mail discussions or to spearhead class research expeditions.

DISTRACTIONS

One of the most powerful aspects of instructional technology is its capacity to enable student-centered activities. There are some drawbacks, however. You may find that the computers become a distraction when you are trying to conduct a face-to-face discussion or present information to your class, or you may notice students drifting away from the task at hand or behaving inappropriately when interacting in electronic forums. A good way to address these potential distractions is to develop rules of decorum as a class. Early in the semester, talk over these concerns and decide upon conventions that you will follow during class activities. You may also want to build those rules right into your course requirements. For problems related to computers in the classroom, ask students to turn off their monitors or close the lids of their laptops when distractions become overwhelming.

INSTITUTIONAL CULTURE

Not only does instructional technology place new demands on your time and energy, but it also prompts you to work in ways that may not be familiar to your colleagues or fit in with traditional categories used for promotion and reward. A related problem some teachers have is that they are isolated from other colleagues in the department, who may not actively be pursuing instructional technologies. Again, explore the context at your school as you consider how the technology-related work you do will fit in with your institution's culture. Ask administrators about their expectations for and ways of evaluating computer-related work. It may also help to establish contact with other members of your institution who use computers in their teaching and/or with Internet communities devoted to technology-based pedagogies. (See the links on pp. 99–100 of this manual.)

THE LITTLE, BROWN HANDBOOK IN THE COMPUTER-ASSISTED CLASSROOM

Many instructors wonder how textbooks fit into the computer-assisted learning environment. At present, it is impossible to predict how soon, or if, the dominant medium for instructional publishing will shift from the bound book to an electronic medium. Remembering that access to computers may vary greatly, the tenth edition of *The Little, Brown Handbook* and its ancillaries provide resources for teaching all phases of the writing process for instructors working in both electronic and traditional classroom environments. Additionally, the book design facilitates quick reference while working online through checklists and other emphasized material set aside in quickly identifiable tinted boxes, a list of which appears in the endpapers. Throughout the handbook are specific strategies for working with computers, and the companion Web site offers video tutorials, Web-only exercises, exercises from the handbook in Word format, and links to relevant Web sites.

BASIC COMPUTER SKILLS FOR WRITERS

Basic computer skills for writers—organizing with a word processor, revising on screen versus on paper, and so on—are covered throughout Part 1 on the writing process. In addition, Chapter 3 emphasizes how computers can help break down the boundaries between prewriting and drafting and support collaborative work. Chapter 3 includes discussions of how students can use file management techniques to work on multiple drafts of papers, which will help them develop the understanding that successful writing results from an evolving and recursive process of prewriting, drafting, and revision. Students can also use file management and naming conventions to share and review one another's papers more easily; this will enable them to strengthen their writing based upon feedback and interaction with their peers. Chapter 3 also instructs students in the use of advanced word-processing features, such as Comment and Track Changes. Teaching students to use just one or two of these advanced functions is an easy way to promote process-oriented writing in a collaborative context.

Later in the book, Chapter 54 discusses options for using computers in the service of collaboration. Students are shown how to collaborate with classmates using e-mail and the Web (including Web-based courseware such as *Blackboard*, *WebCT*, or a Web log). The coverage includes strategies for interacting in class discussions, sharing files, and using online collaboration tools.

EDITING AND OTHER SENTENCE-LEVEL ACTIVITIES

Teaching grammar, mechanics, punctuation, and other sentence-level concerns with computers is a double-edged sword. While functions like spelling and style checkers offer powerful assistance in many situations, they can also lull a student into a false sense of security when it comes to editing her work. Furthermore, they can prove distracting, focusing undeserved attention on surface errors at times when deeper revision or drafting deserves the writer's full attention. Chapter 3 discusses these concerns in detail in order to help students develop a critical understanding of the value of spelling and grammar functions. It also offers instruction in how to customize spelling and grammar functions to maximize their usefulness.

Opportunities for using spelling and style checkers are noted throughout the handbook. These notations also warn students about problems that may arise from uncritical reliance on computer-based editing tools. Links to Web sites that offer additional exercises and instruction on sentence-level writing problems are given on the companion Web site.

RESEARCH-BASED WRITING

The research chapters cover the use of computers in the research process. Beginning with Chapter 42, "Planning a Research Project," the handbook distinguishes between online and print sources and explains how to find bibliographic information for online sources. Chapter 43, "Finding Sources," emphasizes using the library as Web gateway and includes coverage of keyword searches for both library and Internet sources, and the use of electronic catalogs, indexes, abstracts, and subscription services. Chapters 44 and 45, "Working with Sources" and "Avoiding Plagiarisim," discuss ways of evaluating and managing electronic materials, and warn about online plagiarism and explain how plagiarism can be detected by online tools. In addition, the four documentation sections—MLA, Chicago, APA, and CSE—provide the most up-to-date models for citing electronic sources in each style.

DOCUMENT DESIGN

Chapter 5 shows students how to use computers to design academic papers and also provides guidance in the principles of electronic document design (including the role of flow, spacing, emphasis, color, fonts, and illustrations). Chapter 5 also includes guidelines on designing for readers with disabilities.

ONLINE COMMUNICATION AND ELECTRONIC DOCUMENTS

Chapters 54–56 cover a range of opportunities for writing and communicating online. Chapter 54, "Writing Online," focuses on the rhetorical issues of writing e-mail, working in online collaborative writing environments, and composing online papers and original Web sites. Chapter 55, "Public Writing," contains guidelines for preparing an electronic, scannable résumé and a student sample. Chapter 56, "Oral Presentations," provides tips for working with PowerPoint and sample slides from a student presentation.

ANCILLARIES TO *THE LITTLE, BROWN HANDBOOK*

For more ideas on using Internet resources in the writing classroom, Longman offers *Teaching Online: Internet Research, Conversation, and Composition,* prepared by Daniel Anderson, Bret Benjamin, Chris Busiel, and Bill Paredes-Holt. Instructors with little online experience will find basic definitions, numerous examples, and detailed information about using Internet resources in each chapter. Those more familiar with online resources can learn more about using e-mail and discussion lists to foster a workshop atmosphere in the classroom and using the Web to begin a research project. Chapter-end case studies and a sample research paper show numerous applications of online composition, conversation, and research.

Several other important ancillaries can benefit students and instructors alike, most notably the interactive e-book and the *MyCompLab* Web site. See page 23 of this manual for a description. In addition, the handbook's companion Web site, besides offering the student features described on pages 73–96 of this manual, also provides a password-protected copy of this manual as well as transparency masters and *PowerPoint* slides.

OTHER SOFTWARE PROGRAMS: COMPUTER LEARNING ENVIRONMENTS AND GRAMMAR PROGRAMS

Although you can incorporate technology into writing instruction with only a word processor, an e-mail program, and a Web browser, most instructors also have the option of teaching in a computer classroom or using an online learning package. Several software applications have been developed for use in a writing classroom, such as *WebCT* and *Blackboard*. These applications can assist instructors in structuring classroom activities and assignments and provide students and instructors with the opportunity to combine individual writing assignments with collaboration at any point in the writing process. Generally, these learning packages provide a chat option, file-sharing features, a class e-mail system or discussion forum, and the ability to post and collect assignments online. (A proprietary version of *Blackboard, Course Compass*, is available to adopters of the handbook, and the *MyCompLab* online resources are available as content cartridges for instructors who are already using *Blackboard* or *WebCT*.)

Applications devoted to issues of grammar, mechanics, and punctuation generally fall into one of two categories—tutorials or style checkers. Tutorials contain sets of questions (multiple choice, true/false, short answer) on various topics. They may also contain various levels of description and explanation of the topics covered, as well as diagnostic or proficiency tests. Tutorials currently available on the market include *Grammar-ROM, The Grammar Tree, The Grammar Key,* and *Easy English Grammar*, the last designed for ESL and EFL students. Grammar/style checkers examine writing for potential grammatical problems. *Microsoft Word* and *WordPerfect* include style checkers, and others available include *Grammar Slammer, Correct Grammar,* and *Grammatik*. Though occasionally useful in helping students spot specific flaws in their work, these applications should never be viewed as a substitute for careful and thorough editing. (For more information on using word-processor grammar and style checkers, see Chapter 3.)

THE COMPANION WEB SITE

The accompanying companion Web site for *The Little, Brown Handbook* serves as an additional teaching tool for instructors, and a studying and practice tool for students. Here students will be able to practice their grammar skills with exercises, watch video tutorials to guide them through the writing process, and link to resources on the Web. Following is an outline of what can be found on the companion Web site:

1 Assessing the Writing Situation

VIDEO TUTORIALS
Narrowing a subject online
Working with text on a word processor

Exercises

Web-only Exercises
1.1   Identifying subjects for writing
1.2   Considering audience

Exercises from *The Little, Brown Handbook*
1.2   Analyzing a writing situation *6*
1.3   Narrowing subjects *9*
1.6   Considering audience *13*

Checklist from *The Little, Brown Handbook*
Questions about audience *11*

Web Links
Good overall sites on writing
Finding and narrowing a subject
Audience
Purpose

2 Developing and Shaping Ideas

Video Tutorial
Outlining with a word processor

Exercises

Web-only Exercise
2.1   Evaluating thesis statements

Exercise from *The Little, Brown Handbook*
2.9   Organizing ideas *43*

Checklist from *The Little, Brown Handbook*
Questions about patterns *24–25*

Web Links
Discovering ideas
Thesis statements
Organization

3 Drafting and Revising

Video Tutorials
Overcoming writer's block
Revising with a word processor
Using spelling and grammar/style checkers

Exercises

Exercises from *The Little, Brown Handbook*
3.1   Analyzing a first draft *48*
3.4   Analyzing a revised draft *57*
        Sara Ling's formal outline *36*
        Sara Ling's first draft *47–48*
        Sara Ling's revised draft *55–57*
3.9   Proofreading *63*

Checklists from *The Little, Brown Handbook*
Checklist for revision *51*
Checklist for editing *58–59*

Web Links
Drafting

Revising
Word processing and file management
Editing and proofreading
Collaboration
Portfolios

4 Writing and Revising Paragraphs

Video Tutorial
Achieving paragraph unity

Exercises

Web-only Exercises
4.1   Maintaining paragraph unity
4.2   Achieving paragraph coherence
4.3   Developing the paragraph

Exercises from *The Little, Brown Handbook*
4.1   Finding the central idea *75–76*
4.2   Revising a paragraph for unity *76*
4.4   Writing a unified paragraph *77*
4.5   Turning topic sentences into unified paragraphs *77*
4.7   Arranging sentences coherently *88*
4.8   Eliminating inconsistencies *88–89*
4.9   Using transitional expressions *89*
4.11 Writing a coherent paragraph *89*
4.12 Turning topic sentences into coherent paragraphs *90*
4.14 Analyzing and revising skimpy paragraphs *100–101*

Web Links
Good overall sites on writing paragraphs
Paragraph unity
Paragraph coherence
Paragraph development
Introductions and conclusions

5 Designing Documents

Video Tutorials
Working with illustrations on a word processor
Formatting documents on a word processor

Web Links
Good overall sites on document design
Color
Tables, figures, and images
Document and Web page design for readers with disabilities

6 Writing in Academic Situations

Exercises

Web-only Exercises
6.1 Revising in academic writing
Exercises from *The Little, Brown Handbook*
6.1 Using academic language *134*

Web Links
Academic writing

7 Studying Effectively and Taking Exams

Exercises

Web-only Exercises
7.1 Reading main points and supporting ideas
7.2 Summarizing

Web Links
Good overall sites for study skills and essay exams
Time management and organization
Taking notes
Reading
Summary
Essay exams

8 Forming a Critical Perspective

Exercises

Web-only Exercises
8.1 Reading a Web site critically
Exercises from *The Little, Brown Handbook*
8.3 Thinking critically *163–64*
8.9 Responding to critical writing *177–78*

Checklists from *The Little, Brown Handbook*
Guidelines for analysis, interpretation, and synthesis *158*
Guidelines for evaluation *163*

Web Links
Good overall sites on critical thinking
Reading journal
Summary
Analysis, interpretation, synthesis, and evaluation
Working with images
Critical writing

9 Reading Arguments Critically

Video Tutorial
Investigating assumptions

Exercises

Web-only Exercise
9.1 Identifying fallacies

Exercise from *The Little, Brown Handbook*
9.3 Identifying and revising fallacies *198*

Checklist from *The Little, Brown Handbook*
Questions for critically reading an argument *181*

Web Links
Good overall sites on reading arguments
Claims
Evidence
Assumptions
Fallacies

10 Writing an Argument

Video Tutorials
Finding subjects for argument
Answering opposing views

Exercises

Web-only Exercises
10.1 Choosing a suitable subject for argument
10.2 Evaluating thesis statements for argument

Exercises from *The Little, Brown Handbook*
10.1 Finding a subject for argument *200*
10.4 Reasoning inductively *206*
10.5 Reasoning deductively *206–07*
10.7 Identifying appeals *211*
10.11 Critically reading an argument *218*

Web Links
Good overall sites for writing arguments
Argument subjects
Purpose and audience
Thesis statement
Reasoning
Appeals
Organization
Revision

11 Reading and Using Visual Arguments

Exercises

Flash Exercise
Responding to images

Exercises from *The Little, Brown Handbook*

11.1 Reading a visual argument critically *224–25*
11.3 Brainstorming images for a visual argument *230*

Web Links

Reading visual arguments
Using visual arguments

12 Understanding Sentence Grammar

Exercises

Web-only Exercises

12.1 Parts of speech
12.2 Subjects and predicates
12.3 Sentence patterns
12.4 Prepositional phrases
12.5 Verbals and verbal phrases
12.6 Subordinate clauses
12.7 Appositives
12.8 Classifying sentences

Exercises from *The Little, Brown Handbook*

12.1 Identifying subjects and predicates *237*
12.2 Identifying nouns, verbs, and pronouns *237*
12.3 Using nouns and verbs *238*
12.4 Identifying sentence patterns *241*
12.5 Creating sentences *241*
12.6 Identifying and using adjectives and adverbs *243*
12.7 Using verb forms as modifiers *243*
12.8 Sentence combining: Single-word modifiers *244*
12.9 Identifying prepositional phrases *247*
12.10 Sentence combining: Prepositional phrases *247*
12.11 Identifying verbals and verbal phrases *250–51*
12.12 Sentence combining: Verbals and verbal phrases *251*
12.13 Sentence combining: Absolute phrases *252*
12.14 Identifying subordinate clauses *256*
12.15 Sentence combining: Subordinate clauses *256–57*
12.16 Sentence combining: Appositives *258*
12.17 Sentence combining: Compound constructions *262–63*
12.18 Forming questions and commands *265*
12.19 Rewriting passives and expletives *265*
12.20 Identifying sentence structures *266*
12.21 Sentence combining: Sentence structures *266*

Web Links
Good overall sites for grammar
Absolute phrases
Adjectives and adverbs
Appositives
Clauses
Coordinating and correlative conjunctions
Parts of speech
Prepositions and prepositional phrases
Sentence classification
Subordinating conjunctions
Verbals and verbal phrases

13 Case of Nouns and Pronouns

Video Tutorial
Understanding pronouns

Exercises

Web-only Exercises
13.1 Identifying subjects and objects
13.2 Pronoun case: Compound subjects and objects
13.3 Pronoun case: *Who* versus *whom*

Exercises from *The Little, Brown Handbook*
13.1 Choosing between subjective and objective pronouns *270*
13.2 Choosing between subjective and objective pronouns *270–71*
13.3 Choosing between *who* and *whom* *273*
13.4 Sentence combining: *Who* versus *whom* *273–74*
13.5 Revising: Case *274–75*

Web Links
Good overall sites for noun and pronoun case
Who vs. *Whom*

14 Verbs

Video Tutorial
Using irregular verbs

Exercises

Web-only Exercises
14.1 Irregular verbs
14.2 *–s* and *–ed* verb endings
14.3 Helping verbs
14.4 Verbs plus gerunds or infinitives
14.5 Verbs plus particles
14.6 Verb tenses
14.7 Tense sequence

14.8 Subjunctive mood
14.9 Passive and active voice
14.10 Passive voice

Exercises from *The Little, Brown Handbook*
14.1 Using irregular verbs *280–81*
14.2 Distinguishing *sit/set, lie/lay, rise/raise* *282*
14.3 Using *–s* and *–ed* endings *283*
14.4 Using helping verbs *287–88*
14.5 Revising: Helping verbs plus main verbs *288*
14.6 Revising: Verbs plus gerunds or infinitives *290*
14.7 Revising: Verbs plus particles *292*
14.8 Adjusting tense sequence: Past or past perfect tense *298*
14.9 Revising: Tense sequence with conditional sentences *299*
14.10 Revising: Subjunctive mood *301*
14.11 Converting between active and passive voices *303-04*
14.12 Revising: Verb forms, tense, mood *304*

Web Links
Good overall sites on verbs
Active and passive voice
Gerunds and infinitives
Helping verbs
Irregular verbs
Verb forms
Verb mood
Verb tense

15 Agreement

Video Tutorials
Recognizing subject-verb problems
Recognizing pronoun-antecedent problems

Exercises

Web-only Exercises
15.1 Subject-verb agreement
15.2 Subject-verb agreement
15.3 Subject-verb agreement: *–s* or *–es* endings
15.4 Subject-verb agreement: Indefinite pronouns
15.5 Pronoun-antecedent agreement
15.6 Pronoun-antecedent agreement

Exercises from *The Little, Brown Handbook*
15.1 Revising: Subject-verb agreement *312–13*
15.2 Revising: Pronoun-antecedent agreement *317*
15.3 Adjusting for agreement *318*
15.4 Revising: Agreement *318–19*

Web Links
Pronoun-antecedent agreement
Subject-verb agreement

16 Adjectives and Adverbs

Exercises

Web-only Exercises
16.1 Adjectives and adverbs
16.2 Comparatives and superlatives
16.3 Double negatives
16.4 Nouns as modifiers
16.5 Present and past participles as modifiers
16.6 Determiners: *a, an, the*

Exercises from *The Little, Brown Handbook*
16.1 Revising: Adjectives and adverbs *322*
16.2 Revising: Comparatives and superlatives *324*
16.3 Revising: Double negatives *324–25*
16.4 Revising: Present and past participles *326*
16.5 Revising: Articles *330*
16.6 Revising: Adjectives and adverbs *331*

Review
13–16 Revising: Grammatical sentences *331–32*

Web Links
Good overall sites for adjectives and adverbs
Articles and other determiners
Comparatives and superlatives
Double negatives
Participles as adjectives

17 Sentence Fragments

Video Tutorial
Recognizing sentence fragments

Exercises

Web-only Exercises
17.1 Sentence fragments
17.2 Subordinate clauses as sentence fragments
17.3 Other sentence fragments

Exercises from *The Little, Brown Handbook*
17.1 Identifying and revising sentence fragments *337–38*
17.2 Revising: Sentence fragments *340–41*
17.3 Revising: Sentence fragments *341*

Web Links
Sentence fragments

18 Comma Splices and Fused Sentences

Video Tutorial
Recognizing comma splices

Exercises

Web-only Exercises
18.1 Comma splices and fused sentences
18.2 Comma splices and fused sentences: Main clauses without *and, but,*
etc.
18.3 Comma splices and fused sentences: Main clauses with *however, for
example,* etc.

Exercises from *The Little, Brown Handbook*
18.1 Identifying and revising comma splices *347*
18.2 Identifying and revising fused sentences *348–49*
18.3 Sentence combining: Comma splices and fused sentences *349*
18.4 Revising: Comma splices and fused sentences *349*

Web Links
Comma splices and fused sentences

19 Pronoun Reference

Video Tutorial
Recognizing pronoun reference problems

Exercises

Web-only Exercises
19.1 Pronoun reference: Clear and close reference
19.2 Pronoun reference: Specific reference [Indefinite *it, they, you*]

Exercises from *The Little, Brown Handbook*
19.1 Revising: Ambiguous and remote pronoun reference *352–53*
19.2 Revising: Indefinite and inappropriate pronoun reference *356*
19.3 Revising: Pronoun reference *356–57*

Web Links
Pronoun reference

20 Shifts

Exercises

Web-only Exercises
20.1 Shifts in person and number

20.2 Shifts in tense and mood
20.3 Shifts in subject and voice
20.4 Shifts in quotations and questions

Exercises from *The Little, Brown Handbook*
20.1 Revising: Shifts in person and number *359*
20.2 Revising: Shifts in tense and mood *360–61*
20.3 Revising: Shifts in subject and voice *361*
20.4 Revising: Shifts in direct and indirect quotations and questions *362–63*
20.5 Revising: Shifts *363*

Web Links
Shifts

21 Misplaced and Dangling Modifiers

Video Tutorial
Repairing misplaced modifiers

Exercises

Web-only Exercises
21.1 Misplaced modifiers: Unclear placement
21.2 Misplaced modifiers: Awkward placement
21.3 Position of adverbs and adjectives
21.4 Dangling modifiers

Exercises from *The Little, Brown Handbook*
21.1 Revising: Misplaced phrases and clauses *365*
21.2 Using limiting modifiers *366*
21.3 Revising: Squinting modifiers *366*
21.4 Revising: Separated sentence parts *368*
21.5 Revising: Placement of adverbs and adjectives *370*
21.6 Revising: Dangling modifiers *372–73*
21.7 Sentence combining: Placing modifiers *373*
21.8 Revising: Misplaced and dangling modifiers *373*

Web Links
Misplaced modifiers
Adjective order
Adverb order
Dangling modifiers

22 Mixed and Incomplete Sentences

Exercises

Web-only Exercises
22.1 Mixed grammar

22.2   Incomplete compounds and comparisons

Exercises from *The Little, Brown Handbook*
22.1   Revising: Sentences mixed in grammar and meaning *377*
22.2   Revising: Repeated sentence parts *377–78*
22.3   Revising: Incomplete sentences *380–81*
22.4   Revising: Mixed and incomplete sentences *381*

Review
17–22 Revising: Clear sentences *381–82*

Web Links
Mixed and incomplete sentences
Editing and proofreading

23 Emphasizing Ideas

Exercises

Web-only Exercises
23.1   Emphasis
23.2   Emphasis

Exercises from *The Little, Brown Handbook*
23.1   Revising: Emphasis of subjects and verbs *386*
23.2   Sentence combining: Beginnings and endings *388–89*
23.3   Revising: Series and balanced elements *390*
23.4   Emphasizing with repetition or separation *391–92*
23.5   Revising: Conciseness *392*
23.6   Revising: Emphasizing ideas *393–94*

Web Links
Emphasis

24 Using Coordination and Subordination

Exercises

Web-only Exercises
24.1   Coordination
24.2   Subordination

Exercises from *The Little, Brown Handbook*
24.1   Sentence combining: Coordination *397*
24.2   Revising: Excessive or faulty coordination *397–98*
24.3   Sentence combining: Subordination *402*
24.4   Revising: Subordination *403*
24.5   Revising: Faulty or excessive subordination *403*
24.6   Revising: Coordination and subordination *405*

Web Links
Coordination and subordination

25 Using Parallelism

Video Tutorial
Achieving parallelism

Exercises

Web-only Exercises
25.1 Parallelism with *and, both. . . . and,* etc.
25.2 Parallelism for coherence

Exercises from *The Little, Brown Handbook*
25.1 Identifying parallel elements *409*
25.2 Revising: Parallelism *409–10*
25.3 Sentence combining: Parallelism *411*
25.4 Revising: Parallelism *411–12*

Web Links
Parallelism

26 Achieving Variety

Video Tutorial
Achieving variety

Exercises

Web-only Exercises
26.1 Rewriting for variety

Exercises from *The Little, Brown Handbook*
26.1 Revising: Varied sentence structures *415*
26.2 Revising: Varied sentence beginnings *417*
26.3 Revising: Varied sentence beginnings *418*
26.4 Writing varied sentences *419*
26.5 Analyzing variety *419–20*
26.6 Revising: Variety *420*

Review
23–26 Revising: Effective sentences *420–21*

Web Links
Variety

27 End Punctuation

Exercises

Web-only Exercise
27.1 End punctuation

Exercises from *The Little, Brown Handbook*
27.1 Revising: Periods *427*
27.2 Revising: Question marks *428*

27.3   Revising: Exclamation points *429*
27.4   Revising: End punctuation *429–30*

Web Links
End punctuation

28 The Comma

Video Tutorial
Using a grammar checker to spot comma problems

EXERCISES

Web-only Exercises
28.1   Commas with main clauses
28.2   Commas with introductory elements
28.3   Commas with nonessential elements
28.4   Commas with series and coordinate adjectives
28.5   Commas with quotations
28.6   Misuse of commas

Exercises from *The Little, Brown Handbook*
28.1   Punctuating linked main clauses *432–33*
28.2   Sentence combining: Linked main clauses *433*
28.3   Punctuating introductory elements *434*
28.4   Sentence combining: Introductory elements *435*
28.5   Punctuating essential and nonessential elements *439–40*
28.6   Sentence combining: Essential and nonessential elements *440*
28.7   Punctuating absolute phrases and phrases of contrast *441*
28.8   Punctuating series and coordinate adjectives *443*
28.9   Punctuating dates, addresses, place names, numbers *444*
28.10 Punctuating quotations *446–47*
28.11 Punctuating to prevent misreading *447*
28.12 Revising: Needless or misused commas *451*
28.13 Revising: Commas *451–52*

Web Links
Good overall sites for commas
Commas with coordinating conjunctions
Commas with introductory elements
Commas with nonessential elements
Commas with quotations
Unnecessary commas

29 The Semicolon

Exercises
Web-only Exercise
29.1   Semicolons

Exercises from *The Little, Brown Handbook*
29.1   Punctuating between main clauses *453*
29.2   Sentence combining: Related main clauses *454–55*
29.3   Punctuating main clauses related by conjunctive adverbs or transitional expressions *456*
29.4   Sentence combining: Main clauses related by conjunctive adverbs or transitional expressions *456–57*
29.5   Punctuating long main clauses and series items *458*
29.6   Revising: Misused or overused semicolons *460*
29.7   Revising: Semicolons *460*

Web Links
Semicolons

30 The Apostrophe

Video Tutorial
Recognizing apostrophe problems

Exercises

Web-only Exercises
30.1   Apostrophes: Possessives
30.2   Apostrophes: Possessives vs. personal pronouns

Exercises from *The Little, Brown Handbook*
30.1   Forming possessives *463–64*
30.2   Distinguishing between plurals and possessives *465*
30.3   Forming contractions *466*
30.4   Revising: Contractions and personal pronouns *466–67*
30.5   Revising: Apostrophes *467–68*

Web Links
Apostrophes

31 Quotation Marks

Exercises

Web-only Exercise
31.1   Quotation Marks

Exercises from *The Little, Brown Handbook*
31.1   Using double and single quotation marks *471*
31.2   Quoting titles *473*
31.3   Revising: Quotation marks *475–76*
31.4   Revising: Quotation marks *476*

Web Links
Quotation marks

32 Other Punctuation Marks

Exercises

Web-only Exercises
32.1   Colons, dashes, parentheses
32.2   The ellipsis mark

Exercises from *The Little, Brown Handbook*
32.1   Revising: Colons *479*
32.2   Revising: Dashes *481–82*
32.3   Revising: Parentheses *483*
32.4   Using ellipsis marks *486–87*
32.5   Revising: Colons, dashes, parentheses, brackets, ellipsis marks, slashes *487–88*

Review
27–32 Revising: Punctuation *488*

Web Links
Other punctuation marks

33 Capitals

Exercises

Web-only Exercise
33.1   Capitals

Exercise from *The Little, Brown Handbook*
33.1   Revising: Capitals *495–96*

Web Links
Capitals

34 Underlining or Italics

Exercises

Web-only Exercise
34.1   Underlining or italics

Exercise from *The Little, Brown Handbook*
34.1   Revising: Underlining or italics *499–500*

Web Links
Underlining or italics

35 Abbreviations

Exercises

Web-only Exercise
35.1   Abbreviations

Exercise from *The Little, Brown Handbook*
35.1   Revising: Abbreviations *503–04*

Web Links
Abbreviations

36 Numbers

Exercises
Web-only Exercise
36.1   Numbers
Exercise from *The Little, Brown Handbook*
36.1   Revising: Numbers *506–07*
Review
33–36 Revising: Mechanics *507–08*

Web Links
Numbers

37 Using Appropriate Language

Video Tutorial
Using appropriate language

Exercises
Web-only Exercises
37.1   Standard American English
37.2   Unbiased and gender-neutral language
Exercise from *The Little, Brown Handbook*
37.1   Revising: Appropriate words *517–18*

Web Links
Good overall sites
Colloquial language
Slang
Standard American English
Unbiased and gender-neutral language

38 Using Exact Language

Exercises
Web-only Exercises
38.1   Denotation and connotation
38.2   Idioms
Exercises from *The Little, Brown Handbook*
38.1   Revising: Denotation *520*
38.2   Considering the connotations of words *521*

38.3   Revising: Concrete and specific words *522–23*
38.4   Using concrete and specific words *523*
38.5   Using prepositions in idioms *525*
38.6   Analyzing figurative language *527*
38.7   Using figurative language *527*
38.8   Revising: Trite expressions *528–29*

Web Links
Clichés
Denotation and connotation
Idioms

39 Writing Concisely

Video Tutorial
Sentence combining

Exercises

Web-only Exercises
39.1   Focusing on subject and verb
39.2   Cutting empty words and repetition

Exercises from *The Little, Brown Handbook*
39.1   Revising: Subjects and verbs; empty words and phrases *532*
39.2   Revising: Unnecessary repetition *533–34*
39.3   Revising: Conciseness *535–36*
39.4   Revising: Conciseness *536*

Web Links
Good overall sites
Sentence combining

40 Using Dictionaries

Exercise from *The Little, Brown Handbook*
40.1   Using a dictionary *541–42*

Web Links
Using dictionaries

41 Spelling and the Hyphen

Exercises

Web-only Exercises
41.1   Spelling
41.2   The hyphen

Exercises from *The Little, Brown Handbook*
41.1   Distinguishing between *ie* and *ei* *546*
41.2   Keeping or dropping a final *e* *547*

41.3 Keeping or dropping a final *y* *547*
41.4 Doubling consonants *548*
41.5 Forming plurals *549*
41.6 Using hyphens in compound words *556*

Web Links
Good overall sites
Commonly misspelled words
Hyphens in compound words

42 Planning a Research Project

Video Tutorial
Finding source information

Exercises
Web-only Exercise
42.1 Finding source information

Checklists from *The Little, Brown Handbook*
Scheduling steps in research writing *560*
Information for a working bibliography *569*

Web Links
Research journal
Finding a subject and question
Research strategy

43 Finding Sources

Video Tutorial
Using keywords with a search engine

Exercises
Web-only Exercise
43.1 Searching electronically
Exercise from *The Little, Brown Handbook*
43.1 Using the library *597–98*

Web Links
Good overall sites
Keyword searches
Searching the library
Searching the Web
Searching other online sources
Finding images
Conducting interviews
General online sources
Sources in literature and other humanities

Sources in the social sciences
Sources in the natural and applied sciences

44 Working with Sources

Video Tutorial
Evaluating online sources

Exercises
   Web-only Exercises
   44.1 Evaluating Web sites
   44.2 Evaluating an online discussion
   44.3 Effective summaries
   44.4 Effective paraphrases
   44.5 Effective quotations
   44.6 Integrating sources
   Exercises from _The Little, Brown Handbook_
   44.1 Evaluating a source *609*
   44.2 Evaluating Web sites *609–10*
   44.5 Synthesizing sources *611–12*
   44.7 Summarizing and paraphrasing *622–23*
   44.8 Combining summary, paraphrase, and direct quotation *623*
   44.10 Introducing and interpreting borrowed material *628–29*

Checklists from _The Little, Brown Handbook_
Questions for evaluating sources *601*
Questions for evaluating Web sites *602*
Questions for evaluating Web logs and online discussions *608*

Web Links
Evaluating sources
Synthesizing sources
Note taking
Summary, paraphrase, and quotation
Integrating borrowed material

45 Avoiding Plagiarism and Documenting Sources

Video Tutorial
Avoiding plagiarism

Exercises
   Web-only Exercise
   45.1 Detecting plagiarism
   Exercise from _The Little, Brown Handbook_
   45.1 Recognizing plagiarism *635*

Checklist from _The Little, Brown Handbook_
Checklist for avoiding plagiarism *630*

Web Links

Good overall sites on avoiding plagiarism
Documenting sources
Plagiarism-detection sites

46 Writing the Paper

Checklist from *The Little, Brown Handbook*

Checklist for revising a research paper *645*

Web Links

Thesis statement
Outlining
Drafting
Revising
Editing and proofreading

47 Using MLA Documentation and Format

Exercises

Web-only Exercise
47.1 Citing sources using MLA style
Exercise from *The Little, Brown Handbook*
47.1 Writing works-cited entries *686–87*

MLA Style

MLA in-text citations
MLA works cited
Sample MLA works-cited entries

48 Two Research Papers in MLA Style

Sample student papers—MLA style

Gephardt Smith, Julie M. "Here Comes the Bride, All Dressed in Purple?:
   The Inherent Dual Reality of American Women"
Martin, Riley. "Beyond the Words: Diversity in American English"
McElroy, James Jr. "Telecommuting: A Case Study"
Weiss, Ann. "The Editing of the Declaration of Independence: Better or
   Worse?"

MLA Style

49 Working with the Goals and Requirements of the Disciplines

Web Links

Writing in the Disciplines
General online sources
Sources in literature and other humanities

Sources in the social sciences
Sources in the natural and applied sciences

50 Reading and Writing About Literature

Checklists from *The Little, Brown Handbook*
Questions for a literary analysis *741*
Checklist for revising a literary analysis *749*
Questions for analyzing fiction *751*
Questions for analyzing poetry *753*
Questions for analyzing drama *755*

Sample student papers in MLA style from *The Little, Brown Handbook*
Vanessa Haley, "Annie Dillard's Healing Vision" *725–30*
Janet Vong, "Ironies of Life in Kate Chopin's 'The Story of an Hour'" *750–51*
Kenneth Scheff, "Making Time Versus Enduring in Gwendolyn Brooks's
'The Bean Eaters'" *754–55*
Michael Spinter, "Macbeth as Hero" *756–58*

Web Links
Good overall sites on writing about literature
Analyzing literature
Writing about literature
Writing about fiction
Writing about poetry
Writing about drama
Sources in literature and other humanities
General online sources

MLA style

51 Writing in Other Humanities

Sample student paper—Chicago Style
Sample student paper—Columbia Online Style (Humanities)

Web Links
Sources in literature and other humanities
General online sources

Chicago style
Columbia Online Style (COS) in the humanities

52 Writing in the Social Sciences

Sample student paper—APA Style

Web Links
Sources in the social sciences
General online sources

APA style
Columbia Online Style (COS) in the sciences

53 Writing in the Natural and Applied Sciences

Sample student paper—CSE Style

Web Links
> Sources in the natural and applied sciences
> General online sources

CSE style

Columbia Online Style (COS) in the sciences

54 Writing Online

Video Tutorials
> Using e-mail
> Balancing Web design and content

Web Links
> E-mail
> HTML editors
> Web composition
> Online collaboration

55 Public Writing

Sample documents
> Résumés
> Business letter
> Memo
> Report
> Proposal
> Brochure
> Newsletter
> Flyer

Web Links
> Business writing
> Reports and proposals
> Designing flyers, newsletters, brochures, and other public documents
> Writing for community and service learning projects

56 Oral Presentations

Video Tutorial
> Designing a *PowerPoint* presentation

Web Links
> Oral presentations
> Using *PowerPoint*
> Collections of effective speeches

Usage Flashcards

Instructor Resources
Transparency Masters
Web Links

SAMPLE SCHEDULE FOR A FIRST-YEAR COMPOSITION COURSE

The following schedule represents one possible way of structuring a composition course using *The Little, Brown Handbook* and relying on computer-assisted activities. The schedule assumes that you use a course Web site, blog, or e-mail to supplement class activities and that your students have access to computers and support resources. Students will complete four major projects during the course; these may either be graded individually or collectively in a portfolio, depending on your institution's requirements.

In the objectives-and-requirements portion of your syllabus, be sure to explain fully any requirements involving technology as you would any others. For example:

- Require that students back up all their work. Make it known that technical difficulties such as lost or damaged files are unacceptable excuses for not turning in assignments.

- Clarify requirements for participation in online components of the course, while taking into account that some students may need to participate as "lurkers" for a week or two before involving themselves in conversations.

- If you expect students to attend computer-related workshops or complete computer-related tasks such as obtaining e-mail accounts, provide them with handouts and schedules that will help them do so.

Week 2

General course introduction, including objectives; discussion of requirements—assignments, participation, attendance. Complete writing sample, if desired. Introduction to course Web site. Make sure students have e-mail accounts and can check them regularly. Make sure students have access to computers for class activities. Establish conventions for online behavior. Assign Chapter 1.

Week 2

Discussions of purpose and audience in writing, using various examples from online and printed sources. Assign first essay. Discuss invention techniques and have students apply to first assignment. Have students begin using online class discussion e-mail list for brainstorming or to discuss class readings. Assign Chapters 2–4.

Week 3

Draft of first essay due. Discuss and model peer response techniques. Have students review each other's work. Review drafts yourself, focusing on scope and suitability to objectives of the assignment. Establish small groups for semester activities. Conduct peer responses using the Comment and Track Changes functions on a word processor or embedded comments in e-mail or forum postings of papers. Review peer responses, focusing on attention to deepest levels of revision. Continue online discussion exchanges to brainstorm topics or discuss revision strategies.

Week 4

Discuss problem areas individually or in small groups with students, or e-mail suggestions on drafts, focusing on larger organization and meaning problems and one or two sentence-level concerns, and referring students to appropriate handbook chapters. Assign Chapter 5. Continue online discussions to brainstorm topics, discuss class readings, or plan final revision strategies. First essay due.

Week 5

Assign second essay. Employ small groups for pre-writing and invention work using e-mail or class Web tools. Assign Chapter 54. Begin drafting essays. Continue Web forum or class e-mail exchanges to brainstorm topics, discuss class readings, or converse about issues of collaboration.

Week 6

Model successful peer responses using samples from the first essay. Conduct peer response exercise using word-processing Comment and Track Changes functions, embedded comments in e-mail, or forum postings of papers. Revise drafts.

Week 7

Second essay due. Assign third essay (research-based). Assign Chapters 42–43. In-class introduction to research techniques. Continue online discussions to brainstorm topics, discuss class readings, or converse about research issues and strategies.

Week 8

Online discussions of research projects: work in class to compile working bibliography of online and print sources. Discuss bibliographic tools and conventions. Browse discussion-group archives to explore topics. Continue online discussions to brainstorm topics, explore class readings, or discuss assignment.

Week 9

Assign Chapters 44–46. Continue browsing discussion-group archives. Working bibliography due. Begin drafting essay. Continue online discussions to brainstorm topics, explore class readings, or discuss assignment.

Week 10

Individual conferences during class with students on their projects. Model successful integration of quotation, paraphrase, and summary. Continue online discussions to brainstorm topics, explore class readings, or discuss research assignment.

Week 11

Peer response to research projects. Final revisions. Research projects due. Continue online discussions to brainstorm topics, explore class readings, or discuss research assignment.

Week 12

Assign fourth project—a problem/solution proposal, based on research essay, for students not in computer-assisted classrooms, or a Web site exploring the research topic for students in computer-assisted classrooms. Assign Chapter 54 for Web projects. Continue online discussions to brainstorm topics, explore class readings, or discuss final assignment.

Week 13

Web-building workshop for Web project. Additional research and modeling of formats for proposal project. Continue online discussions to brainstorm topics, explore class readings, or discuss research assignment.

Week 14

Drafts due. Discuss and implement uploading of Web projects. Peer reviews in small groups. Continue online discussions to brainstorm topics, explore class readings, or discuss research assignment.

Week 15

In-class editing. Final drafts due. Course evaluations. Final online discussions to evaluate course and assignments.

RESOURCES FOR USING COMPUTERS TO TEACH WRITING

BOOKS

Bolter, Jay David, and Richard Grusin. *Remediation: Understanding New Media.* Cambridge: MIT, 1999.

Borgman, Albert. *Holding on to Reality: The Nature of Information at the Turn of the Millennium.* Chicago: U of Chicago P, 1999.

Hawisher, Gail, and Cynthia Selfe, eds. *Passions, Pedagogies and 21st Century Technologies.* Logan: Utah State UP, 1999.

Hobson, Eric. *Wiring the Writing Center.* Logan: Utah State UP, 1998.

Joyce, Michael. *Of Two Minds: Hypertext, Pedagogy, and Poetics.* Ann Arbor: U of Michigan P, 1995.

Kalmbach, James R. *The Computer and the Page: Publishing, Technology, and the Classroom.* Norwood, NJ: Ablex, 1997.

Kiesler, Sara. *Culture of the Internet.* Mahwah: Erlbaum, 1997.

Landow, George. *Hypertext 2.0: The Convergence of Contemporary Critical Theory and Technology.* Baltimore: Johns Hopkins, 1997.

Nardi, Bonnie A., and Vicki L. O'Day. *Information Ecologies: Using Technology with Heart.* Cambridge: MIT, 1999.

O'Donnell, James J. *Avatars of the Word: From Papyrus to Cyberspace*. Cambridge: Harvard UP, 1997.

Porter, James E., and Patricia Sullivan. *Opening Spaces: Writing Technologies and Critical Research*. Norwood: Ablex, 1997.

Reiss, Donna, and Dickie Self, eds. *Electronic Communication Across the Curriculum*. Urbana: National Council of Teachers of English, 1998.

Snyder, Ilana, and Michael Joyce, eds. *Page to Screen: Taking Literacy into the Electronic Era*. London and New York: Routledge, 1998.

Taylor, Todd W., and Irene Ward, eds. *Literacy Theory in the Age of the Internet*. New York: Columbia UP, 1998.

Tyner, Kathleen. *Literacy in a Digital World: Teaching and Learning in the Age of Information*. Mahwah: Erlbaum, 1998.

Welch, Kathleen. *Electric Rhetoric: Classical Rhetoric, Oralism and a New Literacy*. Cambridge: MIT, 1999.

JOURNALS

CCC
College English
Computers and Composition
Currents in Electronic Literacy
Journal of Advanced Composition
Kairos

LISTSERVS

Rhetnt-L
Devoted to issues of electronic publishing and composition.
web.missouri.edu/~rhetnet/roadmap.html
TESL-L
For educators interested in issues related to teaching English as a second language.
www.hunter.cuny.edu/~tesl-l/
WPA-L
Geared toward issues of teaching writing as they relate to writing centers.
www.english.ilstu.edu/Hesse/listserv.htm

MOOS

Lingua MOO
lingua.utdallas.edu
Diversity University
www.du.org

WEB SITES

Writing@CSU: For Teachers
writing.colostate.edu/instructors.cfm

Computer Teaching Tips
  www.emunix.emich.edu/~krause/Tips
MyCompLab
  www.ablongman.com/mycomplab
Computer Writing and Research Lab
  www.cwrl.utexas.edu
CourseCompass
  www.coursecompass.com
Courses in Cyberculture
  www.com.washington.edu/rccs/courselist.asp
SITES Instructional Tool Resources
  sites.unc.edu/tools
SITES Teaching Pages
  sites.unc.edu
Traci's Lists of Ten
  www.tengrrl.com/tens/index.shtml
The World Lecture Hall
  web.austin.utexas.edu/wlh

CHAPTER 6

Teaching Writing to ESL Students

By Jocelyn Steer and Dawn Schmid

The composition instructor's reaction to having ESL students in a class of native speakers can be a mixture of pleasure and apprehension. On the one hand, students using English as a second language can introduce a fresh perspective to class discussions and in their written work. Competing with this positive response to the richness of cultural diversity, however, may be a feeling of trepidation at entering into the syntactical and lexical labyrinth of the ESL student's written world. There is no question about it: ESL writers struggle with a number of language problems that do not beset native speakers and for which writing instructors may not have quick solutions. However, encouraging ESL writers to become outspoken members of the class and shaping the overall goals of the class to include ESL needs provides benefits for native and nonnative speakers alike.

This chapter is intended to help instructors find their way within that ESL labyrinth. It presents a profile of ESL students, an overview of how culture shapes their notions about learning and composing, a description of effective approaches to teaching writing to ESL students, and some guidelines for evaluating their writing. A cursory look at the most common grammatical errors found in ESL writing and a list of print and online resources for teaching ESL students are also included.

PROFILE OF ESL STUDENTS

The ESL label indicates that a student's first language is not English, but it says nothing about the student's country of origin or reasons for being at college and very little about specific language problems. In fact, ESL students are a remarkably heterogeneous group, about which it is often difficult to make any generalizations. One of the first and most important distinctions to make is between international and permanent resident students.

Generally speaking, international students (also referred to as foreign students) reside permanently in another country and obtain student (F-1) visas in order to study in a school in the United States. Their stay in the United States is usually funded by their families, their place of employment, their government, or their own savings. Their countries of origin

101

vary; they come to the United States in waves, affected by global political and economic events.

Most likely these international students have had previous formal English language instruction in their home country or in the United States. Students trained in their home countries have probably had heavy doses of grammar, vocabulary, and reading, with some translation. Although they will be proficient readers with good command of grammar, they may lack ease and confidence in speaking up in class. Their written work may be mechanically accurate but lack fluency and appropriate organization. International students who have learned English at a language institute in this country will have a higher degree of oral fluency and some basic notions about the conventions of higher education in the United States.

Unlike international students, permanent residents usually do not plan to return to their home country. Their reasons for staying in the United States are varied and may include the need for political asylum, economic advancement, and family ties.

Most students admitted to the United States with refugee status have come for political, not economic, reasons. Refugee students have come from places such as Cambodia, Vietnam, Laos, Eastern Europe, Latin America, Haiti, Ethiopia, and Somalia. Many came to the United States as children and went through the public school system here; others are adults who have decided to return to school to get a better job. Students who graduate from a high school in the United States and who are permanent residents are usually admitted to universities and colleges without submitting a Test of English as a Foreign Language (TOEFL) score, which is required of international students.

Not all permanent residents are refugees seeking political asylum. Many have come to the United States for family or employment reasons. Immigrants are given a resident alien card (a "green card"), which does not grant them citizenship but does allow them to reside permanently in the United States and to work here legally. After a number of years, green card holders may apply for citizenship and become naturalized citizens. Immigrants are given permanent resident status for many reasons; for example, they may have married a US citizen or have been sponsored by a family member. Immigrant students usually acquire English informally, so their spoken English is quite fluent, but their written English requires more formal instruction to achieve the same fluency and accuracy.

Obviously, ESL students have varying degrees of language ability in speaking, reading, and writing. You can also expect to see wide gaps in socioeconomic status among ESL students in the same class, even among those from the same country, and such differences may create friction. ESL students may also hold varying attitudes toward the United States, ranging from open anti-American hostility to a Pollyanna-like view of the United States as the epitome of freedom and opportunity. This range of attitudes can provide an interesting basis for in-class discussions by including a variety of perspectives and by stimulating native speakers to rethink their cultural assumptions.

CROSS-CULTURAL ISSUES

Some ESL students will freely admit to being in a mild state of confusion much of the time during their academic experience. Clearly, a large portion of this confusion may be attributed to having to read and write at a very sophisticated level in a language that they have not yet mastered. There are also cultural factors less visible to the student and the instructor: the unwritten, but well-entrenched, conventions of the academy. These range from the acceptable forms of compiling a research paper to the appropriate ways of addressing an instructor. Because of their prior experience and training, native speakers may be somewhat familiar with these academic conventions, while ESL students may not even know that they exist. However, one advantage in having ESL writers as active participants in a class is that their questions can propel the class as a whole to discover the reasons for conventions that often seem puzzlingly arbitrary. In some cases ESL students know the "rules" of grammar far better than the native speakers and can be called upon to share that expert knowledge.

IDEAS ABOUT LEARNING

ESL students may approach the learning situation from a schema formed largely by their experiences in their first culture. For example, many Latin cultures foster more cooperative learning, whereas Japan adheres to a hierarchical, teacher-dominated model. While these cultural generalities cannot be presumed to apply to individual students, they can be useful in sensitizing us to our own cultural assumptions. The situation in a college classroom may well shock ESL students—the informality of instructors who sit on the desk, classmates who openly disagree with or interrupt their professors. Such students are not comfortable with the open discussion format in which American students feel free to express their opinions, whether or not those opinions align with the professor's. Instructors may view their more quiet ESL students as resistant or unprepared, when in fact these students are showing respect by remaining silent.

In some cultures, professors are expected to mentor and guide students to a greater extent than they do in the United States. Thus, many ESL students may feel that their professors do not do enough for them. It is not unusual for an ESL student to bring in a piece of writing for another class and ask the composition instructor to correct it. Or some students may attempt to negotiate grades because they "need" that grade for a scholarship or admission to a school, and they may be visibly disappointed when an instructor refuses to change a grade. While a teacher in the United States may interpret such behavior as impertinent, the student may view it as a chance for the instructor to use his or her power to further the student's career. And while ESL students may find the informality of the classroom surprising, many find constant testing, penalties for absences, and general surveillance on the part of the instructor to be offensive to their sense of maturity. Many ESL students have attended foreign universities that do not monitor student behavior so closely.

Cross-cultural discussions in which students trace how basic assumptions result in varying styles of learning behavior may be useful for both ESL and native-speaking students. Many ESL students benefit from such discussions because they wish to conform to the conventions of their school in order to enjoy academic success. Similarly, such explorations can help native speakers develop sensitivity to these cross-cultural issues.

CONTRASTIVE RHETORIC

Cross-cultural analyses of ESL–student writing can also be fruitful. Cultures express ideas using different organizational patterns and types of support, and the written and unwritten rules governing what is considered appropriate writing in the culture are transmitted to children in school. It is not surprising, therefore, that ESL students use these first-language writing strategies when they compose in English. The result may be a grammatically correct piece of writing with an idiosyncratic development.

Instructors need to apply the principles of contrastive rhetoric cautiously. Although it is not necessary to undertake an extensive study of the rhetorics of all languages, it is important to recognize how a culture shapes its members' expectations of good writing. An instructional approach that places too much emphasis on contrastive rhetoric, on the other hand, is reductionistic. Such an approach would fail to account for a specific writer's process, potentially misinterpreting a writer's lack of experience as interference from first-language writing strategies. (For a detailed discussion of contrastive rhetoric, consult Ilona Leki's *Understanding ESL Writers: A Guide for Teachers.*)

LEVELS OF SUPPORT AND SPECIFICITY

One important feature of ESL writing that varies among cultures is the level of support and specificity required for assertions. It is not always obvious to ESL writers that facts and statistics are usually considered to be the strongest method of support in English and that when a student makes an assertion, that assertion must be supported with specific examples or quantifiable measures. Other cultures may rely on the hierarchical, rather than the scientific, model of proof. It is not unusual, for example, to have ESL students use quotes from the Koran or statements made by a political leader as evidence for their assertions. Students will need practice in identifying and supplying the kinds of support expected in academic writing in English.

Another central issue in cross-cultural analyses of texts is the level of explicitness expected in academic writing. English is a "writer-responsible" language: the onus is on the writer to present ideas clearly and succinctly. If the reader has difficulty with a text, the blame usually rests with the writer and not the reader. We expect to have the main points stated directly and clearly in a piece of writing, which may help to explain some of our frustration at reading a piece of writing by an ESL student who does not share the same expectation.

This distinction is especially pertinent to native writers of Japanese and Chinese, which are "reader-responsible" languages. Japanese and Chinese readers do not expect the writer to link information and draw conclusions; they expect to do that as readers (Cowie). A Japanese student explained this when asked why she used transitions so sparingly and never seemed to tie up her examples with a general statement: she said that doing so would be insulting to Japanese readers, who are expected to be informed and sensitive enough to be able to make those inferences on their own.

ATTITUDES TOWARD PLAGIARISM

American students who commit plagiarism have a sense that it is an academic offense. ESL students, however, may come from countries where plagiarism, although not completely ethical, is more easily overlooked or accepted. Research and writing in the United States is prized for its originality, but this is not the case in all cultures. Some ESL students may have been taught to incorporate great writing from their culture into their own work out of respect for those scholars. For some students, plagiarism may be a way of coping with their uncertainty about their own lexical abilities (Currie). Other students may be too modest to believe that they can paraphrase the writing of a respected author.

Of course, many ESL students copy for the same reasons American students do—because it's easier, faster, and sure to be more fluent. Whether or not your students are guilty, they need to be warned that plagiarism is unacceptable in a college in the United States. Be sure to discuss the issue of plagiarism early in the semester and invite students to share their understanding of the differences between quoting, paraphrasing, and plagiarizing. Students will benefit from explicit classroom discussion of different cultural attitudes toward what constitutes plagiarism, instruction in how to distinguish between borrowing of words and borrowing of ideas, and plenty of practice with paraphrasing, summarizing, and citing sources. Chapter 45 can be particularly useful here in showing students examples of unacceptable writing with plagiarized sections.

TOPIC SELECTION

Topics that seem to be extremely pertinent to the lives of your native speakers may be inappropriate or difficult for ESL writers. An essay on breaking away from family or living on one's own, for example, may have no meaning for those ESL students who expect to live with their families until they get married. In fact, you may find that your ESL students are more comfortable writing about impersonal subjects than those designed to facilitate self-discovery. Other topics may offend certain groups of students because of their religious beliefs—living together before marriage, gay rights, evolution. We have assigned what seemed to be an innocuous topic— "superstitions in my culture"—only to find out that the Islamic religion does not tolerate superstitions. At the same time, some topics will be more appealing to ESL students, who are often better informed about and more interested in topics dealing with global issues than are American students.

ISSUES IN WORKING WITH ESL WRITING

The above discussion of cross-cultural differences in organization, style, and topic selection underscores the need to provide ESL students with guidelines and models of academic writing so that they can function smoothly and successfully in the college culture. Yet there is a danger—as there is in any acculturation process—of placing too great a value on the expected and accepted form of the writing and too little value on the writer's discovery of voice.

PROCESS VERSUS PRODUCT APPROACH TO WRITING

This dilemma between emphasizing the product over the process of writing is not a new one but one that takes on a slightly different slant when applied to teaching writing to ESL students. An approach that emphasizes the conventions of academic discourse provides ESL students with models of discipline-specific writing that they can emulate, along with guidelines for operating within that discipline. It has been our experience that ESL students welcome this type of instruction. Since they lack the cultural and linguistic schema of native speakers, they benefit from explicit instruction in how to complete academic tasks. Essay-test prompts are an excellent example of this: native speakers have a better notion than ESL students of what is meant by "discuss," for example. By the same token, when ESL students feel free to raise questions about the wording of assignments, the whole class often benefits from the discussion. Assignments that allow students to practice writing essay exams, critical reviews, laboratory reports, case reports, and so on will also help to equip students with the necessary tools for their academic careers.

The danger in such an approach is that students may begin to rely more on the imposed model of academic communication than on their own voice and expression. The result may be mimicry rather than inspiration. This is especially true for ESL students who enter the writing process haltingly. An approach that emphasizes the process of brainstorming, sharing ideas, and collaborating on a topic nurtures ESL students' wavering self-confidence as writers in a second language. By engaging students in the discovery of ideas, this approach also distracts them from ruminating over potential surface errors.

Since a process approach to writing does not outline a single "accepted" product, it encourages students to identify their own personal style first before reconciling that with the models of writing endorsed by the academic community. Yet we would be remiss if we failed to provide our ESL students with those models. Clearly, a combination of the two approaches, without overreliance on product or neglect of process, will serve your ESL students best. As with any student it is important to focus on the strengths of an ESL writer's work and to suggest one or two issues for revision rather than to view the paper as a minefield of errors.

ATTITUDES TOWARD ERRORS

While research indicates that ESL students need more work with actual composing than with language development (Zamel, "Composing"), it may be difficult persuading your ESL students of this. They may believe that good writing means producing grammatically correct sentences. They see errors as obstacles to good writing, and unlike many native speakers, they do not perceive them as symbols of personal failure. They expect to make mistakes since they are learning a second language, and they expect those errors to be corrected. Leki's survey on student perceptions of teacher feedback supports what any ESL teacher might have predicted: students believe that error correction is important. Out of 100 ESL college students surveyed, 91 percent believed that it was very important to have as few errors as possible in their writing, and 93 percent stated that it was important to have the teachers correct the errors.

It was once thought that errors in a second language were the result of interference from the first language. For example, if writers had problems with word order in English, this was because they were applying first-language rules of word order to the second language. Now, however, it is largely believed that most ESL errors are the result of an "interlanguage," a system for communicating in the second language that the student has developed based on what he or she knows about the second language.

Theoretically, this interlanguage is constantly changing as the learner mentally reorganizes what is known about the language. This is an important point and a distinction between the native English and ESL writers. During the course of a semester, your ESL students will probably make a great deal of progress in English because their language-acquisition process is still activated. Their improvement will result not only from your class but also from exposure to other sources of language input. The more that students write, the more likely they are to improve their writing. According to Cowie, the act of writing and revising itself is key to improving student writing at both surface and global levels.

Viewing ESL errors as temporary edifices supporting an ESL writer's ideas lends credence to the argument against correcting every single error in an ESL composition. These errors will disappear as students gain more control over the second language. Errors that seem to be careless mistakes to the reader may not be that at all. They may be the student's individual system for organizing English structure, which will change as the student acquires more language. Nor is it uncommon for advanced ESL students to regress temporarily in their language accuracy as they struggle with new forms and constructions.

You may have some students in your class who have been in the United States for quite some time and who for some reason may have reached a plateau; second-language researchers say that these students' errors are "fossilized." It is not clear why fossilization occurs, but it is clear that working with fossilized errors can be difficult. Distinguishing between errors that occur as the result of fossilization and those that occur because of interlanguage is important; unlike interlanguage errors, which remit spontaneously with increased exposure to the language, fossilized errors require more explicit and direct treatment.

TECHNIQUES FOR RESPONDING TO ESL WRITING

As an experienced composition instructor, you have probably developed a variety of techniques and strategies for providing effective feedback to your students. (In this manual, "Working with Student Writing" on pp. 30–51 provides guidelines for responding to student work.) Below are some suggested techniques and strategies that may be especially helpful in providing feedback to your ESL students.

Sometimes students are confused about what to do with feedback. Research (Conrad and Goldstein) suggests that students have difficulty revising when asked to develop their points by being more explicit, explaining, or analyzing. Providing students with training in how to respond to feedback will enable them to produce better revisions (Currie; Conrad and Goldstein). Moreover, if you use peer feedback in your class, you may find that students from cultures where the teacher is considered the source of knowledge and truth do not take into account their peers' feedback when revising. In this case, it is important to train students in how to give effective peer feedback as well as how to receive it (Cowie; Nelson and Carson).

In general, it is best to provide feedback on grammar, punctuation, and spelling in earlier drafts so that students can incorporate those corrections into subsequent drafts. Students are not as likely to benefit from feedback that is offered on a final draft; they will often look at the grade, read the comments quickly, and file the paper away. However, you can encourage attention to final drafts by asking for localized revisions of a particular pattern of error or of a paragraph. Students can also be encouraged to make note of their common patterns of error and to keep revised examples as a resource for the next paper.

There is no one method for drawing students' attention to sentence-level errors, but generally it is best to locate the error for the student and have the student correct the error on a subsequent draft. Leki's survey found that students like to be given a clue regarding the nature of the error. A numbering system for the most basic errors (for example, verb tense, number agreement, word order, spelling, punctuation, and word form) works well because students seem to respond better to numbers than to abbreviations or words (for example, *sp, awk*), and they become familiar with the errors they tend to make often. The correction code in the handbook is easy to use; it includes a number-and-letter system that directs students to the appropriate section in the handbook that deals with the error. (See pp. 34–35 of this manual for a more detailed description of the correction code.) It is most useful to identify one or two significant patterns of error (subject-verb problems and misused articles, for example) rather than correct every example of error.

Some errors—often those pertaining to sentence boundaries, clause structure, and choice of words—cannot be identified by circling and numbering. When the writer's meaning is unclear, avoid the temptation to rewrite the sentence for the student. You may find your interpretation to be quite different from what the student intended. It's best to ask the student to rewrite the passage.

A concern that continues to surface when dealing with ESL writing is knowing what and how much to correct. As noted earlier, students make many errors; some of them may be careless mistakes, but more likely the sentences were carefully constructed using the students' still-developing knowledge of English structure and vocabulary. Correcting ESL work seems to be more an art than a science because the instructor needs to gauge the particular student's threshold for error correction and identify the errors that the student will benefit from knowing about.

We have also found that students are very receptive to and benefit a great deal from immediate, oral feedback, especially when they solicit it. Students often ask for help with grammar and vocabulary during in-class writing, and they almost always incorporate those revisions into their writing.

Some teachers and students find it helpful to keep track of repeated errors. Using a numbering system such as the one mentioned above can facilitate this process. (See p. 69 in the handbook for a model that can be used to track errors.) In any case, it is very important to recommend or require that students consult the handbook. Not only will it help clarify a confusing grammatical point, but it will also teach students to edit their work independently, an extremely important skill for the ESL student.

EVALUATION

The question of evaluation is a thorny one in composition classes comprising both native and nonnative speakers. Some of the questions that come up are: How do I compare the two? Will I need to lower my standards? Should I expect error-free writing from my ESL students? Should I give a grade to each draft? How many revisions should I allow before assigning a grade?

Keep a few points in mind when deciding how to evaluate ESL writers. First, the ESL student is writing in a second (or third or fourth) language. It is next to impossible to achieve native fluency and accuracy in a second language, especially when the learner began acquisition as an adult. Thus, we need to consider whether it is realistic to expect ESL students to produce error-free writing.

Research (Santos) has indicated that college professors in disciplines other than English tend to be more forgiving of ESL-type errors than of native speakers' errors, which they regard as careless. In addition, although ESL students may not always produce fluent English, their prior training and knowledge in their field of study may far exceed that of their native-speaker classmates. Professors may be delighted to have their input, both in writing and in class discussions, because of the value of their comments and diverse points of view for the class. In such cases, the standards of these professors and their discipline may be less stringent than those maintained in the composition class.

When assigning grades to ESL students, consider a few guidelines that may make the situation more equitable for ESL writers. If at all possible, allow students the opportunity to write multiple drafts that are not graded. This will permit ESL writers the opportunity to refine a piece of writing to their satisfaction. A split grade for the content (for example, organization, development, exemplification) and form (for example, the grammar, spelling, and punctuation) sometimes proves beneficial, especially when ESL students have many good ideas but still struggle with expression. Such a grading system helps students focus on the specific areas in which their writing needs improvement (Song and Caruso). Other solutions include assigning a satisfactory/unsatisfactory grade for work done during the semester and requiring a portfolio of the student's best work at the end of the class. (See pp. 45–47 of this manual for more on portfolios.) The final grade is based on the final portfolio and not the individual assignments.

A final, very important consideration is the time it takes for ESL students to complete written work. It may seem obvious that ESL writers need more time to complete their assignments, but even after many years of teaching ESL students, we are still surprised at the amount of time they actually do need. All writers need help getting started, but ESL writers seem more frightened of that first sentence than native speakers do. It's almost as if they believe that once they put that first sentence down, they are wed to it forever. As Ann Raimes has said, "The first sentence restricts them before they have begun to develop their ideas" (261). This need for more time also has implications for in-class and timed writing assignments. Research (Polio, Fleck, and Leder) has shown that ESL students can self-correct their papers when given extra time, even without feedback from the teacher. If at all possible, allow students a flexible schedule of deadlines.

SENTENCE-LEVEL ERRORS IN ESL WRITING

English composition instructors know a great deal about grammar and punctuation, but many who have not worked extensively with ESL students are puzzled by the errors such students make. Below are a few areas of grammar that are especially troublesome to many ESL students. All these trouble spots are discussed and illustrated in *The Little, Brown Handbook*. For more detailed explanations, consult Marianne Celce-Murcia and Diane Larsen-Freeman's *Grammar Book*, Second Edition, a specialized ESL reference grammar for the instructor, Jocelyn Steer and Karen Carlisi's *Advanced Grammar Book*, Second Edition, an ESL grammar textbook with an accompanying workbook by Jocelyn Steer and Dawn Schmid, or *Teaching English as a Second or Foreign Language*, Third Edition, edited by Marianne Celce-Murcia.

VERB TENSES

ESL students have difficulty with verb tenses and forms of helping verbs. Some tenses in English are straightforward and usually have a direct translation in most languages. These include the past tense, the future tense, and in some cases the present tense. However, other tenses (for example, present progressive and the present perfect) do not have equivalent forms in some languages. (See handbook section 14g.)

HELPING VERBS

Students often have difficulty choosing the appropriate form of the helping verb in a sentence. You may encounter sentences like *He should has been gone* rather than *He should have gone*. (See handbook section 14d.)

VERB ENDINGS

ESL students often leave off the -ed endings on verbs used in the passive (*It was return*) and in the past perfect tense (*I had return it*). One explanation may be that they do not hear the -ed ending in spoken English. (See handbook sections 14c and 14d.) They also often forget to add the -s or -es ending on present-tense verbs in the third-person singular (*He go; it don't work*) but can correct this error immediately when it is pointed out. It's a good idea to have your ESL students check their papers for subject-verb agreement before handing them in to you. (See handbook section 15a.)

VERBS WITH GERUNDS OR INFINITIVES

One particularly difficult area for ESL students to master is the use of a gerund or an infinitive after a verb. Some English verbs may be followed by a gerund (*He recommended going*). Others may be followed by an infinitive (*I want to go*). Some may be followed by either a gerund or an infinitive with no change in meaning (*I continued eating; I continued to eat*). Finally, some verbs may be followed by either form, but with a change in meaning (*I stopped smoking yesterday; I stopped to smoke*). (See handbook section 14e.)

COUNT AND NONCOUNT NOUNS

The distinction between count and noncount nouns in English is especially troublesome for ESL students because correct choice of article or quantifier and agreement with the verb depend on the differences. When ESL students first learn about count and noncount nouns, they are told that count nouns (*book/books; girl/girls*) are easily divided and counted, whereas noncount nouns are not. This rule is fine for the clear-cut examples such as *water, cheese,* or *love*. However, when students learn that *money* is a noncount noun, the rule seems to fall apart: who hasn't counted money easily and successfully? (See handbook section 16h.)

ARTICLES

Choosing an appropriate article is extremely trying for ESL students, especially students whose native language (e.g., Japanese, Chinese) does not have articles. It is equally trying for ESL teachers to explain why a definite article is used instead of an indefinite one. Once again, students learn rules to guide them in their choices. (See handbook section 16h.)

VERBS WITH PARTICLES

Students often complain about prepositions in English. These combinations of verbs and so-called particles (some of them adverbs) are particularly confusing: what may seem to be a simple construction of two (or three) words has a specific meaning that cannot be discerned from the meanings of the specific verb and preposition. There are literally hundreds of these idiomatic constructions. (See handbook section 14f.)

CONCLUSION

Initially, you may feel overwhelmed by the number of errors your ESL students make, and you may even harbor some resentment that you have to spend so much time correcting them. In such cases, it's important to remember that these students are still learning the language as well as writing skills. Don't feel compelled to correct every single mistake. Help students instead to develop and organize their ideas. And keep in mind that it may take your ESL students a long time before they write without making a lot of errors.

As you can see, ESL students—regardless of the cultural or socioeconomic group they may be from—confront a number of obstacles in their daily college lives. Most of these students spend an enormous amount of energy simply listening to lectures and trying to understand the language and the cultural content of what the instructor is saying. Anyone who has lived in a foreign country and listened to a foreign language continuously knows how exhausting negotiating simple tasks in the foreign culture can be. As their instructor, you have a chance to assist your students in this process of acculturation to the academic community and to give them the encouragement they need to succeed in their academic endeavors.

PRINT AND ONLINE RESOURCES FOR TEACHING ESL STUDENTS

PRINT RESOURCES

Auerbach, Elsa Roberts. "The Politics of the ESL Classroom: Issues of Power in Pedagogical Choices." *Power and Inequality in Language Education.* Ed. James Tollefson. Cambridge: Cambridge UP, 1995. 99–133.

Braine, George. "ESL Students in First-Year Writing Courses: ESL Versus Mainstream Classes." *Journal of Second Language Writing* 5 (1996): 91–107. Includes examples of rubrics for evaluating compositions.

Celce-Murcia, Marianne, and Diane Larsen-Freeman. *The Grammar Book.* 2nd ed. Boston: Heinle and Heinle, 1999. The updated edition of an excellent reference book on ESL grammar for instructors.

Connor, Ulla. *Contrastive Rhetoric: Cross-Cultural Aspects of Second-Language Writing.* New York: Cambridge UP, 1996.

Conrad, Susan M., and Lynn M. Goldstein. "ESL Student Revision after Teacher-Written Comments: Text, Contexts, and Individuals." *Journal of Second Language Writing* 8 (1999): 147–79.

Cowie, Neil. "Students of Process Writing Need Appropriate and Timely Feedback on Their Work, and in Addition, Training in Dealing With That Feedback." *Saitama University Review* 31 (1995): 181–94. ERIC Document ED 417581. Includes a summary of the research and practical suggestions for giving effective feedback on student papers.

Currie, Pat. "Staying Out of Trouble: Apparent Plagiarism and Academic Survival." *Journal of Second Language Writing* 7 (1998): 1–18.

Klein, Deborah. "Iago Lives in the Panopticon, or, Teaching Resistance, Granting Respect." *College English* 62 (1999): 169–91.

Kroll, Barbara, ed. *Second Language Writing: Research Insights for the Classroom.* New York: Cambridge UP, 1990. An interesting and often-cited collection of articles by distinguished researchers in second-language writing.

Leki, Ilona. "The Preferences of ESL Students for Error Correction in College Level Writing Classes." *Foreign Language Annals* 24 (1991): 203–14.

———. *Understanding ESL Writers: A Guide for Teachers.* Portsmouth: Boynton/Cook/Greenwood-Heinemann, 1992. An often-cited text.

Matsuda, Paul. "Composition Studies and ESL Writing: A Disciplinary Division of Labor." *College Composition and Communication* 50 (1999): 699–721. A history of the development of ESL instruction as a profession separate from composition instruction; includes a helpful listing of titles of several second-language and composition-study journals.

Mlynarczyk, Rebecca Williams. *Conversations of the Mind: The Uses of Journal Writing for Second-Language Learners.* Mahwah: Erlbaum, 1998.

Nelson, Gayle L., and Joan G. Carson. "ESL Students' Perceptions of Effectiveness in Peer Response Groups." *Journal of Second Language Writing* 7 (1998): 113–31.

Polio, Charlene, Catherine Fleck, and Nevin Leder. "If I Had More Time: ESL Learners' Changes in Linguistic Accuracy on Essay Revisions." *Journal of Second Language Writing* 7 (1998): 43–68.

Raimes, Ann. "Anguish as a Second Language? Remedies for Composition Teachers." *Composing in a Second Language.* Ed. Sandra McKay. Rowley: Newbury, 1984.

———. "Out of the Woods: Emerging Traditions in the Teaching of Writing." *TESOL Quarterly* 25 (1991): 407–30.

Reid, Joy M. *Teaching ESL Writing.* White Plains: Pearson Education ESL, 1993. A comprehensive text with an overview of native speaker and ESL composition; includes specific information for syllabus and course development, responding to and evaluating student writing, and classroom activities.

Santos, Tony. "Professors' Reactions to the Academic Writing of Non-native-Speaking Students." *TESOL Quarterly* 22 (1988): 69–90.

Song, Bailin, and Isabella Caruso. "Do English and ESL Faculty Differ in Evaluating the Essays of Native English-Speaking and ESL Students?" *Journal of Second Language Writing* 5 (1996): 163–82. Includes a sample writing assessment test, evaluation scale, and analytic assessment sheet for rating ten essay components.

Steer, Jocelyn, and Karen Carlisi. *The Advanced Grammar Book.* 2nd ed. Boston: Heinle and Heinle, 1998. Presents grammar principles in context for ESL students.

Steer, Jocelyn, and Dawn Schmid. *The Advanced Grammar Book.* 2nd ed. *Workbook.* Boston: Heinle and Heinle, 1998. Highly contextualized practice of grammar principles for ESL students.

Zamel, Vivian. "The Composing Process of Advanced ESL Students: Six Case Studies." *TESOL Quarterly* 17 (1983): 165–87.

————. "Strangers in Academia: The Experiences of Faculty and ESL Students Across the Curriculum." *The Writing Teacher's Sourcebook.* 4th ed. Ed. Edward P. J. Corbett, et al. New York: Oxford UP, 2000. 100–12.

ONLINE RESOURCES

The ESL Links Site
www.esldesk.com/esl-links/index.htm
A list of online ESL resources. Provides access to grammar resources, online quizzes, games, English dictionaries, and dictionaries that translate from English to other languages. Lists writing, reading, and listening resources. Includes links to related sites.

Purdue University Writing Lab
owl.english.purdue.edu/handouts/esl/eslstudent.html
A directory of Web sites about ESL resources for students, compiled by the Purdue University Writing Lab. Includes links to information about online courses, grammar, vocabulary, quizzes, listservs, and games.

Dave's ESL Cafe
eslcafe.com/ `
A collection of ESL resources for students and teachers. Includes chat rooms and discussion forums, mailing lists, and an ESL quiz center with questions on current news, grammar, idioms and slang, reading comprehension, writing, and world culture. Includes phrasal verbs arranged in a complete list, by meanings and examples, and by random phrasal verbs from the collection. Contains a FAQ section.

PART 1

The Writing Process

CHAPTER 1
Assessing the Writing Sitiuation

CHAPTER 2
Developing and Shaping Ideas

CHAPTER 3
Drafting and Revising

CHAPTER 4
Writing and Revising Paragraphs

CHAPTER 5
Designing Documents

Assessing the Writing Situation

A WRITER'S PERSPECTIVE

I've decided that if you wait for the perfect time to write, you'll never write.

MARGARET ATWOOD

You get all your best ideas in the shower.

CLINT EASTWOOD

CHAPTER HIGHLIGHTS

Teachers know that writing is *not* easy, but students, especially beginning writers, often have the misconception that writing comes easily to experienced writers and is hard only for the untalented or inexperienced. This chapter begins by recognizing the difficulties faced by all writers, experienced and inexperienced alike. Next, the chapter alerts students to the various elements of the writing situation and the writing process and discusses ways to discover and limit subjects. The concluding sections explore flexible strategies for considering audience and defining a purpose for writing. Special features of this chapter are the attention paid to the role of audience and purpose throughout the composition process and the list of "Questions About Audience" (p. 11).

Although Chapters 1 and 2 look at activities typical of the early stages of composing and Chapter 3 treats drafting and revising, the text does not endorse a strictly linear view of the composing process. Instead, all three chapters emphasize the writer's many options and the flexibility of the composing process. They point out that writing is a way of thinking and discovering: that in the middle of drafting an essay a writer may recognize the need to develop new supporting ideas, to make major changes in the organization, or to shift the purpose of the essay and modify the thesis.

MEDIA RESOURCES FOR CHAPTER 1

mycomplab Please visit MyCompLab at *www.mycomplab.com* for more on the writing process.

http://www.ablongman.com/littlebrown ▶ See page 73 of this manual for companion Web site content description.

1a Understanding how writing happens

CLASSROOM IDEA

At ease Students often bring their apprehensions about writing (and writing instructors) with them to class. To create a positive atmosphere for your course, you may wish to establish a setting in which students feel at ease about acknowledging and sharing their apprehensions. One way to do this is to ask them to *list* what they dislike (and like) about writing without worrying about the form or correctness of entries in their lists. Voluntary sharing of the entries can help reduce the isolation many students feel and help you (and them) set priorities for instruction.

ANSWERS

EXERCISE 1.1 Starting a writing journal (p. 3)

Individual responses.

RESOURCES AND IDEAS

Ball, Kevin and Amy Goodburn. "Composition Studies and Service Learning: Appealing to Communities?" *Composition Studies* 28.1 (2000): 79–94. The authors are critical of service learning pedagogy that too often excludes the voices of community participants; they offer suggestions for writing assignments that would include the perspectives of community participants.

Bartholomae, David. "Inventing the University." *When a Writer Can't Write: Studies in Writer's Block and Other Composing Process Problems.* Ed. Mike Rose. New York: Guilford, 1985. 134–65. Bartholomae argues persuasively that many student writers, especially those with little writing experience, need to be taught explicitly the discourse standards of an academic community in order to write successfully for it.

Berlin, James A. "Contemporary Composition: The Major Pedagogical Theories." *College English* 44 (1982): 765–77. Berlin points out that various process approaches have consequences instructors must consider.

Blakeslee, Ann M. "Bridging the Workplace and the Academy: Teaching Professional Genres Through Classroom-Workplace Collaborations." *Technical Communication* 10.2 (2001): 169–92. Using case studies, Blakeslee shows how student writing improves when students work on projects provided by professionals in business and industry.

Deans, Thomas. *Writing Partnerships: Service-Learning in Composition.* Urbana: NCTE, 2000. Deans provides an excellent introduction to the theoretical and pedagogical issues of community writing initiatives.

Durst, Russel K. *Collision Course: Conflict, Negotiation, and Learning in College Composition.* Urbana: NCTE, 1999. Durst advocates that teachers use a "reflective instrumentalism" in order to reconcile students' practical goals with their own desire to teach critical awareness and reflection.

Flower, Linda, and John R. Hayes. "A Cognitive Process Theory of Writing." *College Composition and Communication* 32 (1981): 365–87. This classic article contains what is probably the best-known and most widely accepted discussion of the components of the writing process, though its model is more theoretical than practical.

Lindemann, Erika. "Three Views of English 101." *College English* 57 (1995): 287–302. This article lays out the opposing claims and assumptions of the "process," "product," and "system of social action" approaches to the writing classroom.

McComiskey, Bruce. *Teaching Composition as a Social Process.* Logan: Utah State UP, 2000. McComiskey extends composition theory beyond a discussion of the writing process, re-examining product, in the context of cultural theory, as a cycle of production, distribution, and consumption.

Sherman, Linda K., and Beverly Wall. "The Things that Go Without Saying in Composition Studies: A Colloquy." *Journal of Advanced Composition* 15 (1995): 281–320. The authors assemble a many-voiced critique of some of the current assumptions of composition pedagogy, including the process paradigm.

Tobin, Lad, and Thomas Newkirk, eds. *Taking Stock: The Writing Process Movement in the '90's.* Portsmouth: Boynton, 1994. This collection of essays analyzes the goals of the writing process movement, its application in particular institutions, and the ways in which a focus on the writing process can be adapted for the classrooms of the future.

Yagelski, Robert P. *Literacy Matters: Writing and Reading the Social Self.* New York: Teachers College Press, 2000. Yagelski supports changes to writing curricula to account for the seminal influence of social context on the production and composition of written texts.

1b Analyzing the writing situation

CLASSROOM IDEAS

COMPUTER ACTIVITY Web models Ask students to locate articles or other material on the World Wide Web that can serve as models (having clear subjects, audiences, and purposes) or as negative models (having unclear subjects, purposes, or audiences). Students can share what they find with the rest of the class by e-mailing the URLs to their classmates.

COLLABORATIVE LEARNING Group analysis Break students into small groups and ask them to work together to analyze a writing situation using the questions on pp. 4–5 as a guideline.

ANSWERS

EXERCISE 1.2 Analyzing a writing situation (p. 6)

The assignment specifies the subject (the combinations of client, therapist, and theory that tend to make psychotherapy successful), the audience (the instructor and a "discussion group" of classmates), and the purpose (to explain and support a conclusion about the subject). It requires research into studies of psychotherapy. It specifies a length range and a deadline. It does not specify a format, but APA format could be assumed because the course is in psychology.

RESOURCES AND IDEAS

Brady, Laura. "Overcoming Resistance: Computers in the Writing Classroom." *Computers and Composition* 7:2 (1990): 21–33. Brady found that word processing in the first-year composition classroom increased the volume of student writing, prompted new ways of thinking about topics, encouraged collaboration, and fostered a positive workshop atmosphere.

Brooke, Rupert, Ruth Mirtz, and Rick Evans, eds. *Small Groups in Writing Workshops: Invitations to a Writer's Life.* Urbana: NCTE, 1994. This collection of essays offers many strategies for using collaborative group work to create an active learning situation.

Flower, Linda S., and John R. Hayes. "The Cognition of Discovery: Defining a Rhetorical Problem." *College Composition and Communication* 31 (1980): 21–32. This article reports on a detailed study of how good writers and poor writers conceive of writing tasks as they begin to compose.

Golub, Jeff. *Activities for an Interactive Classroom.* Urbana: NCTE, 1994. Golub provides a number of hands-on suggestions for creating an effective workshop environment.

Hillocks, George, Jr. "Environments for Active Learning." *Theory and Practice in the Teaching of Writing: Rethinking the Discipline.* Ed. Lee Odell. Carbondale: Southern Illinois UP, 1993. 244–70. Hillocks' essay is part case study and part analysis of a classroom structure based on student interactions with each other and with texts.

Summerfield, Judith. "Is There a Life in This Text? Reimagining Narrative." *Writing Theory and Critical Theory: Research and Scholarship in*

Composition. Ed. John Clifford and John Schilb. New York: MLA, 1994. 179–94. Summerfield examines the role of student narratives in the composition classroom, especially the extent to which they can provoke and sustain students' "authentic" voices.

Tedlock, David. "The Case Approach to Composition." *College Composition and Communication* 32 (1981): 253–61. Tedlock argues for the use of cases—detailed, self-contained descriptions of a writing situation—as a basis for assignments and instructions.

1c Discovering and limiting a subject

INSTRUCTOR RESOURCE

The following Presentation Aid is available for download on this book's companion Web site at *http://www.ablongman.com/littlebrown.*

PRESENTATION AID 1.1: Responding to a specific assignment (p. 6)

CLASSROOM IDEAS

COMPUTER ACTIVITY Subject search If your classroom is linked to the Internet, ask your students to do a subject search on a broad topic, like the "environment," and to note the successive points at which they will be able to narrow the topic by choosing among lists of sub-headings. At a later stage you might ask students to create their own hypertext document in which a broad subject heading leads the user to information on more specific topics.

Narrowing subjects to topics Clustering (2a–5) and asking the journalist's questions (2a–6) can also help narrow subjects to topics. For example, the broad subject "Islam" can be the center point of a cluster, and students can write related topic ideas such as "theology of Islam," "Western attitudes toward Muslims and Islam," and "women in Islam" in branches radiating from the center. "Islam" can also be narrowed by asking such questions as "*Who* are major figures in Islam?" "*What* do Muslims believe?" "*How* are Muslims and Islam viewed in the United States?," "*Where* is Islam practiced?," and "*How* and *Why* are women and men treated differently in Islamic tradition?"

Other good subject areas that give students practice in narrowing topics are movies, cars, television programs, and academic fields (for example, sociology, geology).

COLLABORATIVE LEARNING Exercise 1.3 Have students work in groups to find specific topics for the assignments in Exercise 1.3, and then share their conclusions with the class. Students benefit from realizing the numerous and varied options for narrowing a broad subject.

COLLABORATIVE LEARNING Exercise 1.4 Sharing past work can help students connect the writing they are doing in your class to their broader experience as writers, a connection that helps them to gain greater awareness of their own progress as writers. Have students bring in a piece of previous work and present it to their group, describing the context in which that piece was written, their purpose in writing it, what they learned from writing it, and how it differs from other kinds of writing they have done. Ask groups to report on the interesting or unexpected moments that occurred in the group presentations.

COLLABORATIVE LEARNING Exercise 1.5 As part of the process of developing their topics for Exercise 1.5, have students verbally articulate their ideas in small groups and receive suggestions for further developments and focus.

ANSWERS

EXERCISE 1.3 Narrowing subjects (p. 9)

Possible answers:

1. How has direct distribution of popular music on the Web affected consumers' choices?
2. How does slang help to bind members of the college community?
3. How does X's theory about math anxiety apply to me?
4. How might term limits affect the House of Representatives?
5. How has immigration affected food choices?

EXERCISE 1.4 Considering your past work: Discovering and limiting a subject (p. 9)

Individual response.

EXERCISE 1.5 Finding and narrowing a subject for your essay (p. 9)

Individual response.

RESOURCES AND IDEAS

Guiher-Huff, Susan. "Involvement in a Current Problem as a Basis for Writing." *Teaching English in the Two-Year College* 17 (1990): 187–88. Guiher-Huff describes how students used a range of essay formats, made a cause-and-effect oral presentation, and wrote persuasive letters around the topic of pollution. The sustained topic seemed to make the writing meaningful for the students.

Schreffler, Peter H. "'Where All the Children Are Above Average': Garrison Keillor as a Model for Personal Narrative Assignments." *College Composition and Communication* 40 (1989): 82–85. Schreffler discusses the delightful experience personal narrative writing can be as students delve into themselves as well as into the world around them.

Seabury, Marcia Bundy. "The Abstraction Ladder in Freshman Composition." *College Composition and Communication* 40 (1989): 89–92. Seabury has found that teaching S. Hayakawa's abstraction ladder can benefit first-year composition students in their thinking through and writing about their topics.

Wallace, David. "From Intention to Text: Articulating Initial Intentions for Writing." *Research in the Teaching of English* 30 (1996): 182–219. This essay explores the relationship between the planning and composing stages of writing. Wallace's study found that students who were most able to articulate their initial intentions for a writing task were also most able to complete the task effectively.

On limiting subjects:

Coe, Richard M. "If Not to Narrow, Then How to Focus: Two Techniques for Focusing." *College Composition and Communication* 32 (1981): 272–77. Coe describes ways to get students to focus on a particular aspect of a topic as an alternative to the usual approach of narrowing a topic.

Tucker, Amy. *Decoding ESL: International Students in the American College Classroom*. Portsmouth: Boynton, 1995. This book explores the larger issues of how to read and respond to ESL writers, and includes (particularly in Chapter 8) strategies for using readings as the prompts for writing assignments.

1d Considering the audience

INSTRUCTOR RESOURCE

The following Presentation Aid is available for download on this book's companion Web site at *http://www.ablongman.com/littlebrown*.

PRESENTATION AID 1.2: Questions about audience (p. 11)

CLASSROOM IDEAS

Audience inventory Ask students to choose a possible topic for an essay and to list the kinds of people who might be interested in the topic. Tell students that if they wish they may employ the "Questions About Audience" on page 11. (In theory, the lists might be very long. In practice, students soon run out of ideas, but not until they have begun to visualize the audience for their essays.) To extend the exercise, ask students what part of the potential audience they would most like to address or what kinds of people would be most interested in the topic. Then ask them to list either (1) what the restricted audience probably already knows about the topic and what it needs to know or (2) what its attitudes are and what kinds of arguments will be needed to change them.

COLLABORATIVE LEARNING Audience inventory Ask students to compare the lists they developed for the audience inventory and suggest changes, additions, or deletions.

COLLABORATIVE LEARNING Audience assessment Distribute to your class an article from a special-interest magazine, a newspaper feature or editorial, an article from the Internet, or another brief essay whose appeal to a particular audience students will be able to recognize fairly easily. Ask students to read the essay and then to work together to identify the characteristics and attitudes of the intended audience as they think the author viewed it. Ask them also to identify the tone of the essay and to decide whether or not it is appropriate to the subject, the intended audience, and the publication in which the essay appeared. Tell them to be ready to point out what evidence in the essay they used to identify the intended audience and the tone. Rather than bring articles to class yourself, ask students either individually or as teams to bring in a variety of essays or writings aimed at particular audiences. Some target audiences you might pick are consumers, sports fans, parents, businesspeople, patients, and health-care workers.

COMPUTER ACTIVITY Collaborative postings Have your students work together to compose a posting for an Internet newsgroup in which they practice pitching their writing to a nonspecific audience. In their postings they should try to include sufficient (or even extra) information, to assume the role of an equal in the conversation they are entering, and to write in a level tone.

COLLABORATIVE LEARNING Exercise 1.6 Have students work in groups to critique and revise one of their paragraph-length responses to Exercise 1.6. In networked classrooms, students can "publish" the revised paragraphs for the class.

ANSWERS

EXERCISE 1.6 Considering audience (p. 12)

Possible Answers:

1. *For elementary school students:* physical effects in simple terms; statistics in simple figures; difficulty in quitting once addicted; importance of resisting peer pressure.
   Role: combined teacher and parent. Tone: warm, slightly admonitory.
   For adult smokers: graphic depiction of physical effects; detailed statistics; influence on children; effect on smoker's appearance, odor, breath.
   Role: combined friend and lecturer. Tone: no-nonsense.

2. *For cyclists who also oppose the law:* status of law; reasons for opposition; need for action; suggested actions.
   Role: peer, motivator. Tone: informal, urgent.
   For people who favor the law: acknowledgement of pro-law position; disadvantages of helmets; lack of proven need; infringement of cyclists' rights.

Role: Fellow citizen. Tone: informative, reasonable, appealing to shared values.

3. *For your neighbors:* feelings of neighborhood residents; dangers to children and pets; lowered property values; threat of petition to zoning board.
   Role: peer. Tone: direct, a bit angry.

   For the zoning board: violation of zoning regulations; length of time the wrecked truck has been present; number of unsuccessful appeals to neighbors; dangers to children and pets.
   Role: plaintiff. Tone: serious, reasonable.

EXERCISE 1.7 Considering your past work: Writing for a specific audience (p. 13)

Individual response.

EXERCISE 1.8 Analyzing the audience for your essay (p. 13)

Individual response.

RESOURCES AND IDEAS

Bacon, Nora. "Building a Swan's Next for Instruction in Rhetoric." *College Composition and Communication* 51.4 (2000): 589–609. Bacon shows how community-based writing assignments help students understand how purpose and style must change as a result of rhetorical questions.

Ong, Walter J., S. J. "The Writer's Audience Is Always a Fiction," PMLA 90 (1975): 9–21. Ong argues that writers must construct audiences in their imaginations as an essential part of the act of writing and that readers must play the role defined for them by the writer's act of imagination. Of course, students are probably aware that in many writing circumstances, such as writing for a professor or a manager at work, the audience is real, not fictional. It's worth discussing how a writer's task can be shaped by his or her knowledge of actual readers.

Vandenberg, Peter. "Pick Up This Cross and Follow: (Ir)responsibility and the Teaching of 'Writing for Audience.'" *Composition Studies: Freshman English News* 20 (Fall 1992): 84–97. Vandenberg reviews debates over the changing concept of audience and pinpoints some of the contradictions that students face as they try to write for particular audiences.

1e Defining a purpose

CLASSROOM IDEAS

Identifying purpose Use paragraphs drawn from magazine articles, essays in a reader, or student papers as the basis for class discussion of the purposes of writing. You may ask students to work individually or in groups to compare the aims of individual paragraphs with the overall purpose of the essay from which they are taken and to decide what role the paragraphs play within the essay.

COMPUTER ACTIVITY Online purposes Give your students a series of Web pages to look at and ask them to evaluate what they find on each page in terms of purpose.

COLLABORATIVE LEARNING Exercise 1.9 Ask students to develop their responses to Exercise 1.9 in groups, paying particular attention to places where the purposes of a given topic could differ. This discussion will help students to explore ways in which a topic might lend itself to various purposes.

ANSWERS

EXERCISE 1.9 Finding purpose in assignments (p. 15)

Possible answers :

1. *How has direct distribution of popular music on the Web affected consumers' choices?* Explain how the ability to connect directly with musicians on the Web results in more music choices for consumers. Introduce readers to a benefit of the Web.
2. *How does slang help to bind members of the college community?* Explain how the community's unique slang contributes to a sense of belonging. Show readers the value of their slang.
3. *How does X's theory about math anxiety apply to me?* Explain the way X's theory reflects your own experience. Demonstrate to readers the truth of the theory.
4. *How might term limits affect the House of Representatives?* Argue against term limits for legislators. Lead readers to agree that term limits are unnecessary and potentially harmful.
5. *How has immigration affected food choices?* Explain how immigrants have vastly increased the variety of foods available. Help readers appreciate this benefit of immigration.

EXERCISE 1.10 Considering your past work: Defining a purpose (p. 15)

Individual response.

EXERCISE 1.11 Defining a purpose for your essay (p. 15)

Individual response.

RESOURCES AND IDEAS

Ede, Lisa, and Andrea Lunsford. "Audience Addressed/Audience Invoked: The Role of Audience in Composition Theory and Pedagogy." *College Composition and Communication* 35 (1984): 155–71. The authors suggest a negotiated balance between the writer's desires and the audience's needs. See also their "Representing Audience: Successful' Discourse and Disciplinary Critique" in *College Composition and Communication* 47 (1996): 167–79.

Kirsch, Gesa, and Duane H. Roen. *A Sense of Audience in Written Communication*. Newbury Park: Sage, 1990. Sixteen interdisciplinary essays on audience treat the subject from a number of critical perspectives.

Park, Douglas B. "Analyzing Audiences." *College Composition and Communication* 37 (1986): 478–88. Understanding the social context of a writing act helps students define their audiences.

Rieff, Mary Jo. "Rereading 'Invoked' and 'Addressed' Readers Through a Social Lens: Towards a Recognition of Multiple Audiences." *Journal of Advanced Composition* 16 (1996): 407–24. Reiff reviews ways in which the term audience has been evoked by composition theorists and examines ways that writing teachers and students can take multiple audience perspectives into account.

Roth, Robert G. "'The Evolving Audience': Alternatives to Audience Accommodation." *College Composition and Communication* 38 (1987): 47–55. Roth argues that student writers should focus more on how to claim an audience's attention than on heuristics defining the audience.

Trimbur, John. "Composition and the Circulation of Writing." *College Composition and Communication* 52 (December 2000): 188–219. Trimbur suggests that teachers should enrich composition instruction by alerting students to the effects a broader circulation of students' work would have on the manner of composition.

Wells, Susan. "Rogue Cops and Health Care: What Do We Want from Public Writing?" *College Composition and Communication* 47 (1996): 325–41. Wells explores the problems of addressing a "general public" audience in student assignments.

Willey, R. J. "Audience Awareness: Methods and Madness." *Freshman English News* 18:2 (1990): 20+. Willey found that when rhetorical, informational, and social perspectives on audience awareness were considered in the composition classroom, the social perspective was the most productive because of its transactional nature.

CHAPTER 2

Developing
and Shaping Ideas

CHAPTER HIGHLIGHTS

Continuing the discussion of the writing process begun in Chapter 1, this chapter helps students generate and shape their ideas. (2a) Discussion of strategies for exploration, including journal writing, observing, freewriting, listing, clustering, using the journalist's questions, using patterns of development, reading, and thinking critically, begins the chapter. (2b) The next section focuses on conceiving, drafting, and revising thesis statements. (2c) Students then read about how to organize their essays: distinguishing the general and the specific, using organizational tools such as outlines and tree diagrams, and choosing an appropriate structure for an essay. The chapter concludes by addressing unity and coherence and how to check for them.

The exercises for this chapter ask students to reflect on how they have generated ideas for writing in the past and to try out some new techniques as they work on an essay-in-progress.

MEDIA RESOURCES FOR CHAPTER 2

mycomplab Please visit MyCompLab at *www.mycomplab.com* for more on the writing process .

http://www.ablongman.com/littlebrown ▶ See page 73 of this manual for companion Web site content description.

2a Discovering ideas

CLASSROOM IDEAS

Keeping journals Students may have mixed feelings about journal keeping, so it's important to explain to them why writers find keeping journals so valuable. Make clear how journals differ from diaries and how many (and what kind of) entries you expect per week or term. Giving some guidelines or prompts for students to follow helps them get started. Students can also add clippings, photocopies, pictures, and cartoons and even use tapes and videos in their journals as a way of expanding their horizons. (These other media will have to be submitted separately if you have students hand their journals in.)

It's important to make the journal a productive tool, not just make-work. Encourage students to plumb their journals for essay topics and samples of strategies they might use in more formal pieces of writing. You can also make journals productive by encouraging students to write journal entries as letters to you or classmates, then incorporate your or their classmates' answers into the journal as well.

Most instructors react to issues raised or comment on attempts to try new strategies without actually grading the journal. Students will often include very personal material in their journals, so they should be encouraged to fold over, staple, or secure (but not remove) personal material before they show it to you; and they must trust that you will respect their confidentiality.

Computer journals If your students keep their journals on their computers, the Cut-and-Paste function will make it easy for them to mine their journal entries for appropriate material to copy to the document in which they are drafting their paper.

CULTURE LANGUAGE **Writing process as cultural value** Students who have not previously been schooled in the process approach to writing may be surprised by classroom activities that focus on discrete elements of the process. They may be surprised that you as the instructor are interested in the entire process, rather than just the end product, and that you may be reviewing their work on early stages of the process. You may want to spend some time discussing what an original idea is; what a draft is supposed to be; the responsibilities of the teacher and student respectively at various stages of the writing process; and how to determine where the line is between appropriate and inappropriate use of the help of the instructor, peer reviewers, or tutors.

ACTIVITIES THAT SUGGEST TOPICS AND IDEAS

1. Ask students to take a notebook with them to some place likely to be filled with activity and vivid sense impressions—a laundromat, the center of the campus, a busy restaurant. They can record their impressions of the scene in the notebook, later turning those impressions into a structured description or using the material in some other form of writing.

2. Ask students to look at a variety of magazines and to bring in a list of the topics covered in the articles. These topics may in turn suggest topics for student essays. The exercise can be extended by asking students to summarize the contents of one or more of the articles and to indicate how the content might appeal to a particular audience.

3. Check with your audiovisual center or a film rental service for short films that deal with values or controversies. The films or the ensuing discussions can become the basis of student papers.

4. Set up class presentations or debates on an issue in order to provide information and sharpen the focus for papers dealing with the issue or related topics.

Places to write To help students discover interesting topics and ideas through freewriting, you might give them some places to begin. For essays focusing on events:

sports, contests, camping, accidents, storms, childhood experiences, giving a speech, getting lost in a department store, robberies, fires

For writing about a scene or character:

outdoors—woods, seashore, mountains, fields, city streets, parks

indoors—dorm rooms, laundromats

scenes—family gatherings, football games, funerals, a snowy morning people—parents, grandparents, uncles, aunts, childhood friends, people in a public place, teachers, unpleasant people, cartoon characters

For informative or explanatory writing:

hobbies, jobs, investments, fields of study, recent scientific discoveries, places to visit, ways to save money, fishing, gardening, study habits, car repairing, canoeing, audio equipment, magazines

For persuasive writing:

campus issues, environmental concerns, automobile or airline safety, support for education, cost of medical care, regulation of new drugs, specialized education versus liberal arts education, rights of minorities and women, gun control, divorce and child rearing, school prayer, censorship, proposals to improve campus or local services, ways of dealing with a social problem

COLLABORATIVE LEARNING Teamed freewriting A good variation on freewriting is to make it collaborative: have students write freely for five or ten minutes, then pass their freewriting sample to the students sitting next to them. Students should read the freewriting, then reflect on it in another freewriting session. This encourages not only more perspectives on a topic but the notion that writing is a dialogue between writer and reader—and it teaches the value of feedback and audience awareness in writing as well.

COMPUTER ACTIVITY Freewriting in cyberspace Have students freewrite on the computer using the "invisible writing" technique if desired. During the next class period ask students to revise their freewriting into a paragraph, then e-mail that paragraph to another student in the class for a further critique and for revision suggestions. After a final revision, students might "publish" the resulting paragraphs on the network or hand them in for the teacher's evaluation.

COLLABORATIVE LEARNING Topic clusters The topic clusters we show in 2a–5 are very well developed; students need to know it's acceptable to develop smaller or messier clusters. You might ask students to work on topic clusters in groups. If your classroom permits, you might also want to try doing clusters on overhead transparencies or the blackboard, so that students can add to and change their contents more easily.

Using questions and patterns To help students discover the power of sets of questions or the patterns of development for exploring topics, begin by giving them a list of general subjects—music, sports, guns, multiculturalism, the environment—and then ask them to explore each, looking for limited aspects that might make good topics for essays. Do not encourage students to use either the questions or the patterns in probing the topics. Class discussion can focus on how to limit the topics and can indicate how an audience might respond to them.

Following the discussion, ask students to explore the same topics using either the journalist's questions (2a–6) or the patterns of development (2a–7). Ask students to direct their attention to as many different aspects of the topic as they can and at the same time to suggest ways of developing it and organizing an essay around it. Discussion should focus on differences between the "guided" and "unguided" approaches to developing a topic.

Role playing Students often don't know how to respond to readings; role-playing exercises that ask them to pose as book reviewers or discussants on a political talk show may help them find an angle from which to start responding to a reading.

COLLABORATIVE LEARNING Editorial responses Ask students to bring in journal or newspaper articles on controversial topics and work individually or in groups to compose letters of response "to the editor." Students should consult with their groups to determine the appropriate tone and implied journal or newspaper audience for each response.

COMPUTER ACTIVITY Exercise 2.3 Exercise 2.3 can be readily transferred to the computer classroom to encourage students to practice generating material on the computer. At the end of the exercise you might ask students to read through their material to develop ideas and to highlight ideas for future revision, but to avoid deleting material. As a take-home assignment or in the following class, students can revise and delete more extensively; they might then present the resulting material to their groups.

ANSWERS

EXERCISE 2.1 Considering your past work: developing a topic (p. 26)
Individual response.

EXERCISE 2.2 Keeping a journal (p. 26)
Individual response.

EXERCISE 2.3 Using freewriting, brainstorming, or clustering (p. 27)
Individual response.

EXERCISE 2.4 Sending an online query (p. 27)
Individual response.

EXERCISE 2.5 Developing your subject (p. 27)
Individual response.

RESOURCES AND IDEAS

On keeping journals

Fulwiler, Toby, ed. *The Journal Book*. Portsmouth: Boynton/Cook, 1987. The essays in this collection describe the uses of journals for discovering and exploring ideas and as an important strategy for writing and learning in various subject areas.

Gannett, Cinthia. *Gender and the Journal: Diaries and Academic Discourse.* Albany: State U of New York P, 1992. Gannett discusses the development of the genre and how it has been "feminized," with consideration of the pedagogical implications of this history.

White, Fred D. "Releasing the Self: Teaching Journal-Writing to Freshmen." *The Writing Instructor* 1 (1982): 147–54. White offers practical advice on the use of journals: kinds of journals and entries, professional samples, exercises, and a summary of supporting research.

Whitehill, Sharon. "Using the Journal for Discovery: Two Devices." *College Composition and Communication* 38 (1987): 472–74. Whitehill argues that journal assignments calling for lists and for imaginary dialogues can help generate ideas and alleviate writing blocks, and she provides detailed examples of each strategy.

On generative strategies

Flower, Linda S., and John R. Hayes. "Problem-Solving Strategies and the Writing Process." *College English* 39 (1977): 449–61. Flower and Hayes describe techniques for discovering and developing ideas, including cue words, nutshelling, idea trees, role playing, and brainstorming.

Hunter, Susan. "Oral Negotiations in a Textual Community: A Case for Pedagogy and Theory." *Writing Instructor* 8 (1989): 105–10. Hunter states that validating oral communication during the composing process is theoretically sound and helpful in generalizing successful oral communication to successful written communication.

Lackey, Kris. "Amongst the Awful Subtexts: Scholes, The Daily Planet, and Freshman Composition." *College Composition and Communication* 38 (1987): 88–93. In this thought-provoking piece, Lackey suggests encouraging and enabling students to tease out the binary oppositions in texts as a way of discovering various subtexts that suggest topics for students' own writing.

Perrin, Robert. "10:00 and 2:00: A Ten-Paragraph Defense of the Five-Paragraph Theme." *Teaching English in the Two-Year College* 22 (March 2000): 312–14. Perrin defends assigning the infamous five-paragraph essay, showing how, used Judiciously, it does not necessarily stifle creativity.

Qualley, Donna. *Turns of Thought: Teaching Composition as Reflexive Inquiry*. Portsmouth: Boynton/Cook (Heinemann), 1997. Qualley advocates "essayism"—a mode of writing in which students reflect upon and reconsider their own claims in response to an encounter with a new idea or text.

Ratcliffe, Krista. "Rhetorical Listening: A Trope for Interpretive Invention and a 'Code of Cross-Cultural Conduct.'" *College Composition and Communication* 51 (1991): 195–224. Ratcliffe advocates a form of listening (as distinct from reading) in combination with rhetorical invention as a way of creating productive cross-cultural discourse.

Wesley, Kimberly. "The Ill Effects of the Five-Paragraph Theme." *English Journal* 90 (September 2000): 57–60. Wesley argues that students' ability to think critically is stifled when a writing assignment is too prescribed.

On freewriting

Dunn, Patricia. *Talking, Sketching, Moving: Multiple Literacies in the Teaching of Writing.* Portsmouth: Boyton/Cook, 2001. Dunn encourages us to motivate students to write and improve their attitude to writing through prewriting assignments that include oral and visual presentations.

Elbow, Peter. *Writing Without Teachers.* New York: Oxford UP, 1973. In this classic work, Elbow discusses freewriting and other techniques for tapping imagination and creativity during the writing process.

Price, Gayle B. "A Case for a Modern Commonplace Book." *College Composition and Communication* 31 (1980): 175–82. This article reviews freewriting and other techniques for helping students generate ideas and tells how students can use a notebook to record ideas.

Reynolds, Mark. "Make Free Writing More Productive." *College Composition and Communication* 39 (1988): 81–82. Reynolds offers twenty "questions, activities, and guidelines" for drawing useful ideas and promising topics from the often jumbled material provided by freewriting

On clustering

Frye, Bob. "Artful Compositions, Corder's 'Laws of Composition,' and the Weekly Letter: Two Approaches to Teaching Invention and Arrangement in Freshman English." *Journal of Teaching Writing* 8 (1989): 1–14. Frye argues that having students write replies to the instructor's weekly letters allows them to experience genuine rhetorical invention rather than experiencing closure, often the product of structure.

Rico, Gabriele Lusser. *Writing the Natural Way.* Los Angeles: Tarcher, 1983. Rico draws on research about brain functions as the basis for advice about strategies—especially clustering—that encourage creativity in expression.

On heuristics

Kneupper, Charles W. "Revising the Tagmemic Heuristic: Theoretical and Pedagogical Considerations." *College Composition and Communication* 31 (1980): 160–68. Kneupper offers a simplified version of the powerful question system introduced by Young, Becker, and Pike in their text, *Rhetoric: Discovery and Change* (New York: Harcourt, 1970).

Washington, Eugene. "WH-Questions in Teaching Composition." *College Composition and Communication* 28 (1977): 54–56. Washington suggests using what, why, where, and how questions to increase density of information in essays and clarify structure.

On patterns of development

D'Angelo, Frank J. *A Conceptual Theory of Rhetoric*. Cambridge: Winthrop, 1975. D'Angelo argues that rhetorical patterns of organization (e.g., analysis, classification, and description) are also patterns of thought and invention and can be used to probe experience as part of the composing process. See also D'Angelo's "Topoi and Form in Composition," *The Territory of Language*. Ed. Donald A. McQuade. Carbondale: Southern Illinois UP, 1986. 114–22.

Podis, Leonard A. "Teaching Arrangement: Defining a More Practical Approach." *College Composition and Communication* 31 (1980): 197–204. Podis describes a teaching sequence designed to make students aware of the basic principles of organization, and he reviews some standard patterns of arrangement useful for academic and professional writing.

Wilcox, Lance. "Time Lines in the Composing of Narratives: A Graphic Aid to Organization." *The Writing Instructor* 6 (1987): 162–73. Wilcox describes in detail the use of time lines to help develop and organize narrative essays.

2b Developing a thesis

INSTRUCTOR RESOURCES

The following Presentation Aids are available for download on this book's companion Web site at *http://www.ablongman.com/littlebrown*.

PRESENTATION AIDS 2.1: Functions of the thesis statement (p. 28)

PRESENTATION AID 2.2: Checklist for revising the thesis statement (p. 30)

CLASSROOM IDEAS

Implicit thesis versus explicit thesis Students need to understand that all good writing has a controlling idea (an implied thesis) but that some good writing doesn't have an explicit thesis. Asking students to look for theses in various kinds of writing (from textbooks to novels to travel articles to junk mail) is one way of showing them that a writer must decide whether to use an explicit thesis based on his or her purpose and audience.

Oral progress reports Have students report orally to the class or to their peer writing groups on topics and thesis statements for a coming paper.

Giving an oral presentation forces students to focus their ideas and adopt a stance. As they speak, moreover, students may sense difficulties with the topic or thesis. Comments from classmates can help identify strengths and weaknesses and suggest an appropriate tone for the essay.

Condensing the argument Often the exercise of condensing the main ideas of a paper in a separate forum can help writers recognize and articulate their thesis. Ask students to set their paper-in-progress aside and write a short (three sentences to one paragraph) abstract summarizing its central argument.

Student models You may wish to copy effective thesis statements from student papers to use in class discussion or small-group work. The statements will provide positive models and may suggest topics for future essays. You can vary this exercise by copying ineffective statements and discussing how they may be revised. Be sure to keep the discussion of ineffective statements positive in tone, however.

Supplying an omitted thesis statement Ask students to read their papers to the class or to a peer group, deliberately leaving out the thesis statement. Ask the other students to supply a thesis for the essay. If the original thesis and the one supplied by the students match, fine. If not, the thesis a student has chosen may be inappropriate for the paper and the discussion that follows can suggest possible revisions.

COLLABORATIVE LEARNING Agreement on thesis Ask students to read an essay from a collection or a fellow student's paper and then to state its thesis in their own words. Divide students into small groups and ask the group members to come up with a thesis statement together. Next have the groups try to identify a thesis statement in the essay. If the essay has an explicit thesis statement, ask if they consider it effective or if the thesis statement they produced would be more effective. If the thesis is implicit, ask students whether or not the essay would benefit from an explicit thesis statement.

COLLABORATIVE LEARNING Thesis checklist Divide students into pairs or small groups and ask them to use the Checklist for revising the thesis statement (p. 30) as a tool for peer review. They can trade essays and use the checklist to evaluate one another's thesis statements.

COMPUTER ACTIVITY Thesis archive On your class Web site, have students compile an archive of thesis statements they have found in print or electronic sources. Each submission should include an annotation that evaluates the functionality of the thesis statement (see the functions list on p. 28).

COMPUTER ACTIVITY Collaborative documents If you have the capacity to have multiple authors of a computer document, create a document consisting of a thesis statement in need of revision. Circulate it online and ask students to suggest revisions and recirculate them.

ANSWERS

EXERCISE 2.6 Evaluating thesis statements (p. 31)

1. The statement lacks unity because the two halves do not seem to relate to each other.

   Possible revision: We should channel our natural feelings of aggression toward constructive rather than destructive ends.

2. The statement needs to be more significant and specific: How is Islam misunderstood? So what?

   Possible revision: Americans' misconceptions about Islam – especially that it is fanatical and oppressive—contribute to global instability.

3. The statement needs to be more specific: How do manners work as "social glue"?

   Possible revision: Manners are a kind of social glue, binding people together by regulating the interactions of acquaintances and strangers alike.

4. Good thesis statement: significant, specific, and unified.

5. The sentence simply states a fact.

   Possible revision: The poem depicts motherhood as a saintly calling.

EXERCISE 2.7 Considering your past work: developing a thesis (p. 31)
Individual response.

EXERCISE 2.8 Drafting and revising your own thesis statement (p. 32)
Individual response.

RESOURCES AND IDEAS

Liszka, Thomas R. "Formulating a Thesis for Essays Employing Comparison." *College Composition and Communication* 38 (1987): 474–77. Liszka offers a method that helps students to generate theses and guides them in organizing and developing their essays; the method appears to be adaptable to various kinds of essays.

2c Organizing ideas

CLASSROOM IDEAS

COLLABORATIVE LEARNING Assessing structures Ask students to find (in newspapers or magazines) essays that use a general-to-specific, specific-to-general, or problem-solution structure. Working in pairs, they can discuss the appropriateness and effectiveness of each essay's structure.

COMPUTER ACTIVITY Bold highlights Ask students to use the Bold function or particular fonts to highlight general ideas and distinguish them from specific ideas.

COLLABORATIVE LEARNING Practicing outlining strategies Ask each group of students to outline the same essay. Then have the entire class compare the outlines—where they agree and where they differ. This exercise helps students see how different readers perceive different kinds of organizational cues and react to them.

COMPUTER ACTIVITY Tree, branch, web Ask students to do Web research on the use of child labor by multinational corporations in their Third World factories. They can begin by making a tree diagram. Then have them do a Web search and find links that go with the branches on their diagram. They may also find that the Web search gives them new branches to add to their diagram.

COMPUTER ACTIVITY Cut-and-paste outlines The flexibility of the computer software's Cut-and-Paste or Block-and-Move features allows students to arrange ideas in various orders and then to consider the result. As a follow-up to Exercises 2.9 and 2.10, pose a thesis statement (such as one of the revised examples from Exercise 2.6), then have students brainstorm on the computer to come up with a related list of ideas and organize them into several possible outlines.

CULTURE LANGUAGE **Writing patterns** In some cultures, expository writing patterns are circular rather than linear: students will repeat or restate the topic sentence before going on to the next topic. As a result, students seem to be "writing in circles" when they are simply following the pattern they have been taught. Explain to students that in American expository writing development is linear; that transitions, not restated topics, link ideas together in a paper; and that the conclusion is the point at which ideas are restated or summarized.

   I. Introduction with thesis
     A. Idea 1
       1. Support
     B. Idea 2 (with transition)
       1. Support
  II. Conclusion
     A. Summarize ideas
     B. Restate thesis in a fresh way

Purpose outlines Some students have trouble maintaining unity of purpose and coherent organization even after they have outlined an essay because the outline describes the content of the essay but does not indicate the function of each part. To help students overcome this problem, ask them to add a statement of purpose to each major section of their outlines and to indicate how the section will carry out the purpose of the paper, as in this example:

> In this section I plan to explain how much money industries lose by failing to treat industrial waste to recover precious metals like chromium, gold, silver, and platinum. This will be the second of the three little-known costs of pollution that my thesis statement promises the paper will discuss.

Statements of purpose can alert students to potential problems in the organization or unity of an essay, and they can provide instructors with a quick way to spot the problems. Some instructors even ask students to submit "purpose outlines" in place of formal outlines:

> In this section of the paper, I plan to show that there is a real need for this university to provide more funds for the library. To support my point, I plan to explore three serious effects of underfunding—lack of basic reference materials, lack of staff to shelve books properly and check for missing volumes, and poor maintenance of the library building.

Using visual cues Some students find it handy to write their purpose statement or thesis on squares of stick-on paper and post these on their drafts, over their desks, or on the monitor of their word processors, in order to keep these ideas clearly in mind.

MODELS OF STUDENT WRITING

While "A Picture of Hyperactivity" is included here for its ways of achieving unity and coherence, its argument and tone are also worthy of consideration. If your students have had any experience with ADHD themselves, they may have a lot to say about the argument of this essay. If they knew nothing about ADHD before reading Linda Devereaux's essay, they might want to do additional research about learning disabilities. You might also want to ask your students to discuss how well the emotional tone of the piece advances its argument, and this might lead to a more general discussion of how to write about emotionally laden topics.

COLLABORATIVE LEARNING Exercises 2.9 and 2.10 Ask students to compare their responses to Exercise 2.9 and then to work in pairs to create the formal outline described in Exercise 2.10. The discussions necessitated by this collaborative project encourage students to think through and articulate an organizational logic.

ANSWERS

EXERCISES 2.9 AND 2.10 Organizing ideas AND Creating a formal outline (pp. 43–44)

Possible answer:

I. Fans resist [new general idea].
  A. Sports seasons are already too crowded for fans.

      1. Baseball, football, hockey, and basketball seasons already overlap.
      2. Fans have limited time to watch.
      3. Fans have limited money to pay for sports.
   B. Soccer is unfamiliar [new general idea].
      1. A lot of kids play soccer in school, but the game is still "foreign."
      2. Soccer rules are unfamiliar.
 II. Backers resist [new general idea].
   A. Sports money goes where the money is.
      1. Soccer fans couldn't fill huge stadiums.
      2. Backers are concerned with TV contracts.
      3. TV contracts almost matter more than live audiences.
      4. American soccer fans are too few for TV interest.
   B. Backers are wary of losing money on new ventures.
      1. Failure of the US Football League was costly.
      2. Previous attempts to start a pro soccer league failed.

EXERCISE 2.11 Considering your past work: Organizing ideas (p. 44)

Individual response.

EXERCISE 2.12 Organizing your own essay (p. 44)

Individual response.

RESOURCES AND IDEAS

On organizational strategies

Lotto, Edward. "Utterance and Text in Freshman English." *College English* 51 (1989): 677–87. Lotto analyzes the differences between spoken and written language as they relate to the difficulties students have in supporting generalizations with concrete examples. He makes suggestions for helping students become aware of text and concrete expression.

Perdue, Virginia. "The Politics of Teaching Detail." *Rhetoric Review* 8 (1990): 280–88. Perdue provides methods for using detail to arrive at broader thoughts in the composing process.

Walvoord, Barbara, Virginia Johnson Anderson, John R. Breihan, Lucille Parkinson McCarthy, Susan Miller Robinson, and A. Kimbrough Sherman. "Functions of Outlining Among College Students in Four Disciplines." *Research in the Teaching of English* 29 (1995): 390–421. The authors demonstrate the varying functions served by outlining across the disciplines and explore the strategies that students use in different situations.

On unity and coherence

Sloan, Gary. "The Frequency of Transitional Markers in Discursive Prose." *College English* 46 (1984): 158–79. Sloan shows how infrequently explicit transition markers are used by either professional or student writers.

Smith, Rochelle. "Paragraphing for Coherence: Writing as Implied Dialogue." *College English* 46 (1984): 8–21. Smith uses reader-response theory and the notion of author-reader dialogue to improve paragraph cohesion.

Witte, Stephen P., and Lester Faigley. "Coherence, Cohesion, and Writing Quality." *College Composition and Communication* 32 (1981): 189–204. Students need to learn the features of coherence that extend across sentence boundaries; the article stresses ways to make them aware of coherence strategies.

Drafting
and Revising

I've never thought of myself as a good writer; anyone who wants reassurance of that should read one of my first drafts. But I'm one of the world's great rewriters.

JAMES MICHENER

How can I know what I think until I see what I say?

E. M. FORSTER

CHAPTER HIGHLIGHTS

This chapter continues the exploration, begun in Chapters 1 and 2, of writing as a flexible process and looks in detail at strategies for drafting, revising, editing, and proofreading. The journey from initial draft to finished essay may involve many decisions and changes of direction for which there are no firm rules. To alert student writers to the options available to them, the chapter provides lists of strategies for drafting an essay and checklists for revising (p. 51) and editing (p. 58). It also provides concrete advice for the stages of composing that many writers find the most difficult: getting started and completing the initial draft.

Students who view revision as an expendable stage in the writing process may benefit from following, draft by draft, the development of Sara Ling's essay (begun in Chapter 2) on Internet communication. Like most initial efforts, Ling's early draft can benefit from revisions in organization, content, tone, and approach to clarify the essay's purpose and the relationships among its ideas and also to make it easier for readers to share Ling's perspective. The revised draft, in turn, needs editing for clarity, style, and correction of errors in grammar, usage, punctuation, and spelling—changes that appear in the final version of the essay. Ling's paper can provide material for small-group discussion and evaluation, and the section on benefiting from criticism (3g) can help students learn to work effectively in peer critique groups. "Commenting on others' writing" and

"Benefiting from comments on your writing" on pages 67 and 68 clarify peer review in a helpful list format.

MEDIA RESOURCES FOR CHAPTER 3

mycomplab📝 Please visit MyCompLab at *www.mycomplab.com* for more on the writing process.

http://www.ablongman.com/littlebrown ▶ See page 73 of this manual for companion Web site content description.

3a Writing the first draft

INSTRUCTOR RESOURCE

The following Presentation Aid is available for download on this book's companion Web site at *http://www.ablongman.com/littlebrown*.

PRESENTATION AID 3.1: Ways to start drafting (p. 45)

CLASSROOM IDEAS

Overcoming writing blocks Many students have a hard time writing first drafts because they try to get everything right the first time. They end up writing sentences and then crossing out what they have written so often that they have no time left to revise their thoughts in a second draft. Sometimes the pressure of perfection is so great that students become blocked writers, unable to finish even a single draft before the deadline. Here are four ways to help students get started and to help them develop flexibility and self-confidence in their approach to the task:

1. Show them copies of your own first and final drafts to indicate that you were not afraid to make mistakes in the initial draft because you had a chance to correct them in the later versions.
2. Give students a time limit for the first draft, perhaps an hour and a half or two hours, depending on the length of the assignment. Require them to hand in the draft with the final paper so that you can see how they approached the task of writing.
3. Have students start writing in class, where you can encourage them to get ideas down on paper before they try to perfect the wording.
4. Require students to spend some time either jotting down ideas and phrases or freewriting so that they will be loosened up before tackling the initial draft.

COMPUTER ACTIVITY Keeping track of ideas Writers can often become anxious about adding in or losing track of ideas that don't seem to fit as they write out a rough draft. Students who are composing on the computer might keep a notebook nearby to scrawl down extra ideas that occur as they write. If your students' computer programs have a Second Document feature, you can also encourage students to shift quickly to a second document to note ideas that don't seem to fit into the document they're composing.

MODELS OF STUDENT WRITING

Sara Ling's essay Sara Ling's essay is one of several models of student writing that appear throughout *The Little, Brown Handbook*. Reading these examples of student writing may give your students a better idea of what you expect from their writing. Even when your students are not yet able to produce papers as strong as these sample papers, they may find it helpful to have concrete examples to emulate.

The inclusion of multiple drafts of Sara Ling's essay is intended to help students understand the process by which a paper is formulated, developed, and polished. Several of this chapter's exercises ask students to evaluate drafts of the paper; you might want to supplement these exercises by asking your students what they think about the final draft. If your students are well versed in the five-paragraph essay, they may be particularly interested to see how Ling's essay departs from that structure while still maintaining a coherent organization and a measure of fluidity.

You may also find the topic of this essay and its argument about the Internet to be very interesting to students. The essay might be a springboard for class debate on the topic; you could ask students to compose a rebuttal to Ling's essay, or you could allow them to use it to begin to formulate their own research projects.

ANSWERS

EXERCISE 3.1 Analyzing a first draft (p. 48)

Possible answers

Some significant differences between Ling's outline and her first draft:

- In paragraph 1, Ling explicitly addressed the essay by M. Kadi.
- In paragraph 2, she added an explanation of how the Internet allows anonymity.
- In paragraph 3, she added a long example from her experience.
- In paragraph 4, she omitted planned examples and focused on working out her larger ideas. (Her readers objected to the lack of examples. See p. 54 in the handbook.)

EXERCISE 3.2 Considering your past work: Drafting (p. 48)

Individual response.

EXERCISE 3.3 Drafting your essay (p. 48)

Individual response.

RESOURCES AND IDEAS

On writer's block

Bartholomae, David. "Inventing the University." *When a Writer Can't Write: Studies in Writer's Block and Other Composing Process Problems*. Ed. Mike Rose. New York: Guilford, 1985. 134–65. Bartholomae points out that one of the factors causing blocks or writing anxiety may be an unfamiliarity with the community for which the writer is writing, and he suggests ways to familiarize writers with the discourse expectations of academic writing.

Bloom, Lynn Z. "Research on Writing Blocks, Writing Anxiety, and Writing Apprehension." *Research in Composition and Rhetoric*. Ed. Michael G. Moran and Ronald F. Lunsford. Westport: Greenwood, 1984. 71–91. Bloom surveys research on the fears and blocks that many writers encounter and examines strategies, similar to those presented in this chapter, for overcoming the difficulties.

Rose, Mike. *Writer's Block: The Cognitive Dimension*. Carbondale: Southern Illinois UP, 1984. The case studies of student writers that Rose discusses demonstrate that blocked writers often follow rigid, absolute rules about the forms and process of writing, whereas fluent writers use flexible, enabling strategies.

———. "Writing Around Rules." *Patterns in Action*. 2nd ed. Ed. Robert A. Schwegler. Glenview: Scott, 1988. 473–80. As an illustration of the kinds of rules that block writing and the kinds of strategies that enable it, Rose tells of the difficulties he encountered in titling a poem.

3b Revising the first draft

INSTRUCTOR RESOURCES

The following Presentation Aids are available for download on this book's companion Web site at *http://www.ablongman.com/littlebrown*.

PRESENTATION AID 3.2: Ways to gain distance from your work (p. 49)

PRESENTATION AID 3.3: Checklist for revision (p. 51)

CLASSROOM IDEAS

COLLABORATIVE LEARNING Exercise 3.1 Ask students to work in groups to complete Exercise 3.1 and to use that exercise as the occasion to discuss their own drafting processes (Exercise 2.3). Students can benefit a great deal both from articulating their habits, choices, and difficulties throughout the writing process and hearing how others writer work.

Revision activities Here are a few revision activities for students working on their own or in groups:

Making out an inventory After students have written an initial draft, ask them to complete a brief version of the audience inventory described in Chapter 1 (p. 11). Their completed inventory can help guide the choices they make during revision. Students may wish to share drafts and inventories with other students.

Using dialog For narrative writing, ask students to circle every use of "He said that" and "She thought that" or similar phrases in their own or someone else's paper. Then ask them to consider replacing the indirect discourse with dialogue and direct quotations to make the writing more vivid and realistic.

Using the senses For narrative and descriptive writing, ask students to check how many of the senses they have drawn on: then ask them to consider making use of the other senses.

Adding other arguments For argumentative essays, have students list all the arguments they could use but have not yet included in the paper; they may wish to turn to other students for advice about including these arguments.

Soliciting class suggestions For argument essays, ask students to summarize their theses and supporting arguments for their classmates. Then ask the other students to suggest more supporting arguments and opposing arguments the writer might consider during revision.

Answering more questions For expository essays, ask students to answer these questions for their own or someone else's paper: What five things do you know about this topic that are not included in the draft? Which ones could be put into the essay without harming its unity or coherence? What three things are readers most likely to find interesting, useful, or surprising about this topic? Could these three things be given more emphasis without disrupting the organization or clarity of the essay?

Questioning taboos A good way to emphasize the distinction between revising and editing is to ask students to brainstorm a list of the taboos they've been taught about writing: "Don't begin sentences with I"; "Don't end sentences with prepositions"; "Never use contractions"; and so on. Then discuss the possible reasons for these rules and the occasions when they would apply. Once students understand the reasons for the rules they are much more able to check for usage errors in the editing process and to avoid allowing such taboos to hamper their revision processes.

Encouraging revision The only way to get students to revise regularly is to require it. You may need some ingenuity; one strategy that works is to require students to revise each graded essay and return it to you. Only when the essay is revised do you formally record a grade. Then students who don't revise won't get credit for their papers.

Another method for encouraging revision efforts is to focus your written comments on the areas that students have revised effectively or failed to revise. Later in the semester it can also be useful to ask students to choose one of their own earlier papers to revise in the light of further reading or increased skills. This practice helps students to gain confidence in their own revision skills.

Revision checklist The revision checklist provides an effective worksheet for collaborative revision groups. If groups have trouble working through the entire checklist in one class session, you might have students begin by looking at each other's work for thesis, structure, and paragraph development, then have them read for additional elements like overall coherence, organization, introduction, title, and conclusion in a later session.

COLLABORATIVE LEARNING Choosing titles Ask students to work with their revision group to create several possible titles for each other's revised drafts. This kind of discussion often helps the writer of each paper to reconsider and articulate the central aims of the piece.

RESOURCES AND IDEAS

On revision generally

Bishop, Wendy, ed. *Elements of Alternate Style: Essays on Writing and Revision*. Portsmouth: Boynton/Cook (Heinemann), 1997. A collection of essays offering hands-on approaches to recovering play and joy in the writing and revision processes.

Elbow, Peter. *Writing with Power: Techniques for Mastering the Writing Process*. New York: Oxford UP, 1981. Elbow's book offers detailed, practical, and often innovative advice on drafting, revising, shaping for an audience, and making use of feedback, including several chapters on revising ("Quick Revising," "Thorough Revising," "Revising with Feedback," and "Cut and Paste Revising and the Collage").

Harris, Muriel. "Composing Behaviors of One- and Multi-Draft Writers." *College English* 51 (1989): 174–91. Harris emphasizes the differences in revision techniques and success of student writers.

Laib, Nevin. "Conciseness and Amplification." *College Composition and Communication* 41 (1990): 443–59. Laib argues for a balance between brevity and abbreviation.

Schwartz, Mimi. "Revision Profiles: Patterns and Implications." *College English* 45 (1983): 549–58. Schwartz maintains that revisers can be grouped by the revision strategies they use.

Sommers, Nancy. "Revision Strategies of Student Writers and Experienced Adult Writers." *College Composition and Communication* 31 (1980): 378–88. According to Sommers, students see revision as changes in small units—words and sentences. Experienced writers see it as a recursive process directed at larger units of the text and the meaning it conveys.

Welch, Nancy. *Getting Restless: Rethinking Revision in Writing Instruction*. Portsmouth: Boynton/Cook (Heinemann), 1997. Welch looks at what student writers have to say about their own attempts at revision. She concludes that revision engages the domain of the emotional/personal, a domain which makes most academics uncomfortable.

On computers and the revision process

Many writers find that the computer facilitates their composing and revision processes without realizing the extent to which the medium has changed the way we think and write. In "The Metaphor of Collage: Beyond Computer Composition," Russel Wiebe and Robert S. Dornsife, Jr., argue that computers are not simply an addition to the classroom; rather, they revolutionize the way we and our students write and think about texts. The authors use the metaphor of a multimedia collage to describe the best pedagogical approach to these changes (Journal of Advanced Composition 15 (1995): 131–37). See also, Cynthia Selfe and Susan Hilligoss, *Literacy and Computers: the Complications of Teaching and Learning with Technology* (New York: MLA, 1994).

On collaborative revision

Peer editing and collaborative learning have become regular features of many composition courses over the past two decades, and these approaches are particularly well suited to drafting and revising activities. Section 3g coaches students in giving and receiving criticism. And the chapter "Using Collaborative Learning with the Handbook" on pages 49–62 of this manual offers detailed advice about designing collaborative activities and preparing students to work in groups. It also provides sample reader response forms, which you may wish to copy and use in your class.

Much has been written recently about collaborative learning and peer writing groups. See, for example, the *Journal of Advanced Composition* 14:1 (1994); the entire issue is devoted to issues of collaboration. The following two works offer good starting points for someone interested in examining both the opportunities offered by this approach and the controversies that it has created:

Gere, Anne Ruggles. *Writing Groups: History, Theory, and Implications.* Carbondale: Southern Illinois UP, 1987. Gere reviews the history, theory, and practice of writing groups and collaborative learning; she also provides a useful annotated bibliography of research and pedagogy.

Trimbur, John. "Collaborative Learning and Teaching Writing." *Perspectives on Research and Scholarship in Composition.* Ed. Ben W. Mcclelland and Timothy R. Donovan. New York: MLA, 1985. 87–109. Trimbur offers a compact survey of the history and theories behind collaborative learning and raises important questions about the roles of response and evaluation in a student- (rather than teacher-) centered classroom.

On independent revision

Even though you encourage students to revise and offer them detailed advice about what and when to revise, you may still find that their revisions are limited to superficial changes. Part of the problem may be that students have not yet become good enough readers of their own texts to identify features that might be altered or dropped and to identify places where something might be added. Here are some resources for helping students to become active readers and writers, aware of what they have written and how it might be changed:

Beck, James P. "Asking Students to Annotate Their Own Papers." *College Composition and Communication* 33 (1982): 322–26. Beck asks students to identify specific techniques they have used in their writing (including features of structure, detail, argument, and style) and to evaluate how well they have used those techniques.

Sommers, Jeffrey. "The Effects of Tape-Recorded Commentary on Student Revision: A Case Study," *Journal of Teaching Writing* 8 (1989): 49–75. Sommers argues that students can misunderstand instructor response to their writing and demonstrates how tape-recorded responses led one student through a series of successive revisions.

Straub, Richard. "The Concept of Control in Teacher Response: Defining the Varieties of 'Directive' and 'Facilitative' Commentary." *College Composition and Communication* 47 (1996): 223–51. Straub reviews the influential studies on teacher response in an effort to identify the kinds of comments that encourage students to produce effective independent revisions.

3c   Examining a sample revision

CLASSROOM IDEAS

COLLABORATIVE LEARNING Exercise 3.4 Exercise 3.4 works well as a small-group project. Encourage students to discuss their differing ideas for further revisions and then have each group present their conclusions to the class.

ANSWERS

EXERCISE 3.4 Analyzing a revised draft (p. 57)

Individual response.

EXERCISE 3.5 Considering your past work: Revising (p. 57)

Individual response.

EXERCISE 3.6 Revising your own draft (p. 57)

Individual response.

3d   Editing the revised draft

INSTRUCTOR RESOURCES

The following Presentation Aids are available for download on this book's companion Web site at *http://www.ablongman.com/littlebrown.*

PRESENTATION AID 3.4: Ways to find what needs editing (p. 58)

PRESENTATION AID 3.5: Checklist for editing (p. 58)

CLASSROOM IDEAS

Individualized checklists Since most students' work demonstrates patterns of repeated error, have them keep ongoing lists of their recurring editing errors and stylistic problems. Ask them to bring their lists to class for in-class revision and editing sessions and to have their revision group help them look particularly for those errors.

COMPUTER ACTIVITY An archive for rejected passages Having labored so hard to produce a first draft, writers are sometimes reluctant to cut passages when revising their drafts. Your students may find it easier to make cuts if they paste the cut passages into a blank document, saving that document as part of their own personal writing archive. They can choose to replace the cut passages later or use them for a different piece of writing altogether.

COMPUTER ACTIVITY Editing vehicles To help students explore how editing on a computer may produce different results from editing hard copy, ask students to edit a sample paper, but ask half of them to edit it on the computer and half to edit it by hand. Then, in small groups, have them compare their edits and discuss the differences.

COMPUTER ACTIVITY Human versus machine Have a contest between student proofreaders and the spell check or grammar check program of their word processing software, to see which method produces the cleanest copy.

COLLABORATIVE LEARNING Exercise 3.7 Have students respond individually to the questions in Exercise 3.7 and then return to those questions as they work through drafts in their revision groups. Especially if students are working regularly with a particular group, they can be extremely helpful in pointing to one another's recurring strengths and problems.

ANSWERS

EXERCISE 3.7 Considering your past work: Editing (p. 62)
Individual response.

EXERCISE 3.8 Editing your own draft (p. 62)
Individual response.

3e Preparing and proofreading the final draft

INSTRUCTOR RESOURCE

The following Presentation Aid is available for download on this book's companion Web site at *http://www.ablongman.com/littlebrown*.

PRESENTATION AID 3.6: Techniques for proofreading (p. 63)

CLASSROOM IDEAS

Individualized proofreading lists Students often struggle to recognize common proofreading errors in their own work. Ask students to keep an ongoing list of the misspellings, typos, and minor grammatical errors that occur frequently in their own work and use that list for proofreading.

RESOURCES AND IDEAS

Harrington, Jane. "Editing: the Last Step in the Process." *Nuts and Bolts: a Practical Guide to Teaching.* Ed. Thomas Newkirk. Portsmouth: Boynton, 1993. 151–78. Harrington defines the editing process and provides practical suggestions for making editing a familiar part of classroom practice.

Harris, Jeanette. "Proofreading: A Reading/Writing Skill." *College Composition and Communication* 38 (1987): 464–66. Harris argues that proofreading is a reading skill, a process of looking at each word and punctuation mark rather than of paying attention to the meaning of the text; and she suggests teaching students strategies like those outlined in this chapter—using a pointer (finger, pencil), reading aloud, reading in reverse order, and letting time elapse between writing and proofreading—in order to develop the specialized skill of proofreading.

Horner, Bruce. "Rethinking the 'Sociality' of Error: Teaching Editing as Negotiation." *Rhetoric Review* 11 (1992): 172–99. Horner argues for a consideration of editing as a process of social exchange best supported by peer groups and one-on-one conferences.

3f Examining a final draft

CLASSROOM IDEAS

COLLABORATIVE LEARNING **Exercises 3.9 and 3.10** Exercises 3.9 and 3.10 make for productive collaborative projects. Ask students to revise the sample paragraph together and then to proofread each other's work.

ANSWERS

EXERCISE 3.9 Proofreading (p. 65)

An environmental group, Natural Resources Defense Council, has estimated that 5,500 to 6,200 children who are in preschool today may contract cancer during their lives because of the pesticides they consume in their food. In addition, these children will be at greater risk for kidney damage, problems with immunity, and other serious impairments. The government bases its pesticide-safety standards on adults, but children consume many more of the fruits and fruit products likely to contain pesticides.

EXERCISE 3.10 Preparing your final draft (p. 66)
Individual response.

3g Giving and receiving comments

INSTRUCTOR RESOURCES

The following Presentations Aids are available for download on this book's companion Web site at *http://www.ablongman.com/littlebrown*.

PRESENTATION AID 3.7: Commenting on others' writing (p. 67)

PRESENTATION AID 3.8: Benefiting from comments on your writing (p. 68)

CLASSROOM IDEAS

Constructive criticism Students sometimes initially think of "criticizing" as a negative activity rather than a supportive practice. These "suggestions for commenting" on each other's writing can help set a supportive tone for collaborative revision groups. Criticism that is given in a helpful and careful manner is perhaps the easiest kind of criticism to benefit from. You can also encourage student writers to take an active role by bringing in questions and concerns about their own papers and by probing their peers' comments for specific examples and explanations: "Can you show me the places where my organization starts to break down?" See the chapter "Using Collaborative Learning with the Handbook" on pages 49–62 of this manual for a detailed discussion on preparing students to provide and receive peer criticism. You may wish to draw on this discussion as a way of helping your students learn how to benefit from criticism and learn how to offer their classmates advice that can lead to real improvements in expression.

COMPUTER ACTIVITY Electronic feedback If students have easy access to e-mail, it's possible to post drafts or sample essays on a bulletin board or class account to receive comments and feedback. See Daniel Anderson's essay on "Using Computers to Teach Writing" on pages 63–75 of this manual for more information on working in a computer classroom.

RESOURCES AND IDEAS

Gilliam, Alice M. "Returning Students' Ways of Writing: Implications for First-Year College Composition." *Journal of Teaching Writing* 10:1 (1991): 1–20. Gilliam discusses the stresses and constraints returning students face and suggests ways to help such students succeed in the classroom.

Greenwood, Claudia M. "'It's Scary at First': Reentry Women in College Composition Classes." *Teaching English in the Two-Year College* 17 (1990):

133–42. Greenwood identifies several constant negative internal factors—feelings of guilt, inferiority, doubt, of being out of place—among women reentering higher education, but she finds that the positive internal factors outweigh the negative.

Grimm, Nancy. "Constructing Ideas of the Social Self." *Journal of Teaching Writing* 8 (Spring 1989): 11–20. Social pressures, social rules, and social values are at work in the composition classroom and may interfere in collaborative learning, particularly in classes made up of a culturally diverse student population. The classroom composition must be considered when instructors expect students to think critically and to question dominant cultural values.

Johnson, T. R. "School Sucks." *College Composition and Communication* 52 (June 2001): 620–30. Johnson explains why so many students dislike writing classes and provides advice on improving students' attitudes.

McKendy, Thomas F. "Legitimizing Peer Response: A Recycling Project for Placement Essays." *College Composition and Communication* 41 (1990): 89–91. Mckendy found that when students in a remedial writing course holistically scored placement essays, their scoring correlated closely with that of trained readers. This exercise led to the students' being more accepting of their placement in the course and more trusting of each others' responses to their writing.

Simmons, Robin L. *http://www.chompchomp.com.* Because it is interactive, this is an especially good Web site to send students to for help with a variety of writing problems.

Sirc, Geoffrey, and Tom Reynolds. "The Face of Collaboration in the Networked Writing Classroom." *Computers and Composition* 7 (1990): 53–70. Sirc and Reynolds discuss the use of networked classrooms in peer response to compositions.

Sperling, Melanie. "Constructing the Perspective of Teacher as Reader: A Framework for Studying Response to Student Writing." *Research in the Teaching of English* 28 (1994): 175–223. This article studies one teacher's responses to student papers in order to evaluate the impact of teacher comments on student writing.

Weissberg, Bob. "Speaking of Writing: Some Functions of Talk in the ESL Composition Class." *Journal of Second Language Writing* 3 (1994): 1121–39. This essay examines class discussion and peer input as learning factors, particularly in the ESL context.

Welch, Nancy. "Sideshadowing Teacher Response." *College English* 60 (1998): 374–95. Welch suggests the technique of "sideshadowing," in which students make marginal comments on their own drafts.

Yancey, Kathleen Blake, and Irwin Weiser, eds. *Situating Portfolios: Four Perspectives.* Logan: Utah State UP, 1996. This collection of essays explores the issues of power and authority in portfolio evaluation.

3h   Preparing a writing portfolio

CLASSROOM IDEA

COLLABORATIVE LEARNING Portfolio presentation Ask students to prepare to hand in their portfolios by making an oral presentation to their regular revision group. Each student can briefly describe the pieces she has chosen to include in her portfolio and explain how each piece has contributed to her progress. Revision group members can often remind writers of noticeable overall strengths that they might have overlooked.

CHAPTER 4

Writing and Revising Paragraphs

A WRITER'S PERSPECTIVE

The purpose of paragraphing is to give the reader a rest. The writer is saying . . . : "Have you got that? If so, I'll go on."

H. W. FOWLER

CHAPTER HIGHLIGHTS

The writing some American high school students do is no more than a paragraph in length, and even older or nontraditional students may have had little writing experience. So learning to think of paragraphs as units in larger pieces of discourse may be a challenge for your students. If they have written longer essays, these probably have been in the familiar "five-paragraph theme" pattern of introduction, three paragraphs of development, and conclusion. ESL students may conceptualize and shape paragraphs differently or may not be used to writing in paragraphs at all. Don't be surprised, then, if learning to use paragraphs in different ways presents a challenge for your students.

Here we present a strategy of developing paragraphs as mini-essays, each with a generalization (topic sentence) supported by limitations and evidence. Practicing these essays-in-miniature can help students develop longer essays as they gain more skill. Of course, not all paragraphs in professional writing conform in length, structure, or purpose to the models this chapter provides.

The chapter reviews strategies for improving paragraph unity, achieving paragraph coherence, developing paragraph content, and writing special-purpose paragraphs. It concludes by showing how paragraphs can be linked within the larger context of the essay. Helping students learn and practice the standard paragraphing strategies elaborated in this chapter can be a good way to help them improve their writing. The annotations provided for sample paragraphs help students see the strategies explained in the chapter "in practice."

MEDIA RESOURCES FOR CHAPTER 4

mycomplab Please visit MyCompLab at *www.mycomplab.com* for more on the writing process.

| http://www.ablongman.com/littlebrown | ▶ See page 73 of this manual for companion Web site content description.

INSTRUCTOR RESOURCE

The following Presentation Aid is available for download on this book's companion Web site at *http://www.ablongman.com/littlebrown*.

PRESENTATION AID 4.1: Checklist for revising paragraphs (p. 72)

CLASSROOM IDEA

COMPUTER ACTIVITY Evaluating Web pages Have students print out Web pages and bring them into class. Individually or as a class, they can evaluate the paragraphs for unity, coherence, and development. Students can make suggestions for how to revise each page's paragraphs and for where to position links to other pages.

RESOURCES AND IDEAS

Knoblauch, C. H. "The Rhetoric of the Paragraph." *Journal of Advanced Composition* 2 (1981): 53–61.

Stern, Arthur A. "When Is a Paragraph?" *College Composition and Communication* 27 (1976): 253–57. Stern argues for the rhetorical flexibility of paragraphs as development devices.

4a Maintaining paragraph unity

SECTION HIGHLIGHTS

Section 4a of this chapter addresses the need for a paragraph to focus on a topic and to make the focus clear to the reader through an explicit statement in the form of a topic sentence. It introduces the basic form of the expository paragraph—topic sentence, illustrations, and details—and indicates how this pattern can be varied to suit a writer's purpose and to fit within the context created by the surrounding paragraphs.

The concept of a clearly stated and variously placed topic sentence that controls the shape of a paragraph is an oversimplification. But it appears to help students a great deal to think of the paragraph as a unit dominated and controlled by an expressly stated generalization. Students can see the topic sentence as a commitment they make to the reader, with the rest of the paragraph following through on the commitment. Seeing the obvious parallel between the paragraph's topic sentence and the essay's thesis statement is also helpful to many students. Finally, stating a central point in a single sentence and marshaling support for it enables students to see more clearly what is required for unity.

The exercises for this section ask students to identify the central idea in unified paragraphs, to revise paragraphs, to build a paragraph by combining and revising kernel sentences, and to write their own paragraphs. These exercises can be easily adapted to small-group work: in coming to understand how others view paragraphs, students may more readily understand the influence of paragraph structure and unity on readers.

CLASSROOM IDEAS

COLLABORATIVE LEARNING Using student writing Ask students to choose key paragraphs from their works-in-progress and read them aloud to their groups. The listeners should take notes on the effectiveness of the various unity strategies they hear in each paragraph. If students have trouble responding without seeing a written text, you can have them work in pairs to critique and revise the unity of each other's paragraphs.

COLLABORATIVE LEARNING Coloring paragraphs Bring in copies of sample paragraphs and felt-tipped pens or pencils in two colors. Split the class into groups and ask each group to underline topic sentences in one color and examples and details in another color. Students should then be able to discover the arrangement of each paragraph, the placement of the topic sentence, and the way the parts fit together to form a unified whole. Students working in a computer classroom can use the Bold feature and designated fonts instead of pens to identify each of these elements.

COLLABORATIVE LEARNING Using student writing Ask students to bring in paragraphs from writings in other classes or other disciplines to use in the "coloring paragraphs" activity. They will find it instructive to note how different writers decide to place, emphasize, or omit topic sentences. They can also perform this exercise on the paragraphs in their drafts.

Seeing paragraphs Visually, students may find it easier to understand topic sentence placement and paragraph arrangement by using these diagrams as guides:

Topic sentence at the beginning:	▲
Topic sentence at the beginning and in the middle:	▲▲
Topic sentence at the end:	▼
Topic sentence at the beginning and the end:	◆

COLLABORATIVE LEARNING Topic sentence omission Some research suggests that the necessity of a topic sentence is determined by the author's relation to his or her readers; a writer writing to less expert or more expert readers is more likely to use a topic sentence than one writing for peers, for instance. Ask students to work in groups to collect examples of topic sentence use and omission, then analyze the different author-reader relationships implied in each example. Encourage students to collect samples from their own journals and papers, but also from various kinds of published writing, to get the best results from this survey.

COMPUTER ACTIVITY Reorganizing paragraphs For students working on computers, the reorganization of paragraphs is particularly easy. Encourage students to select one or two paragraphs from their drafts and reorganize them with the controlling idea at the end, as Reston does. Then ask them to judge whether they gain any rhetorical advantage from such a rearrangement. Leonard A. Podis suggests some other exercises of this nature in "Teaching Arrangement: Defining a More Practical Approach," *College Composition and Communication* 31 (1980): 197–204, and JoAnne M. Podis and Leonard A. Podis present more exercises in "Identifying and Teaching Rhetorical Plans for Arrangement," *College Composition and Communication* 41 (1990): 430–42.

COLLABORATIVE LEARNING Exercise 4.1 Ask students to work in groups to complete Exercise 4.1. Ask each group to discuss what effect the particular placement of each topic sentence has, and then report back to the class on the sentences that best express the central idea of each paragraph.

COLLABORATIVE LEARNING Exercise 4.2 Have students work in groups to complete Exercise 4.2. Ask groups to consider how they might revise and expand the deleted material to include it in a following paragraph.

COMPUTER ACTIVITY Rearranging paragraphs Exercises 4.4 and 4.5 work well in a computer classroom because students have the flexibility to rearrange sentences multiple times without retyping them. Students can print out the results in order to compare their differing responses in groups. In a networked classroom you might ask students to e-mail their responses to a partner in the class, or you could post several volunteer responses on the network for the whole class to read and discuss.

ANSWERS

EXERCISE 4.1 Finding the central idea (pp. 75–76)

1. The central idea is sentence 8: The black bourgeoisie feel a sense of shame about their own identity.
2. The central idea is sentence 1: Scientists know something about the song of the humpback whale.

EXERCISE 4.2 Revising a paragraph for unity (p. 76)

The topic sentence is sentence 1. Unrelated are sentences 4 and 7.

EXERCISE 4.3 Considering your past work: Paragraph unity (p. 76)

Individual response.

EXERCISE 4.4 Writing a unified paragraph (p. 77)

Delete statements not pertaining to Mozart's accomplishments: when he was born, where he lived, when he married, his debts. Possible paragraph:

Mozart's accomplishments in music seem remarkable even today. At the age of six he made his first concert tour of Europe, playing harpsichord, organ, and violin. He had begun composing music at the age of five, and by adolescence he had published numerous musical compositions. When he died at thirty-five, his work included over six hundred compositions, most notably operas, symphonies, quartets, and piano concertos.

EXERCISE 4.5 Turning topic sentences into unified paragraphs (p. 77)

Individual response.

RESOURCES AND IDEAS

Rhetorical scholarship is split on a number of the "givens" of paragraphing: whether paragraphs are self-contained units or building blocks of larger discourses, whether topic sentences are needed, and so on. These references offer you a fairly mainstream view of research into paragraphing.

Becker, A. L. "A Tagmemic Approach to Paragraph Analysis." *College Composition and Communication* 16 (1965): 237–42. Becker observes that expository paragraphs generally follow a variation of one of two patterns: topic-restriction-illustration (TRI) or problem-solution (PS).

Wiener, Harvey S. "The Single Narrative Paragraph and College Remediation." *College English* 33 (1972): 660–69. Wiener suggests using paragraph-length narrative themes to help students develop both paragraph and essay skills.

4b Achieving paragraph coherence

INSTRUCTOR RESOURCE

The following Presentation Aid is available for download on this book's companion Web site at *http://www.ablongman.com/littlebrown*.

PRESENTATION AID 4.2: Ways to achieve coherence (p. 78)

SECTION HIGHLIGHTS

This section of the chapter deals with paragraph coherence, addressing it from the reader's perspective as well as the writer's. Students are shown how the devices they use to achieve paragraph coherence help readers to follow the arguments or information being presented.

The discussion emphasizes the need to maintain a clear organizational pattern as one of the principal ways to ensure coherence, and it presents examples of two basic ways of organizing paragraphs: organizing by space or time and organizing for emphasis. Students who have difficulty organizing their own writing can usually see the pattern of organization in a well-made example from another writer's work.

Following the discussion of patterns, the section takes up and illustrates other methods of achieving coherence: parallelism; repetition of words; careful use of pronouns; consistency in person, tense, and number; and transitional expressions. Analysis of paragraphs can help students understand these explicit and implicit means by which individual sentences are held together so that the reader effortlessly follows the flow of ideas and information. As in the preceding section, the exercises move from analysis to revision to production and are useful in small-group activities as well as individual work.

CLASSROOM IDEAS

Picturing the paragraph A good metaphor to use with students is that of cinematography and film. Remind them how in movies the camera can give wide shots, pan in for close-ups, or sweep across a scene for effect. A writer chooses similar "shots" (i.e., positions from which to view the material) in order to organize paragraphs.

Paragraph patterns I Give students a topic sentence and a set of assertions, facts, and details in undeveloped form. Tell them to use the material to write a coherent paragraph, following one of the patterns described in the handbook: spatial, chronological, general-to-specific, specific-to-general, problem-solution, climatic, most familiar to least familiar, or simplest to most complex. Students can manipulate the material however they wish to achieve an effect that is appropriate to the pattern. You may want to ask for several paragraphs, each using the same content but a different pattern.

Paragraph patterns II Write a paragraph following one of the basic organizational schemes discussed in 4b–1. Leave the subject and content of the paragraph up to the individual student. If they wish, students may make up information, as long as they keep it plausible. Students can compare results in group, then work together to revise one of those responses into a paragraph to be "published" on the class computer network or printed out and distributed.

Extra examples The following examples illustrate the specific-to-general pattern in a sentence and may be extended to short sample paragraphs:

> (specific) + good study habits
> (specific) + consistent effort
> (specific) + curiosity
> _____
> (general) = good grades

> Good study habits, consistent effort, and intellectual curiosity will result in good grades.

> (specific) + seeds
> (specific) + soil
> (specific) + sunlight
> (specific) + water
> _____
> (general) = good vegetable crop

A combination of fresh seeds, well-balanced soil, and adequate sunlight and water results in a good vegetable crop.

Paragraph scrambles These activities are suitable for students working individually; when assigned to small groups, however, the activities work even better by encouraging considerable discussion and discovery.

1. Take a good paragraph, by either a student or a professional, and rearrange the sentences. Then ask students to unscramble the sentences and make a clear, coherent paragraph. This exercise will make students aware of the flow of a coherent paragraph and will alert them to the number of examples and details found in a well-developed paragraph.

2. Choose a paragraph that lacks coherence and rearrange the sentences. Tell students to unscramble the sentences to form a coherent paragraph. Indicate that students are free to add any transitions, sentences, illustrations, or details they feel are necessary to make the paragraph both coherent and well developed. Students will quickly spot any coherence problems in the original paragraph, and unless the topic of the paragraph is quite unusual, they will be able to add any necessary content.

Dramatic examples Climatic order is a form of structuring that moves from least to most important. To help explain this strategy you may wish to draw examples from drama, particularly from the structure of tragedy. Othello provides an obvious example of structuring that moves from least dramatic/tension-filled to most dramatic/tension-filled.

Least dramatic—Othello marries Desdemona
More dramatic—Othello suspects Desdemona of infidelity
More dramatic—Desdemona defends her chastity and argues for her life
Most dramatic (climax)—Othello kills Desdemona and then realizes that she has been faithful to him

Listening to the music To recognize the power of repetition, students need only turn to popular music. Have them begin by listing the titles of popular songs whose lyrics they know by heart. Then ask them to identify words and phrases that they remember best from the songs or that they learned first. Chances are that they will identify the chorus because it is the element of the song most often repeated. You might point out that choruses help unify songs. Students may also note that the considerable amount of repetition in many songs makes them easy to remember and helps create a unified effect. This exercise may also be used to point out the difference between effective use of repetition and overuse.

He's on second To illustrate the importance of clear pronoun reference in paragraphs, try to locate a recording or transcript of the famous Abbott and Costello skit, "Who's on First." While humorous, this skit demonstrates the frustration a reader can feel when encountering a series of pronouns with unclear antecedents. Keep in mind that students' use of unclear pronoun antecedents may signal a larger difficulty in defining or expanding on their subject matter.

Reading aloud Often students can spot a lack of transitions in their own writing if they read their papers aloud. If you ask students to read one another's papers aloud, the student writers will often be able to recognize missing or unclear transitions at those points where the readers stumble over a passage or have to stop to puzzle out the meaning.

COLLABORATIVE LEARNING Transitional expressions Ask students to work in groups to analyze what happens when they substitute another transition from the same group into one of the sentences from Kathleen LaFrank's paragraph. How can a transitional word affect the meaning of that sentence and of the relationships between sentences?

Highlighting transitions Encourage students to use highlighting pens or the Highlighting feature on a word processor to mark where transitional expressions appear in their texts; if they think too few "highlights" show up, students can add more.

CULTURE LANGUAGE **Cross-cultural communication** Pan-cultural examples lend themselves to collaborative discussion; students might collect and discuss examples of mistranslations from other languages to English or from English to other languages. For instance, the Chevy Nova was a failure when it was introduced in Puerto Rico because *No va* means "It doesn't run" in Spanish. Students for whom English is a second language can contribute many examples of idioms that give them trouble.

COMPUTER ACTIVITY Scrambling sentences The computer makes scrambling exercises particularly viable. Ask each student to scramble the sentence order deliberately in one of their own paragraphs and then present that exercise in "unscrambling" to their group. It can be very useful for each writer to hear their own coherence "clues" being analyzed and debated.

COLLABORATIVE LEARNING Analyzing for coherence Exercise 4.6 works well as a group exercise because students have more opportunity to debate and explore options. Have each group report back to the class on the different methods each writer uses to achieve coherence.

Transitional expressions Ask students to compare answers to Exercise 4.9 and discuss the effects of each student's choices on the meaning of the sentences and of the paragraph.

COMPUTER ACTIVITY Rearranging sentences Exercise 4.11 is particularly feasible on the computer since students can rearrange the information in multiple ways without retyping.

Coherent paragraphs The kind of coherence achieved in Exercises 4.11 and 4.12 will depend a great deal on each individual's choice of connective strategies. When students compare their responses to Exercises 4.11 and 4.12 in groups, it is beneficial for them to note the results of other writers' differing choices.

ANSWERS

EXERCISE 4.6 Analyzing paragraphs for coherence (p. 88)

1. Lieber paragraph (p. 76): Organization: general to specific. Parallelism after first sentence: *They have measured . . . recorded and studied . . . learned.* Repetition: *whale, sings, song.* Pronoun: *they.* Transitional expression: *And.*
2. Begas paragraph (p. 91): Organization: chronological. Parallelism: *They persuaded . . . they deprived; Jill became . . . she dropped out.* Repetition: *lonely, college/school.* Pronouns: *Jill/she; men and women/they.* Transitional expressions: *Between . . . , increasingly, Before long, too.*
3. Dyson paragraph (p. 93): Organization: climactic. Parallelism and repetition: *reason is the need . . . reason is the need . . . reason is our spiritual need.* Further repetition: *space, earth/this planet.* Pronouns: *we, our, us.* Transitional expressions: *first, second, third.*

EXERCISE 4.7 Arranging sentences coherently (p. 88)

The coherent order would be 1, 2, 5, 3, 6, 4

EXERCISE 4.8 Eliminating inconsistencies (pp. 88–89)

The Hopi tihu, or kachina likeness, is often called a "doll," but its owner, usually a girl or woman, does not regard it as a plaything. Instead, she treats it as a valued possession and hangs it out of the way on a wall. For its owner the tihu represents a connection with the kachina's spirit. It is considered part of the kachina, carrying a portion of the kachina's power.

EXERCISE 4.9 Using transitional expressions (p. 89)

Possible answers

1. *Yet, However, Even so,* or *Nevertheless*
2. *even, also,* or *further*
3. *As a result, Consequently,* or *Therefore*

EXERCISE 4.10 Considering your past work: Paragraph coherence (p. 89)

Individual response.

EXERCISE 4.11 Writing a coherent paragraph (p. 89)

Possible paragraph

Hypnosis is far superior to drugs for relieving tension. It is inexpensive even for people who have not mastered self-hypnosis, whereas drugs are expensive. It is nonaddictive, whereas drugs foster addiction. And most important, hypnosis has none of the dangerous side effects of drugs, such as weight loss or gain, illness, and even death.

> **EXERCISE 4.12 Turning topic sentences into coherent paragraphs** (p. 90)
> Individual response.

RESOURCES AND IDEAS

These two sources draw on current linguistic and rhetorical theory to provide frameworks for describing patterns of coherence and development in paragraphs:

Coe, Richard M. *Toward a Grammar of Passages*. Carbondale: Southern Illinois UP, 1988.

Markels, Robin Bell. *A New Perspective on Cohesion in Expository Paragraphs*. Carbondale: Southern Illinois UP, 1984.

Other good readings on paragraph coherence include the following:

Brostoff, Anita. "Coherence: 'Next to' Is Not 'Connected to.'" *College Composition and Communication* 32 (1981): 278–94. Brostoff discusses the causes of lack of coherence in writing and describes a program for helping students achieve coherence.

Christensen, Francis. "A Generative Rhetoric of the Paragraph." *Notes Toward a New Rhetoric: Nine Essays for Teachers*. 2nd ed. Ed. Francis Christensen and Bonniejean Christensen. New York: Harper & Row, 1978. 74–103. Christensen views paragraphs as a series of statements on differing levels of generality, often moving from more general toward the specific.

Sloan, Gary. "The Frequency of Transitional Markers in Discursive Prose." *College English* 46 (1984): 158–79. Sloan shows how infrequently explicit transition markers are used by either professional or student writers.

Smith, Rochelle. "Paragraphing for Coherence: Writing as Implied Dialogue." *College English* 46 (1984): 8–21. Smith uses reader-response theory and the notion of author-reader dialogue to improve paragraph cohesion.

Winterowd, W. Ross. "The Grammar of Coherence." *College English* 31 (1971): 828–35. This article describes the kinds of relations that link sentence to sentence and paragraph to paragraph.

Witte, Stephen, and Lester Faigley. "Coherence, Cohesion, and Writing Quality." *College Composition and Communication* 32 (1981): 189–204.

4c Developing the paragraph

SECTION HIGHLIGHTS

Section 4c looks at ways to convey the central idea of a paragraph fully and convincingly to the reader. Developing paragraphs and essays fully is often difficult for students. One of the important differences between casual conversation and formal writing is the degree to which ideas must be concretely developed in writing. Because students are more experienced in conversation than in writing, they find generalizations much easier to come by than the details, examples, and reasons to support them.

All of us must grapple with the student essay or single paragraph that is largely a succession of generalizations without support or explanation. Part of the solution to such problem paragraphs is to make students aware of readers as a special kind of audience for ideas. Another part is to make them aware of different strategies for developing paragraphs or essays.

The ways to develop ideas are infinite, but this section focuses on a limited number. The initial emphasis falls on the use of details, examples, and reasons, which are essential to any more specific method of development. Students are encouraged to follow the standard methods or patterns of development by posing questions about an idea, event, or object in order to uncover concrete information about it.

You may wish to ask students to spend time in class or in groups working with sample topics to discover how the methods of development can be used to probe a topic and how the questions reveal different aspects of a topic. This discussion may help students see how the process of development can be an act of discovery. You will probably want to stress, however, that the methods of development covered in the handbook are not the only ones writers can use and that most paragraphs use more than a single method.

The exercises for this section range from analyzing paragraphs to producing them, and whether used in groups or by students working individually, they encourage students to treat the patterns of development as different ways of viewing a topic.

CLASSROOM IDEAS

What and why Students from non-Western cultures may be unaccustomed to analysis that involves critical thinking. They may know how to describe an item or text by listing component parts, for instance, but they may not be accustomed to including discussion of why the thing or text is important. A quick way to help these students learn to distinguish between "what" a thing is and "why" it is important is to ask them the following series of questions about a flag:

What is the object attached to the tall pole in the quad? (Describe its appearance, give its name, discuss the component colors and shapes.)

How does the object work? (How is it attached? How is it raised and lowered? When is it raised and lowered?)

Why does it get flown? (This question will lead students into a discussion of the symbolism and meaning of the flag and of its being flown on campus.)

The subject-object boundary Students may find that the subjective-objective boundary is sometimes fuzzy. Even the objective paragraph (p. 92) has judgmental language like "piercing" in it. Perhaps a way of solving this dilemma is to say that in *subjective* description, the writer's intention is to interpret experience for readers, while in *objective* description, the writer's intention is to allow the audience to interpret the reported experiences themselves.

Paragraph coherence Students sometimes have the idea that "next to" means "connected to" as far as coherence goes; this is emphatically not the case. Take a paragraph like this one and have students mark the coherence devices used; or sabotage a paragraph by removing or disguising the coherence devices, and ask students to put them back in.

COMPUTER ACTIVITY Paragraph revision In a networked classroom, students might complete the draft of their paragraphs, then e-mail them to a revision partner for comments and suggestions before reworking them. It is important for students to recognize that a well-developed paragraph generally emerges from successive drafts. You can dramatize this process by posting student paragraphs at various stages of revision on the class network and holding discussions about strategies for developing each example further.

Extra example

Division: Face

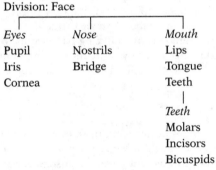

Eyes	Nose	Mouth
Pupil	Nostrils	Lips
Iris	Bridge	Tongue
Cornea		Teeth

Teeth
Molars
Incisors
Bicuspids

Classification practice Other topics to be classified might include car models, job categories, types of music, and local restaurants. (You might want to bring in the Yellow Pages for the last topic.)

Extra example

Classification:

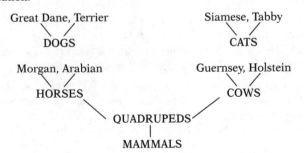

COLLABORATIVE LEARNING Team classification Ask teams of students to compile the group of sentences or facts from an area they know well (for instance, sports, business, entertainment, social groups, or activities). Have the groups exchange sets of sentences and then attempt to assemble them into paragraphs. When the paragraphs are written, the "expert" collectors should critique the perspective each offers.

COLLABORATIVE LEARNING Combining for emphasis Put together a group of sentences or bits of information about a topic, perhaps drawing the material from an essay in a reader or a magazine article. Ask students, working individually or in groups, to combine the material into a paragraph that has a distinct point of view. You might, for example, provide information about a recent controversial incident and ask for a paragraph emphasizing one perspective toward the incident or one perspective on its causes and effects.

COLLABORATIVE LEARNING Practical instructions The most hilarious process exercise is one of the oldest: bring the ingredients for peanut butter and jelly sandwiches to class. Have each group write instructions for making a peanut butter and jelly sandwich. Then have the groups exchange instructions and make the sandwich exactly according to instructions they receive. (Typically, students' instructions will omit using a knife to spread the fillings, or putting together the sides with fillings.) The results are usually hilarious—and messy—but prove the point that process paragraphs must be complete to be effective.

Imitating paragraphs Choose a successful paragraph (student or professional) with a clear pattern, and discuss it in class. Then ask students to write paragraphs imitating the pattern but not the content of the model paragraph.

Developing paragraphs Take underdeveloped paragraphs on subjects likely to be familiar to students and ask them to develop the paragraphs fully by drawing on their own knowledge. Student paragraphs often provide good material for this exercise. Students can work collaboratively in groups of two or three to develop each person's paragraph. Alternatively, groups can supply a list of questions for each paragraph based on the questions provided in this chapter. Then each student can brainstorm responses to the questions and use that material to revise his or her own paragraph.

COLLABORATIVE LEARNING Analyzing paragraphs When students work together to analyze the paragraphs in Exercise 4.13 they benefit by discovering a broader range of interpretive responses. Those discoveries can be put to work in revising the underdeveloped paragraphs in Exercise 4.14 either individually or in groups.

COLLABORATIVE LEARNING Developing paragraphs In exercises like 4.15 and 4.16, where students may find it difficult to develop their own paragraphs, they can work initially with their revision groups to pinpoint unsupported statements, highlight unclear claims, and create a list of specific questions to aid each writer in a further revision.

ANSWERS

EXERCISE 4.13 Analyzing paragraph development (p. 101)

1. Gates paragraph (p. 76): Patterns of development: cause-and-effect analysis and illustration. Supporting information: mainly the example in sentences 4–8.
2. Wax paragraph (p. 81): Pattern of development: cause-and-effect analysis. Supporting information: first three sentences.

EXERCISE 4.14 Analyzing and revising skimpy paragraphs (p. 100)

Possible answers

1. Sentence 1 requires some expansion to explain *quality of communication*. Each of the next two sentences needs to be supported with specific examples of the two qualities named.
2. Sentences 2, 3, and 4 should each be followed by at least two specific examples of gestures to make the writer's meaning concrete.
3. Sentences 2 and especially 3 require specific support: examples of easy changes, advantages of trying out different versions, and clarification of *the hard work of revising*. What does it involve? Why is it *hard*? Why is it different from what a word processor can do?

EXERCISE 4.15 Considering your past work: Paragraph development (p. 101)

Individual response.

EXERCISE 4.16 Writing with the patterns of development (p. 101)

Individual response

RESOURCES AND IDEAS

Cohan, Carol. "Writing Effective Paragraphs." *College Composition and Communication* 27 (1976): 363–65. Cohan suggests encouraging paragraph development by treating topic sentences as questions to be answered by the paragraph that follows.

Eden, Rick, and Ruth Mitchell. "Paragraphing for the Reader." *College Composition and Communication* 37 (1986): 416–30. The authors suggest that judgments about length and paragraph decisions should be made with the readers in mind.

Lanham, Richard. *Analyzing Prose.* New York: Scribner, 1983. Lanham offers extensive advice on revising paragraphs for stylistic effect.

Witte, Stephen, and Lester Faigley. "Coherence, Cohesion, and Writing Quality." *College Composition and Communication* 32 (1981): 189–204. Students need to learn the features of coherence that extend across sentence boundaries; the article stresses ways to make them aware of coherence strategies.

4d   Special kinds of paragraphs

INSTRUCTOR RESOURCES

The following Presentation Aids are available for download on this book's companion Web site at *http://www.ablongman.com/littlebrown*.

PRESENTATION AID 4.3: Some strategies for opening paragraphs (p. 103)

PRESENTATION AID 4.4: Openings to avoid (p. 105)

PRESENTATION AID 4.5: Some strategies for closing paragraphs (p. 106)

PRESENTATION AID 4.6: Closings to avoid (p. 108)

SECTION HIGHLIGHTS

This section addresses introductory and concluding paragraphs, the occasionally useful transitional and short emphatic paragraphs, and the conventions of paragraphing in dialogue. The emphasis you give to introductory and concluding paragraphs may vary with the experience of your students. For some, writing a straightforward introductory paragraph that simply sets the stage for the essay and presents a thesis statement will be an accomplishment. Others will benefit from experimenting with some of the variations illustrated. Most, however, will appreciate the list of don'ts for introductory paragraphs.

Because concluding paragraphs often present a special problem, you may wish to highlight the common inept endings that trap students and then suggest satisfactory alternatives.

CLASSROOM IDEAS

Using journals Encourage students to collect a repertoire of introduction strategies in their journals. They can draw these strategies from class readings, other courses, and their outside reading. They might also make a log of the ways television news or tabloid shows introduce various subjects and add them to this repertoire. This strategy can also be applied to conclusions.

Magazine models Magazines like *Time, Glamour, Outdoor Life, Ebony* and *Self* contain a variety of informative articles. The authors of these articles and students writing expository essays face a similar problem—how to get readers interested enough to keep reading. Have students collect effective openings and bring them to class for discussion. Students can also comb editorials and magazine articles for openings of argumentative essays.

Learning strategies To help students learn effective strategies for writing opening paragraphs, give the class outlines of well-known essays and ask students to construct opening paragraphs based on the information provided. Compare students' opening paragraphs with those of the essays.

This exercise will expose students to the numerous possibilities for creating good opening paragraphs and will promote discussion of the relative merits of different techniques for a specific subject, essay, or audience.

Imitating openings and closings When experienced writers have trouble beginning or ending essays, they usually turn to strategies that have been successful on other occasions. To help student writers develop similar resources, distribute opening and closing paragraphs that demonstrate particularly effective strategies and ask students to write their own paragraphs using the same strategies but containing different content.

COLLABORATIVE LEARNING Comparing closings Using the same essays gathered for the preceding activity, ask students to read all but the conclusions. Then have them underline the thesis statement and the main ideas of each paragraph. Finally, have students write their own conclusions. This exercise will help students to recognize the structure, effectiveness, and importance of concluding paragraphs and will provide diverse examples of how key information may be arranged for variety and emphasis.

Opening and closings Students can work together effectively to analyze the introductory and concluding paragraphs of the student essay in Chapter 3, the openings and closings of published essays and the opening and closing paragraphs from their own papers. Ask each group of students to create their own list of effective opening and concluding strategies accompanied by quoted examples from those various readings.

Pairs of ideas Students may hone their skills with transitional paragraphs by being given pairs of seemingly unrelated ideas and being asked to link them. For example, using the topic of global sweatshop labor, have students create a transitional paragraph linking the discussion of legal implications to the discussion of moral implications.

One-sentence paragraphs Students may be confused about the use of one-sentence paragraphs. Take time to discuss publicly the uses of such paragraphs and to make them aware of any taboos or restrictions you place on such paragraphs; this will save you and your students time and grief later.

COMPUTER ACTIVITY Navigation markers Ask students to locate sample Web pages and bring them to class. Together, the class can evaluate the effectiveness of the navigational markers in the text of each Web page and discuss how to use paragraphing to optimize the reader's ease of navigation.

ANSWERS

EXERCISE 4.17 Analyzing an introduction and conclusion (p. 109)

Possible answer

The introduction in the first draft rushes to Kadi's essay without first securing the reader's interest, and it summarizes and dismisses Kadi's point too tersely. In contrast, the final introduction approaches readers with a statement and question of general interest, more fully explains Kadi's point, and grants it some value.

The conclusion in the first draft is abrupt, does not pick up both of the essay's main points (becoming more tolerated as well as more tolerant), and does not clearly link tolerance to community. The final conclusion solves these problems (especially with the addition of common ground) and finishes strongly.

EXERCISE 4.18 Considering your past work: Introductions and conclusions (p. 109)

Individual response.

RESOURCES AND IDEAS

Fulkderson, Richard. "Composition at the Turn of the Twenty-First Century." *College Composition and Communication* 56 (June 2005): 654–87. Fulkerson provides an excellent introduction to current key issues in composition theory and pedagogy, including the influence on curriculum of critical/cultural studies and genre analysis and the continuing popularity of expressive approaches to teaching writing.

McClish, Glen. "Of Attention-Getting Openers and Contracts: A Reassessment of an Introductory Dilemma." *Journal of Teaching Writing* 13:1 (1996): 197–207. McClish discusses the metaphor of the "contract" as a way to teach students about the rhetorical impact of introductions without prompting clichés.

Platz, Judith. "Revision and Process: 'Round Robin' Group Writing." *Teaching English in the Two-Year College* 22 (March 2000): 342. Platz shows how a collaborative writing activity can improve the structure and content of student writing.

4e Linking paragraphs in the essay

CLASSROOM IDEAS

COMPUTER ACTIVITY Paragraphs in the essay Ask your students to visit each other's Web sites (for those who already have them) and give feedback on the smoothness of the page-to-page transitions.

ANSWERS

EXERCISE 4.19 Analyzing paragraphs in an essay (p. 110)

Possible answer

Throughout the essay the author repeats or restates her key terms: *communication/interaction, community, anonymous/anonymity, physical barriers/physical appearance/the way they look/physical bias, pre-judged/prejudge, tolerance/tolerated/tolerant,* and so on. For each main point, the opening sentence specifically connects to the thesis statement. The pronouns *we, us,* and *our* appear consistently. Transitional expressions (*Instead, Because of . . . , For example, Granted, However,* and many others) explicitly link sentences and paragraphs. And parallelism links sentences in the second, third, and fifth paragraphs (for instance, *The people we communicate with do not know* and *reader's don't even know* in the second paragraph). (Further analysis of this essay appears in Chapter 3 of the handbook and in the preceding answer to Exercise 4.17.)

EXERCISE 4.20 Considering your past work: Paragraphs in the essay (p. 110)

Individual response.

CHAPTER 5

Designing Documents

A WRITER'S PERSPECTIVE

[After revising.] Nothing should then remain that offends the eye.

ROBERT GRAVES

CHAPTER HIGHLIGHTS

Document design is increasingly important to the creation of written documents, as technology gives the individual computer user access to increasingly powerful design tools. If the courses you teach include diverse forms of writing, or if you teach journalism, technical writing, or business writing, you may wish to ask your students to put together a smart-looking newsletter, report, or brochure, and they will need to know how to design their projects. Even if you are teaching a course strictly focused on argument and academic prose, your students can benefit from understanding how to design their documents.

The chapter begins by referencing various academic formatting styles that will probably be useful to your student. Section 5b explains the principles of good document design: creating flow, using good spacing techniques, grouping related elements, emphasizing important elements, and standardizing the appearance of elements. Section 5c covers application of design principles using specific tools and features, including print quality, margins, text, lists, headings, tables, figures, images, and color. Section 5d has an expanded treatment of using illustrations, with examples of tables, figures, and photographic or other images. A new section (5e) on considering readers who have vision disabilities ends the chapter.

MEDIA RESOURCES FOR CHAPTER 5

mycomplab Please visit MyCompLab at *www.mycomplab.com* for more on the writing process.

http://www.ablongman.com/littlebrown ▶ See page 73 of this manual for companion Web site content description.

5a Designing academic papers and other documents

CLASSROOM IDEA

Packaging sells Students who have written résumés probably understand how important formatting is to a résumé (both because of the multilayered nature of résumé text and because hiring decisions are at stake), but they may not be used to thinking about college papers as having comparable requirements. A moment's reflection will probably produce the realization that almost all of the written material they encounter in their daily lives, from cereal-box blurbs to the newspaper, is formatted in some way.

RESOURCES AND IDEAS

Connors, Robert J. "Actio: A Rhetoric of Manuscripts." *Rhetoric Review* 2 (1983): 64–73. Connors discusses the rhetorical effect of typefaces, paper, and format on readers.

Flammia, Madelyn. "Avoiding Desktop Disasters: Why Technical Communication Students Should Learn About Mechanical Paste-Up Techniques." *Journal of Technical Writing and Communication* 23 (1993): 287–95. Flammia discusses a group of assignments intended to make students more aware of the principles of page design and layout.

Harris, Jeanette. "Proofreading: A Reading/Writing Skill." *College Composition and Communication* 38 (1987): 464–66. Harris discusses why students have proofreading problems and how they can improve their editing skills.

Henry, Mathew. "Advertising and Interpretive Analysis: Developing Reading, Thinking, and Writing Skills in the Composition Course." *Teaching English in the Two-Year College* 31 (May 2002): 355–66. Henry explains how he helps students develop critical thinking, writing, and reading skills by having them analyze advertisements.

Madroso, Jan. "Proofreading: The Skill We've Neglected to Teach." *English Journal* 82.2 (1993): 32–41. Madroso suggests ways to make this activity more productive for students.

Norton, Robert. "Commentary: Graphic Excellence for the Technical Communicator." *Journal of Technical Writing and Communication* 23 (1993): 1–6. Norton reminds students how good visuals can contribute to a better understanding of difficult concepts.

5b Considering principles of design

INSTRUCTOR RESOURCE

The following Presentation Aid is available for download on this book's companion Web site at *http://www.ablongman.com/littlebrown*.

PRESENTATION AID 5.1: Principles of document design (p. 113)

CLASSROOM IDEAS

COMPUTER ACTIVITY Previous work Students who have already written papers using one of the academic formats can send their old papers as e-mail attachments to the rest of the class. Ask them to write a cover note explaining why the document format standards are useful within the discipline.

Newsletter Critique If any student organization on your campus produces a newsletter, bring in copies of one issue and ask the class to critique it from a document design standpoint.

Alternative formats Demonstrate to students the effect of different arrangements and presentations of the same text. Comparing formats in this way teaches them the importance of good manuscript presentation. You might handwrite, type, and print out a simple passage on several types of computer printers (with and without corrected errors), then display these on overhead transparencies for class discussion.

COLLABORATIVE LEARNING Design analysis Have students bring to class a brochure, advertisement, or announcement. In small groups, ask them to discuss each document and evaluate it for flow, spacing, grouping, emphasis, and standardization of elements. Each group might also write up a report of their analysis and present it to the class.

Campus flyer service I Set up a flyer designing service for your campus, perhaps located at the college writing center. Campus groups that need a flyer designed for an event can bring content and ideas to your students, the designers. As a first step, have teams of students use the "Principles of document design" list on p. 113 to plan the flyer they will be designing. (A sample flyer appears on p. 852.)

COMPUTER ACTIVITY Revising design Have students locate a brochure, ad, or announcement that they think has an ineffective design. On their computers, they can redesign the document, using the comment function of their word processing software to insert notes about what they changed and why.

5c Using the elements of design

CLASSROOM IDEAS

COMPUTER ACTIVITY Tool tutorials Have students work in pairs to teach each other how to use computer tools such as the Table function of their word processor or the tool that imports graphics files into a document. Each partner can master one tool and then teach the other partner in a hands-on session.

COLLABORATIVE LEARNING Campus flyer service II As a follow-up to the "Campus flyer service I" exercise in 5b, have student teams create a design for a flyer, attending to print quality, margins, text, lists, headings, graphics, and color.

COMPUTER ACTIVITY Fooling with the margins Students who have ever tried to stretch out a short paper to meet a page minimum will probably already know how to alter the margins and font on their computers, but they may not be aware that teachers can usually spot those papers by glancing at them. Have students print out a paper-in-progress using different margin and font settings and then decide which one looks the most appropriate. If you give word lengths for your assignments, students can use the word count function of their word processing software to check the length of their papers.

Brochure services If your college has a student activities fair toward the beginning of the year, you can have your students create a brochure for a campus group to which they belong. They can print out copies and distribute them at the student activities fair.

COLLABORATIVE LEARNING Class Newsletters Have each peer group put together a short newsletter for the rest of the class. Each student should write a different part of the cop, and then all can work together on the document design.

COLLABORATIVE LEARNING Current issue reports Have groups of students work together to write a brief report on a current campus issue. Reports should include summary, statement of problem, and solution, and their design features should be appropriate to the topic.

COMPUTER ACTIVITY Campus Flyer service III As a follow-up to the previous "flyer service" exercises in 5c, have your students create a mock-up of a flyer on their computers. They should plan to revise it based upon feedback from you, the class as a whole, and the campus group that commissioned the flyer.

COLLABORATIVE LEARNING Overkill Some students use underlining, boldface, or italics liberally without being aware that the more highlights they use, the less each one will mean, and that highlighting is no substitute for choosing the right words. To help convey this, have them print out two versions of the same paper, one version with multiple highlights and the other with only one highlight. Then have their peer groups read the papers and respond.

Proofreading for format Students might not be aware that their document may come out of the printer with slightly different formatting (page breaks, for instance) than it had on the screen. They should be cautioned to check hard copy for formatting inconsistencies and make any necessary adjustments on screen.

Listing the reasons The occasional student may submit a paper entirely in list form, not understanding that a list is an inappropriate format for an academic paper. To illustrate that point, you might give them two versions of a sample paragraph, one with the evidence in list form and the other written conventionally, and discuss how the list affects the flow of the paragraph. Students should also identify any information the list leaves out such as transitions or logical connections.

Exercise 5.1 Redesigning a paper (p. 120)
Individual response.

5d   Using illustrations

CLASSROOM IDEAS

COMPUTER ACTIVITY Instructions for making a hot fudge sundae Have students create an instructional document on how to "build" a hot fudge sundae (or other dessert of their choice). They should apply elements of design appropriately and create the document on their computer. They can include illustrations, color, highlighting, numbered lists, or other elements they think will make for a well-designed document. The goal is for the document to be visually appealing and easy to read.

COMPUTER ACTIVITY Excelling at tables Spreadsheet software often contains different options for creating tables and charts from data. Your students can experiment with different presentations of the same data to see which conveys the information best or to emphasize different aspects of the data.

A thousand words Students who are not strong writers may like the idea of allowing a visual image to speak for them in their own papers. You may need to show them that, while images can add to readers' understanding of your writing, they are not a substitute for clear, developed prose.

Web site recommendations Ask students to evaluate the photographs and illustrations on your college's Web site and to make recommendations for additional illustrations where appropriate. You might even have the class present their top three recommendations to your campus computer services department for consideration when the college Web site is next updated.

COMPUTER ACTIVITY Clearly designed Web sites In a networked classroom, take your students on a tour of Web sites and ask them to evaluate each site in terms of its accessibility to vision-impaired readers.

RESOURCES AND IDEAS

Draga, Sam and Van Doss. "Cruel Pies: The Inhumanity of Technical Illustrations." *Technical Communication* 48.3 (2001): 265–74. The authors' review of the research on the ethics of visual communication suggests that visual information is not always presented accurately and honestly; they suggest ways of correcting the problem.

Williams, Robin. *The Non-Designer's Design Book.* 2nd ed. Berkeley: Peachpit, 2003. This is an accessible beginner's guide to modern document design.

PART 2

Reading and Writing in College

CHAPTER 6
Writing in Academic Situations

CHAPTER 7
Studying Effectively and Taking Exams

CHAPTER 8
Forming a Critical Perspective

CHAPTER 9
Reading Arguments Critically

CHAPTER 10
Writing an Argument

CHAPTER 11
Reading and Using Visual Arguments

Writing in Academic Situations

CHAPTER HIGHLIGHTS

Chapter 6 is new to the tenth edition of the *Little, Brown Handbook*. Because beginning students often have difficulty assuming an academic writing stance, this chapter begins with a detailed discussion of how students can make the transition. The "Tips for becoming an academic writer" checklist can give students strategies that will help prepare them for academic writing. Subsequent chapter sections cover analyzing audience, determining purpose, choosing structure and content, and use of academic language.

MEDIA RESOURCES FOR CHAPTER 6

mycomplab Please visit MyCompLab at *www.mycomplab.com* for more on the writing process.

`http://www.ablongman.com/littlebrown` ▶ See 73 of this manual for companion Web site content description.

6a   Becoming an academic writer

INSTRUCTOR RESOURCE

The following Presentation Aid is available for download on this book's companion Web site at *http://www.ablongman.com/littlebrown*.

PRESENTATION AID 6.1: Tips for becoming an academic writer (p. 129)

RESOURCES AND IDEAS

Rose, Shirley K. "The Voice of Authority: Developing a Fully Rhetorical Definition of Voice in Writing." *Writing Instructor* 8 (1989): 111–18. Rose argues that voice, or authority over one's texts, is a measure of effective writing, and shows how this quality can be developed in students' writing in a fifteen-week time period.

Valerie-Gold, Marie and Mary P. Demming. "Reading, Writing, and the College Developmental Student." *Handbook of College Reading and Study Strategy Research*. Ed. Rona F. Flippo and David C. Caverly. Mahwah: Lawrence Earlbaum, 2000: 149–57. The authors show how focused, critical reading can benefit students.

6b Analyzing audience

CLASSROOM IDEAS

Building the role Students may be surprised to find that becoming an academic writer is dependent upon these collateral activities. Share with them the analogy of an actor who does background work to prepare for a role. The actor might read historical works about the time period; might work with a dialect coach to understand the meaning of lines and how to say them; might visit the place in which the play takes place to absorb the atmosphere; might become familiar with their character's profession by shadowing a real professional in that field. These activities take place before rehearsals begin and help the actor to make the role believable.

Crossover writers Many academic professionals write successfully for different audiences. Stephen Jay Gould, Carl Sagan, and Deborah Tannen are well known for their crossover writings, but there are many others as well. Show your students two samples of a single author's writing on the same subject but pitched to different audiences, to help them see the difference.

Classroom audience The members of your classroom, including the students and you, constitute an educated or academic audience (albeit less specialized or sophisticated than an audience composed of academic professionals.) Asking students to read their papers aloud in class, standing at the front of the class or a podium, can be a way to establish a more formal atmosphere. The experience of making a formal oral presentation may help them get a better feeling for the formal qualities of academic writing.

6c Determining purpose

CLASSROOM IDEA

COMPUTER ACTIVITY Interpreting assignments Post a number of sample assignments from disciplines on your class Web site. You can either create your own, hunt for sample online, or ask your colleagues if they will provide a sample assignment for this purpose. Ask students to post on the Web site their interpretations of purpose as implied by each sample assignment.

6d Choosing structure and content

CLASSROOM IDEAS

COLLABORATIVE LEARNING Disciplinary differences Give students samples of discipline-specific academic writing. In small groups, they can compare the samples, locating differences in structure and content conventions. They can use this section's bulleted list of guidelines to help them evaluate the samples.

Culturally specific conventions If you have international students in your course, you might invite them to bring in samples of writing they did for teachers in their home country, and to explain to the rest of the class any structure or content conventions in their culture that differ from U.S. conventions.

5e Using academic language

CLASSROOM IDEAS

COMPUTER ACTIVITY Web site prose/academic prose Ask students to bring to class a paragraph taken from a Web site of their choice. Then ask them to evaluate the degree to which the excerpt adheres to, or departs from, academic conventions of content, structure, and language.

COLLABORATIVE LEARNING Formality tree Put mural paper on a classroom wall and ask students to bring in examples of formal and informal writing on a current events topic. They may collect samples from a wide range of sources, but they must include the source citation with the source itself. Draw a tree on the mural paper, with branches devoted to different categories of discourse (media, government publications, academic writing, etc.). Then put samples on the appropriate branches. You can further subdivide the tree such that the more formal in language a source is, the higher it goes on its particular branch.

Persuasion and neutrality If the subject matter is a hot-button issue, students may have difficulty assuming a neutral tone in their writing. Help them understand that a balanced, informed content and a dispassionate tone can often help persuade readers better than an obviously biased content and angry tone.

ANSWERS

EXERCISE 6.1 Using academic language (p. 134)

Possible revision

The stereotype that women talk more on cell phones than men do turns out to be false. In a five-year study of 1021 cell phone owners, a major wireless company found that men spend 35 percent more time on their phones, talking an average of 571 minutes a month compared to women's average of 424 minutes a month. Women do talk more on home phones than men do, but that difference is declining.

EXERCISE 6.2 Considering your past work: Writing in academic situations (p. 134)

Individual response.

EXERCISE 6.3 Considering your native language or dialect (p. 134)

Individual response.

Studying Effectively and Taking Exams

A WRITER'S PERSPECTIVE

Those who fail to reread are obliged to read the same story everywhere.

ROLAND BARTHES

CHAPTER HIGHLIGHTS

Chapter 7 is new to the tenth edition of the *Little, Brown Handbook*. The first three sections cover successful study methods, from time management and organization to reading and writing, including discussion of summary and note-taking techniques. Section 7d contains a discussion, expanded in this edition of the Handbook, of how to prepare for and take essay examinations. The sample instruction chart on page 145 provides hypothetical essay questions and strategies for answering them. There are also two sample answers (successful and unsuccessful) to an essay question, with marginal annotations for each.

MEDIA RESOURCES FOR CHAPTER 7

my**complab**²⁰ Please visit MyCompLab at *www.mycomplab.com* for more on the writing process.

http://www.ablongman.com/littlebrown ▶ See page 73 of this manual for companion Web site content description.

7a Managing your time

CLASSROOM IDEAS

ADD & time management Students with attention deficit disorder often have difficulty with time management. For these students, time management strategies (alarm clocks or other external cueing devices, planners, and study schedules) are essential. Most campuses have a learning center or academic assistance office that can provide additional support to these students.

Writing chunks Remind your students that paper-writing usually requires multiple sessions, with time for incubating thoughts in between. So when they are planning their weekly work schedule, they will do best to break a paper assignment into chunks, such as brainstorming, outlining, drafting, and revising. Chunks can be spread out over several days or longer.

7b Listening and taking notes in class

INSTRUCTOR RESOURCE

The following Presentation Aid is available for download on this book's companion Web site at *http://www.ablongman.com/littlebrown.*

PRESENTATION AID 7.1: Tips for taking class notes (p. 137)

CLASSROOM IDEA

Differentiated instruction techniques Students who are visual or global learners may have difficulty taking notes from an oral class lecture without supplementary materials. To help reach students with these learning styles, you might pass out a written version of lecture notes or post notes on your class Web site so that students can review them later.

7c Reading for comprehension

INSTRUCTOR RESOURCE

The following Presentation Aid is available for download on this book's companion Web site at *http://www.ablongman.com/littlebrown.*

PRESENTATION AID 7.2: Writing a summary (p. 140)

CLASSROOM IDEAS

COLLABORATIVE LEARNING Reading notes Have students read a short article in class and take reading notes on it. Then ask them to use their reading notes to discuss the article in small groups.

Practice previewing Give your students practice in previewing techniques by bringing in a collection of books to class (on per student) and asking them each to preview one. Then ask them to present the book to the rest of the class.

Reading goals Reading with a goal in mind can help students focus their reading process. You could give students a list of study questions before they read to help them focus their reading to extract key ideas. Alternatively, you could ask each student to bring to class one discussion question base on the reading.

Summary assignment A summary can make a good short writing assignment, especially for beginning writers. Students can focus on comprehending another writer's argument without the additional task of making their own argument in a written assignment.

COMPUTER ACTIVITY Summary contest Ask students to submit summaries anonymously to your class Web page and then have the class vote on which summary is the best. Follow up with a discussion of why the winning summary was successful.

Casual summarizing You can point out to students that they summarize all the time when telling friends about movies they've seen or books they've read. Have them summarize a favorite book from memory, and then revise the summary to make sure it's comprehensive and succinct.

7d Preparing for and taking exams

A WRITER'S PERSPECTIVE

> *The papers they had been written lay*
> *In piles of blue and white*
> *But though they wrote it all by rote*
> *They did not write it right*
>
> ANONYMOUS

CLASSROOM IDEAS

COLLABORATIVE LEARNING Study groups Study groups are a time-honored way for students to collaborate. You may want to set up formal study groups that will work together throughout the semester. Using online real-time chat software (if your class has a Web site) can help study groups meet if they are commuter students and can't stay on campus after class.

Aural and kinesthetic memory Repeating facts out loud may work for some students. They may retain an aural memory of the sound of the words, or a kinesthetic memory of how their mouth feels shaping the words.

COLLABORATIVE LEARNING Study group questions A good way for a study group to review material together is for each member of the group to come up with some study questions to ask the other members.

COLLABORATIVE LEARNING Essays in the disciplines Divide students into groups according to their intended majors (humanities majors, education majors, and so on). Ask them to bring in examples of essay questions from examinations in their major discipline courses. (Some campus libraries or tutoring groups keep old copies of exams on file for student use; these can be valuable sources of information). Have each group determine the kinds of questions and keyboards used most often in their disciplines; then they can prepare a short report for the rest of the class on the best strategies for writing successful essay answers for these questions.

What works and what doesn't Comparing these sample "successful" and "unsuccessful" essay exam answers should help students get a better idea of what to strive for in their own essay exam answers. The successful answer is direct, substantive, and well structured. You may also want to have students take a closer look at the use of transitions in the successful essay; they provide coherence within and among paragraphs, giving the reader essential information about how the various pieces of information in the essay are interrelated.

Achievable standards Both of the sample essay answers here (successful and unsuccessful) are clearly written and correct in grammar and usage. Your students may think they set a standard impossible to achieve. You can reinforce the idea that content and structure are the most important elements in a good essay exam answer and that they should not waste valuable exam time trying to perfect grammar, sentence structure, or mechanics. If they leave time at the end they can do a quick clean-up to catch any egregious errors.

COMPUTER ACTIVITY Online exams If your students are going to compose and submit their essay exams using a computer, have them do a dry run with a practice document to make sure they know how to save, format, and submit it according to your specifications.

CHAPTER 8

Forming a Critical Perspective

CHAPTER HIGHLIGHTS

Becoming explicitly aware of their critical powers, and then learning to use them, may seem an overwhelming task to students who are already coping with other changes brought on by the first year of college. However, developing a critical awareness is one of the most important things first-year students need to do to make the transition to college.

This chapter begins with the sometimes challenging concept of being critical without being negative. Thomas Sowell's provocative essay, "Student Loans," models truly academic critical reading. The essay is printed in full, and it is also used as an example throughout the chapter's coverage of active reading, summarizing, and constructing a critical response with the use of analysis, interpretation, synthesis, and evaluation.

An expanded section on "Viewing images critically" discusses writing while reading an image; previewing, interpreting, analyzing, and evaluating an image; and synthesizing ideas about an image. Several illustrations provide examples for this section.

Finally, the chapter covers ways of communicating the results of critical thinking and reading to an audience through critical writing. Two annotated students papers, one responding to Sowell's essay and the other responding to the *Time* magazine advertisement, provide models of how to shape and produce a coherent critical response.

MEDIA RESOURCES FOR CHAPTER 8

mycomplab Please visit MyCompLab at *www.mycomplab.com* for more on the writing process.

http://www.ablongman.com/littlebrown ▶ See page 73 of this manual for companion Web site content description.

8a Thinking and reading critically

INSTRUCTOR RESOURCES

The following Presentation Aids are available for download on this book's companion Web site at *http://www.ablongman.com/littlebrown*.

PRESENTATION AID 8.1: Techniques for critical reading (p. 151)

PRESENTATION AID 8.2: Questions for previewing a text (p. 153)

PRESENTATION AID 8.3: Guidelines for analysis, interpretation, and synthesis (p.159)

PRESENTATION AID 8.4: Questions for previewing an image (p. 165)

PRESENTATION AID 8.5: Elements of images (p.167)

CLASSROOM IDEAS

The meaning of *critical* One of the greatest difficulties in teaching critical strategies is the problems students have with the negative connotations of the word *critical*. Brainstorm all the meanings and uses of the word they know; beyond those implying value judgments, some students will come up with "critical temperature," "critical mass," "critical condition," "critical point of the game," and so on. By showing how these terms connect to discernment, or important stages of development, you can demonstrate that the word need not always have negative overtones and thus help students to study these techniques with a better attitude.

Matthiessen's mistake One good anecdote to share with students concerns F. O. Matthiessen's classic work of literary criticism, *American Renaissance*. When it first appeared in 1941, it contained a passage praising the irony in Herman Melville's metaphor "the soiled fish of the sea" (describing an eel). When readers rushed to read the Melville passage in question, however, they found that "soiled" was actually a typographical error; the correct reading was "coiled." Matthiessen's brilliant critique of Melville's irony was founded on a typesetter's mistake. Students find it comforting to know that great critics can make mistakes, too; you can point out that it was, in fact, people employing critical reading who found Matthiessen's misreading!

CULTURE LANGUAGE **Challenging texts** Critical activities may provide an additional hurdle for students whose first language is not English or who come from cultures outside the United States. In many cultures, students are taught not to challenge ideas in print; such questions may be considered disrespectful by some who see print as an indication of authority and value. (This is especially true if the text refers to religious beliefs.) Other students, especially those who grew up in nondemocratic societies, may know from experience how dangerous it can be to challenge the "party line" espoused in school. And depending on the area of the United States you teach in, you may find students who believe in the "inerrancy of the word," even if the text is not biblical. Discuss the students' right to ask questions about, respond to, and challenge printed works, whether in published texts or in personal manuscripts.

COLLABORATIVE LEARNING Group practice Even after they work through the materials in this chapter, students will need to practice critical reading until it becomes a familiar process. Having students work in groups to answer previewing questions or to create questions for rereading can make the critical approach to reading more accessible, and it will result in a broader range of interpretive responses.

COLLABORATIVE LEARNING Complex texts Choose a relatively complex essay from your reader or another published collection. Ask students to work through various sections of the essay in small groups, then present their findings to the class. After those presentations, students might reread the essay and write an interpretive response to a short passage from the essay, which they again can share and critique in groups. Students can also use the essay as the basis for the appropriate exercises in this chapter. This will give them further confidence in their critical skills.

COLLABORATIVE LEARNING Exercise 8.1 Since students in your class will have different abilities as well as different levels of experience with texts like Sowell's, their responses in Exercise 8.1 may be widely different. Having students discuss their responses in small groups lets them see a variety of reading and understanding strategies at work; students who had difficulty with the passage should be encouraged to talk about the part(s) that gave them trouble and ask for suggestions on how to tackle similar readings in the future. You might ask each group to create a list of key quotes, questions, and comments, which they can later summarize for the class.

If possible, avoid giving students a "correct" response (usually one you've written) to this exercise and the other exercises in this chapter, since it subconsciously but powerfully reinforces the mistaken stereotype that there is one right way to read an essay—the teacher's.

Wearing the film critic's hat To help students understand the concept of "misreading," try the "movie critic" exercise: a movie critic writes that a film is "one of the really great awful films of the decade." An ad for the film that claims "Critic So-and-So calls this 'one of the really great . . . films of the decade'" is a deliberate misreading. Ask students to construct deliberate misreadings of reviews or critiques as a way of teaching them what not to do in their own summaries.

COLLABORATIVE LEARNING Comparing summaries Ask students to compare their summaries in groups and list points that are similar and different among the summaries in their group. Then, as a way of deciding how much information is needed to create an effective summary, have each student defend the places where his or her summary differs from the group consensus.

Summary strategies Students learning standard American English may find synonyms for some key words in the sentences that express the main points of a source, but they may feel insecure about using other sentence structures. Encourage students to change the sentence structure as well as the vocabulary of the original in writing summaries. Working collaboratively on summaries helps students see alternative ways to express ideas; in addition, stronger students (and native speakers) can help the weaker students and, in so doing, reinforce their own writing skills. Alice Oshima and Ann Hogue, in *Writing Academic English*, 3rd ed. (New York: Longman, 1999), include useful exercises for students who need additional practice in summarizing.

COLLABORATIVE LEARNING Exercise 8.2   Make Exercise 8.2 collaborative by asking each group of students to write a collective summary; then switch summaries among groups and have the readers decide how effective the other group's effort is in conveying the essential information in Sowell.

COLLABORATIVE LEARNING Magazine collection   Encourage students to bring magazines of various kinds to class. Have students work in groups to brainstorm lists similar to the one shown here for reach magazine they collected. Each group might present their most surprising or revealing findings to class.

COMPUTER ACTIVITY AND COLLABORATIVE LEARNING Web threads   Have students visit an online discussion group and follow a "thread" of conversation. Ask them to list some of the assumptions made by individual writers, make inferences about those writers' beliefs, and then evaluate whether or not most of the participants seem to share those beliefs.

COMPUTER ACTIVITY Networked inferences   Having students summarize and draw inferences from one another's work can be a useful exercise for both reader and writer. Have students work in pairs (either on the computer or on printed copy) to summarize, then practice reasonable and deliberately faulty inferences of passages from each other's work. In each case, the writer of the passage can argue for his or her intention in writing the passage and evaluate the effectiveness of the summary, while the reader can point to evidence or lack of evidence for the inference. Particularly in a networked classroom, each student pair can send two passages with attached summary and inferences to another group for evaluation, and/or the instructor can post one or two examples for the entire class. See Rick Monroe's *Writing and Thinking with Computers: A Practical and Progressive Approach* (Urbana: NCTE, 1993). Monroe lays out the nuts and bolts of establishing a networked computer lab and of rethinking classroom practice in relation to computer use.

COLLABORATIVE LEARNING Exercises 8.3, 8.4, 8.5   When students have completed Exercise 8.3, 8.4, and 8.5 individually, it is beneficial to have them share their analyses in small groups so that they are able to note and discuss the differing conclusions that each student may have reached. In a networked classroom, this sharing can take place by email, which encourages dialogue and helps students deepen their critical analyses.

The Onion   It may help students to understand previewing if they think of an onion. Their job in looking at the image is to work their way from the outside (the most striking elements of the image, the publication and authorship information, and their first response) to deeper, internal layers of meaning.

List of reading questions Students may want to use the questions on pages 165–66 about purpose, audience, words and symbols, subject, and form as a guideline to help them in their notetaking. These questions would also be helpful if students are creating annotated lists of images.

Change the caption To help students understand how images and words work together, ask them to write some alternative captions for the *Time* magazine photo. The class can then discuss how the new captions help influence the meaning of the visual image.

Comparing images To give students practice in analyzing elements of images, give them several images and ask them to compare a single element in all the images. By focusing on one element at a time, you can help students develop their ability to analyze that element. You could also ask them to find examples of images that have a distinctive use of an element, such as an image with an unusual point of view, a compelling narration, or a good use of tension or allusion.

COLLABORATIVE LEARNING Poster images Posters often abound on college campuses, and they provide legitimate fodder for image analysis. Ask students to bring in one of their favorite posters and have them work in small groups to analyze the elements.

COMPUTER ACTIVITY Views of the web The Web, so abundant in visual images, is an ideal place to practice critical viewing. You can create a guided tour for your students through some choice Web pages. As they follow the links in order, students can answer worksheet questions or just record their interpretations of the images they see.

COMPUTER ACTIVITY Personal web pages Some of your students may have their own Web pages with graphics or other visual images. Ask for volunteers to have their Web pages viewed and evaluated by the rest of the class. Alternatively, if your students are building their own Web pages, you can ask them to experiment with images and try them out on their classmates.

Claims and evidence These examples of reasonable and faulty inferences should be familiar to students who have been writing thesis and topic sentence claims supported by evidence. Some students may be adept at interpreting images but less so at interpreting the written word. If so, have them practice first on images. IF they can understand how to draw reasonable inferences from an image, they may be able to apply that understanding to interpretations of written texts.

COLLABORATIVE LEARNING Group ads Have students work in pairs to create their own ad or editorial cartoon on a subject of their choosing. Ask them to submit a rationale along with the ad, in which they explain what they were trying to achieve visually. The class as a whole can critique or respond to the submissions.

COLLABORATIVE LEARNING Image auction Have your students imagine they are the auctioneer for an estate sale of images (you provide the collection of images). Ask them each to select an image they think is excellent in quality and/or high in significance, and to write a blurb for the auction program in which they describe the image and try to "sell" their classmates on its value and significance. You can put the image online and the class can work together to create an online auction program including each of their entries.

COLLABORATIVE LEARNING Exercise 8.6 Exercise 8.6 can work well as a group activity. Have students discuss the *Time* advertisement in small groups, using the list of visual elements, to develop alternative interpretations.

COLLABORATIVE LEARNING Exercise 8.8 Exercise 8.8 can work well as a group exercise. Each group member can supply one image, and then the group can perform the analysis together.

COLLABORATIVE LEARNING Polling students Have each student solicit critical responses to Sowell's article from their roommates or friends. Then have students work in pairs to compare the responses of their friends to that of Robinson. This exercise will help students get a sense of the range of responses a written argument can engender.

MODELS OF STUDENT WRITING

"Weighing the Costs" Charlene Robinson's essay is an excellent example of critical writing, combining a well-developed critique with good organization, effective transitions, and balanced tone. Particularly if they are not strong writers, your students may feel that their own efforts (in Exercises 8.4 and 8.10) do not measure up. In order to emphasize for your students that Robinson's approach is but one possible way of critiquing Sowell, you might want to spend some time as a class developing alternative critiques. For instance, you might point out to your students that Robinson does not provide statistical evidence of her own, and ask them to test her assertions by doing some further research on student loans.

Illustrated arguments Ask your students to find or create a visual image (photograph, graphic, drawing, etc.) that could accompany Robinson's essay. They can compare the image they chose with members of their small group, and this could prompt discussion of the different merits of written and visual critiques.

COMPUTER ACTIVITY Summary to argument On your class Web site or through e-mail, post a summary of a course reading of your choice. Then ask students to begin the process of converting the summary to a written critical response. They can begin with some online discussion and then propose arguments that would form the basis of a response essay.

MODELS OF STUDENT WRITING

"Playing It Safe" John Latner's essay analyzing the *Time* magazine advertisement offers an example of a very well-developed interpretation and analysis of an image. It has a bold thesis which is well supported by evidence. Students who are not accustomed to writing about images may be surprised at how much mileage Latner gets out of the magazine ad, but they should soon see that all the preparatory work they do when they view an image (such as keeping a response journal or writing down analysis of the elements of the image) is indispensable when they being to write their own critical essay.

Because of its timely and nationally significant subject matter, Latner's essay may make for a lively classroom discussion. Latner makes a compelling argument, but your students may want to propose alternative interpretation of the image.

COLLABORATIVE LEARNING Exercise 8.9 Have students form a networked chatgroup (or work in small groups) to discuss the questions for Exercise 8.9 and come up with a number of responses to each question. Then ask each student to revise those responses individually into a brief essay. When students exchange the completed essays in their group they are often surprised by the varying interpretations developed by the individual essays.

If time and your classroom situation permit, you might put students into groups to compare their answers to these questions, and post the group's consensus on the class web site so that students can compare their responses with those of their classmates. Encourage students to focus not only on points on which they agree but on their disagreements. Such differences of opinion indicate where their analytical frameworks and assumptions vary, even though they may consider themselves all part of the same "audience."

COLLABORATIVE LEARNING Exercises 8.10 and 8.11 Exercise 8.10 and 8.11 may be particularly difficult for students if their perspectives are similar to Charlene Robinson's or John Latner's. Beginning students especially may find it difficult to define a distinct perspective of their own in the face of a well-argued example they have just read. You might work with them as a group to brainstorm some alternative (but not too dissimilar) perspective.

ANSWERS

EXERCISE 8.1 Reading (p. 155)

Individual response.

EXERCISE 8.2 Summarizing (p. 157)

As their support of the government's student loan program illustrates, politicians ignore the economic reality that using resources to benefit one group (students in debt) involves taking the resources from another group (taxpayers). Students' average debt is not even that high, and college graduates can afford to pay it off. The greatest attention is paid to the graduate with a large debt, but the law also allows affluent students to borrow, even if their parents profit and the students drop out of school or waste time there. Funded by taxpayers, the loan program has contributed to declining educational standards, rising tuitions, and rising professors' salaries. Taxpayers should balk at funding the program further.

EXERCISE 8.3 Thinking critically (p. 163)

Possible answers

1. *Analysis:* What is the basis for the author's comparison of print and televised journalism? The key words are *demand reading, not just viewing.*

   Interpretation: Are better . . . than implies a value judgment. *Demand reading, not just viewing* reveals the author's assumption that viewing is somehow less worthy than reading, perhaps because viewing is more passive.

   Synthesis: This author prefers print journalism and disparages television journalism because of the different activities needed to partake of them.

   Evaluation: This statement shows the author's bias in favor of written news and implies some contempt for TV news. The author's reasons for preferring reading over viewing are not evident and require explanation. Some other questions: Are people who get their news from TV less well-informed than those who get it from reading? Even if television news is inferior, isn't it better than no news at all (for those who won't or can't read)? Might television news be preferable for its immediacy?

2. *Analysis:* What is the author's purpose? The key words are *true, democratic, giving voice to,* and *people of all persuasions.*

   Interpretation: Democratic means "of or for the people." *True democratic forum* means that there are competing, perhaps misleading, forums. *Giving voice to people* appeals to a sense of fair play and belief in free speech, while *all persuasions* implies open-mindedness. The author assumes that people need a public forum where they can voice their opinions. Because it is immediate, radio gives people the freedom to say what they want. Other forums may censor or restrict who can say what.

   Synthesis: The writer values radio call-in shows for affording all kinds of people a chance to express themselves without censorship.

   Evaluation: This writer evidently believes that radio is somehow freer than other places for people to speak their minds. What other forums for freespeech are there? Does radio censor or alter the opinions expressed? (What about the time delays for objectionable language?) Are "people of all persuasions" really calling such shows, or just some kinds of people? Are unedited, inexpert opinions a democratic necessity?

3. *Analysis:* What is the author's attitude toward online communication? The key words are *threaten, undermine, ability,* and *interact face to face.*

Interpretation: Threaten and *undermine* imply danger; *ability* and *interact face to face* imply that face-to-face communication is a kind of skill or talent. Together the words imply that the skill or talent is vulnerable, subject to some kind of destruction. The author's assumptions: Online and face-to-face communication are different. Face-to-face interaction has an intrinsic value. Online communication does not have this value. Communicating online diminishes this value.

Synthesis: The author believes that something valuable will be lost to online communication.

Evaluation: This statement indicates a preference for face-to-face interaction over online communication and a concern about the latter overwhelming the former. But what exactly is special about face-to-face interaction? What does it provide that online communication doesn't? Won't people continue to meet face to face even if they also communicate online? Will online communication necessarily undermine face-to-face interaction? Might online communication also contribute something positive of its own, adding to rather than subtracting from the ways people interact?

EXERCISE 8.4 Reading an essay critically (p. 164)
Individual response.

EXERCISE 8.5 Reading a magazine critically (p. 164)
Individual response.

EXERCISE 8.6 Viewing an image critically (p. 172)
Individual response.

EXERCISE 8.7 Viewing an image critically (p. 172)
Individual response.

EXERCISE 8.8 Comparing images critically (p. 172)
Individual response.

EXERCISE 8.9 Responding to critical writing (p. 177)
Individual response.

EXERCISE 8.10 Writing critically about a text (p. 178)
Individual response.

EXERCISE 8.11 Writing critically about an image (p. 178)
Individual response.

EXERCISE 8.12 Writing critically about an image (p. 178)
Individual response.

EXERCISE 8.13 Writing critically about several images (p. 178)
Individual response.

RESOURCES AND IDEAS

On approaches to teaching critical thinking

Anson, Chris M., ed. *Writing and Response: Theory, Practice, and Research.* Urbana: NCTE, 1989. A collection of essays that explore the practical and theoretical issues involved in reading and commenting on student texts.

Brookfield, Stephen D. *Developing Critical Thinkers.* San Francisco: Jossey-Bass, 1987. Brookfield encourages connections between critical skills developed in school and their applications in daily life.

Chambers, Marilyn J. "Text Cues and Strategies Successful Readers Use to Construct the Gist of Lengthy Written Arguments." *Reading Research Quarterly* 30 (1995): 778–807. Chambers examines students' strategies for identifying argument structure, claim, and evidence in lengthy texts.

Elbow, Peter. "Ranking, Evaluating, and Liking: Sorting Out Three Forms of Judgment." *College English* 55 (1993): 187–206. Elbow's essay is largely concerned with these three activities as part of teacher assessment of student writing, but it gives many ideas that can be translated into classroom practice.

Fiske, John. *Introduction to Communication Studies.* New York: Routledge, 1990. Fiske provides a general overview (for students and teachers) of the methods of cultural criticism, with explicit connections to the teaching of writing.

Foehr, Regina Paxton, and Susan A. Schiller, eds. *The Spiritual Side of Writing: Releasing the Learner's Whole Potential.* Portsmouth: Boynton/Cook (Heinemann), 1997. Essays exploring how writing, learning, and teaching may be experiences that lead to spiritual and ethical awareness and growth.

Golub, Jeff, and the NCTE Committee on Classroom Practices, eds. *Activities to Promote Critical Thinking.* Urbana: NCTE, 1986. The authors have compiled a collection of essays focusing on practical advice and teaching strategies.

Jenseth, Richard. "Understanding Hiroshima: An Assignment Sequence for Freshman English." *College Composition and Communication* 40 (1989): 215–19. Jenseth describes a course wherein students focus on one work (or theme) for an entire semester, considering and reconsidering issues from various critical perspectives.

Jones, Libby Falk. "Exploring Beliefs Through Dialectical Thinking." *The Critical Writing Workshop: Designing Writing Assignments to Foster Critical Thinking.* Ed. Toni-lee Capossella. Portsmouth: Boynton, 1993. 17–34. This essay and the collection as a whole offer general discussion and practical examples of how to structure thought-provoking assignments.

Kline, Nancy. "Intertextual Trips: Teaching the Essay in the Composition Class." *Journal of Teaching Writing* 8 (1989): 15–37. Kline describes an "active and playful" strategy used by writers of essays and suggests ways to help students detect and appreciate it.

Marzano, Robert J. *Cultivating Thinking in English: The Language Arts.* Urbana: NCTE, 1991. Marzano explores strategies for enhancing student learning, emphasizing ways in which students can analyze their own values and responses to class texts and discussions.

Matthews, Mitford M. "The Freshman and His Dictionary." *About Language.* Ed. William H. Roberts and Gregoire Turgeon. Boston: Houghton, 1986. Matthews outlines three categories of information students can find in dictionaries; useful on inference.

McLeod, Susan H. "Cultural Literacy, Curricular Reform, and Freshman Composition." *Rhetoric Review* 8 (1990): 270–78. McLeod argues that students can move beyond personal experience in writing essays by reading scholarly materials and responding to them.

Mirskin, Jerry. "Writing as a Process of Valuing." *College Composition and Communication* 46 (1995): 387–410. Mirskin argues that because values shape meaning, teachers must learn to recognize students' systems of value in order to best help them make meaningful connections within an academic environment.

Nelson, Jennie. "Reading Classrooms as Text: Exploring Student Writers' Interpretive Practices." *College Composition and Communication* 46 (1995): 411–29. Nelson examines four case studies to show students' strategies for reading and responding to assignments, grading practices, and teacher comments.

Odell, Lee. "*Strategy* and *Surprise* in the Making of Meaning." *Theory and Practice in the Teaching of Writing: Rethinking the Discipline.* Ed. Lee Odell. Carbondale: Southern Illinois UP, 1993. 213–43. This essay explores the debates over fostering spontaneity and intuitive insights in the teaching of writing as opposed to teaching conscious control, and identifies several approaches that work to do both.

Qualley, Donna. "Using Reading in the Writing Classroom." *Nuts and Bolts: A Practical Guide to Teaching College Composition.* Ed. Thomas Newkirk. Portsmouth: Boynton, 1993. Qualley lays out strategies for integrating critical reading and writing using journals, reading conferences, and small group discussions.

Robertson, Julie Fisher, and Donna Rane Szotstak. "Using Dialogues to Develop Critical Thinking Skills: A Practical Approach." *Journal of Adolescent and Adult Literacy* 39 (April 1996): 552–56. Robertson and Szotstak describe how students can write, analyze, and perform dialogues in order to develop critical thinking skills.

Shaughnessy, Mina. *Errors and Expectations: A Guide for the Teacher of Basic Writing.* New York: Oxford UP, 1977. This pathbreaking study of the challenges faced by basic writers reveals the connections between student error and issues of critical thinking.

Shor, Ira. *Empowering Education: Critical Teaching for Social Change.* Chicago: U of Chicago P, 1992. Shor promotes critical thinking as a part of a pedagogy designed to empower students and citizens.

Tierney, Robert J., John E. Readence, and Ernest K. Dishner, eds. *Reading Strategies and Practices: A Compendium.* 3rd ed. Boston: Allyn and Bacon, 1990. This textbook approach to reading offers a number of exercises and worksheets that help to focus students on particular aspects of the reading process.

Toulmin, Stephen, Richard Rieke, and Allan Janik. *An Introduction to Reasoning.* 2nd ed. New York: Macmillan, 1984. Toulmin et al. detail the reasoning processes involved in making claims, supplying evidential backing, and preparing for rebuttal.

Tripp, Ellen L. "Speak, Listen, Analyze, Respond: Problem-Solving Conferences." *Teaching English in the Two-Year College* 17 (1990): 183–86. Tripp suggests collaborative and individual activities to be completed before students write final papers proposing solutions.

Wiley, Mark. "How to Read a Book: Reflections on the Ethics of Book Reviewing." *Journal of Advanced Composition* 13 (1993): 477–92. Wiley discusses communities of inquiry and why we grant some readers more authority over texts than others.

On writing and critical reading

Berrent, Howard I. "Open to Suggestion: OH RATS—A Note-taking Technique." *Journal of Reading* 27 (1984): 548–50. This essay outlines a useful note-taking strategy to complement critical reading.

Berthoff, Ann E. "A Curious Triangle and the Double-Entry Notebook: Or, How Theory Can Help Us Teach Reading and Writing." *The Making of Meaning: Metaphors, Models, and Maxims for Writing Teachers.* Upper Montclair: Boynton/Cook, 1981. Berthoff shows how use of a double-entry journal can help students improve critical reading skills.

Emig, Janet. "Writing as a Mode of Learning." *College Composition and Communication* 28 (1977): 122–28. A seminal analysis of the ways in which writing facilitates mental processes like intuition, reformulation, and the construction of meaningful relationships between ideas.

Greene, Stuart, and John M. Ackerman. "Expanding the Constructivist Metaphor: A Rhetorical Perspective on Literary Research and Practice." *Review of Educational Research* 65 (Winter 1995): 383–420. This review essay evaluates a number of constructivist explanations of the relationship between reading and writing as a learning model.

Price, Gayle B. "A Case for a Modern Commonplace Book." *College Composition and Communication* 31 (1980): 175–82. Price suggests using classic techniques for commonplace books in conjunction with other journal activities.

Walsh, John A. "Circle Diagrams for Narrative Essays." *Journal of Reading* 32 (1989): 366–68. Use of a graphic technique of concentric circles (similar to Venn diagrams) helps students comprehend and analyze narrative events, relationships, and significance.

On discourse communities

Carter, Duncan. "Critical Thinking for Writers: Transferable Skills or Discipline-Specific Strategies?" *Composition Studies: Freshman English News* 21 (1993): 86–93. Carter explores the question of whether critical thinking skills are transferable across discourse communities.

Killingsworth, M. Jimmie. "Discourse Communities—Global and Local." *Rhetoric Review* 11 (Fall 1992): 110–22. Killingsworth makes readers aware that they are members of both kinds of communities, and he suggests ways to negotiate the bridge(s) between the two.

Morris, Barbara S. *Disciplinary Perspectives on Thinking and Writing.* Ann Arbor: U of Michigan English Composition Board, 1989. This essay collection demonstrates different modes of inquiry and acceptable responses among various disciplines.

Williams, James D., David Huntley, and Christine Hanks. *The Interdisciplinary Reader: A Collection of Student Writing.* New York: HarperCollins, 1992. The editors provide a collection of student essays from various disciplines, accompanied by critiques of their effectiveness in writing critically for particular discourse communities.

On summaries

Carella, Michael J. "Philosophy as Literacy: Teaching College Students to Read Critically and Write Cogently." *College Composition and Communication* 34 (1983): 57–61. Carella argues that students can be taught not only to summarize complex arguments but to respond critically to them.

Lambert, Judith R. "Summaries: A Focus for Basic Writers." *Journal of Developmental Education* 8 (1984): 10+. Lambert reviews advantages of teaching students to summarize.

Sherrard, Carol. "Summary Writing: A Topographical Study." *Written Communication* 3 (1986): 324–43. Sherrard shows that assigning longer summaries forces students to use their own words instead of copying from the source.

8b Viewing images critically

RESOURCES AND IDEAS
Suggested Readings

George, Diana. "From Analysis to Design: Visual Communication in the Teaching of Writing." *College Composition and Communication* 54 (2000): 11–39. Excellent explanation of how instruction in visual literacy can inform the composition curriculum.

Soleil, Naome. "Reflective Reading: A Study in (Tele)literacy." *Journal of College Reading and Learning* 30 (Fall 1999): 5–16. Soleil shows how a reflective reading of television texts can provide a bridge to link oracy and literacy.

Zeller, Robert. "Developing the Inferential Reasoning of Basic Writers." *College Composition and Communication* 38 (1987): 343–46. Zeller suggests that asking students to make connections between visual prompts like photographs and writing helps their critical thinking skills.

CHAPTER 9

Reading
Arguments Critically

A WRITER'S PERSPECTIVE

A great many people think they are thinking when they are merely rearranging their prejudices.

WILLIAM JAMES

CHAPTER HIGHLIGHTS

This chapter presents a discussion of reading arguments critically. The first section describes the elements of arguments: assertions, evidence, and assumptions (9a). The next section offers techniques for testing assertions, for identifying fact, opinion, belief, and prejudice, and for looking at a writer's definition of terms, use of evidence, and appeals to beliefs or needs (9b). Discussions of weighing evidence, analyzing underlying assumptions, attending to language and tone, and judging reasonableness round out the first part of this chapter. Ways for students to recognize logical fallacies—various kinds of evasions and oversimplifications—comprise the second half of this chapter.

The need to read arguments critically is becoming ever more important as argumentation proliferates online. Web sites and online discussion groups are breeding grounds for arguments based on poor evidence, prejudice, or false authority. Exercises and teaching tips offer suggestions for helping students become more critical users of cyberspace.

This chapter assumes that students have read Chapter 8, "Forming a Critical Perspective," and are familiar with its terminology and research.

MEDIA RESOURCES FOR CHAPTER 9

mycomplab Please visit MyCompLab at *www.mycomplab.com* for more on the writing process.

http://www.ablongman.com/littlebrown ▶ See page 73 of this manual for companion Web site content description.

9a   Recognizing the elements of argument

CLASSROOM IDEAS

COMPUTER ACTIVITY Highlighting the elements Create a computer document out of an assigned reading, or ask students to find an argument-based text of their own. Using the highlight function of their word processor, students can highlight the elements of argument in the text, using different colors for claims, evidence, and assumptions.

COMPUTER ACTIVITY Missing elements On your class Web site or via e-mail, post an essay from which you have deleted necessary evidence. Then ask your students to insert comments into their copy of the essay where they think evidence is necessary, and send their commented versions back to you.

RESOURCES AND IDEAS

Bator, Paul. "Aristotelian and Rogerian Rhetoric." *College Composition and Communication* 31 (1980): 427–32. Bator describes the differences between the two schools of argument and helps students understand when each strategy is most appropriate.

Brent, Doug. "Young, Becker, and Pike's 'Rogerian' Rhetoric: A Twenty-Year Reassessment." *College English* 53 (1991): 452–66. Brent reassesses the usefulness of argument based on common views and values in a culturally diverse world.

Ferris, Dana R. "Rhetorical Strategies in Student Persuasive Writing: Differences Between Native and Non-native Speakers." *Research in the Teaching of English* 28 (1994): 45–65. Ferris analyzes sixty persuasive essays by first-year composition students to show the particular difficulties that nonnative speakers can encounter in formulating claims, using data, and anticipating counterarguments.

Katula, Richard A., and Richard W. Roth. "A Stock-Issues Approach to Writing Arguments." *College Composition and Communication* 31 (1980): 183–96. The authors use problem-solving strategies as ways to build arguments.

Maxley, John M. "Reinventing the Wheel or Teaching the Basics: College Writers' Knowledge of Argumentation." *Composition Studies: Freshman English News* 21 (1993): 3–15. Maxley reviews various approaches to teaching argument, including the "Toulmin model" in an effort to identify the most effective strategies.

Rapkins, Angela A. "The Uses of Logic in the College Freshman English Classroom." *Activities to Promote Critical Thinking: Classroom Practices in Teaching English.* Urbana: NCTE, 1986. Rapkins argues that students should be introduced to logic early in the semester, even if writing arguments comes later.

Toulmin, Stephen, Richard Rieke, and Allan Janik. *An Introduction to Reasoning*. New York: Macmillan, 1979. This is a classic textbook exposition of reasoning.

9b Testing claims

INSTRUCTOR RESOURCE

The following Presentation Aid is available for download on this book's companion Web site at *http://www.ablongman.com/littlebrown*.

PRESENTATION AID 9.1: Questions for critically reading an argument (p. 181)

COLLABORATIVE LEARNING "Stump the class" game show Students can benefit from lots of practice in distinguishing between facts, opinions, beliefs, and prejudices. Divide your class into two teams and give each team a set of statements. The team members have to decide on whether the statement is a fact, opinion, belief, or prejudice. The team that gets the most right answers in the shortest amount of time wins.

COMPUTER ACTIVITIY Web claims Ask students to locate and visit an online discussion group on an assigned topic (environmentalism, for instance) and follow a thread of conversation. Have them make a list of claims they find and then evaluate whether each claim is one of fact, opinion, belief, or prejudice. Students may find that opinion statements rely upon facts presented in earlier entries by other thread participants, so they should make sure to look beyond a single entry or writer for facts.

Defining argument Some students may need instruction on the technical meaning of argument, since their view of this rhetorical mode may include only vehement disagreement. Ask students to look up *argument* in various dictionaries and bring a number of definitions of this word to share with their group. Have them discuss how all come into play in persuasive writing.

COLLABORATIVE LEARNING Cut and paste Ask groups of students to identify an issue, collect newspaper or magazine articles on it, and bring the articles to class (in photocopied form, if possible). Then ask them to work in groups to identify what the articles say on the different sides of the issue and to cut out the assertions and paste them in columns (or simply write them out) according to the particular perspective on the argument they represent.

COLLABORATIVE LEARNING Analyzing issues Break students into groups to discuss a campus issue such as residential policies, parking arrangements, or library or computer services. The goal of students' discussion should be to identify the assertions and supporting evidence on each side of the argument. As each group reports back on their findings, list the assertions and evidence on the board so that students can distinguish fact from opinion and identify terms that need defining. If students know enough about issues of public policy (such as gun control, capital punishment, or nuclear disarmament), these topics, too, can be used for discussion.

COLLABORATIVE LEARNING Reassembling an argument Select a short text that contains claims and evidence. Put each claim or item of evidence on a separate clip of paper and shuffle them. Give a set of randomized slips to each small group of students and ask them to sort the slips into two piles: one pile of claims and another of evidence. If they like, they can then try to match each claim with its appropriate evidence.

COLLABORATIVE LEARNING Peer review for undefined terms Ask students to work with their peer review partner to identify abstract terms in their own essays. They can work collaboratively on creating or revising definitions for those key terms.

COMPUTER ACTIVITIY Terms needing definitions Ask students to go online to locate op-ed articles that contain abstract terms. If the author has provided the definition, the student can highlight the definition and insert a comment evaluating the usefulness of the definition. If the author has not defined the term, the student can propose a definition they think would be appropriate in context.

9c   Weighing evidence

INSTRUCTOR RESOURCES

The following Presentation Aids are available for download on this book's companion Web site at *http://www.ablongman.com/littlebrown.*

PRESENTATION AID 9.2: Evidence for argument (p. 184)

PRESENTATION AID 9.3: Criteria for weighing evidence (p. 186)

CLASSROOM IDEAS

COLLABORATIVE LEARNING Editorial evidence Distribute copies of newspaper editorials and ask students, in groups, to examine the evidence the editorials contain in order to (1) identify facts, statistics, examples, and expert opinions and (2) evaluate the evidence for accuracy, relevance, representativeness, adequacy, and reliability. Then ask the groups to compare the results of their analysis and evaluation.

COMPUTER ACTIVITY Fact checking Students can locate a Web site (commercial, educational, or informational) that presents evidence and then go to an authoritative source to verify that the evidence is true and quoted accurately. Together, the class can start a collection of Web sites that present false or misleading evidence.

Expert opinion? A common variation of the expert opinion is a celebrity endorsement. Students should be asked to decide what various celebrities' credentials are for offering their opinions and why the persuaders thought celebrities were the best people to endorse their respective products.

◀ CULTURE LANGUAGE ▶ Attitudes toward sources The ideas that some sources are more authoritative than others and that part of the reader's job is to evaluate the accuracy and veracity of evidence may be counterintuitive to students from Asian or Middle Eastern countries. You may want to spend some time discussing your students' attitudes toward various kinds of sources.

Surveying persuasion Assign students to keep track of all the persuasive communications they are exposed to in the course of one day and to share that list with their groups. (Examples may include advertisements, conversations, television programs, junk mail, songs on the radio, Internet ads, and so on.) Then ask each group to classify and weigh the kinds of evidence used to support each of these persuasive appeals. Which kinds are used most and least often?

RESOURCES AND IDEAS

Chambers, Marilyn J. "Text Cues and Strategies Successful Readers Use to Construct the Gist of Lengthy Written Arguments." *Reading Research Quarterly* 30 (1995): 778–807. Chambers examines students' strategies for comprehending the argument structure, claims, and evidence in lengthy texts.

McCormick, Kathleen. "Teaching Critical Thinking and Writing." *The Writing Instructor* 2 (1983): 137–44. McCormick suggests having students develop critical and analytical skills by critiquing flawed essays, and she describes several units in a course employing this strategy.

9d Discovering assumptions

INSTRUCTOR RESOURCE

The following Presentation Aid is available for download on this book's companion Web site at *http://www.ablongman.com/littlebrown*.

PRESENTATION AID 9.4: Guidelines for analyzing assumptions (p. 188)

CLASSROOM IDEA

COLLABORATIVE LEARNING Technology assumptions Have students engage in a group discussion about the relationship between computer technology and Western cultural and economic dominance around the globe. (For instance, students might consider to what degree computer technology would empower Third World countries, and to what degree it would contribute to global dominance by the West.) Students can do reading on their own in order to explore this issue and then formulate assertions which can be presented and discussed in small groups. Finally, have students identify the underlying assumptions upon which their classmates base their assertions.

9e Watching language, hearing tone

CLASSROOM IDEAS

Advertising tone People who have something to sell provide examples of subtle or not-so-subtle tone. Have students evaluate print advertisements, commercial Web sites, television ads, even junk mail. How does each solicitor try to persuade the reader to buy/use/subscribe to his or her product?

COLLABORATIVE LEARNING Euphemism hunting Have students work in small groups to find examples of euphemisms common in public discourse. They can mine the newspaper or other current events organs; speeches made by politicians or government officials; the nightly newscast; or even sources closer to home such as documents produced on campus by student groups. See which group can collect the most examples.

COMPUTER ACTIVITY Flames on the Web Many discussion groups on the Web have "no flaming" rules—participants are expected to maintain a civil tone when they post messages to the group. But there is still room for a range of tones. Ask your students to shadow a discussion group and collect samples of postings written using various tones.

9f Judging reasonableness

CLASSROOM IDEA

COLLABORATIVE LEARNING Exercise 9.1 Students will benefit from working together on Exercise 9.1. In discussing possible responses and debating the evidence for each response they will learn even more about how each argument is crafted and its effects on different readers. Since the skill of analyzing arguments in these terms is a crucial and challenging one, you might expand on Exercise 9.1 by bringing in other examples of persuasive argumentation and asking students to analyze further examples using these terms.

ANSWERS

EXERCISE 9.1 Reading arguments critically (pp. 190–91)

Possible answers

Kirkpatrick Sale essay

Claims: Thesis (paragraph 5): Individuals' conservation efforts do not raise the consciousness necessary to solve the ecological crisis. Supporting claims: Individuals' conservation does not make a significant dent in energy consumption dominated by industry and government (1, 2). The ecological crisis requires a *drastic overhaul of this civilization,* not individual *life-style solutions* (3). Such solutions divert individuals from *the hard truths and hard choices* of truly changing consciousness (4).

Evidence: Statistics and other facts: 2–5. Examples: 1, 3–5. Appeals to beliefs or needs: mainly, we should do what's necessary to solve the ecological crisis (throughout).

Assumptions: Notably: There is an environmental crisis. It must be solved. Ozone depletion and rain forest destruction are *corporate crimes* (2). Industry and government are powerful and self-protective. They will not respond appropriately to the ecological crisis unless forced to do so by the people. The people are unwilling to make more than life-style changes to solve the crisis.

Tone: No-nonsense (*I don't . . . believe that I am saving the planet*), unrestrained (*patently corporate crimes; truly pernicious*), sardonic (*"all of us"; "our" control; life-style solutions; write-your-congressperson solutions*).

Reasonableness: Sale is obviously biased, so his reasonableness will probably reside in the eye of the beholder. He does offer evidence for his key assertion about the environmental responsibility of industry and government, and his examples show him to be familiar with the mentality of most recyclers (a group he even includes himself in). He acknowledges the opposition most clearly in paragraph 5, where he rebuts the claim that the individualistic approach is at least a start on consciousness raising.

Fallacies: See the answer to Exercise 9.4.

Evaluation: Answers will vary.

Oil corporation advertisement

Claims: Thesis (paragraphs 2, 6, 10, 13): Myths about oil exploration, waste, and conservation do not address America's true energy needs. Supporting claims: Offshore drilling is necessary and does not unduly pollute (4). Though heavy, America's energy use is appropriate for the nation's size and productivity (7, 9). Favoring conservation over exploration would increase oil imports or stop economic growth (12).

Evidence: Statistics and other facts: 3–4, 7–9, 12. Examples: 3. Appeals to beliefs or needs: Mainly, America is a strong country whose economic health is crucial for all (throughout).

Assumptions: Notably: Policy needs to be guided by truths, not myths. Importing foreign oil is undesirable. Some pollution is inevitable and acceptable. America is justified in using energy proportionate to its size and productivity. Conservation is desirable. Economic growth is essential.

Tone: Sincere (*a mystery we hope puzzles others as much as it does us; We probably can—and should—do more*), candid (*Truth is; The fact is; In fact; Let's face it; No doubt about it*), perplexed (*We always have such a problem; where is the waste*).

Reasonableness: Like Sale's essay, the ad is strongly biased, but the statistics and other facts and the sincere tone contribute to a sense of reasonableness. So do the several bows to the opposition, including the statements of the objectionable myths themselves and the support for conservation.

Fallacies: See the answer to Exercise 9.4.

Evaluation: Answers will vary.

9g | Recognizing fallacies

INSTRUCTOR RESOURCE

The following Presentation Aid is available for download on this book's companion Web site at *http://www.ablongman.com/littlebrown*.

PRESENTATION AID 9.5: Checklist of fallacies (p. 193)

CLASSROOM IDEAS

Naming fallacies Many students are put off by the terminology used to classify fallacies. Let them know that the fallacies sometimes overlap and that it is more important for them to recognize and avoid oversimplifications and evasions than to know the correct terms for them.

COMPUTER ACTIVITY Fallacy hunting To sharpen student sensitivity to fallacies, tell your students to go "fallacy hunting" on the Web. Each student should try to collect at least one example of each fallacy on the checklist. You can prepare a "dictionary of fallacies" to be posted on your class Web site.

Keeping the fallacies straight Students can keep a copy of the "Checklist of fallacies" (p. 193) on their computers, and refer to it when they are writing their own papers. If they find they have made a fallacious statement in a draft of their paper, they can paste into the "Checklist" document to keep as an example.

COLLABORATIVE LEARNING Exercise 9.2 Have students work in groups to list and analyze the fallacies found in Exercise 9.2. Ask each group to present the advertisement with the most blatant or surprising fallacy to the class.

COLLABORATIVE LEARNING Exercise 9.4 Ask students to work in groups on Exercise 9.4. After completing the exercise each group might go on to compose an advertisement in which the argument for the product contains each of these fallacies.

ANSWERS

EXERCISE 9.2 Analyzing advertisements (p. 197)

Individual response.

EXERCISE 9.3 Identifying and revising fallacies (p. 198)

Possible answers

1. Begged question, argument ad populum, and false analogy.

   A revision: The fact that individuals in the United Stated cannot legally sell nuclear technology to nonnuclear nations, which the government can, points up a disturbing limit on individual rights.

2. Sweeping generalization and begged question.

A revision: A successful marriage demands a degree of maturity.

3. Hasty generalization and non sequitur.

   A revision: Students' persistent complaints about the unfairness of the grading system should be investigated.

4. Either/or fallacy and hasty generalization.

   A revision: People watch television for many reasons, but some watch because they are too lazy to talk or read or because they want mindless escape from their lives.

5. Reductive fallacy and begged question.

   A revision: Racial tension may occur when people with different backgrounds live side by side.

EXERCISE 9.4 Identifying fallacies in arguments (p. 198)

Possible answers

Though free of the most egregious appeals, the Sale essay and the advertisement both demonstrate several basic fallacies. Most notably:

Kirkpatrick Sale essay

Either/or: Either we achieve a *drastic overhaul of our civilization* or the environment will be destroyed (paragraph 3).

Begged question: The individualistic approach to environmental problems does not *challenge the belief in technofix or write-your-Congressperson solutions* [Do these not work?] or achieve an essential, fundamental change in thinking [Is the change essential?] (5).

False analogy: The analogy between recycling centers and hospitals (5) implies that a preventive approach (*ecological criteria* for packaging and production; preventive medicine) would eliminate the need for the institution. This isn't true of hospitals (people would still get sick), so how is it true of recycling centers?

Oil corporation advertisement

Begged question: The fact is, oil industry offshore drilling operations cause less pollution than other sources of pollution (4). [But how much pollution do the drilling operations cause?]

Either/or: Either we move everyone to one place or we continue to use a disproportionate amount of the world's energy (7).

Either/or: Either we find more energy or the economy will not grow; either we find more energy or we will have to increase imports (2).

Begged question: Despite good conservation efforts, we still need petroleum exploration (12). [But why can't conservation be improved to eliminate the need for risky exploration?]

EXERCISE 9.5 Identifying fallacies online (p. 198)

Individual response.

RESOURCES AND IDEAS

Moore, Vincent. "Using Role Playing in Argument Papers to Deconstruct Stereotypes." *Teaching English in the Two-Year College* 22 (1995): 190–96. Moore argues for the efficacy of role-playing to help students gain flexibility in seeing multiple perspectives when developing an argument.

Rapkins, Angela A. "The Uses of Logic in the College Freshman English Curriculum." *Activities to Promote Critical Thinking.* Ed. Jeff Golub. Urbana: NCTE, 1986. 130–35. Rapkins suggests emphasizing logic in all the papers in a course and describes in detail the use of ads in a final argumentation unit, a strategy that expands awareness of the logical fallacies students have been developing throughout the course.

CHAPTER 10

Writing an Argument

CHAPTER HIGHLIGHTS

This chapter introduces students to the process of conceiving their own written arguments. Discussions of subject, thesis, purpose, and audience are considered before the chapter turns to the concepts of inductive and deductive argumentation. As they construct their own arguments, students will consider their own use of evidence, the most effective kinds of appeals to readers, how to deal with opposing views, how to organize their arguments, and how to revise their arguments. A helpful checklist for revising an argument appears on p. 213. The chapter concludes with an annotated sample argument written by a student.

The Internet can be particularly useful for the novice argument-builder. A series of computer exercises in this chapter's annotations asks students to work with Internet discussion list postings to evaluate subjects, theses, purposes, and audience. You could create an extended project in which students mine an Internet discussion list for the elements of argument and then construct one of their own.

MEDIA RESOURCES FOR CHAPTER 10

mycomplab™ Please visit MyCompLab at *www.mycomplab.com* for more on the writing process.

http://www.ablongman.com/littlebrown ▶ See page 73 of this manual for companion Web site content description.

10a Finding a subject

INSTRUCTOR RESOURCE

The following Presentation Aid is available for download on this book's companion Web site at *http://www.ablongman.com/littlebrown*.

PRESENTATION AID 10.1: Tests for an argument subject (p. 199)

CLASSROOM IDEAS

Listing priorities and values Ask groups of students first to list the five (or ten) issues they consider most worth arguing about and then to record their different opinions about the top two or three.

Restricted lists Ask students to prepare lists as above, but to restrict the list to a specific area, such as sports, the economy, or drugs. In so doing, you will create a situation in which students will need to go beyond obvious issues and opinions to complete their lists.

COLLABORATIVE LEARNING The art of lampoon In the course of your work on what makes a good topic for argument, you might ask your students to come up with a subject that is ridiculous but nonetheless is technically possible to argue. (Give them a copy of Jonathan Swift's "A Modest Proposal" as an example). Ask them to work in partners to write an argument based upon their subject and then to read it aloud to the class. The results can be hilarious.

COMPUTER ACTIVITY Internet debates Internet discussion lists are prime sites for argumentation, both the elegant and the sophomoric. Have your students explore some hotly debated topics on their favorite discussion lists and compile a list of the best and worst subjects for argument.

COLLABORATIVE LEARNING Exercise 10.1 Have students work on Exercise 10.1 in groups and then share their group's findings with the rest of the class.

ANSWERS

EXERCISE 10.1 Finding a subject for argument (p. 200)

Possible answers

Topics that are not appropriate for argument:

  2. A matter of facts, and few people would disagree.
  4. A matter of facts, and few people would disagree.
  8. A matter of personal preference.
  9. A matter of facts.
  10. A matter of personal belief.

10b Conceiving a thesis statement

CLASSROOM IDEAS

COMPUTER ACTIVITY Internet theses As a follow-up to the "Internet debates" exercise suggested in 10a (see above), ask your students to find examples of good thesis statements among the Internet discussion-list debates they have been shadowing.

COMPUTER ACTIVITY Thesis posting If you are working in a networked classroom, you might post the list of potential subjects to your web site and ask students to add thesis statements with analyses of purpose and audience.

COLLABORATIVE LEARNING Televised arguments Ask small groups of students to gather outside of class to watch C-Span, which airs many varieties of political and academic speeches. Ask them to see if they can agree on what the thesis statement is for each speech they watch, and keep a class collection of those thesis statements.

COLLABORATIVE LEARNING Exercise 10.2 For Exercise 10.2 encourage groups to come up with more than one possible thesis for each appropriate topic, then have each group present their most compelling thesis statements.

ANSWERS

EXERCISE 10.2 Conceiving a thesis statement (p. 201)

Possible answers

Thesis statements for appropriate topics in Exercise 10.1:

1. An athletic scholarship should be what the term implies: an award to one who is both a superior athlete and a superior scholar.
3. Although censoring the Web sites of hate groups might offer some protection to persecuted groups or individuals, such censorship would be far too costly to free speech.
5. Until the city can construct private housing for the homeless, it must do more to make public shelters safe and clean.
6. Billboards help to destabilize urban neighborhoods by creating the impression that the neighborhoods are mere roadways.
7. Humane testing methods are adequate enough that cosmetics companies do not have to abuse animals in testing.

10c Analyzing your purpose and your audience

ANSWERS

EXERCISE 10.3 Analyzing purpose and audience (p. 202)

Individual response.

10d Using reason

INSTRUCTOR RESOURCES

The following Presentation Aids are available for download on this book's companion Web site at *http://www.ablongman.com/littlebrown*.

PRESENTATION AID 10.2: Figure 10.1 (p. 203)

PRESENTATION AID 10.3: Figure 10.2 (p. 204)

CLASSROOM IDEAS

COLLABORATIVE LEARNING Audience appeals Have the class select two or three broad subjects; then, in small groups, have them decide what more focused purposes they could have in writing about such subjects and what evidence and appeals they would choose in writing for different audiences. If the topic is "censorship," for instance, you might have groups arguing for or against certain kinds of censorship for audiences ranging from the library trustees to the city council to the manager at a local videotape rental store.

COMPUTER ACTIVITY Internet purposes and audiences As a follow-up to the "Internet debates" and "Internet theses" exercises suggested for 10a and 10b, ask your students to describe the purpose and intended audience of each thesis statement they collect from the Internet discussion groups they have been shadowing.

COLLABORATIVE LEARNING Checking the logic Ask students to work in pairs to evaluate each other's use of logic in an assigned essay. Each partner can read the other's paper and use the "Tests for inductive and deductive reasoning" list (p. 205) to evaluate the paper's use of logic. For inductive reasoning, the reader can list the evidence, assumption, and claim. For deductive reasoning, the reader can construct a syllogism. After readers have had a chance to evaluate the logic, they can share their findings with their partner, the writer.

COMPUTER ACTIVITY Computer templates and outline tools Outlining tools of word-processing programs can help students work through inductive or deductive schema. Students can make templates in their word-processing programs, with categories for evidence, assumptions, and assertions (induction) and for premises and conclusions (deduction). Then they can use the templates to plug in data to build specific logical arguments.

COMPUTER ACTIVITY Internet logic As a follow-up to the "Internet debates," "Internet theses," and "Internet purposes and audiences" exercises suggested for 10a, 10b, and 10c, ask your students to find good examples of inductive and deductive reasoning in the Internet discussion groups they have been shadowing.

COLLABORATIVE LEARNING Exercises 10.4 and 10.5 Students can work effectively together on Exercises 4 and 5. To foster a more active discussion of likely inferences and deductions, ask each group to note places where individuals disagree and to pose those cases to the class as a whole.

ANSWERS

EXERCISE 10.4 Reasoning inductively (p. 206)

The unreasonable generalizations from the given evidence are statements 2 (can't be inferred from the facts), 3 (contradicted by the facts), and 5 (can't be inferred from the facts).

EXERCISE 10.5 Reasoning deductively (pp. 206–07)

Possible answers

1. **Premise:** Anyone who has opposed pollution controls may continue to do so.
   Premise: The mayor has opposed pollution controls.
   Conclusion: The mayor may continue to do so.
   The statement is valid and true.

2. **Premise:** Corporate Web sites are sponsored by for-profit entities.
   Premise: Information from for-profit entities is unreliable.
   Conclusion: Information on corporate Web sites is unreliable.
   The statement is untrue because the second premise is untrue.

3. **Premise:** Many good artists trained at Parsons.
   Premise: Schroeder trained at Parsons.
   Conclusion: Schroeder is a good artist.
   The statement is invalid because the first premise does not necessarily apply to the second.

4. **Premise:** Those who use their resources to help others deserve our particular appreciation.
   Premise: Some wealthy athletes use their resources to help others.
   Conclusion: Some wealthy athletes deserve our particular appreciation.
   The statement is valid and, if the first premise is accepted, true.

5. **Premise:** Any employer who has hired only one woman is sexist.
   Premise: Jimson is an employer who has hired only one woman.
   Conclusion: Jimson is sexist.
   The statement is untrue because the first premise is not true: there may be other reasons besides sexism for hiring only one woman.

RESOURCES AND IDEAS

Kasterly, James L. "From Formalism to Inquiry: A Model of Argument in *Antigone.*" *College English* 62 (1999): 222–41. Kasterly takes an anti-formalist (non-Toulminian) approach to argument, presenting a reading of *Antigone* as a case in point.

Kneupper, Charles W. "Teaching Argument: An Introduction to the Toulmin Model." *College Composition and Communication* 29 (1978): 237–41. Kneupper provides a brief review of Stephen Toulmin's simplified, practical logic, a system based primarily on three elements: data, claim, and warrant.

Lamb, Catherine E. "Beyond Argument in Feminist Composition." *College Composition and Communication* 42 (1991): 11–24. Lamb finds that the oral discourse modes of negotiation and mediation can be effectively used in conceiving the purpose and audience of a written argument. She says, "Argument still has a place, although now as a means, not an end. The end—a resolution of conflict that is fair to both sides—is possible even in the one-sidedness of written communication."

10e Using evidence

CLASSROOM IDEAS

COMPUTER ACTIVITY Internet evidence As a follow-up to the "Internet debates," "Internet theses," "Internet purposes and audiences," and "Internet logic" exercises suggested for 10a, 10b, 10c, and 10d, ask your students

to find examples of good and poor use of evidence in the Internet discussion groups they have been shadowing.

COLLABORATIVE LEARNING Exercise 10.6 After students have drafted an argument as suggested in Exercise 10.6, ask them to work in groups to help one another to test and to develop the evidence for each argument further. Then ask each student to revise his or her argument using the group's comments.

ANSWERS

EXERCISE 10.6 Using reasoning and evidence in your argument (p. 208)

Individual response.

RESOURCES AND IDEAS

Corrigan, Dagmar Stuehrk, and Chidsey Dickson. "Ezines and Freshman Composition." *Kairos* (Summer 2002) <http://english.ttu.edu/kairos7 .2binderhtml?sectiontwo/corrigan/description.html>. The authors show how course content is enriched with theadditions of assignments that ask students to contribute to electronic magazines.

Gage, John T. "Teaching the Enthymeme: Invention and Arrangement" *Rhetoric Review* 2 (1983): 38–50. Gage argues that students can gain awareness and control over the context, logic, and structure of their arguments by stating their reasoning in enthymemic fashion, as a sentence containing an assertion and a because clause.

Geisler, Cheryl, et al. "Itext: Future Directions for Research on the Relationship Between Information Technology and Writing." *Journal of Business and Technological Communication* 15.3 (2001): 269–309. The authors argue that texts such as e-mail are altering the nature of written communication and recommend a variety of ways to monitor such changes and to assess their social impact.

George, Diana. "From Analysis to Design: Visual Communication in the Teaching of Writing." *College Composition and Communication* 54 (September 2002): 11–39. In this review of current theory and research and the pedagogical history of visual literacy, George provides an excellent introduction for writing teachers who want to include instruction in visual literacy in curricula.

Porter, Jeffery. "The Reasonable Reader: Knowledge and Inquiry in Freshman English." *College English* 49 (1987): 332–44. Porter argues that enthymemes organize readers' "participation in the text."

10f Reaching your readers

CLASSROOM IDEAS

COLLABORATIVE LEARNING Collecting appeals Ask students to read, on their own, a relatively long and complex argumentative essay from a reader or a magazine of political or social opinion. In class, assign students to groups and ask each group (1) to identify purely logical appeals, purely emotional appeals, and mixed appeals in the essay and (2) to describe, if they can, the effect of each appeal on average readers (like the members of the group).

COMPUTER ACTIVITY Polling the online audience The Web offers access to audiences beyond the classroom community, which can help students learn how to assess the needs of audiences as they build arguments. Students whose personal Web sites include arguments or claims can solicit responses from their audiences which will help them evaluate the effectiveness of their audience appeals. They can survey visitors to their Web site to find out whether they have targeted their audience accurately and to find out how visitors respond to the appeals made on the Web site. Composing the survey is the first component of this exercise; collecting and interpreting the information is the second; revising the Web site to use more effective appeals is the third.

COMPUTER ACTIVITY Internet appeals As a follow-up to the "Internet debates," "Internet theses," "Internet purposes and audiences," "Internet logic," and "Internet evidence" exercises suggested for 10a, 10b, 10c, 10d, and 10e, ask your students to find examples of rational and emotional appeals in the Internet discussion groups they have been shadowing.

Anticipating opposition A good strategy for teaching students to anticipate opposition is to have them generate "yes, but" lists. Ask them to list all the strong points supporting their argument, then think of a counterargument for each point. (Sometimes they will be able to overcome these counterarguments; at other times they may have to concede the point.) For instance, if their thesis is "Raising the tuition at Golden College will reduce enrollment," they might produce a "yes, but" list like this:

Supporting point	"Yes, but" objection
Tuition rose 3 percent last year, and enrollment dropped by 2 percent.	Yes, but the recession and the lack of financial aid may also have contributed to lower enrollment.
There are cheaper schools in area.	Yes, but Golden College is rated in the top ten of small schools in the area.
Students can't afford higher tuition costs.	Yes, but they seem to afford all the clothes, cars, and CDs they want to buy. Where are their priorities?

COLLABORATIVE LEARNING Devil's advocate Group work is particularly useful in helping students to anticipate opposition to an argument. Ask the groups to play devil's advocate in order to test each writer's reasoning processes and use of evidence. To ensure that this is a supportive experience, remind groups to frame their questions about each writer's argument as a series of productive revision suggestions.

COLLABORATIVE LEARNING Exercise 10.7 Ask students to work in small groups to identify the emotional, rational, and ethical appeals of the passages in Exercise 10.7 and then to identify similar grounds for appeal in their own arguments (as specified in Exercise 10.8).

ANSWERS

EXERCISE 10.7 Identifying appeals (p. 211)

Possible answers
1. Primarily emotional appeal. Ethical appeal: knowledgeable, concerned, reasonable (at least in the two uses of *may*), slightly sarcastic (*most essential of skills*).
2. Primarily rational appeal. Ethical appeal: knowledgeable, reasonable.
3. Primarily rational appeal. Ethical appeal: knowledgeable, fair, willing to acknowledge opposing views.
4. Primarily emotional appeal. Ethical appeal: sympathetic toward animals (but perhaps unfair to *so-called scientists*).
5. Primarily rational appeal. Ethical appeal: knowledgeable, fair, willing to acknowledge opposing views.

EXERCISE 10.8 Reaching your reader (p. 211)

Individual response.

RESOURCES AND IDEAS

Winder, Barbara E. "The Delineation of Values in Persuasive Writing." *College Composition and Communication* 29 (1978): 55–58. Winder asks writers to spell out both sides of an argument to make them sensitive to their own values and those of their readers.

10g Organizing your argument

INSTRUCTOR RESOURCE

The following Presentation Aid is available for download on this book's companion Web site at *http://www.ablongman.com/littlebrown*.

PRESENTATION AID 10.4: Organizing an argument's body and response to opposing views (p. 212)

CLASSROOM IDEAS

COLLABORATIVE LEARNING Organizing together Many students have difficulty organizing their papers. Allow them to work in pairs on organizing each of their papers in turn. Ask them to pay special attention to anticipating opposing views.

COMPUTER ACTIVITY Electronic organizing tools Students who have access to computers can use the Outlining function of their word-processing software to organize the introduction, body, and conclusion of their papers, to outline a traditional or problem-solution scheme, and to cut and paste supporting claims and evidence to find the optimum arrangement.

ANSWERS

EXERCISE 10.9 Organizing your argument (p. 213)
Individual response.

10h Revising your argument

INSTRUCTOR RESOURCE

The following Presentation Aid is available for download on this book's companion Web site at *http://www.ablongman.com/littlebrown*.

PRESENTATION AID 10.5: Checklist for revising an argument (p. 212)

CLASSROOM IDEAS

Peer outlining Making an outline of a draft of a paper is a challenging to do, but a very powerful tool for revision. To make it easier for students, have them work with a partner to construct an outline of the draft. Then, the writer can revise the outline before writing the next draft.

COMPUTER ACTIVITY Revision checklist Revision tools like the "Checklist for revising an argument" (p. 212) can be kept on the computer for easy access during the revision process.

COLLABORATIVE LEARNING Exercise 10.11 Students can work effectively together using the questions about Holbrook's in Exercise 10.11 to critique each other's final arguments. If students have worked continuously with the same group throughout the process of developing their arguments, you might rearrange the groups for this exercise so that each writer experiences a fresh set of responses to his or her argument.

ANSWERS

EXERCISE 10.10 Writing and revising your argument (p. 214)
Individual response.

10i Examining a sample argument

MODELS OF STUDENT WRITING

Craig Holbrook's essay "TV Can Be Good for You" is a strong example of student writing featuring an introductory hook, a tight structure (with topic sentence claims at the ends of some paragraphs), extensive research, and effective appeals to reason. It may serve as a model of writing as engagement in reasoned debate, especially for students whose own writing overuses emotional appeals. It may also serve as a model of writing that goes against the grain of received wisdom, and does so persuasively.

To help your students formulate their own responses to the paper (especially in Exercise 10.11, questions 6 and 7), you might begin with classroom discussion about television's effects on viewers. Students generally love to talk about television, although they may have an emotional stake in believing that their own watching habits are not harmful. You might compile anecdotal data about class members, and then discuss whether that evidence seems to confirm or refute Holbrook's findings. On the basis of this discussion, you might also introduce the concept of evidence gathered in controlled studies versus anecdotal evidence.

ANSWERS

EXERCISE 10.11 Critically reading an argument (p. 218)

1. *Claims* related to the thesis statement: the last sentences of paragraphs 3, 5, and 7; the first and last sentences of paragraph 8; and the conclusion. *Evidence*: studies cited in paragraphs 2, 3, 4, 5, 7, and 9; evidence gathered by the author in paragraphs 4 (comedy programming) and 6 (educational programming).
2. *Appeals to reason:* mainly, the use of studies as evidence (pars. 2, 3, 4 5, 7), the tempered claim (pars. 8, 9), and the deductive argument (replacement voices can be helpful; television provides replacement voices; therefore, television can be helpful). *Appeals to emotion:* sympathy for the lonely (par. 2), appreciation of children (par. 6). The argument is mainly rational.
3. The ethical appeal is that of a fair-minded, reasonable person.
4. *Appeals made by the illustrations:* Responses about the effectiveness of the illustrations will vary. Some of the appeals:
   Fig. 1 backs up the claim that TV can ease loneliness (rational appeal), shows the man enjoying himself (emotional appeal), and conveys the writer's competence in choosing an appropriate image (ethical appeal).
   Fig. 2 strengthens the claim that laughter is healthful with information from a reliable source (rational appeal), arouses curiosity with an unusual combination of photograph and diagram (emotional appeal), and proves the writer trustworthy and fair with the caption's acknowledgement that the source does not merit TV watching (ethical appeal).
   Fig. 3 supports the claim that TV can educate children by showing children with a character from a respected educational program (rational appeal), depicts a familiar, comfortable character, and cute, smiling children (emotional appeal), and shows sensitivity to readers' probable knowledge as well as seriousness.
5. The objections are raised and answered in paragraph 8: too much TV is harmful, and replacement voices are not enough. Both objections are accepted as valid.
6. Individual response.
7. Individual response.

CHAPTER 11

Reading and Using Visual Arguments

CHAPTER HIGHLIGHTS

This chapter is new to the tenth edition of *The Little, Brown Handbook*. Its coverage of visual argument should be very timely for students who are bombarded with visual images on television, in the print media, and online. The first half of the chapter teaches students how to read images for their underlying claims; how to evaluate the kinds of evidence used by a visual argument; how to identify the underlying assumptions upon which the image's claims are based; and how to recognize fallacies in visual arguments.

The chapter's second half focuses on how to use visual arguments to optimum effect. Students are shown how to use images, how to use them as evidence, and how to evaluate their appeal to readers. Throughout the chapter, examples of visual arguments are provided as concrete illustrations of the concept presented in each section.

MEDIA RESOURCES FOR CHAPTER 11

mycomplab Please visit MyCompLab at *www.mycomplab.com* for more on the writing process.

http://www.ablongman.com/littlebrown ▶ See page 73 of this manual for companion Web site content description.

11a Reading visual arguments critically

CLASSROOM IDEAS

Image captioning Collect a group of magazine ads that make claims visually. Cover the captions or text of each image so only the image is visible. Then have your students try to guess what the caption is by looking at the image alone. This exercise might produce hilarious results, and you can use it to help students understand how text and picture work together.

Get more milk The celebrities of milk ads are so abundant that students may know of many additional examples. Ask them to bring those in and compare their claims to that of the Oscar de la Hoya example provided in this section. Most will be similar, but subtle differences in claims may be enlightening to students. They can also find many of the ads at *whymilk.com/celebrity_archive.htm.*

Fashion design examples If your students are interested in fashion, you could ask them to bring in flyers or catalogs from their favorite designers or stores. Photographic examples of clothing can be compared from designer to designer or store to store.

Pseudo-experts Students are very savvy about advertising claims. Ask them to locate an image using an expert opinion that they find suspect, and to explain to the rest of the class why they think the "expert" may not be credible.

COMPUTER ACTIVITY Gallery of appeals Ask students to look around on the Web and collect visual appeals that reinforce readers' values. They can provide links to the Web site and a brief analysis on your class Web site of the values to which the images appeal.

COLLABORATIVE LEARNING Riis's images Jacob Riis, the famous photo-journalist, provides an excellent example of using visual images to advance an argument in his classic text *How the Other Half Lives* (New York: Charles Scribner's Sons, 1890). Have students work together to evaluate selected images and the accompanying data and text.

COLLABORATIVE LEARNING Riis's images II As a follow-up to the previous exercise, have student groups evaluate Riis's assumptions about who his readers are, what they know about his subject, and how readily they will be persuaded by the images he presents.

COMPUTER ACTIVITY The Dinner party Locate images from artist Judy Chicago's famous installation *The Dinner Party*, and show them to students. Chicago's triangular table, with place settings for famous women from history, is an excellent example of visual art used for persuasion and social commentary. Lead a class discussion about why Chicago's audience was, how sympathetic they were likely to be to her claims, and what kinds of images appealed to them. You can also talk about the way she used an unfamiliar format to provoke interest and response from her viewers.

Economic trends Economists often use graphs or charts showing changes in tax spending over time, budget deficit projections, cost of living changes over time, or other financial trends affecting the populace. However, some images may be misleading. If your course focuses one economics, you may want to spend some time looking at competing visual evidence from different economic think tanks (liberal and conservative).

Contemporary propaganda The propaganda sources listed in Exercise 11.2 are for World War II, but propaganda has arguably been used by the United States in more recent wars (Vietnam, Persian Gulf, Iraq). The validity of these wars and the US role in them are matters highly contested by the American public. Students may hold strong opinions that impair their ability to evaluate US documents about these wars or to entertain the notion that the US might have engaged in propaganda activities. However, if your students are able to handle such controversial issues, it could be productive to bring in some examples of government-produced images about these wars.

ANSWERS

EXERCISE 11.1 Reading a visual argument critically (p. 224)

Possible answers

1. The audience seems to be people who are serving or might serve as Big Brothers or Big Sisters (primarily the latter since the people depicted are female). The happiness and togetherness of the subjects would reinforce the commitment of current volunteers and invite the participation of others.
2. The organization fosters pairings of adults and children and emphasizes togetherness and having fun.
3. The main claim is in the large text: "Time spent with you is like a day on the beach." In other words, the relationship of volunteer and child is carefree, invigorating, and fun.
4. The photograph provides the evidence for the claim: the beach is inviting, the subjects are happy, lively, and affectionate.
5. Some assumptions: Happy, affectionate relationships are good for adults and children. The smiling subjects are in fact a volunteer and her "little sister." A day at the beach is an appealing prospect and a desirable parallel for a relationship.
6. The most noticeable elements of the image are subjects' feet, the subjects' smiles and windblown hair, and the bright background, all conveying beach fun. The foregrounded bare feet, especially, emphasize freedom and playfulness. The large type across the woman's feet further focuses attention on them.
7. Individual response.

EXERCISE 11.2 Identifying fallacies in visual arguments (p. 225)

Individual response.

11b Using visual arguments effectively

CLASSROOM IDEAS

Over-reliance upon the visual Caution your students that a visual image is not usually an adequate substitute for verbal argument, and that they should be careful not to rely upon images to convey what they find difficult to say in words. Images should always be tied closely into the argument with captioning or prose.

COLLABORATIVE LEARNING Testing images on peers Peer groups can function as test audiences for student authors using images. Have each student bring to class an image he or she plans to use in a paper and show the image to their peer group (which will already have read their paper draft). The peer group can help to evaluate the usefulness of the image and how the author has linked it to the paper's argument.

Searching for visuals Some search engines, such as *Google*, allow users to limit a search to images only, which can help students search more efficiently.

COLLABORATIVE LEARNING Testing appeal Divide students into small groups, and give each group a visual image to view. Ask them to make a list of feelings or ideas evoked by the image. Each group can then use its list to help assess the rational, emotional, and/or ethical appeal of the images.

COLLABORATIVE LEARNING Contest of images After students have completed Exercise 11.3, have each group find or create an image to go with each of the five argument subjects. Hold a class contest to choose the best image for each argument subject.

COMPUTER ACTIVITY Exercise 11.4 As a follow-up to Exercise 11.4, ask students to conduct a Web search to find additional images to support the argument about cosmetic procedures.

COLLABORATIVE LEARNING Daily shows Television comedians like Jon Stewart often use visual images in a deliberately bad way to expose ironies and poke fun at public images. As a follow-up to Exercise 11.6, have your class create and perform its own daily news spoof show, juxtaposing images and text for satirical effect.

ANSWERS

EXERCISE 11.3 Brainstorming images for a visual argument (p. 230)

Possible answers

1. Images helpful: photographs of seniors and their pets; graph relating pet care and life improvement.
2. Images somewhat helpful: photographs of people gathered in building entrances or other places were smokers congregate; emphasizing variety of people and obvious interactions.
3. Images essential: Military recruitment ads targeted to certain kinds of people.
4. Images helpful: photograph of solid-waste landfill; chart showing current and proposed volume of campus waste; diagram showing proposed recycling process.
5. Images not helpful unless data demonstrate relation of music listening and information retention.

EXERCISE 11.4 Filling gaps in a visual argument (p 230)

Additional images might include a graph showing the increase in viewers watching TV makeover shows (to complement the graph showing an increase in cosmetic procedures) and additional before and after photographs of women having makeovers on such shows (to reinforce the claim that the shows encourage a "particular beauty standard").

EXERCISE 11.5 Revising an oversimplified visual argument (p. 230)

Individual response.

EXERCISE 11.6 Creating a deliberately bad visual argument (p. 230)

Individual response.

EXERCISE 11.7 Revising an ineffective visual argument (p. 230)

Individual response.

RESOURCES AND IDEAS

Suggested Readings

Langrehr, Don. "From a Semiotic Perspective: Inference Formation and the Critical Comprehension of Television Advertising." *Reading Online* 9 (May 2003). Langrehr illustrates the difficulty students have "reading" television advertisements and offers advice on improving this dimension of visual literacy.

Sellen, Mary. "Information Literacy in the General Education: A New Requirement for the 21st Century." *Journal of General Education* 51 (2002): 115–26. Sellen suggests that there is a need for instruction in multimedia literacy because students can now incorporate visual and aural information into their texts.

Stroupe, Craig. "Visualizing English: Recognizing the Hybrid Literacy of Visual and Verbal Authorship on the Web." *College English* 62 (May 2000): 602–32. Stroupe presents a method for combining verbal and nonverbal features in students texts, made possible by the advances in visual digitality.

PART 3

Grammatical Sentences

CHAPTER 12
Understanding Sentence Grammar

CHAPTER 13
Case of Nouns and Pronouns

CHAPTER 14
Verbs

CHAPTER 15
Agreement

CHAPTER 16
Adjectives and Adverbs

Understanding Sentence Grammar

CHAPTER HIGHLIGHTS

In this chapter, students will encounter a brief descriptive grammar that can serve as a reference for explanations of basic grammatical terms and as a guide to how sentences are constructed and their major elements punctuated. The chapter builds cumulatively from the simplest sentence to increasingly complex expansions rather than compartmentalizing grammar into parts of speech and kinds of phrases, clauses, and sentences. Moreover, it treats punctuation in context, as part of the discussion of word groups and syntactic relationships that may require it.

Because of its whole sentence approach and because of the many sentence-combining and -modeling exercises it contains, this chapter can be useful for a wide range of students. Those whose writing displays fundamental problems with sentences will benefit from its clear treatment of sentence parts and structure and from the exercises that require manipulation of sentence elements. Those who have mastered basic sentence strategies will be able to develop many options for expression through sentence-combining exercises that introduce elements like verbal phrases, absolute phrases, and appositives. And all students will gain a greater understanding of punctuation when they see how it grows out of and communicates a sentence's structure and meaning.

This chapter uses almost entirely traditional terminology because such terminology, despite its weaknesses, is still the most widely used and most likely to be familiar to students and instructors. The overall description largely reflects a structural view of English grammar. It is as simple as possible while still including all the word classes and syntactic structures needed by the student to understand the twenty successive chapters on sentences and punctuation.

You may wish to emphasize or de-emphasize the chapter, depending in part on the preparation of your students and on how much you think an understanding of grammar can contribute to their writing. As may be obvious, this chapter of the handbook was prepared in the belief that a clear understanding of the essential structure of English sentences and of the uses of syntactic groups and compound structures can help many students not only to punctuate correctly but also to gain greater control of subordination and emphasis within their sentences. This process will take place only if students get a chance to put knowledge into action through exercises that ask them to manipulate and create sentences. In this regard, the sentence-combining exercises in the chapter can be coordinated with those in other chapters of the text to create a program of sentence combining designed to complement instruction in essay and paragraph writing.

MEDIA RESOURCES FOR CHAPTER 12

mycomplab Please visit MyCompLab at *www.mycomplab.com* for more on the writing process.

http://www.ablongman.com/littlebrown ▶ See page 73 of this manual for companion Web site content description.

12a Understanding the basic sentence

INSTRUCTOR RESOURCES

The following Presentation Aids are available for download on this book's companion Web site at *http://www.ablongman.com/littlebrown*.

PRESENTATION AID 12.1: The parts of speech (p. 235)

PRESENTATION AID 12.2: The five basic sentence patterns (p. 239)

CLASSROOM IDEAS

Dictation Read to your class the words in the list below (or in a similar one) and then go through the list again, giving students a minute or two to write sentences using the words in as many different roles (parts of speech) as they can. The word good, for example, can be an adjective or a noun.

well	needle
post	while
set	bit
bill	turn
that	

CULTURE ▲ LANGUAGE **Articles and languages** Students who are native speakers of such languages as Russian, Korean, and Japanese may have difficulty understanding the concept of the article, and you may need to work on this basic concept before moving on to the distinction between definite and indefinite articles. Students who are native speakers of Spanish or Italian may have difficulty hearing the difference between "this" and "these" because of the way "i" is pronounced in those languages.

Transitive and intransitive verbs Remind students that intransitive verbs *cannot* be followed by a direct object. Transitive verbs, in contrast, *must* have a direct object to complete the meaning of a sentence. Some transitive verbs can have both a direct object and an indirect object. For students who need additional practice with transitive and intransitive verbs and passive voice, Jocelyn Steer and Karen Carlisi include useful exercises in Chapters 5 and 11 of *The Advanced Grammar Book* (Boston: Heinle, 1991).

To be test Advise students that one way to determine whether a sentence fits into pattern 5 (p. 239) is to insert the words *to be* between the first noun and the following noun or adjective: *The citizens considered the earthquake to be a disaster.*

ANSWERS

EXERCISE 12.1 Identifying subjects and predicates (p. 237)

1. The leaves|fell.
   SUBJECT | PREDICATE
   Sample imitation: The kite soared.
2. October|ends soon.
   SUBJECT | PREDICATE
   Sample imitation: My class begins soon.
3. The orchard owners|made apple cider.
   SUBJECT | PREDICATE
   Sample imitation: The couple grew summer squash.
4. They|examined each apple carefully before using it.
   SUBJECT | PREDICATE
   Sample imitation: They dried each glass gingerly after washing it.
5. Over a hundred people|will buy cider at the roadside stand.
   SUBJECT | PREDICATE
   Sample imitation: Few pool owners will swim at the public beach.

EXERCISE 12.2 Identifying nouns, verbs, and pronouns (p. 237)

1. The trees died.
   N V
2. They caught a disease.
   P V   N
3. The disease was a fungus.
   N   V   N
4. It ruined a grove that was treasured.
   P V   N   P V   V
5. Our great-grandfather planted the grove in the last century.
   P   N   V   N   N

EXERCISE 12.3 Using nouns and verbs (p. 238)

Possible answers

1. Noun and verb.
   Blow out the candles and make a wish. [Noun.] The child wished for a new bicycle. [Verb.]
2. Noun and verb.
   Many people purchase ties as Father's Day presents. [Noun.] Tie the rope into a square knot. [Verb.]

3. Noun and verb.
   The <u>swing</u> hung from a large oak tree. [Noun.] Ted picked up his niece and <u>swung</u> her around and around. [Verb.]
4. Noun and verb.
   The <u>mail</u> does not come on national holidays. [Noun.] <u>Mail</u> the package to her home address. [Verb.]
5. Verb.
   He <u>spends</u> his free time doing volunteer work.
6. Noun and verb. The <u>label</u> bore a poison warning. [Noun.] The companies must <u>label</u> their products. [Verb.]
7. Noun.
   The <u>door</u> flew open by itself.
8. Noun.
   My younger sister was good <u>company</u>.
9. Noun and verb.
   The <u>whistle</u> released us from work. [Noun.] We <u>whistle</u> all the way home. [Verb.]
10. Noun and verb.
   The <u>glue</u> stuck to my hands. [Noun.] We <u>glue</u> our models together. [Verb.]

EXERCISE 12.4 Identifying sentence patterns (p. 241)

1. <u>Find</u> is transitive.

   Many people find <u>New York City</u> <u>exciting</u>.
                   DO   OC

2. <u>Flock</u> is intransitive.

   No objects or complements.

3. <u>Visit</u> is transitive.

   Often they visit <u>Times Square</u> first.
                  DO

4. <u>Are</u> is linking.

   The Square's lights are <u>astounding</u>.
                           SC

5. <u>Sell</u> is transitive.

   The flashing signs sell <u>visitors</u> <u>everything</u> from TVs to underwear.
                       IO   DO

EXERCISE 12.5 Creating sentences (p. 241)

Possible answers

1. The audience laughed.
2. The town elected Flynn mayor.
3. Pip stole the pie.
4. Josie caught the ball.
5. My uncle brought me a cake.

6. Marilou seems unhappy.
7. One candidate called the other a crook.
8. We became reckless.
9. We bought ourselves a television set.
10. No one studied.

RESOURCES AND IDEAS

Grammar instruction

Does grammar instruction help? The effectiveness of grammar instruction in improving writing and in helping students achieve correctness in their prose is still a hotly debated issue. The essays in *The Place of Grammar in Writing Instruction: Past, Present, Future,* edited by Susan Hunter and Ray Wallace, explore the various possibilities for integrating grammar into writing instruction, including Eric H. Hobson's "Taking Computer-Assisted Grammar Instruction to New Frontiers" (Portsmouth: Boynton, 1995). A recent issue of *English Journal* (85:7, Nov. 1996) is devoted to considerations surrounding the teaching of grammar. These essays range from historical overviews like Martha Kolln's "Rhetorical Grammar: A Modification Lesson" to the debates surrounding grammar instruction in Ed Vavra's "On Not Teaching Grammar" to specific discussions of how best to teach pronoun and verb usage.

Other useful works on grammar instruction include the following:

Connors, Robert, J. "The Erasure of the Sentence." *College Composition and Communication* 52 (September 2001): 96–128. Connors suggests that sentence combining and imitation of exercises, which fell out of favor after the paradigm shift in composition theory, remain useful for improving student writing.

Enos, Teresa, ed. *A Sourcebook for Basic Writing Teachers.* New York: Random, 1987. This collection of essays explores the debates over the efficacy of grammar instruction for standard and for nonstandard dialect speakers. The collection includes Sarah D'Eloia's "The Uses—and Limits—of Grammar," which suggests ways to integrate instruction in writing and grammar, including dictation, paraphrase and conversion, imitation, follow-ups to writing assignments, and exercises that ask students to "discover" a rule from examples of it in operation (373–416).

Farr, Marcia, and Harvey Daniels. *Language Diversity and Writing Instruction.* New York: ERIC Clearinghouse on Urban Education, 1986. Though the issue is clearly far from resolved, the perspective offered in this work is promising. The authors look at standard and nonstandard dialects in the context of linguistic research and provide suggestions for shaping writing instruction as a whole (including instruction in formal grammar) in ways that are likely to benefit speakers of nonstandard dialects.

Gorrell, Donna. "Controlled Composition for Basic Writers," *College Composition and Communication* 32 (1981): 308–16. Gorrell argues that students who learn to correct the grammar of their peers become more skilled in producing their own error-free sentences.

Newman, Michael. "Correctness and Its Conceptions: The Meaning of Language Form for Basic Writers." *Journal of Basic Writing* 15 (Summer 1996): 23–38. Newman discusses changing views on "correctness" and "error" since Mina Shaughnessy's pathbreaking *Errors and Expectations.*

Noguchi, Rei. R. *Grammar and the Teaching of Writing: Limits and Possibilities.* Urbana: NCTE, 1991. Noguchi has made an important contribution in helping teachers conceive of grammar instruction as a conceptual issue, and of student errors as an inseparable part of the larger concerns with meaning-making in writing instruction.

Online Writing Center of the University of Wisconsin at Madison. *http://www.wisc.edu/writing.* This site is especially helpful to students with grammar problems.

Purdue University Online Writing Lab. *http://owl.English.purdue.edu.* This site is one of our profession's most respected OWLs.

Sams, Lynn. "How to Teach Grammar, Analytical Thinking, and Writing: A Method That Works." *English Journal* 92 (January 2003): 57–65. Sams rejects instruction in prescriptive grammar and in-context grammar instruction in favor of a sequenced approach to grammar instruction designed to build students' competence gradually.

Dealing with error

Bartholomae, David. "The Study of Error." *College Composition and Communication* 31 (1980): 253–69. Bartholomae suggests that asking basic writers to read their papers aloud helps identify sources of error and can contribute to improvement in writing.

Horner, Bruce. "Discoursing Basic Writing." *College Composition and Communication* 47 (1996): 199–222. Horner discusses the larger trends in the basic writing movement since the 1970s, including changing approaches to error.

Shaughnessy, Mina P. *Errors and Expectations: A Guide for the Teacher of Basic Writing.* New York: Oxford UP, 1977. This valuable book focuses on basic writing but is also an important work for teachers of writing at all levels. It provides a detailed analysis of the causes of student errors as well as useful strategies for dealing with writing problems.

Viera, Carroll. "Helping Students to Help Themselves: An Approach to Grammar." *College Composition and Communication* 37 (1986): 94–96. Viera suggests having students analyze their own grammatical problems, do research in their handbooks, and present mini-lessons in small groups.

12b Expanding the basic sentence with single words

CLASSROOM IDEA

COLLABORATIVE LEARNING Exercise 12.8 Students can work effectively in pairs or small groups on Exercise 12.8. Encourage the groups to be imaginative about combining each sentence in more than one way, and to report back to the class on their most innovative combinations.

ANSWERS

EXERCISE 12.6 Identifying and using adjectives and adverbs (p. 243)

      ADJ   ADJ   ADJ

1. The blue water glistened in the hot afternoon sunlight.
   Sample imitation: The blue bird perched on a thin leafy branch.

     ADV   ADJ

2. Happily, children dipped their toes in the cool lake.
   Sample imitation: Quietly, we peeked into the silent cathedral.

     ADV

3. Excitedly, some of the children hopped into the water.
   Sample imitation: Impatiently, two of the children howled for the candy.

   ADJ   ADV

4. Cautious parents watched from their shady porches.
   Sample imitation: Ambitious runners train for every marathon.

               ADV   ADV

5. The children played contentedly until the day finally ended.
   Sample imitation: The babies lay still while the singer quietly crooned.

EXERCISE 12.7 Using verb forms as modifiers (p. 243)

Possible answers

1. Jack woke up craving scrambled eggs.
2. The twitching limb relaxed when the sedative took effect.
3. The treasurer's rambling speech covered more topics than I can remember.
4. The typed manuscript contained many errors.
5. Painted birds decorate the window.
6. He wanted to know the origins of the written word.
7. The man escaped the charging animal.
8. We picked the ripened fruit.
9. All the known facts contradict his theory.
10. Driven people may have hypertension.

EXERCISE 12.8 Sentence combining: Single-word modifiers (p. 244)

Possible answers

1. The turn of the twentieth century ushered in improved technology and new materials.

2. A sturdy steel skeleton made the construction of skyscrapers possible.
3. By 1913 the towering Woolworth Building, with its Gothic ornaments, stood 760 feet (55 stories).
4. At 1450 feet the Sears Tower in Chicago now doubles the relatively puny height of the Woolworth Building.
5. Skyscrapers would not have been practical if Elisha Graves Otis had not built the first safe passenger elevator in 1857.

RESOURCES AND IDEAS

Bushman, Donald, and Elizabeth Ervin. "Rhetorical Contexts of Grammar: Some Views from Writing Emphasis Instructors." *The Place of Grammar in Writing Instruction: Past, Present, Future.* Ed. Susan Hunter and Ray Wallace. Portsmouth: Boynton, 1995. 136–58. This essay explains strategies for teaching grammar in cross-disciplinary rhetorical contexts.

Hashimoto, I. "Sentence Variety: Where Theory and Practice Meet and Lose." *Composition Studies: Freshman English News* 21 (Spring 1993): 66–77. Hashimoto explores the contradictions between the common injunctions to students about sentence variation and stylistic choices of professional writers.

Herriman, Jennifer, and Aimo Seppänen. "What Is an Indirect Object?" *English Studies* 77 (1996): 484–500. This essay contrasts the consensus on defining and teaching the "direct object" with the vaguer approaches to the indirect object.

Herrington, Anne J. "Grammar Recharted: Sentence Analysis for Writing." *Writing Exercises from "Exercise Exchange."* Ed. Charles R. Duke, vol. 2. Urbana: NCTE, 1984. 276–87. Herrington suggests using a five-column chart to analyze sentence patterns and help make students aware of syntax. The five columns in the chart—Preceding Subject, Subject, Between Subject and Verb, Verb, and Following Verb—allow the system to account for both relatively simple sentences and those to which considerable information has been added. The columns can be layered as well to account for compound sentences.

12c   Expanding the basic sentence with word groups

INSTRUCTOR RESOURCES

The following Presentation Aids are available for download on this book's companion Web site at *http://www.ablongman.com/littlebrown.*

PRESENTATION AID 12.3: Tests for finite and nonfinite verbs (verbals) (p. 248)

PRESENTATION AID 12.4: Common subordinating conjunctions (p. 253)

CLASSROOM IDEAS

CULTURE LANGUAGE **Prepositions and dialects** Regional and social dialects may contribute to prepositional confusion: for instance, students may become sick *in*, *on* ,or *to* their stomachs. In parts of the Northeast, people stand *on*, not *in*, line. This issue is given full coverage in 38c.

CULTURE LANGUAGE **Prepositional problems** Prepositions follow few specific rules, and, because of idiomatic usage, often cannot be translated directly into students' first languages. As a result, even advanced ESL students find prepositions difficult. Refer students who need additional practice to Unit 6 of Len Fox, *Focus on Editing: A Grammar Workbook for Advanced Writers* (White Plains: Longman, 1992), and to Alan Meyers, *Writing with Confidence* (6th ed., New York: Longman, 2000).

Grammar terms Terminology like *gerund* is one reason why so many students are convinced that they can't "do" grammar, despite the fact that they construct sophisticated sentences every days. You may want to use a synonym like *verbal* or *–ing noun* to help students become more comfortable with this term.

COLLABORATIVE LEARNING Exercises 12.11 and 12.12 Students might work independently on Exercise 12.11, then compare answers in small groups and work together on Exercise 12.12. Encourage each group to create more than one combination for each pair of sentences in Exercise 12.12.

Expecting problems As students begin practicing use of absolute phrases, you may find more comma splices and fragments in their essays. Warn students to expect these errors, so that they can proofread for such problems more carefully. Be understanding as you evaluate student papers in which the students are practicing these strategies for the first time. If you focus on grammar faults, they may lose the incentive to take further stylistic risks.

COLLABORATIVE LEARNING Exercises 12.13 Students can work productively in pairs or small groups to combine the sentences in Exercise 12.13. The collaborative effort and consequent discussion can be useful for students who are having difficulty with absolute phrases.

COLLABORATIVE LEARNING Create your own Divide the class into groups. Ask each group to create its own set of sentence-combining exercises following the pattern of the exercises in the handbook. Then ask the groups to trade exercises, work on them, and return them to the authors with both answers and constructive feedback.

CULTURE LANGUAGE **Clause connectors** ESL students may try unsuccessfully to use ellipsis in writing. Remind students that generally, in formal writing, clause connectors such as *that* and the relative pronouns *that*, *which*, and *whom* are not omitted. Students *will not* go wrong if they keep the clause connectors in their writing, but they *may* be wrong if they omit them.

COLLABORATIVE LEARNING Exercises 12.14 and 12.15 Exercises 12.14 and 12.15 work well as collaborative projects. In particular, students with varying grammatical skills have the opportunity to discuss the parts of speech and their relative functions.

COLLABORATIVE LEARNING Expecting problems As students begin using appositives, you may find more comma splices and fragments in their essays. Warn students to expect these errors, so that they will proofread more carefully. Be understanding as you evaluate student papers in which the students are practicing these strategies for the first time. If you focus on grammar faults, they may lose the incentive to take stylistic risks.

ANSWERS

EXERCISE 12.9 Identifying prepositional phrases (p. 247)

On July 3, 1863 [ADVERB], at Gettysburg, Pennsylvania [ADVERB], Robert E. Lee gambled unsuccessfully for a Confederate victory [ADVERB] in the American Civil War [ADJECTIVE]. Called Pickett's Charge, the battle was one of the most disastrous conflicts [ADJECTIVE] of the war [ADJECTIVE]. Confederate and Union forces faced each other on parallel ridges [ADVERB] separated by almost a mile [ADVERB] of open fields [ADJECTIVE]. After an artillery bombardment [ADVERB] of the Union position [ADJECTIVE], about 12,000 Confederate infantry marched toward the Union ridge [ADVERB].

The Union guns had been silent but suddenly roared, mowing the approaching Confederates. Within an hour [ADVERB], perhaps half of the Confederate [ADJECTIVE] soldiers lay wounded or dead.

EXERCISE 12.10 Sentence combining: Prepositional phrases (p. 247)

Possible answers

1. The slow loris of Southeast Asia protects itself well with a poisonous chemical.
2. To frighten predators, the loris exudes the chemical from a gland on its upper arm.
3. Unlike a skunk's spray, the loris's chemical is highly toxic even in small quantities.
4. A tiny dose in the mouth can send a human into shock.
5. Predators probably can sense the toxin at a distance with their nasal organs.

EXERCISE 12.11 Identifying verbals and verbal phrases (p. 250)

1. Written in 1850 by Nathaniel Hawthorne [ADJ], *The Scarlet Letter* tells the story of Hester Prynne.
2. Shunned by the community [ADJ], Hester endures her loneliness.

ADV
3. Hester is humble enough to withstand her Puritan neighbors' cutting remarks.

ADJ   N
4. Despite the cruel treatment, the determined young woman refuses to leave her home.

N
5. By living a life of patience and unselfishness, Hester eventually becomes the community's angel.

EXERCISE 12.12 Sentence combining: Verbals and verbal phrases (p. 251)

Possible answers

1. Air pollution is a health problem affecting millions of Americans.
2. Polluted mainly by industries and automobiles, the air contains toxic chemicals.
3. Environmentalists pressure politicians to pass stricter laws.
4. Wavering politicians are not necessarily against environmentalism.
5. The problems are too complex to be solved easily.

EXERCISE 12.13 Sentence combining: Absolute phrases (p. 252)

Possible answers

1. Her face beaming, Geraldine Ferraro enjoyed the crowd's cheers after her nomination for Vice President.
2. A vacancy having occurred, Sandra Day O'Connor was appointed the first female Supreme Court justice.
3. Her appointment confirmed, Condoleezza Rice became the first female national security advisor.
4. The midterm elections over, Nancy Pelosi was elected the first female minority leader of the House of Representatives.
5. The election won, Elizabeth Dole was a US senator from North Carolina.

EXERCISE 12.14 Identifying subordinate clauses (p. 256)

ADJ
1. Scientists who want to catch the slightest signals from space use extremely sensitive receivers.

ADV
2. Even though they have had to fight for funding, these scientists have persisted in their research.

ADJ
3. The research is called SETI, which stands for Search for Extraterrestrial Intelligence.

N (SUBJECT COMPLEMENT)
4. The theory is that intelligent beings in space are trying to get in touch with us.

N (DIRECT OBJECT)
5. The challenge is to guess what frequency these beings would use to send signals.

EXERCISE 12.15 Sentence combining: Subordinate clauses (p. 256)

Possible answers

1. Moviegoers expect that movie sequels should be as exciting as the original films.
2. Although a few sequels are good films, most are poor imitations of the originals.
3. Whenever a sequel to a blockbuster film arrives in the theater, crowds quickly line up to see it.
4. Viewers pay to see the same villains and heroes whom they remember fondly.
5. Afterward, viewers often grumble about filmmakers who rehash tired plots and characters.

EXERCISE 12.16 Sentence combining: Appositives (p. 258)

Possible answers

1. Some people, geniuses from birth, perform amazing feats when they are very young.
2. John Stuart Mill, a British philosopher, had written a history of Rome by age seven.
3. Paul Klee and Gustav Mahler, two great artists, began their work at age four.
4. Mahler, a Bohemian composer of intensely emotional works, was also the child of a brutal father.
5. As a child the Swiss painter Paul Klee was frightened by his own drawings of devils.

RESOURCES AND IDEAS

Sentence combining: Background and suggestions

Many of the exercises in this chapter can be used as the basis for a sequence of sentence-combining activities. The appropriate exercises are 12.8, 12.10, 12.12, 12.13, 12.15, 12.16, 12.17, 12.21. Exercises in other chapters that can be part of a sentence-combining sequence are listed in the discussion "A Sequence for Sentence Combining" in the chapter "Using *The Little, Brown Handbook*," pages 24–25 of this manual. Much has been written about sentence combining over the past two decades. The twenty-three essays in *Sentence Combining: A Rhetorical Perspective*, ed. Donald A. Daiker, Andrew Kerek, and Max Morenberg (Carbondale: Southern Illinois UP, 1985) provide excellent perspectives on the strengths and weaknesses of sentence combining as a way of improving the quality of writing and of developing an understanding of language and style.

The following articles are also useful resources:

Daiker, Donald, Andrew Kerek, and Max Morenberg. "Sentence-Combining and Syntactic Maturity in Freshman English." *College Composition and Communication* 29 (1978): 36–41. The authors discuss the results of an experiment demonstrating the effectiveness of sentence combining over fifteen weeks of intensive instruction.

Johnson, Karen E. "Cognitive Strategies and Second Language Writers: A Re-evaluation of Sentence Combining." *Journal of Second Language Writing* 1 (1992): 61–75. This essay reviews debates over the effectiveness of sentence combining in the context of ESL writers.

Larsen, Richard B. "Sentence Patterning." *College Composition and Communication* 37 (1986): 103–04. Larsen describes a sequence in which students are introduced to a variety of sentence patterns and then asked to use the patterns in their writing, including paragraph-length compositions.

Solomon, Martha. "Teaching the Nominative Absolute." *College Composition and Communication* 26 (1975): 356–61. Solomon offers advice on analyzing and teaching the absolute.

12d Compounding words, phrases, and clauses

CLASSROOM IDEAS

Using readings Students can analyze passages from any essay in a reader (or some other source), looking for verbal phrases, passive sentences, compound and complex sentences, or any other features that you feel contribute to the effect of the essay and should be part of the students' prose style.

COLLABORATIVE LEARNING Redo the readings Using the passages from the "Using readings" activity above (or other passages), ask students to work together to transform each occurrence of a structure—verbal phrases or compound sentences, and so on—into alternate structures of their choice without changing the meaning of the passage. Then have students comment on how the changes affect the passage, if at all. This activity is particularly well suited for collaborative work.

Grammar terms Terminology like *conjunctive adverb* is another reason that many students are convinced they can't "do" grammar, despite the fact that they construct sophisticated sentences every day. You may want to use a synonym like *movable adverb* or *floating adverb* to help students become more comfortable with this term.

COLLABORATIVE LEARNING Exercise 12.17 Students can work effectively in groups on Exercise 12.17. Have each group try the effect of different conjunctive adverbs and coordinating and correlative conjunctions from the lists on pages 259–61 and discuss the effect that each change has on the meaning of the sentence.

EXERCISE 12.17 Sentence combining: Compound constructions (p. 262)

Possible answers

1. All too often people assume that old age is not a productive time; however, many people in their nineties have had great achievements.
2. In his nineties the philosopher Bertrand Russell spoke vigorously for both international peace and nuclear disarmament.
3. Grandma Moses did not retire to an easy chair; instead, she began painting at age seventy-six and was still going at one hundred.
4. The British general George Higginson and the British archaeologist Margaret Murray published their memoirs after they were ninety.
5. The architect Frank Lloyd Wright designed his first building at age twenty and his last at age ninety.

12e Changing the usual word order

CLASSROOM IDEA

CULTURE LANGUAGE Expletives Remind students that because English is a subject-verb-object language, something must fill the subject position when the subject is delayed. *There* and *it* fulfill this requirement by acting as dummy subjects.

EXERCISE 12.18 Forming questions and commands (p. 264)

Possible answers

1. Will the water boil?
   Boil the water, please.
2. Did the music stop?
   Stop the music.
3. Have you set the table?
   Set the table.
4. Have you rolled the dice yet?
   Roll the dice.
5. Who can use the telephone?
   Use the telephone.

EXERCISE 12.19 Rewriting passives and expletives (p. 264)

1. Milo Addica and Will Rokos cowrote the screenplay for *Monster's Ball.*
2. Marc Foster directed the film.
3. Only one performance in the movie received an Academy Award.
4. Halle Berry won the award for best actress.
5. The press congratulated Berry for being the first African American to win the award.

RESOURCES AND IDEAS

Gorrell, Donna. "Controlled Composition for Basic Writers," *College Composition and Communication* 32 (1981): 308–16. Gorrell argues that students who learn to correct the grammar of their peers become more skilled in producing their own error-free sentences.

12f Classifying sentences

A WRITER'S PERSPECTIVE _____

> *Prose is architecture, and the Baroque is over.*
>   ERNEST HEMINGWAY

CLASSROOM IDEAS

COLLABORATIVE LEARNING Decoding the sentence Divide the class into small groups and have each group write a set of nonsense sentences that conform to English syntax and punctuation. Students should be sure to include nonsense prepositional phrases, verbals, appositives, absolutes, and subordinate and coordinate structures. Warn students to punctuate the sentences carefully. Students can use the nonsense sentence at the beginning of Chapter 12 as a model.

Parts of speech Once the sentences are written, have groups exchange sentences or write them on the board and try to identify the part of speech for each nonsense word. If the creators of the sentences have made errors in punctuation, the puzzle-solvers should be prepared to correct them. This exercise should help students see how grammar and punctuation work together to define a word's role in a sentence and to create different kinds of sentences.

SUMMARY GUIDES

The guides on this and the next five pages appear only in this manual. They are included here for use in conferences and labs. Each guide collects all the descriptions and conventions for a different element: nouns, pronouns, verbs and verbals, and modifiers. Thus the guides provide convenient indexes or texts for students having difficulty with, say, identifying and placing modifiers or distinguishing verbs and verbals. The listings under "Conventions" in each guide contain at least one example showing correct or preferred usage. For additional examples or detailed explanations, consult the sections or pages given in parentheses.

GUIDE TO NOUNS

Summary and index of information in the student text (consult sections or pages in parentheses).

Description of nouns
Nouns as sentence subjects (12a-1, 12a-2)

Nouns as direct and indirect objects (12a-3), object complements (12a-3), objects of prepositions (12c-1), appositives (12c-5), modifiers (16f)

Classes of nouns: proper, common, collective, count, mass, concrete, abstract (12a-2)

Forms of nouns: subjective and objective case (13a, 13b), possessive case (30a), and plural (41b-6)

Other structures serving as nouns: gerunds and gerund phrases (12c-2), infinitives and infinitive phrases (12c-2), subordinate clauses (12c-4)

Conventions regarding nouns
Forms of nouns
Possessive forms: *boy's* vs. *boys'; Park's* vs. *Parks's* vs. *Parkses'* (30a)

Possessives before gerunds: *Nguyen's writing is clear.* (13h)

Plurals of nouns and compound nouns: *dish, dishes; child, children; mother-in-law, mothers-in-law* (43b-6)

Nouns and other sentence parts
Agreement of subjects and verbs: *The towel was wet. The towels were wet.* (15a)

Agreement of antecedents and pronouns: *The children surrounded their father.* (15b)

Grammatical fit between subjects and predicates (avoiding mixed grammar): *In the supervision of others is the best preparation for a management career.→The supervision of others is the best preparation for a management career.* (22a)

Fit in meaning of subjects and predicates (avoiding faulty predication): *The use of the airwaves is the ideal medium for campaigning.→The airwaves are the ideal medium for campaigning.* (22b)

Clarity and effectiveness
Nouns as modifiers (avoiding overuse): *adult education grants workshop→workshop on grants for adult education* (16f)

Consistency in subjects and the voice of verbs: *Tony woke suddenly, but his eyes were kept shut.→Tony woke suddenly, but he kept his eyes shut.* (20c)

GUIDE TO PRONOUNS

Summary and index of information in the student text (consult sections or pages in parentheses).

Description of pronouns
Pronouns as substitutes for nouns (12a-2; 15b)

Pronouns as subjects, objects, complements, appositives, modifiers (Chapter 13)

Case forms of pronouns: subjective, objective, possessive (Chapter 13)

Person, number, and gender of personal pronouns (12a-2; 15b)

Conventions regarding pronouns
Forms of pronouns

Subjective case for subjects and subject complements: *You and I can talk. It was she.* (13a)

Objective case for objects: *Ken gave me a dog. He gave her to me.* (13b)

We or *us* with nouns: *We drivers like highways. Many of us drivers like highways.* (13c)

Case in appositives: *Two drivers, she and Nell, won the award. The state rewarded two drivers, her and Nell.* (13d)

Case after *than* or *as*: *Nell likes Buddy more than [she likes] him. Nell likes Buddy more than he [likes Buddy].* (13e)

Objective case for subjects and objects of infinitives: *We invited him to meet her.* (13f)

Who vs. *whom*: *Who can predict whom he will ask?* (13g)

Possessives before gerunds: *his working* (13h)

Possessive forms of personal pronouns: *hers* (not *her's*); *theirs* (not *their's*) (30b)

Possessive pronouns vs. contractions: *its* vs. *it's; your* vs. *you're; their* vs. *they're* (30c)

Pronouns and other sentence parts

Agreement of pronoun subjects and verbs: *Neither he nor they are late. Everybody is finished.* (15a)

Agreement of pronouns and antecedents: *Everybody finished his or her paper. Lisa or Maria left her notebook.* (15b)

Reference of pronouns to antecedents (avoiding unclear or remote reference): *The first act of the play seemed weak, but then it improved.→The first act of the play started weakly but then improved. Or: Though the first act was weak, the play then improved.* (19a–19e)

GUIDE TO VERBS AND VERBALS

Summary and index of information in the student text (consult sections or pages in parentheses).

Description of verbs and verbals

Verb as sentence predicate (12a-1, 12a-2, 12a-3)

Transitive, intransitive, and linking verbs (12a-3)

Forms of verbs: infinitive, past tense, past participle, present participle, *-s* form (pp. 284–302)

Regular vs. irregular verbs (14a)

Finite vs. nonfinite verbs (12c-2)

Helping (auxiliary) verbs (14d)

Tense of verbs: present, past, future, etc. (pp. 303–11)

Mood of verbs: indicative, imperative, subjunctive (pp. 312–14)

Voice of verbs: active and passive (pp. 314–17)

Verbals and verbal phrases: participles, gerunds, infinitives (12c-2)

Conventions regarding verbs and verbals
Forms and tenses of verbs

Principal parts of common irregular verbs: e.g., *begin, began, begun; run, ran, run* (14a)

Sit vs. *set, lie* vs. *lay,* and *rise* vs. *raise* (14b)

Needed -*s* and -*ed* endings: *He asks/asked too much.* (14c)

Needed helping verbs: *He is asking too much.* (14d)

Present tense (*runs*) and perfect tenses (*has/had/will have run*). (14g)

Sequence of tenses: e.g., *We would like to have gone* vs. *We would have liked to go.* (14h)

Subjunctive mood: *I wish I were there.* (14i)

Verbs and other sentence parts

Agreement of verbs and subjects: *The guests are here. Nobody is missing.* (15a)

Unseparated verb phrases and infinitives: *They had before long agreed to voluntarily surrender.→Before long they had agreed to surrender voluntarily.* (21e)

Grammatical fit between subjects and predicates (avoiding mixed grammar): *By saving is how they could buy a car.→By saving, they could buy a car.* (22a)

Fit in meaning of subjects and predicates (avoiding faulty predication): *The reason is because they were frugal.→The reason is that they were frugal.* (22b)

Problems with verbals

Verbs required in complete sentences (avoiding sentence fragments with verbals): *Rain falling silently.→Rain fell silently.* (17a, 17c)

Clear and logical modifiers (avoiding dangling modifiers): *Flying home, her thoughts remained behind.→As she flew home, her thoughts remained behind.* (21h)

Punctuation with verbals

Commas after introductory verbal modifiers: *Struggling for air, the climbers reached the summit.* (28b)

Commas to set off nonessential verbal modifiers: *The climbers, struggling for air, reached the summit.* (28c)

Clarity and effectiveness

Active rather than passive voice: *Hands were raised by the students.→The students raised their hands.* (14j)

Consistency in voice: *Before you tighten the bolts, the car should be lowered to the ground.→Before you tighten the bolts, you should lower the car to the ground.* (20c)

Consistency in tense: *The hero escapes, but he was captured. →The hero escapes, but he is captured.* (20b)

Consistency in mood: *Unscrew the bolts, and then remove the wheel.→Unscrew the bolts and then remove the wheel.* (20b)

Strong rather than weak verbs (avoiding wordiness): *The book is a depiction of family strife.→The book depicts family strife.* (23a, 40a)

GUIDE TO MODIFIERS

Summary and index of information in the student text (consult sections or pages in parentheses).

Description of modifiers

Functions of adjectives: modifying nouns and pronouns (p. 334)

Functions of adverbs: modifying verbs, adjectives, other adverbs, phrases, and clauses (pp. 333–35)

Forms of adjectives and adverbs: positive, comparative, superlative (16d)

Irregular adjectives and adverbs (16d-1)

Classes of adjectives: descriptive, limiting, proper, attributive, predicate (pp. 333–36, 932–33)

Classes of adverbs: modifiers of verbs, adjectives, and other adverbs (pp. 333–36); transitional and parenthetical expressions (28b); conjunctive adverbs (12d-2)

Other structures serving as modifiers: nouns (16f); prepositional phrases (12c-1); participles and participial phrases (12c-2); infinitives and infinitive phrases (12c-2); subordinate clauses (12c-4)

Conventions regarding modifiers

Distinctions between adjectives and adverbs

Adverbs (not adjectives) to modify verbs, adjectives, adverbs: *Susan writes well* [not *good*]. (16a)

Adjectives after linking verbs, adverbs to modify other verbs: *I feel bad. She sings badly.* (16b)

Adjectives to modify objects, adverbs to modify verbs: *We believed him honest. We treated him honestly.* (16c)

Forms of adjectives and adverbs

Comparatives and superlatives: *steady, steadier/more steady, steadiest/most steady; good/well, better, best* (16d-1); *most steadiest→most steady* (16d-2); *the bigger of two and the biggest of three* (16d-3); *most unique→unique* (16d-4)

Modifiers and other sentence parts

Clear placement of modifiers: *We waited for the rain to stop in a doorway.→We waited in a doorway for the rain to stop.* (21a–21e)

Clear and logical modifiers (avoiding dangling modifiers): *Watching the rain, our hands and feet froze.→As we watched the rain, our hands and feet froze.* (21h)

Punctuation and mechanics with modifiers

Commas after most introductory modifiers: *Happily, we have friends.* (28b)

Commas to set off nonessential modifiers: *Ellen, who is our best friend, checks in every day.* (28c)

Commas to set off absolute phrases: *Her workday finished, she calls us.* (28d)

Commas for coordinate adjectives: *She is a steady, reliable friend.* (28f-2)

Commas with conjunctive adverbs and transitional and parenthetical expressions: *Traffic was bad; we left, however, before it could get worse.* (28c-3, 29b)

Semicolons between clauses related by conjunctive adverbs: *We did not leave right away; instead, we waited for Ellen.* (18b, 29b)

Capital letters for proper adjectives: *Indian tea; Buddhist chant* (33d)

Figure vs. words for numbers: *327* vs. *twenty-three* (36a)

Hyphens in compound adjectives and numbers: *well-spoken words* vs. *words well spoken* (43d-1); *thirty-two minutes* (43d-2)

Clarity and effectiveness

Clear negation (avoiding double negatives): *They don't want no interruptions.* →*They don't want any interruptions.* Or: *They want no interruptions.* (16e)

Nouns as modifiers (avoiding overuse): *business managers spreadsheet analysis seminar*→*seminar in spreadsheet analysis for business managers* (16f)

Complete and logical comparisons: *The value of friendship is greater than money.*→*The value of friendship is greater than the value of* [or *that of*] *money.* (22d)

ANSWERS

EXERCISE 12.20 Identifying sentence structures (p. 266)

1. *Simple:* Joseph Pulitzer endowed the Pulitzer Prizes. [MAIN]

2. *Simple:* Pulitzer, incidentally, was the publisher of the New York newspaper *The World.* [MAIN]

3. *Complex:* Although the first prizes were for journalism and letters only, [SUBORDINATE] Pulitzers are now awarded in music and other areas. [MAIN]

4. *Compound:* For example, Berke Breathed won for his *Bloom County* comic strip, [MAIN] and Roger Reynolds won for his musical composition *Whispers Out of Time.* [MAIN]

5. *Compound-complex:* Although only one prize is usually awarded in each category, [SUBORDINATE] in 1989 Taylor Branch's *Parting the Waters* won a history prize, [MAIN] and it shared the honor with James M. McPherson's *Battle Cry of Freedom.* [MAIN]

EXERCISE 21 Sentence combining: Sentence structures (p. 266)

Possible answers

1. Recycling takes time, but it reduces garbage in landfills.
2. After people begin to recycle, they generate much less trash.
3. Although white tissues and paper towels biodegrade more easily than dyed ones, people still buy dyed papers.
4. Aluminum cans bring recyclers good money.
5. Environmentalists hope that more communities will recycle newspaper and glass, but many citizens refuse to participate.

RESOURCES AND IDEAS

Dawkins, John. "Teaching Punctuation as a Rhetorical Tool." *College Composition and Communication* 46 (1995): 533–48. Dawkins makes a case for teaching the rhetorical thinking processes that accompany decisions about punctuation marks.

Herrington, Anne J. "Grammar Recharted: Sentence Analysis for Writing." *Writing Exercises from "Exercise Exchange."* Vol. 2. Urbana: NCTE, 1984. 276–87. Herrington offers a number of useful classroom activities.

CHAPTER 13

Case of Nouns and Pronouns

CHAPTER HIGHLIGHTS

The forms that nouns and pronouns take according to their role in a sentence are relatively few in English when compared with some other languages. Nonetheless, most students are likely to find compound subjects and objects or questions of *who* and *whom* occasionally troublesome. Others may need to review pronoun forms more extensively to gain control over this part of their writing.

This chapter opens with a review of the functions a pronoun can perform, functions that determine the form, or case, of the pronoun. In addition to the familiar list of forms of the personal pronouns, the chapter provides sentences illustrating the wide variety of uses for pronouns. Following this are brief discussions of the proper case for pronouns in contexts that usually cause difficulty for student writers, including compound subjects and objects, appositives, comparisons using *than* or *as*, possessive case with gerunds, and the different uses of *who* and *whom*.

The exercises ask students to select the appropriate forms of pronouns in the troublesome contexts treated in the discussion, to correct any case errors in a paragraph, and to combine sentences so as to use *who* or *whom* in relative clauses.

MEDIA RESOURCES FOR CHAPTER 13

mycomplab Please visit MyCompLab at *www.mycomplab.com* for more on the writing process.

http://www.ablongman.com/littlebrown ▶ See page 73 of this manual for companion Web site content description.

INSTRUCTOR RESOURCE

The following Presentation Aid is available for download on this book's companion Web site at *http://www.ablongman.com/littlebrown*.

PRESENTATION AID 13.1: Case forms of nouns and pronouns (p. 268)

CLASSROOM IDEAS

The chart Students may be tempted to skip over the chart giving the case forms of nouns and pronouns. Get them to pay attention by asking them to

247

fill out the whole chart in class—without looking at the text. The act of remembering the forms or figuring them out will be more valuable than listening to an explanation. Students who have trouble completing the chart probably need to spend time reviewing the chapter.

CULTURE LANGUAGE **Noun-noun possessives** Students who are nonnative speakers of English learn that people and animals go in possessive case ("Phoebe's phone," "the ferret's fur") but that inanimate objects take "of" formations ("the end of the line"). Students may be confused by the exceptions to this rule ("table top," "car engine.") Have your students keep a list of exceptions to this rule and see how long the list grows by the end of your course.

RESOURCES AND IDEAS

Redfern, Richard K. "Pronouns Are Highly Personal." *English Journal* 85 (1996): 80–81. Redfern presents further strategies for teaching pronoun usage.

13a Use the subjective case for compound subjects and for subject complements.

INSTRUCTOR RESOURCE

The following Presentation Aid is available for download on this book's companion Web site at *http://www.ablongman.com/littlebrown*.

PRESENTATION AID 13.2: A test for case forms in compound constructions (p. 269)

CLASSROOM IDEAS

Back to nouns Distribute copies of a paragraph taken from a magazine article, an essay in a reader, or a student paper. Ask students to rewrite it, substituting the appropriate noun for each pronoun. This exercise will help students to understand the role of pronouns and see the relationship between the case of a pronoun and the function of the noun it stands for.

13b Use the objective case for compound objects.

ANSWERS

EXERCISE 13.1 Choosing between subjective and objective pronouns (p. 270)

1. I	4. her, me
2. she, I, we	5. her, me
3. She, I	

13c Use the appropriate case when the plural pronoun *we* or *us* occurs with a noun.

CLASSROOM IDEA

Us the people If students try out pronoun forms in sentences, they can often "hear" the contrast between correct and incorrect forms by relying on their implicit understanding of the language or by using familiar phrases as touchstones:

> *Us* the people.
> *Us* are the world.
> Are you going with *we?*
> Take *we* to the movies.

This approach will not work with students for whom standard English is a second language or a second dialect.

13d In appositives the case of the pronoun depends on the function of the word described or identified.

ANSWERS

EXERCISE 13.2 Choosing between subjective and objective pronouns (p. 270)

1. us	4. us
2. we	5. we, I
3. him	

13e The case of a pronoun after *than* or *as* in a comparison depends on the meaning.

CLASSROOM IDEA

Make up your own test Give students time in class to write out five to ten sentences in quiz form. The easiest way for students to do this is to pattern their questions after the exercises and sample sentences in the handbook:

> Most of [*we, us*] college students realize that finding a good job isn't easy.
> There is a five-hundred-dollar reward for [*whomever, whoever*] finds the missing stock certificates.

Students can use the handbook in preparing the questions, and as long as they know that one of the possible answers they have provided must be right, they need not be sure which one it is.

When the tests are completed, students should exchange them and fill them out. Correcting the tests is best done in small groups so that students can help one another or turn to the instructor for any information necessary to provide answers to the toughest questions.

13g The case of the pronoun *who* depends on its function in its clause.

INSTRUCTOR RESOURCES

The following Presentation Aids are available for download on this book's companion Web site at *http://www.ablongman.com/littlebrown*.

PRESENTATION AID 13.3: A test for *who* versus *whom* in questions (p. 272)

PRESENTATION AID 13.4: A test for *who* versus *whom* in subordinate clauses (p. 273)

CLASSROOM IDEA

COLLABORATIVE LEARNING Exercises 13.3 and 13.4 Students might complete Exercise 13.3 independently, then compare answers and work on Exercise 13.4 in pairs or in small groups. Ask each group to create several sentences of their own using *who* and *whom,* and based on the models provided in Exercise 13.4. Each group might present some of their most inventive responses to the class by writing them on the chalkboard, making transparencies, or posting them on the network.

ANSWERS

EXERCISE 13.3 Choosing between *who* and *whom* (p. 273)

1. who
2. who
3. whoever
4. Who
5. Whom

EXERCISE 13.4 Sentence combining: Who versus whom (p. 273)

1. Some children who have undetected hearing problems may do poorly in school.
2. They may not hear important instructions and information from teachers who speak softly.
3. Classmates whom the teacher calls on may not be audible.
4. Some hearing-impaired children who get a lot of encouragement at home may work harder to overcome their disability.
5. Some hearing-impaired children may take refuge in fantasy friends whom they can rely on not to criticize or laugh.

13h Ordinarily, use a possessive pronoun or noun immediately before a gerund.

CLASSROOM IDEA

COLLABORATIVE LEARNING Create a story On the board, write a sentence or two that introduces as many people's names as possible. For example, you might write,

Bob went to a party last night, and there he saw his first-grade teacher, Mrs. West; his neighbor George; his old girlfriend Sarah; and her children Susan and Jason. In the middle of the party, Bob's dog Bowser came racing into the living room.

Divide the class into small groups and ask each group to write a one-paragraph story that grows out of the sentences on the board. (In the example above, students would probably describe what happened after the dog's entrance.) In writing their story, students should try to use as many pronouns as possible without introducing any ambiguity into the tale.

Groups should then read their stories aloud or write them on the board so that other students can try to understand the stories and verify that all the pronoun cases are accurate.

ANSWERS

EXERCISE 13.5 Revising: Case (p. 274)

Written four thousand years ago, *The Epic of Gilgamesh* tells of the friendship of Gilgamesh and Enkidu. Gilgamesh was a bored king who his people thought was too harsh. Then he met Enkidu, a wild man who had lived with the animals in the mountains. Immediately, he and Gilgamesh wrestled to see who was more powerful. After hours of struggle, Enkidu admitted that Gilgamesh was stronger than he. Now the friends needed adventures worthy of the two strongest men on earth. Gilgamesh said, "Between you and me, mighty deeds will be accomplished, and our fame will be everlasting." Among their acts, Enkidu and he defeated a giant bull, Humbaba, and cut down the bull's cedar forests. Their bringing back cedar logs to Gilgamesh's treeless land won great praise from the people. When Enkidu died, Gilgamesh mourned his death, realizing that no one had been a better friend than he. When Gilgamesh himself died many years later, his people raised a monument praising Enkidu and him for their friendship and their mighty deeds of courage.

CHAPTER 14

Verbs

CHAPTER HIGHLIGHTS

Verbs can cause trouble for writers regardless of their level of skill. For some writers, choosing the correct tense or form of a verb can be a formidable challenge. In addition, certain regional and social dialects of English have different patterns for marking verb tenses and forms, which may add to the confusion. Even experienced writers may occasionally stumble over the choice between *sit* and *set* or struggle to maintain the correct sequence of tenses in a complex sentence.

For all these needs (and many others as well) this chapter can be useful, although it must be supplemented to provide the more sustained support and practice some students may require. Students whose first language is not English may benefit from the ESL coverage and the worksheets by Jocelyn Steer and Dawn Schmid. If your campus is fortunate enough to have a writing center, your students may benefit from the extra support it can provide.

Students looking for help with verb *forms* will benefit from the chapter's thorough explanations, list of the principal parts of frequently used irregular verbs, discussion of the troublesome pairs *sit/set* and *lie/lay*, and treatment of two problems often associated with dialect interference: omitted -*s* and -*ed* endings and omitted helping verbs.

Students looking for help with verb *tense* can make use of the chapter's discussion of the major tenses and of appropriate sequences of tenses. Tense sequence becomes increasingly important as students begin to write ambitious narratives and expository or argumentative essays.

MEDIA RESOURCES FOR CHAPTER 14

mycomplab Please visit MyCompLab at *www.mycomplab.com* for more on the writing process.

http://www.ablongman.com/littlebrown ▶ See page 73 of this manual for companion Web content description.

INSTRUCTOR RESOURCE

The following Presentation Aid is available for download on this book's companion Web site at *http://www.ablongman.com/littlebrown*.

PRESENTATION AID 14.1: Terms used to describe verbs (p. 276)

CLASSROOM IDEA

One-form paragraphs Choose groups of three to five verbs and have students create paragraphs using only one form of the verbs. Then have students rewrite the paragraphs using a different verb form. This exercise will reinforce consistent use of form and may make students more aware of the element of time in verb usage. Following are student-written examples that use the past-participle form of the verbs *break, bring, burst, buy,* and *catch.*

> *Because his bubble had burst and she had broken his heart, he had caught the next train home and had brought his mother some flowers.*
> —Jennifer Haas

> *We had brought the dishes out to the table to set it. When we looked we realized that we had broken some of them. We had burst out laughing, but it wasn't too funny when we realized that my mother had caught us.*
> —Nicole Hanna

> *He had broken the vase that she had brought. She had burst into tears. If only he had caught it.*
> —Jim Rosen

RESOURCES AND IDEAS

Yoder, Rhoda Byler. "Of Fake Verbs and Kid Words: Developing a Useful Grammar." *English Journal* 85 (1996): 82–87. Middle school teacher develops a simplified language for teaching students the functions of verbs and verbals.

14a Use the correct forms of regular and irregular verbs.

CLASSROOM IDEAS

The origin of irregular verbs Irregular verbs are antiques reflecting the history of English well before the Norman Conquest of England in 1066. In the first few centuries AD, speakers of the Germanic languages that evolved into English used changes in the internal vowel structure of words to show tense. Thus, verbs like *drink, throw,* and especially *be* preserve a little of the linguistic history of our ancestors. A very readable account of this period is found in Joseph Williams, *Origins of the English Language* (New York: Free Press, 1975).

Hypothetical verbs A good game to play to show students how well they intuitively understand how irregular verbs are formed is to invent some (e.g., *flink*) and ask students to decide what their other forms would be (*flink, flank, flunk* or *flink, flought, flought*). A variation is to take a more regular verb and pretend it's irregular: *My engine won't crank in cold weather; My engine hadn't crunk.*

ANSWERS

EXERCISE 14.1 Using irregular verbs (p. 280)

1. The world population has grown by two-thirds of a billion people in less than a decade. (Past participle.)
2. Recently it broke the 6 billion mark. (Past tense.)
3. Experts have drawn pictures of a crowded future. (Past participle.)
4. They predict that the world population may have slid up to as much as 10 billion by 2050. (Past participle.)
5. Though the food supply rose in the last decade, the share to each person fell. (Both past tense.)

14b **Distinguish between *sit* and *set*, *lie* and *lay*, and *rise* and *raise*.**

CLASSROOM IDEA

Irregular verbs and the dictionary The need to learn the uses of *sit* and *set*, *rise* and *raise*, and *lie* and *lay* makes a great excuse to introduce students to the wonders of the *Oxford English Dictionary*, in either its first or its second edition. The entries for these words, among the longest in the OED, will show students the number of meanings words can have and the reasons all writers find these particular words so difficult.

ANSWERS

EXERCISE 14.2 Distinguishing *sit/set, lie/lay, rise/raise* (p. 282)

1. Yesterday afternoon the child lay down for a nap.
2. The child has been raised by her grandparents.
3. Most days her grandfather has sat with her, reading her stories.
4. She has risen at dawn most mornings.
5. Her toys were laid out on the floor.

14c **Use the *-s* and *-ed* forms of the verb when they are required.**

CLASSROOM IDEA

CULTURE LANGUAGE Speakers of Black English Vernacular may tend to use the verb forms of this dialect in their writing rather than those of standard written English, particularly by dropping *-s* and *-ed* endings. Becoming aware of the verb system of standard written English and the differences between it and the verb system of Black English Vernacular is an important step for students seeking control over their writing. But as Marcia Farr and Harvey Daniels point out in *Language Diversity and Writing*

Instruction (New York: ERIC Clearing House on Urban Education and Urbana: NCTE, 1986), awareness of and practice in identifying and using the verb forms are useful only if they take place in a context that includes a wide range of reading and writing experiences; substantial practice in writing; collaborative activities; sentence combining or similar activities; and flexible, sensitive feedback from the instructor. Farr and Daniels also offer a detailed discussion of dialects and language variations, along with concrete suggestions for teaching.

ANSWERS

EXERCISE 14.3 Using *-s* and *-ed* verb endings (p. 283)

A teacher sometimes asks too much of a student. In high school I was once punished for being sick. I had missed some school, and I realized that I would fail a test unless I had a chance to make up the classwork. I discussed the problem with the teacher, but he said I was supposed to make up the work while I was sick. At that I walked out of the class. I received a failing grade then, but it did not change my attitude. Today I still balk when a teacher makes unreasonable demands or expects miracles.

14d Use helping verbs with main verbs appropriately.

ANSWERS

EXERCISE 14.4 Using helping verbs (p. 287)

1. Each year thousands of new readers have been discovering Agatha Christie's mysteries.
2. The books were written by a prim woman who had worked as a nurse during World War I.
3. Christie never expected that her play *The Mousetrap* would be performed for decades.
4. During her life Christie was always complaining about movie versions of her stories.
5. Readers of her stories have been delighted to be baffled by her.

EXERCISE 14.5 Revising: Helping verbs plus main verbs (p. 288)

1. A report from the Bureau of the Census has confirmed a widening gap between rich and poor.
2. As suspected, the percentage of people below the poverty level did increase over the last decade.
3. More than 17 percent of the population is making 5 percent of all the income.
4. About 1 percent of the population will be keeping [*or* will keep] an average of $500,000 apiece after taxes.
5. Sentence correct.

14e Use a gerund or an infinitive after a verb as appropriate.

CLASSROOM IDEA

CULTURE LANGUAGE Choosing between gerunds and infinitives ESL students generally find gerunds more problematic than infinitives, perhaps because gerunds occur less frequently; as a result, students may use infinitives where gerunds are required. According to Marianne Celce-Murcia and Diane Larsen-Freeman in *The Grammar Book* (Boston: Heinle, 1983), gerunds tend to express "fulfilled action," whereas infinitives tend to express "unfulfilled action":

> I *enjoyed meeting* your brother at the party. (The action, the meeting, was fulfilled.)
>
> I *hoped to meet* your brother at the party. (The action, the hoped-for meeting, was unfulfilled.)
>
> I'll always *remember calling* my son when he was overseas. (The action, calling, was fulfilled before the remembering.)
>
> I *remembered to call* my son on his birthday. (The action, calling, was unfulfilled until after the remembering.)

Refer students who need additional practice distinguishing gerunds and infinitives to Unit 8 of Carroll Washington Pollock, *Communicate What You Mean: Grammar for High-Level ESL Students* (Englewood Cliffs: Prentice-Hall, 1982), and Chapter 14 of Jocelyn Steer and Karen Carlisi, *The Advanced Grammar Book* (Boston: Heinle, 1991).

ANSWERS

EXERCISE 14.6 Revising: Verbs plus gerunds or infinitives (p. 290)

1. A program called HELP Wanted tries to encourage citizens <u>to take</u> action on behalf of American competitiveness.
2. Officials working on this program hope <u>to improve</u> education for work.
3. American businesses find that their workers need <u>to learn</u> to read.
4. In the next ten years the United States expects <u>to face</u> a shortage of 350,000 scientists.
5. Sentence correct.

14f Use the appropriate particles with two-word verbs.

INSTRUCTOR RESOURCE

The following Presentation Aid is available for download on this book's companion Web site at *http://www.ablongman.com/littlebrown*.

PRESENTATION AID 14.2: Tenses of a regular verb (active voice) (p. 293)

ANSWERS

EXERCISE 14.7 Revising: Verbs plus particles (p. 292)

1. American movies treat everything from going out with [correct] someone to making up [correct] an ethnic identity, but few people <u>look into</u> their significance.
2. While some viewers stay away from [correct] topical films, others <u>turn up at the theater</u> simply because a movie has sparked debate.
3. Some movies attracted rowdy spectators, and the theaters had to <u>throw them out</u>.
4. Filmmakers have always been eager to <u>point their influence out</u> [cor rect; *or* <u>point out their influence</u>] to the public.
5. Everyone agrees that filmmakers will <u>keep on creating controversy</u>, if only because it can fill up [correct] theaters.

14g Use the appropriate tense to express your meaning.

CLASSROOM IDEAS

Memory aid To help students remember special uses of the present tense, you might suggest that they use the acronym FACT as a memory aid:

> Future time
> Action recurring
> Content of literature
> Truth, general

Invented verbs Concoct some plausible English verbs like *fliggle, displore,* or *frink*. Ask students to work out their forms and use them in all possible tenses. Students might then work in groups on the computer or on paper to concoct a story around their invented verb.

◄CULTURE LANGUAGE► **Time lines** Tense use varies widely among languages; as a result, ESL students may have difficulty distinguishing tenses. Point out that the present perfect tense relates past events to present time and implies that an event may continue to occur in the future. Certain time words often accompany the present perfect, including *already, before, for, recently, (ever) since, so far,* and *ever* and *yet* (for questions and negative statements such as *Have you ever seen that dancer perform? No, I haven't seen her yet, but hope to*). Students often find time lines helpful in distinguishing the present perfect from the simple past tense:

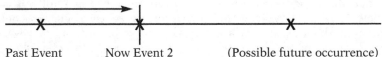

Past Event   Now Event 2   (Possible future occurrence)

Past: The dancer performed here a year ago.

Present perfect: Critics have written about it ever since (and may continue to write about it).

In *The Advanced Grammar Book* (Boston: Heinle, 1991), Jocelyn Steer and Karen Carlisi include useful time lines for distinguishing tenses.

CULTURE LANGUAGE The use of progressive tenses Some languages (for example, Arabic) use progressive tenses to express habitual activities, whereas English uses simple tenses. Explain to students that in English, the progressive tenses emphasize the *duration* or *continuous nature* of an action. Perfect progressive tenses are also used for ongoing action that is intersected by another action.

Exceptions As the text notes, verbs that express mental states or activities are generally not used in the progressive tenses. However, there are some exceptions:

> *see = date or consult:* Marsha isn't <u>seeing</u> John any more. Gina is <u>seeing</u> a doctor about her allergies.
> *think = consider:* I'm <u>thinking</u> about taking a literature course next term.
> *cumulative effects:* I'm <u>understanding</u> English better and better as I go through this course.

14h Use the appropriate sequence of verb tenses.

CLASSROOM IDEAS

COLLABORATIVE LEARNING Imaginary reporting A good activity is to ask students, either individually or in groups, to construct some imaginary event (an episode from a TV show, a football game, a newscast) and recount its chronology using the correct sequence of tenses. Students can work together to revise their reported events, and volunteer groups might read their responses to the class or post them on the network.

Creating a story Write on the board a sentence containing one or more characters and an action. Here are some examples:

> As he rounded the corner, John heard a loud noise, somewhere between a crash and a bang.
> As he came into the classroom, Jim noticed that Carolyn was already there reviewing her notes.

Ask students to form groups, and then require the groups to write paragraph-length (seven to eight sentences) stories. The stories should begin with the sentence you have provided, and individual members of the group should add sentences to the narrative one by one until it is complete. The final story should maintain a correct sequence of tenses, contain proper verb forms, and use a variety of action verbs. Students may wish to use ideas or episodes from their journals in completing this exercise.

COLLABORATIVE LEARNING Discussion story Put a lead sentence (as in "Creating a Story," above) on the board and ask the class as a whole to decide on the events that follow it. Summarize the events briefly; then ask groups of students to write out the story as in the preceding activity, making it as vivid as they can. This entire exercise will provide both oral and written practice with verb tense and sequence.

COLLABORATIVE LEARNING AND COMPUTER ACTIVITY Indirect quotations Ask students to complete Exercise 14.10 individually and compare answers in pairs. Then have each pair create five additional examples, in which students take turns inventing direct quotes and then rephrasing them in indirect quotations. This exercise also works well in a computer classroom.

COMPUTER ACTIVITY Networked stories Both the "Creating a Story" and the "Discussion Story" work well as electronic exercises. In each case, the teacher posts the opening prompt for the story, then asks students to work collaboratively or individually on their responses. Periodically, the teacher might post the entire story (or one group's version of the story) for the whole class to read and discuss. For related activities, see Daniel Anderson's chapter on "Using Computers to Teach Writing," beginning on page 66 of this manual.

COLLABORATIVE LEARNING Three moods Ask students to work together to scan their own work for examples of the indicative, imperative, and subjunctive moods. Have each group put one or two examples on the board, on transparencies, or on the network for the class.

ANSWERS

EXERCISE 14.8 Adjusting tense sequence: Past or past perfect tense (p. 298)

1. Diaries that Adolf Hitler was supposed to have written had surfaced in Germany.
2. Many people believed that the diaries were authentic because a well-known historian had declared them so.
3. However, the historian's evaluation was questioned by other authorities who called the diaries forgeries.
4. They claimed, among other things, that the paper was not old enough to have been used by Hitler.
5. Eventually, the doubters won the debate because they had the best evidence.

EXERCISE 14.9 Revising: Tense sequence with conditional sentences (p. 299)

1. When an athlete turns professional, he or she commits to a grueling regimen of mental and physical training.
2. If athletes were less committed, they would disappoint teammates, fans, and themselves.
3. If professional athletes are very lucky, they may play until age forty.
4. Unless an athlete achieves celebrity status, he or she will have few employment choices after retirement.
5. If professional sports were less risky, athletes would have longer careers and more choices after retirement.

14i   Use the subjunctive forms appropriately.

INSTRUCTOR RESOURCE

The following Presentation Aid is available for download on this book's companion Web site at *http://www.ablongman.com/littlebrown*.

PRESENTATION AID 14.3: Active and passive voice (p. 302)

CLASSROOM IDEAS

The disappearing subjunctive The blurring of the subjunctive mood is swiftly spreading; in another half-century it may be gone in all but the most formal writing. Linguistically this change is understandable; English has simplified its forms more than most other languages. The disappearance of the subjunctive is another example of this natural process. A very readable book on this subject is Jean Aitchison's *Language Change: Progress or Decay?* (Suffolk: Fontana, 1981).

COLLABORATIVE LEARNING Exercise 14.10 If students are struggling with the subjunctive mood, have them work in small groups on Exercise 14.10, then ask each group to compose three additional sentences in the subjunctive mood.

Passive sentences—count the words Write on the board a number of sentences in the active voice, the sentences ranging from simple to relatively complex. Ask students to change the sentences into the passive voice and then to count the number of words in each version. Finally, ask students to read some of the passive sentences aloud and comment on their effectiveness. This exercise will allow you to check students' understanding of the passive voice and at the same time demonstrate its wordiness.

⟨CULTURE LANGUAGE⟩ Problems with the past participle Not all languages include a passive voice. As a result, ESL students are not always certain about when passive voice is appropriate. Also, because ESL students do not always hear the past-participle *-ed* ending, particularly when *-ed* sounds like *t*, they may omit *-ed* in writing passive voice. Encourage students to listen for the use of the passive voice *-ed* ending in political speeches or in news programs or documentaries. Unit 5 of Carroll Washington Pollock, *Communicate What You Mean: Grammar for High-Level ESL Students* (Englewood Cliffs: Prentice Hall, 1982), and Chapter 11 of Jocelyn Steer and Karen Carlisi, *The Advanced Grammar Book* (Boston: Heinle, 1991), include useful exercises both in writing and in determining when to use passive voice.

ANSWERS

EXERCISE 14.10 Revising: Subjunctive mood (p. 301)

1. If John Hawkins <u>had known</u> of the dangerous side effects of smoking tobacco, would he <u>have introduced</u> the dried plant to England in 1565?

2. Hawkins noted that if a Florida Indian were to travel for several days, he would smoke tobacco to satisfy his hunger and thirst.
3. Early tobacco growers feared that their product would not gain acceptance unless it were perceived as healthful.
4. To prevent fires, in 1646 the General Court of Massachusetts passed a law requiring that colonists smoke tobacco only if they were five miles from any town.
5. To prevent decadence, in 1647 Connecticut passed a law mandating that one's smoking of tobacco be limited to once a day in one's own home.

14j Generally, prefer the active voice. Use the passive voice when the actor is unknown or unimportant.

CLASSROOM IDEAS

COLLABORATIVE LEARNING Passive sentences—finding passages Have students, working in groups, locate passive sentences in an essay from a reader or a similar source. Ask them to decide if the passive voice provides emphasis appropriate for the essay or if the active voice would be better. Tell them to be ready to defend their choice of the passive or to offer a revision of the sentence in the active voice. Have each group present its most hotly debated case to the class.

COLLABORATIVE LEARNING Scientific style Many editors of scientific journals now recommend that authors use first person pronouns and active verbs where possible instead of relying on the passive. They recommend that authors use the passive when the performer of the action is unknown or unimportant or when emphasis should be placed on the recipient of the action. Students writing in science courses should check with their instructors to see what stylistic guide they should follow; see also Chapters 52 and 53.

COLLABORATIVE LEARNING Active/passive Ask students to work on Exercise 14.11 in small groups; then ask each group to compose additional examples of active- and passive-voiced sentences.

COLLABORATIVE LEARNING Verbs and adverbs Ask students to compare their response to Exercise 14.2 and then to circle and revise the verbs and verbals in one paragraph from each student's work. This kind of application of skills learned in an exercise to examples from students' own work can be extremely beneficial.

ANSWERS

EXERCISE 14.11 Converting between active and passive voices (p. 303)

1. When engineers built the Eiffel Tower in 1889, the French thought it was ugly.
2. At that time industrial technology was still resisted by many people.

3. This technology was epitomized by the tower's naked steel construction.
4. People expected beautiful ornament to grace fine buildings.
5. Further, people could not even call the tower a building because it had no solid walls.

EXERCISE 14.12 Revising: Verb forms, tense, mood (p. 304)

For centuries the natives of Melanesia, a group of islands lying northeast of Australia, have practiced an unusual religion. It began in the eighteenth century when European explorers first visited the islands. The natives were fascinated by the rich goods or "cargo" possessed by the explorers. They saw the wealth as treasures of the gods, and cargo cults eventually arose among them. Over the centuries some Melanesians turned to Christianity in the belief that the white man's religion would bring them the white man's treasures. During World War II, US soldiers, having arrived by boat and airplane to occupy some of the islands, introduced new and even more wonderful cargo. Even today some leaders of the cargo cults insist that the airplane be worshipped as a vehicle of the Melanesians' future salvation.

CHAPTER 15

Agreement

CHAPTER HIGHLIGHTS

Some students may have difficulty with basic subject-verb agreement, particularly with the *-s* or *-es* endings that mark plural nouns and singular verbs in English. Almost all students encounter problems with subject-verb and pronoun-antecedent agreement when they begin writing complicated, information-filled sentences. This chapter addresses the needs of both groups of writers, paying special attention to sentence structures that make it difficult for student writers to determine the correct relationship in number between subjects and verbs or pronouns and antecedents.

Rather than treating agreement problems as errors resulting from ignorance, the chapter treats such problems as areas requiring special attention, even by experienced writers. Among the troublesome structures covered are compound subjects, collective nouns, relative and indefinite pronouns, phrases like "one of the," and widely separated subjects and verbs.

Recent changes in the language have given rise to some confusion over pronoun-antecedent agreement with indefinite pronouns. Moreover, in English, subjects that are singular in form, like *audience* or *the faculty,* may be plural in meaning. In speech, even educated speakers sometimes treat indefinite pronouns like *anybody* and *everybody* as plural: "Everybody ought to pay attention to their own business." This change in part reflects a desire to avoid the generic *he,* a form of usage many people regard as sexist. The discussions present alternatives designed to avoid sexist language, while at the same time making clear the need to treat *everybody, someone,* and the like as singular, at least in the more conservative written medium.

MEDIA RESOURCES FOR CHAPTER 15

mycomplab²⁰ Please visit MyCompLab at *www.mycomplab.com* for more on the writing process.

http://www.ablongman.com/littlebrown ▶ See page 73 of this manual for companion Web site content description.

INSTRUCTOR RESOURCE

The following Presentation Aid is available for download on this book's companion Web site at *http://www.ablongman.com/littlebrown*.

PRESENTATION AID 15.1: Agreement (p. 305)

15a Make subjects and verbs agree in number.

CLASSROOM IDEAS

CULTURE LANGUAGE The rule of one *-s* Remind students that this is "the rule of one *-s*"—in the present tense, English sentences require one *-s* in the third person:

> Singular noun + verb + *s*
> Noun + *s* (plural noun) + verb

Refer students who need additional practice to Unit 3 of Len Fox, *Focus on Editing: A Grammar Workbook for Advanced Writers* (White Plains: Longman, 1992), and to Alan Meyers, *Writing with Confidence* (6th ed., New York: Longman, 2000).

Widely separated subjects and verbs Ask students (working individually or in groups and using the handbook as a guide) to identify the sentence strategies that often result in widely separated subjects and verbs. Then ask them to write in their own words a description of these strategies (i.e., the grammatical rules governing them). Finally, ask students to write sentences using the strategies and containing proper subject-verb agreement. (This exercise can also be used with compound subjects, collective nouns, inverted word order, or other strategies that frequently lead to agreement problems.)

True complexity Sometimes the sample sentences we offer to students by way of illustrating a point of grammar or style seem a bit artificial or a bit too simple. Writers such as Charles Dickens and Henry James offer sentences with considerable variety and flair in structure that can be used either as models themselves or as patterns for sentences with a more contemporary content and cast. The following sentence, from James's preface to *The Princess Casamassima*, illustrates tight control of subject-verb and pronoun-antecedent agreement:

> The troubled life mostly at the center of our subject—whatever our subject, for the artistic hour, happens to be—embraces them [fools] and deals with them for its amusement and its anguish: they are apt largely indeed, on a near view, to be all the cause of its trouble.

Although students often produce grammatically complex sentences, particularly in response to readings, it can be fun and enlightening for them to practice different kinds of complexity. Copy a sentence like this one on the board, on a transparency, or on the network, and ask students to compose sentences that mimic, even parody, its complex structure.

Are everyone ready? Though many students will not, at first, hear anything wrong with sentences like "Everyone ought to pay attention to their own business" (a pattern that has wide acceptance in speech), almost all will find sentences like these unacceptable: "Are everyone ready for lunch?" "Do everybody have enough money to buy tickets for the rides?" Anyone who finds the latter sentences acceptable is probably having trouble recognizing the singular and plural forms of verbs. Sample sentences can, therefore, help you identify the real source of a student's problems with agreement.

CULTURE LANGUAGE Separated by a common language? In British usage, collective nouns are treated as plurals; students educated in British usage (such as those from former British dependencies) may use constructions like *The team were ready for the game.* Such constructions also appear in the works of British authors.

A little intervention Agreement problems with *who, which,* and *that* are often the result of a phrase's separating the subject from the relative clause. Give students a few examples of such phrases:

> is one of those people who
> is the only one of the workers who
> are often believed to be creatures that
> are generally considered to be people who
> is representative of those executives who

Then ask them to write sample sentences of their own employing these or similar phrases and avoiding problems of agreement.

CULTURE LANGUAGE Reminder Remind students that phrases like *one of* also require *the* before the noun: *Bardini is one of the aides* [not *one of aides*] *who work unpaid.*

COLLABORATIVE LEARNING Exercise 15.1 Ask students to work together on Exercise 15.1 and then to look for agreement problems in each other's journal writing, drafts, or completed work.

ANSWERS

Exercise 15.1 Revising: Subject-verb agreement (pp. 312–13)

1. Weinstein & Associates is a consulting firm that tries to make business-people laugh.
2. Statistics from recent research suggest that humor relieves stress.
3. Reduced stress in businesses in turn reduces illness and absenteeism.
4. Reduced stress can also reduce friction within an employee group, which then works more productively.
5. In special conferences held by one consultant, each of the participants practices making the others laugh.
6. One consultant to many companies suggests cultivating office humor with practical jokes such as a rubber fish in the water cooler.
7. When the manager or employees regularly post cartoons on the bulletin board, office spirit usually picks up.
8. Sentence correct.
9. In the face of levity, the former sourpuss becomes one of those who hide bad temper.
10. Every one of the consultants cautions, however, that humor has no place in life-affecting corporate situations such as employee layoffs.

RESOURCES AND IDEAS

Kolln, Martha. "Everyone's Right to Their Own Language." *College Composition and Communication* 37 (1986): 100–02. The frequency with which students treat indefinite pronouns as plural suggests that the widely accepted rules of usage discussed in this section may in some ways conflict with practice. Kolln takes a radical stance, arguing that "dicta that designate all indefinite pronouns as singular have no basis either in actual usage or in the rules of logic" (102).

Sklar, Elizabeth S. "The Tribunal of Use: Agreement in the Indefinite Constructions." *College Composition and Communication* 39 (1988): 410–22. Sklar reviews historical and textbook treatments of agreement with indefinites and offers some pragmatic strategies for teachers to use.

15b Make pronouns and their antecedents agree in person, number, and gender.

INSTRUCTOR RESOURCES

The following Presentation Aids are available for download on this book's companion Web site at *http://www.ablongman.com/littlebrown*.

PRESENTATION AID 15.2: Ways to correct agreement with indefinite words (p. 316)

PRESENTATION AID 15.3: Exercise 15.2 Revising: Pronoun-antecedent agreement (p. 317)

CLASSROOM IDEAS

COLLABORATIVE LEARNING Using magazines or a reader Using essays from a reader or magazine articles, have students work in groups to find sentence structures often associated with agreement problems. Ask the groups to decide how important these structures are for expository prose and to write out what they consider to be the rules governing agreement within these structures.

CULTURE LANGUAGE Confusion over indefinite pronouns ESL students may be confused by the indefinite pronouns *everyone, everybody,* and *everything* because they mean *all* of a group but are grammatically singular. Explain to students that the *endings* to these words—*one, body,* and *thing*—cause them to be singular rather than plural.

COLLABORATIVE LEARNING Exercises 15.2, 15.3, and 15.4 Ask students to work on Exercises 15.2, 15.3, and 15.4 in groups and then to read examples from their own work looking for subject-verb and pronoun-antecedent problems.

ANSWERS

EXERCISE 15.2 Revising: Pronoun-antecedent agreement (p. 317)

1. Each girl raised in a Mexican American family in the Rio Grande Valley of Texas hopes that one day she will be given a *quinceañera* party for her fifteenth birthday.
2. Such a celebration is very expensive because it entails a religious service followed by a huge party. *Or:* Such celebrations are very expensive because they entail a religious service followed by a huge party.
3. A girl's immediate family, unless it is wealthy, cannot afford the party by itself.
4. Her parents will ask each close friend or relative if he or she can help with the preparations. *Or:* Her parents will ask close friends or relatives if they can help with the preparations.
5. Sentence correct.

EXERCISE 15.3 Adjusting for agreement (p. 318)

1. Biologists wish to introduce captive red wolves into the Smoky Mountains in order to increase the wild population of this endangered species.
2. When freed, the wolves naturally have no fear of humans and thus are in danger of being shot.
3. The first experiments to release the wolves were failures.
4. Now researchers pen the wolf puppies in the wooded area that will eventually be their territory.
5. The wolves have little contact with people, even their own keeper, during the year of their captivity.

EXERCISE 15.4 Revising: Agreement (p. 318)

The writers Richard Rodriguez and Maxine Hong Kingston, despite their differences, share one characteristic: their parents were immigrants to California. A frequent theme of their writings is the difficulties of growing up with two languages and two cultures.

A child whose first language is not English is often ridiculed because he or she cannot communicate "properly." [*Or:* Children whose first language is not English are often ridiculed because they cannot communicate "properly."] Rodriguez learned Spanish at home, but at school classmates and teachers expected him to use their language, English. He remembers his childish embarrassment because of his parents' poor English. College and graduate school, which usually expand one's knowledge, widened the gap between Rodriguez and his Latino culture. His essays suggest that he lost a part of himself, a loss that continues to bother him.

Kingston spoke Chinese at home and also learned her first English at school. She sometimes writes of these experiences, but more often she writes to recover and preserve her Chinese culture. *The Woman Warrior,* which offers a blend of autobiography, family history, and mythic tales, describes the struggle of Kingston's female relatives. *China Men* focuses on Kingston's male ancestors; each one traveled to Hawaii or California to make money for his wife back in China. Kingston's work, like Rodriguez's essays, reflects the tension and confusion that the child of immigrants often feels when he or she tries [*or:* that the children of immigrants often feel when they try] to blend two cultures.

CHAPTER 16

Adjectives and Adverbs

CHAPTER HIGHLIGHTS

Many readers view misuse of adjectives and adverbs as a sign of ignorance or carelessness. You should alert students to the potential effect of errors, of course, and remind them that this text offers helpful advice.

Yet fear of failure can disrupt the writing process and cause students to drop effective phrases and sentences from an essay because they are uncertain about the correct form of a word. This chapter therefore takes a positive approach, showing students the correct way to use adjectives and adverbs rather than emphasizing the *don't's*. It also offers easily remembered advice to guide writers over trouble spots. The exercises in the chapter ask students not only to recognize errors but also to revise sentences to make sure adjectives and adverbs are used appropriately.

MEDIA RESOURCES FOR CHAPTER 16

mycomplab Please visit MyCompLab at *www.mycomplab.com* for more on the writing process.

http://www.ablongman.com/littlebrown ▶ See page 73 of this manual for companion Web site content description.

INSTRUCTOR RESOURCE

The following Presentation Aid is available for download on this book's companion Web site at *http://www.ablongman.com/littlebrown*.

PRESENTATION AID 16.1: Functions of adjectives and adverbs (p. 319)

16a Use adjectives only to modify nouns and pronouns.

CLASSROOM IDEA

Homemade quizzes Ask students to follow the pattern of the sample sentences and exercises in the chapter and make up sentences containing common errors in the use of adjectives and adverbs. The uses of *well* and *good, bad* and *badly* are good starters. Collect the papers and distribute them as quizzes during the next class. Ask students to correct them in small groups.

16c After a direct object, use an adjective to modify the object and an adverb to modify the verb.

ANSWERS

EXERCISE 16.1 Revising: Adjectives and adverbs (p. 322)

1. King George III of England declared Samuel Johnson <u>suitable</u> for a pension.
2. Johnson was taken <u>seriously</u> as a critic and dictionary maker.
3. Thinking about his meeting with the king, Johnson felt <u>proud</u>.
4. Sentence correct.
5. After living <u>cheaply</u> for over twenty years, Johnson finally had enough money from the pension to eat and dress <u>well</u>.

16d Use the comparative and superlative forms of adjectives and adverbs appropriately.

INSTRUCTOR RESOURCE

The following Presentation Aid is available for download on this book's companion Web site at *http://www.ablongman.com/littlebrown*.

PRESENTATION AID 16.2: Degrees of irregular adjectives and adverbs (p. 323)

CLASSROOM IDEA

COLLABORATIVE LEARNING Sabotaging essays Give each group a different short essay and have them introduce a number of errors into its adjective and adverb use. (They may want to use correction fluid for this task.) Then have students copy the essay so their corrections won't show and give it to a different group, which attempts to find all the changes the first group made. The first group comments on and critiques the "corrected" essay by comparing it to the original version. If students are working in a computer classroom, they can print out the error-ridden version of the essay for the other group.

ANSWERS

EXERCISE 16.2 Revising: Comparatives and superlatives (p. 324)

Possible answers

1. Charlotte was the <u>oldest</u> of the three Brontë sisters, all of whom were novelists.
2. Some readers think Emily Brontë's *Wuthering Heights* is the <u>saddest</u> novel they have ever read.
3. Sentence correct.
4. Critics still argue about whether Charlotte or Emily wrote <u>better</u>.
5. Certainly, this family of women novelists was <u>unique</u>.

16e Watch for double negatives.

ANSWERS

EXERCISE 16.3 Revising: Double negatives (p. 324)

Interest in books about the founding of the United States seems to vary with the national mood. Americans show hardly any interest [or little interest] in books about the founders when things are going well in the United States. However, when Americans can barely [or cannot] agree on major issues, sales of books about the Revolutionary War era increase. During such periods, one cannot go to a bookstore without seeing several new volumes about John Adams, Thomas Jefferson, and other founders. When Americans feel they have nothing [or don't have anything] in common, their increased interest in the early leaders may reflect a desire for unity.

16g Distinguish between present and past participles as adjectives.

CLASSROOM IDEA

CULTURE LANGUAGE Participles Present participles generally describe inanimate or nonhuman nouns: The *storm was frightening.* Past participles generally describe animate nouns (since only animate beings experience feelings): The *horses were frightened.*

ANSWERS

EXERCISE 16.4 Revising: Present and past participles (p. 326)

1. Several critics found Alice Walker's *The Color Purple* to be a fascinating book.
2. Sentence correct.
3. Another critic argued that although the book contained many depressing episodes, the overall impact was exciting.
4. Since other readers found the book annoying, this critic pointed out its many surprising qualities.
5. In the end most critics agreed that the book was a satisfying novel.

16h Use *a, an, the,* and other determiners appropriately.

CLASSROOM IDEAS

CULTURE LANGUAGE Article use As the text notes, because other languages use articles differently from English or not at all, even advanced ESL students may find articles difficult; some students may never completely master article use. Refer students who need additional practice with article use to Unit 2 of Len Fox, *Focus on Editing: A Grammar Workbook for Advanced Writers* (White Plains: Longman, 1992), and Chapter 10 of Jocelyn Steer and Karen Carlisi, *The Advanced Grammar Book* (Boston: Heinle, 1991).

CULTURE LANGUAGE Categories of noncount nouns Refer students who need additional practice with count and noncount nouns to Unit 2 of Len Fox, *Focus on Editing: A Grammar Workbook for Advanced Writers* (White Plains: Longman, 1992), and Chapter 1 of Jocelyn Steer and Karen Carlisi, *The Advanced Grammar Book* (Boston: Heinle, 1991).

CULTURE LANGUAGE *A lot of* ESL students tend to use *a lot of* in formal writing because they are unaware that it is an informal, conversational phrase. Give students formal substitutes for *a lot of,* such as *a large amount of* before noncount nouns and *many* before plural count nouns.

COLLABORATIVE LEARNING Exercises 16.5 and 16.6 Students can work in small groups to complete Exercises 5 and 6, then read each other's work to check article, adjective, and adverb usage.

ANSWERS

EXERCISE 16.5 Revising: Articles (p. 330)

From the native American Indians who migrated from Asia 20,000 years ago to the new arrivals who now come by planes, the United States is a nation of foreigners. It is a country of immigrants who are all living under a single flag.

Back in the seventeenth and eighteenth centuries, at least 75 percent of the population came from England. However, between 1820 and 1975 more than 38 million immigrants came to this country from elsewhere in Europe. Many children of the immigrants were self-conscious and denied their heritage; many even refused to learn the native language of their parents and grandparents. They tried to "Americanize" themselves. The so-called Melting Pot theory of social change stressed the importance of blending everyone together into a kind of stew. Each nationality would contribute its own flavor, but the final stew would be something called "American."

This Melting Pot theory was never completely successful. In the last half of the twentieth century, an ethnic revival changed the metaphor. Many people now see American society as a mosaic. Americans are once again proud of their heritage, and ethnic differences make the mosaic colorful and interesting.

EXERCISE 16.6 Revising: Adjectives and adverbs (p. 331)

Americans often argue about which professional sport is best: basketball, football, or baseball. Basketball fans contend that their sport offers more action because the players are constantly running and shooting. Because it is played indoors in relatively small arenas, basketball allows fans to be closer to the action than the other sports do. Fans point to how gracefully the players fly through the air to the hoop. Football fanatics say they hardly stop yelling once the game begins. They cheer when their team executes a really complicated play well. They roar more loudly when the defense stops the opponents in a goal-line stand. They yell most loudly when a fullback crashes in for a score. In contrast, the supporters of baseball believe that it might be the perfect sport. It combines the one-on-one duel of pitcher and batter struggling valiantly with the tight teamwork of double and triple plays. Because the game is played slowly and carefully, fans can analyze and discuss the manager's strategy. Besides, they never know when they might catch a foul ball as a souvenir. However, no matter what the sport, all fans feel happy only when their team wins!

EXERCISE ON CHAPTERS 13-16 Revising: Grammatical sentences (p. 331)

Occasionally, musicians become "crossover artists" who can perform well in more than one field of music. For example, Wynton and Branford Marsalis were trained in jazz by their father, the great pianist Ellis Marsalis. Both of the sons have become successful classical artists. Branford's saxophone captures the richness of pieces by Ravel and Stravinsky. Wynton's albums of classical trumpet music from the Baroque period have brought him many awards. Still, if he were to choose which kind of music he likes better, Wynton would probably choose jazz. In contrast to the Marsalises, Yo-Yo Ma and Jean-Pierre Rampal grew up studying classical music. Then in the 1980s they were invited by Claude Bolling, a French pianist, to record Bolling's jazz compositions. In fact, Rampal's flute blended with Bolling's music so well that the two men have done three albums.

Such crossovers are often harder for vocalists. Each type of music has its own style and feel that are hard to learn. For example, Luciano Pavarotti and Kiri te Kanawa, two great opera performers, have sung popular music and folk songs in concerts and on albums. On each occasion, their technique was nearly perfect, yet each sounded as if he or she were simply trying to sing properly. It is even more difficult for pop or country vocalists to sing opera, as Linda Ronstadt and Gary Morris found when they appeared in *La Bohème*. Each of them has a clear, pure voice, but a few critics said that he and she lacked the vocal power necessary for opera. However, Bobby McFerrin has been successful singing both pop and classical pieces. He won a Grammy award for his song "Don't Worry, Be Happy." But he is equally able to sing classical pieces *a cappella* (without musical accompaniment). His voice's remarkable range and clarity allow him to imitate many musical instruments.

No matter how successful, all of these musicians have shown great courage by performing in a new field. They are willing to test and stretch their talents, and each of us music fans benefits.

PART 4

Clear Sentences

CHAPTER **17**
Sentence Fragments

CHAPTER **18**
Commas Splices and Fused Sentences

CHAPTER **19**
Pronoun Reference

CHAPTER **20**
Shifts

CHAPTER **21**
Misplaced and Dangling Modifiers

CHAPTER **22**
Mixed and Incomplete Sentences

Sentence Fragments

CHAPTER HIGHLIGHTS

This chapter opens with a positive approach, showing students how to test sentences for completeness, revise any fragments, and punctuate revised fragments. Following the opening section are discussions of particular structures that are often mispunctuated as complete sentences: subordinate clauses; verbal and prepositional phrases; and other word groups such as appositives, parts of compound predicates, and nouns plus modifiers. The chapter concludes with a discussion of the acceptable uses of incomplete sentences.

MEDIA RESOURCES FOR CHAPTER 17

mycomplab Please visit MyCompLab at *www.mycomplab.com* for more on the writing process.

http://www.ablongman.com/littlebrown ▶ See page 73 of this manual for companion Web site content description.

INSTRUCTOR RESOURCE

The following Presentation Aid is available for download on this book's companion Web site at *http://www.ablongman.com/littlebrown.*

PRESENTATION AID 17.1: Complete sentence versus sentence fragment (p. 334)

RESOURCES AND IDEAS

Harris, Muriel. "Mending the Fragmented Free Modifier." *College Composition and Communication* 32 (1981): 175–82. Harris presents strategies for identifying kinds of fragments and correcting them.

Noguchi, Rei R. "Fragments and Beyond." Chapter 5 in *Grammar and the Teaching of Writing: Limits and Possibilities*. Urbana: NCTE, 1991. 84–112. Noguchi outlines a positive approach to teaching students how to recognize, revise, or make use of sentence fragments.

17a Test your sentences for completeness, and revise any fragments.

INSTRUCTOR RESOURCE

The following Presentation Aid is available for download on this book's companion Web site at *http://www.ablongman.com/littlebrown.*

Presentation Aid 17.2: Tests for complete sentences (p. 335)

CLASSROOM IDEAS

Fragments Students have been bombarded with so many fragments in advertising and popular prose ("Less filling! Tastes great!") that they may in fact not realize that using subordinate clauses as complete sentences is usually unacceptable. Your first job may be to convince them that what is acceptable in speech and informal writing is not always desirable in formal writing.

Newscasters The breathless style of radio and television newscasters often includes fragments. Ask students to write down examples from the evening news. Newspapers, especially tabloids, can be a good source, too.

Subordinating-word clues Encourage students to look for subordinating words—that is, subordinating conjunctions or relative pronouns—as they read their papers. Remind students that a complete sentence with a subordinating word must include two subjects and verbs, one subject and verb in the subordinate clause and one subject and verb in the main clause. Reading papers backward, from last sentence to first, may help some students find sentence fragments.

ANSWERS

Exercise 17.1 Identifying and revising sentence fragments (p. 337)

Possible answers

1. Lacks a subject and a verb.
   Complete: An article about vandalism against works of art was interesting.
   Combined: In an interesting article about vandalism against works of art, the author says the vandals' motives vary widely.
2. Lacks a verb.
   Complete: The motives of the vandals vary widely.
   Combined: The motives of the vandals varying widely, researchers can make few generalizations.
3. Complete sentence.
4. Lacks a subject and a verb.
   Complete: But the vandal is not necessarily angry at the artist or the owner.
   Combined: Whoever harms artwork is usually angry, but not necessarily at the artist or the owner.
5. Lacks a verb for the subject man.
   Complete: For instance, a man hammered at Michelangelo's *Pietà*.
   Combined: For instance, a man who hammered at Michelangelo's *Pietà* was angry at the Roman Catholic Church.

6. Lacks a subject.
   Complete: And he knocked off the Virgin Mary's nose.
   Combined: A man hammered at Michelangelo's *Pietà* and knocked off the Virgin Mary's nose.
7. Begins with a subordinating conjunction.
   Complete: He was angry at the Roman Catholic Church.
   Combined: A man hammered at Michelangelo's *Pietà* because he was angry at the Roman Catholic Church.
8. Begins with *which* but is not a question.
   Complete: The Church knew nothing of his grievance.
   Combined: He was angry at the Roman Catholic Church, which knew nothing of his grievance.
9. Begins with a subordinating conjunction.
   Complete: Many damaged works can be repaired.
   Combined: Although many damaged works can be repaired, even the most skillful repairs are forever visible.
10. Complete sentence.

17b A subordinate clause is not a complete sentence.

CLASSROOM IDEAS

COLLABORATIVE LEARNING Exercise 17.1 After students have completed Exercise 17.1 independently, have them compare responses in small groups and then read each other's work for examples of sentence fragments. For students who are struggling with the concept of sentence structure and of the sentence fragment, the move to recognize errors in their own work can be extremely helpful.

Analyzing patterns If students are keeping an error log in their journals, ask them to analyze the pattern(s) that lead them to commit fragments. Most students will commit fragments with only one or two of the problem sentence patterns discussed in 17b–17d.

17d Any word group lacking a subject or a verb or both is not a complete sentence.

INSTRUCTOR RESOURCE

The following Presentation Aid is available for download on this book's companion Web site at *http://www.ablongman.com/littlebrown.*

Presentation Aid 17.3: Exercise 17.3 Revising: Sentence fragments (p. 340)

CLASSROOM IDEA

COLLABORATIVE LEARNING Exercises 17.2 and 17.3 Students can work productively together on Exercises 17.2 and 17.3. Encourage each group to experiment with more than one response to each sentence.

ANSWERS

Exercise 17.2 Revising: Sentence fragments (p. 340)

1. Human beings who perfume themselves are not much different from other animals.
2. Animals as varied as insects and dogs release *pheromones*, chemicals that signal other animals.
3. Human beings have a diminished sense of smell and do not consciously detect most of their own species' pheromones.
4. The human substitute for pheromones may be perfumes, especially musk and other fragrances derived from animal oils.
5. Some sources say that humans began using perfume to cover up the smell of burning flesh during sacrifices to the gods.
6. No sentence fragment.
7. The earliest historical documents from the Middle East record the use of fragrances, not only in religious ceremonies but on the body.
8. In the nineteenth century chemists began synthesizing perfume oils, which previously could be made only from natural sources.
9. The most popular animal oil for perfume today is musk, although some people dislike its heavy, sweet odor.
10. Synthetic musk oil would preserve a certain species of deer whose gland is the source of musk.

17e Be aware of the acceptable uses of incomplete sentences.

CLASSROOM IDEA

Creating problems If students have been assigned Chapter 18, "Comma Splices and Fused Sentences," along with this chapter, ask them to write sample sentences containing fused sentences, comma splices, and fragments. Then have them exchange papers and check to see if the errors have been executed properly. This exercise will help students recognize fused sentences, comma splices, and fragments. (It's much harder to create intentional errors, particularly sentence fragments, than most students will think.)

ANSWERS

Exercise 17.3 Revising: Sentence fragments (p. 341)

Possible revision

   Baby red-eared slider turtles are brightly colored. Bold patterns on their yellowish undershells serve as a warning to predators. The bright colors of skunks and other animals signal that the animals will spray nasty chemicals. In contrast, the turtle's colors warn largemouth bass that the baby turtle will actively defend itself. When a bass gulps down a turtle, the feisty baby claws and bites, forcing the bass to spit it out. To avoid a similar painful experience, the bass will avoid other baby red-eared slider turtles. The turtle loses its bright colors as it grows too big for a bass's afternoon snack.

CHAPTER 18

Comma Splices
and Fused Sentences

CHAPTER HIGHLIGHTS

This chapter begins with a summary of the accepted methods for punctuating consecutive main clauses and follows with advice for recognizing and correcting comma splices and fused sentences. Correction of comma splices and fused sentences may involve strategies that students should employ more frequently in their sentences, particularly subordination and use of the semicolon. To encourage variety in sentence structure along with the avoidance of error, exercises for the chapter ask students to combine sentences following different strategies as well as to recognize and revise comma splices and fused sentences.

It's important to remember that students will naturally commit more of these errors as they struggle to master more complex syntactic patterns. Although you want to point out their mistakes, be careful not to focus too tightly on punctuation errors that occur as they strive for stylistic growth.

MEDIA RESOURCES FOR CHAPTER 18

mycomplab Please visit MyCompLab at *www.mycomplab.com* for more on the writing process.

http://www.ablongman.com/littlebrown ▶ (See page 73 of this manual for companion Web site content description.

INSTRUCTOR RESOURCE

The following Presentation Aid is available for download on this book's companion Web site at *http://www.ablongman.com/littlebrown*.

PRESENTATION AID 18.1: Situations that may produce comma splices and fused sentences (p. 343)

CLASSROOM IDEA

Knowing your errors Writers tend to produce repeated patterns of error (comma splices or sentence fragments, for example) and may struggle to recognize as well as to correct occurrences of those particular patterns of error in their work. It can be extremely helpful for students to learn which errors frequently occur in their work and to keep a list of corrected examples of those errors from previous work in order to look for those particular errors in future work.

RESOURCES AND IDEAS

Teachers and tutors who have little trouble punctuating sentences themselves may find it difficult to understand why some students have such difficulty with punctuation. In *The Practical Tutor* (New York: Oxford UP, 1987, 177–201), Emily Meyer and Louise Z. Smith offer detailed explanations of the causes of error and advice for diagnosing the roots of a student's punctuation difficulties. The teaching strategies they suggest include reading aloud, reading unpunctuated passages, asking probing questions (examples provided), and using simple diagrams. Rei R. Noguchi also offers innovative approaches to these errors in "Run-ons, Comma Splices, and Native-Speaker Abilities" in *Grammar and the Teaching of Writing: Limits and Possibilities* (Urbana: NCTE, 1991, 64–83).

18a **Separate two main clauses with a comma *only* when they are joined by a coordinating conjunction.**

CLASSROOM IDEAS

CULTURE LANGUAGE Fanboys A mnemonic that helps students remember the coordinating conjunctions is *fanboys*, which is the first letter of each coordinating conjunction. Put the following chart on the board to illustrate:

	for	
	and	
	nor	
Sentence 1	*but*	Sentence 2
	or	
	yet	
	so	

Remind ESL students that after *nor*, English requires inverted word order.

In context Identifying sentence problems in the context of an essay can be more challenging and rewarding than working with single-sentence examples. The content and flow of an essay can draw attention away from punctuation and sentence structure, making it hard to identify errors but also providing an experience similar to that of proofreading. To supplement the paragraph exercise at the end of this chapter (or at the end of Chapter 17), revise part of a professional essay to introduce errors (or find an error-filled student essay) and then distribute the essay to the class, asking students to locate and revise the errors.

Separate main clauses related by *however, for example,* and so on.

CLASSROOM IDEA

COLLABORATIVE LEARNING Exercises 18.1, 18.2, 18.3, and 18.4 Ask students to complete Exercises 18.1 and 18.2 independently and compare their responses in small groups. Then ask each group to work together on Exercises 18.3 and 18.4. Finally, have the groups examine each other's work to find and revise examples of comma splices and fused sentences. For students who are having difficulty with these errors, the move from the handbook exercises to their own work can be extremely beneficial.

ANSWERS

EXERCISE 18.1 Identifying and revising comma splices (p. 347)

Possible answers

1. Money has a long history. It goes back at least as far as the earliest records.

   Money has a long history that goes back at least as far as the earliest records.

2. Many of the earliest records concern financial transactions; indeed, early history must often be inferred from commercial activity.

   Many of the earliest records concern financial transactions. Indeed, early history must often be inferred from commercial activity.

3. No comma splice.

4. Sometimes the objects have had real value. In modern times, however, their value has been more abstract.

   Sometimes the objects have had real value; in modern times, however, their value has been more abstract.

5. Cattle, fermented beverages, and rare shells have served as money, and each one had actual value for the society.

   Cattle, fermented beverages, and rare shells have served as money. Each one had actual value for the society.

18c Combine two main clauses only with an appropriate conjunction or punctuation mark between them.

INSTRUCTOR RESOURCE

The following Presentation Aid is available for download on this book's companion Web site at *http://www.ablongman.com/littlebrown*.

PRESENTATION AID 18.2: Exercise 18.4: Revising: Comma splices and fused sentences (p. 349)

CLASSROOM IDEA

Creating problems If students have been assigned Chapter 17, "Sentence Fragments," along with this chapter, ask them to write sample sentences containing comma splices, fused sentences, and fragments. Then have them exchange papers and check to see if the errors have been executed properly. This exercise will help students recognize comma splices, fused sentences, and fragments. (It's much harder to create intentional errors, particularly fused sentences and sentence fragments, than most students will think.)

ANSWERS

EXERCISE 18.2 Identifying and reviving fused sentences (p. 348)

1. Throughout history money and religion were closely linked because there was little distinction between government and religion.

   Throughout history money and religion were closely linked, for there was little distinction between government and religion.

2. The head of state and the religious leader were often the same person. All power rested in one ruler.

   The head of state and the religious leader were often the same person; all power rested in one ruler.

3. These powerful leaders decided what objects would serve as money, and their backing encouraged public faith in the money.

   These powerful leaders decided what objects would serve as money. Their backing encouraged public faith in the money.

4. When coins were minted of precious metals, the religious overtones of money were strengthened.

   Coins were minted of precious metals. The religious overtones of money were then strengthened.

5. People already believed the precious metals to be divine, so their use in money intensified its allure.

   People already believed the precious metals to be divine; their use in money intensified its allure.

EXERCISE 18.3 Sentence combining: Comma splices and fused sentences (p. 349)

1. The exact origin of paper money is unknown because it has not survived as coins, shells, and other durable objects have.

2. Perhaps goldsmiths were also bankers; thus they held the gold of their wealthy customers.

3. The goldsmiths probably gave customers receipts for their gold, and these receipts were then used in trade.
4. The goldsmiths were something like modern-day bankers; their receipts were something like modern-day money.
5. The goldsmiths became even more like modern-day bankers when they began issuing receipts for more gold than they actually held in their vaults.

EXERCISE 18.4 Revising: Comma splices and fused sentences (p. 349)

All those parents who urged their children to eat broccoli were right; the vegetable really is healthful. Broccoli contains sulforaphane; moreover, this mustard oil can be found in kale and Brussels sprouts. Sulforaphane causes the body to make an enzyme that attacks carcinogens, substances that cause cancer. The enzyme speeds up the work of the kidneys so that they can flush harmful chemicals out of the body. Other vegetables have similar benefits; however, green, leafy vegetables like broccoli are the most efficient. Thus wise people will eat their broccoli; it could save their lives.

CHAPTER 19

Pronoun Reference

CHAPTER HIGHLIGHTS

Writers at all levels—advanced or struggling—will be likely to consult this chapter often, for problems with pronoun reference can arise in short, uncomplicated sentences as well as in papers that are ambitious in style and content. The discussion covers a number of particularly troublesome problems: unclear or ambiguous antecedents; broad reference with *this, that, which,* and *it*; indefinite use of *it* and *they*; and inappropriate use of *who, which,* and *that.* In each case, the discussion stresses the need for precision in reference as a way of ensuring that readers can follow the meaning of a passage. The examples and exercises mostly show reference problems within sentences as a way of keeping the discussion as simple and accessible as possible; however, the text points out that reference problems are just as likely to occur between sentences, and the paragraph exercise at the end of the chapter stresses this fact.

Because strings of pronouns are an important device for creating coherence over long stretches of discourse, reference problems between or among sentences can cause considerable misunderstanding. In this sense, pronoun reference errors can point to students' larger conceptual difficulties (such as defining or elaborating on key terms or thinking through a transition). This means that when students learn to recognize their pronoun reference errors, that recognition can provide the occasion for substantive revision and paragraph development.

MEDIA RESOURCES FOR CHAPTER 19

mycomplab[20] Please visit MyCompLab at *www.mycomplab.com* for more on the writing process.

http://www.ablongman.com/littlebrown ▶ See page 73 of this manual for companion Web site content description.

19a Make a pronoun refer clearly to one antecedent.

CLASSROOM IDEAS

Retrieving sentences Reverse the process of sentence combining by asking students to reconstruct (or retrieve) the shorter (kernel) sentences that lie behind a long sentence containing a reference error. You may wish to use sentences from the text as a basis for the exercise. This activity will help students spot ambiguity or vague reference in the long sentence. After they have found the shorter sentences, ask students to recombine, this time avoiding the reference problem.

> *Original sentence:* After the van hit John's car, its engine stopped running and its radiator started leaking.
>
> *Kernels:* The van hit John's car. The van's engine stopped running. The van's radiator started leaking.
>
> *Recombined sentence:* After the van hit John's car, the van's engine stopped running and its radiator started leaking.

CULTURE LANGUAGE Omitted relative clause pronouns Sentences in which the relative clause pronoun is omitted often give ESL students difficulty, and they may make the mistake of adding an extra redundant pronoun. Give them a model sentence to help them remember the rule, such as the following:

> We are going to the flea market that we read about in the newspaper.

This can be especially helpful when they are doing sentence-combining exercises, and they may want to keep a few of their own models in a computer file for handy reference. (See also 22a-2 for more on repeated sentence parts.)

19b Place a pronoun close enough to its antecedent to ensure clarity.

ANSWERS

EXERCISE 19.1 Revising: Ambiguous and remote pronoun reference (p. 352)

Possible answers

1. There is a difference between the heroes of the twentieth century and the heroes of earlier times: twentieth-century heroes have flaws in their characters.
2. Sports fans still admire Pete Rose, Babe Ruth, and Joe Namath even though none of these heroes could be perfect.
3. Fans liked Rose for having his young son serve as batboy when Rose was in Cincinnati.
4. Rose's reputation as a gambler and tax evader may overshadow his reputation as a ballplayer, but the latter will survive.
5. Rose amassed an unequaled record as a hitter, using his bat to do things no one else has ever done. The record stands even though Rose has been banned from baseball.

19c Make a pronoun refer to a specific antecedent, not an implied one.

CLASSROOM IDEA

Correcting a narrative Find or write a brief narrative containing several events and more than one character. Introduce enough reference problems so that readers have difficulty unraveling the events. If you wish, include dialogue in the narrative in such a way that the reference problems make it hard to identify the speakers. (Using "He said" as a tag when there are two men in the narrative is one possibility.) Ask students to work in groups to untangle the problems in the narrative and to rewrite it, removing vague and ambiguous references.

RESOURCES AND IDEAS

Moskovit, Leonard. "When Is Broad Reference Clear?" *College Composition and Communication* 34 (1983): 454–69. The question of the acceptability of broad reference is a complicated one, as Moskovit points out, and anyone interested in looking at how broad reference operates in sophisticated prose will enjoy his essay.

19d Use *it* and *they* to refer to definite antecedents.

CLASSROOM IDEA

It, which, and they Distribute copies of a student paper that uses *it, which, they,* and other pronouns in sentences without supplying clear antecedents in preceding sentences. Ask students to work in groups to revise the reference problems. In each case ask the group to consider whether the revision simply involves correcting the error or whether it calls for the writer to clarify and develop his or her transition between sentences or paragraphs.

19e Use *who, which,* and *that* for appropriate antecedents

CLASSROOM IDEAS

Use of *that* or *which* Students are often confused about whether to use *which, who,* or *that* because they misunderstand essential and nonessential elements. Students who suffer from this confusion should also consult Chapter 28 and *that/which* in the Glossary of Usage.

COLLABORATIVE LEARNING Exercises 19.2 and 19.3 Students can work productively together on Exercises 19.2 and 19.3. After they have completed both exercises, ask them to look for and revise instances of unclear pronoun references in other examples from each other's work. Each group might present one example of an unclear pronoun reference discovered in a student paper to the class.

ANSWERS

EXERCISE 19.2 Revising: Indefinite and inappropriate pronoun reference (p. 356)

Possible answers

1. "Life begins at forty" is a cliché many people live by, and this saying may well be true.
2. When Pearl Buck was forty, her novel *The Good Earth* won the Pulitzer Prize.
3. Buck was a novelist who wrote primarily about China.
4. In *The Good Earth* the characters have to struggle, but fortitude is rewarded.
5. Buck received much critical praise and earned over $7 million, but she was very modest about her success [*or* the praise *or* the money].
6. Kenneth Kaunda was elected to the presidency of Zambia in 1964, at age forty.
7. When Catherine I became empress of Russia at age forty, the Russians feared more than loved her.
8. At forty, Paul Revere made his famous ride to warn American revolutionary leaders that the British were going to arrest them. His warning gave the colonists time to prepare for battle.
9. The members of the British House of Commons did not welcome forty-year-old Nancy Astor as the first female member when she entered in 1919.
10. In AD 610, Muhammad, age forty, began to have a series of visions that became the foundation of the Muslim faith. Since then, millions of people have become Muslims.

EXERCISE 19.3 Revising: Pronoun reference (p. 357)

Possible revision

In Charlotte Brontë's *Jane Eyre*, Jane is a shy young woman who takes a job as governess. Her employer is a rude, brooding man named Rochester. He lives in a mysterious mansion on the English moors, and both the mansion and the moors contribute an eerie quality to Jane's experience. Eerier still are the fires, strange noises, and other unexplained happenings in the house; but Rochester refuses to discuss them. Eventually, Jane and Rochester fall in love. On the day they are to be married, however, Jane learns that Rochester has a wife hidden in the house. The wife is hopelessly insane and violent and must be guarded at all times, circumstances that explain Rochester's strange behavior. Heartbroken, Jane leaves the moors, and many years pass before she and Rochester are reunited.

Shifts

CHAPTER HIGHLIGHTS

Shifts in person and number, in tense and mood, in subject and voice, or between direct and indirect quotation can be irritating to readers and occasionally make it hard to follow the meaning of a passage. Often, however, students are not fully aware of the shifts or their effect on a reader. This chapter describes in detail and illustrates the various shifts so that students can learn to identify the problems in their own writing. The exercises ask students to revise sentences and a longer passage, much as they will need to do in revising their own work.

MEDIA RESOURCES FOR CHAPTER 20

mycomplab Please visit MyCompLab at *www.mycomplab.com* for more on the writing process.

http://www.ablongman.com/littlebrown ▶ See page 73 of this manual for companion Web site content description.

20a Keep a sentence or related sentences consistent in person and number.

CLASSROOM IDEAS

COLLABORATIVE LEARNING Check your own If shifts are a problem in the essays your class submits, go over the chapter in detail in class, and then ask students to go through their papers and circle each shift they find. This activity can be done on the day papers are to be handed in or with a set of graded papers on which you have not marked the shifts. The activity is also a good small-group exercise; students are often good at spotting shifts in someone else's writing.

COMPUTER ACTIVITY Highlighting agreement Encourage students who compose on a word processor to use its highlighting or boldface capabilities to mark person and number, tense, or subject-verb agreement markers in a draft; this helps students see at a glance where they may need to revise.

ANSWERS

Exercise 20.1 Revising: Shifts in person and number (p. 359)

1. When a taxpayer is waiting to receive a tax refund from the Internal Revenue Service, he or she begins to notice what time the mail carrier arrives. *Or:* When taxpayers are waiting to receive tax refunds . . . , they begin to notice what time the mail carrier arrives.
2. If the taxpayer does not receive a refund check within six weeks of filing a return, he or she may not have followed the rules of the IRS. *Or:* If taxpayers do not receive refund checks within six weeks of filing a return, they may not have followed the rules of the IRS.
3. If taxpayers do not include their Social Security numbers on returns, they will have to wait for refunds. *Or:* A taxpayer who does not include a Social Security number on a return will have to wait for a refund.
4. When taxpayers do not file their returns early, they will not get refunds quickly.
5. If taxpayers make errors on the tax forms, they might even be audited, thereby delaying refunds even longer. *Or:* If one has made errors on the tax form, he or she might even be audited, thereby delaying a refund even longer.

20b Keep a sentence or related sentences consistent in tense and mood

CLASSROOM IDEA

CULTURE LANGUAGE Tense sequencing and shifts ESL students may be particularly confused about how to tell the difference between correct tense sequencing and incorrect tense shifting. You might need to include a review of section 14h when you are teaching this topic.

ANSWERS

EXERCISE 20.2 Revising: Shifts in tense and mood (p. 360)

1. When your cholesterol count is too high, adjusting your diet and exercise level reduces it.
2. After you lower your cholesterol rate, you decrease the chances of heart attack and stroke.
3. First eliminate saturated fats from your diet; then consume more whole grains and raw vegetables.
4. To avoid saturated fats, substitute turkey and chicken for beef, and use cholesterol-free salad dressing and cooking oil.
5. A regular program of aerobic exercise, such as walking or swimming, improves your cholesterol rate and makes you feel much healthier.

20c   Keep a sentence or related sentences consistent in subject and voice.

CLASSROOM IDEA

Class reading Use the passage below, or find or write another that contains several kinds of shifts. Distribute copies to the class and read through the passage with students, asking them to identify the problems. This exercise will help make students aware of the different kinds of shifts as they appear in the context of an essay.

As soon as the avalanche was over, Jim pulls himself out of the snowbank and yells, "Where's everybody?" and were we still alive. As each of us in turn started digging out, you could see the damage the huge wall of snow had caused. The snow had destroyed the lodge and cars were swept away.

ANSWERS

EXERCISE 20.3 Revising: Shifts in subject and voice (p. 361)

1. If students learn how to study efficiently, they will make much better grades on tests.
2. Conscientious students begin to prepare for tests immediately after they attend the first class.
3. Before each class the students complete all reading assignments, outline the material, and answer any study questions.
4. In class they listen carefully and take good notes.
5. The students ask questions when they do not understand the professor.

20d   Keep a quotation or a question consistently direct or indirect.

CLASSROOM IDEA

COLLABORATIVE LEARNING Exercise 20.4 Students can create their own examples of direct and indirect quotations and questions, using the models provided in Exercise 20.4. Ask students to work through Exercise 20.4 in small groups and then to create two or three additional examples.

Alternatively, you might ask students to compare their independent responses to Exercises 20.1–20.4, then work in small groups to revise the paragraph in Exercise 20. 5. This gives students the opportunity to help each other recognize shifts and to discuss the effects of unnecessary shifts. You might have each group present their responses to one or two sentences of the paragraph in Exercise 20.5 and encourage the presenters to foreground the group's questions and comments.

EXERCISE 20.4 Revising: Shifts in direct and indirect quotations and questions (p. 362)

1. *Direct:* One anthropologist says, "The functions of marriage have changed, nowhere more dramatically than in industrialized cultures."
Indirect: One anthropologist says that the functions of marriage have changed, most dramatically in industrialized cultures.
2. *Direct:* May siblings marry? Would the union be immoral?
Indirect: The question even arises of whether siblings may marry and whether the union would be immoral.
3. *Direct:* The author points out, "Sibling marriage is still illegal everywhere in the United States, and people are still prosecuted under the law."
Indirect: The author points out that sibling marriage is still illegal everywhere in the United States and that people are still prosecuted under the law.
4. *Direct:* She says, "Incest could be considered a universal taboo. The questions asked about the taboo vary widely."
Indirect: She says that incest could be considered a universal taboo and that the questions asked about the taboo vary widely.
5. *Direct:* Is the taboo a way of protecting the family? Might it be instinctive?
Indirect: Some ask whether the taboo is a way of protecting the family or whether it may be instinctive.

EXERCISE 20.5 Revising: Shifts (p. 263)

Possible revision

Driving in snow need not be dangerous if you practice a few simple rules. First, avoid fast starts, which prevent the wheels from gaining traction and may result in the car's getting stuck. Second, drive more slowly than usual, and pay attention to the feel of the car: if the steering seems unusually loose or the wheels do not seem to be grabbing the road, slow down. Third, avoid fast stops, which lead to skids. Be alert for other cars and intersections that may necessitate applying the brakes suddenly. If you need to slow down, reduce the car's momentum by downshifting as well as by applying the brakes. When braking, press the pedal to the floor only if you have antilock brakes; otherwise, pump the pedal in short bursts. If you feel the car skidding, release the brakes, turn the wheel into the direction of the skid, and then press or pump the brakes again. Repeating these motions will stop the skid and reduce the speed of the car.

CHAPTER 21

Misplaced and Dangling Modifiers

CHAPTER HIGHLIGHTS

Misplaced and dangling modifiers often interest students because the faulty constructions can be amusing. To tie together all the different problems discussed in the chapter, however, you may want to point out that they all illustrate the importance of position and arrangement in sentences. Split constructions (21d and 21e) conveniently emphasize the need to keep the parts of related syntactic groups clearly unified. Yet both standard speech and formal writing provide frequent examples of freely placed limiting modifiers and of split infinitives. Part of our difficulty in teaching composition is in giving students effective advice about when freedom is constructive and when it is confusing. As in all such matters, the advice of the handbook is largely conservative; you may therefore want to modify it somewhat.

MEDIA RESOURCES FOR CHAPTER 21

mycomplab™ Please visit MyCompLab at *www.mycomplab.com* for more on the writing process.

http://www.ablongman.com/littlebrown ▶ See page 73 of this manual for companion Web site content description.

21a Place modifiers where they will clearly modify the words intended.

ANSWERS

EXERCISE 21.1 Revising: Misplaced phrases and clauses (p. 365)

1. Women have contributed much of great value to knowledge and culture.
2. In 1821 Emma Willard founded the Troy Female Seminary, the first institution to provide a college-level education for women.
3. Sixteen years later Mary Lyon founded Mount Holyoke Female Seminary, the first true women's college with a campus and directors who would sustain the college even after Lyon's death.

4. *Una,* which was founded by Pauline Wright Davis in 1853, was the first US newspaper that was dedicated to gaining women's rights.
5. Mitchell's Comet, which was named for Maria Mitchell, was discovered in 1847.

21b Place limiting modifiers carefully.

CLASSROOM IDEA

Moving *only* Ask students to create sentences whose meaning changes as a modifier like only moves from place to place:

Only students were asked to bring gym shorts and running shoes.

Students were *only* asked to bring gym shorts and running shoes.

Students were asked *only* to bring gym shorts and running shoes.

Students were asked to bring *only* gym shorts and running shoes.

21c Make each modifier refer to only one grammatical element.

CLASSROOM IDEA

COLLABORATIVE LEARNING Limiting and squinting modifiers Students can work productively together (in pairs or small groups) on Exercises 21.2 and 21.3. This collaborative effort can be particularly useful when students are asked to create more than one possible revision.

ANSWERS

EXERCISE 21.2 Using limiting modifiers (p. 366)

1. Almost everybody hates him.
   Everybody almost hates him.
2. Even now I remember the details of the event.
   Now I remember even the details of the event.
3. We hardly heard him call our names.
   We heard him hardly call our names.
4. Write simply.
   Simply write.
5. I nearly missed the performance that was booed off the stage.
   I missed the performance that was nearly booed off the stage.

EXERCISE 21.3 Revising: Squinting modifiers (p. 366)

1. People who often sunbathe can damage their skin. *Or:* People who sunbathe can often damage their skin.

2. Sunbathers who frequently apply a sunscreen block some of the sun's harmful rays. *Or:* Frequently, sunbathers who apply a sunscreen block some of the sun's harmful rays.
3. Men and women who often lie out in the sun have leathery, dry skin. *Or:* Often men and women who lie out in the sun have leathery, dry skin.
4. Doctors tell sunbathers they risk skin cancer when they are older. *Or:* Doctors tell older sunbathers they risk skin cancer.
5. People who usually stay out of the sun will have better skin and fewer chances of skin cancer. *Or:* People who stay out of the sun will usually have better skin and fewer chances of skin cancer.

21d Keep subjects, verbs, and objects together.

CLASSROOM IDEAS

The media Radio and television newscasts are rich sources of dangling and misplaced modifiers, perhaps because reporters have little time to pay attention to the structure of their sentences. Have students listen to newscasts and record errors: doing so will help them to understand the perspective of a reader who comes across similar errors in an essay. Newspaper headlines and public announcements are also rich sources; from time to time, magazine articles and paperback books appear with collections of particularly humorous errors. But students will be able to find many on their own by looking at the newspaper for headlines like *Young man slain with flowers*.

COLLABORATIVE LEARNING Home-grown star reporters Ask students to form groups in order to write their own newscasts filled with the kinds of errors they might spot through the activity above. The newscasts (and the errors) should be plausible in style and content, though the content will probably have to be the product of students' imaginations. Having heard many newscasts, however, students will probably have little trouble parodying them in form and matter.

21e Keep parts of infinitives or verb phrases together.

ANSWERS

EXERCISE 21.4 Revising: Spearated sentence parts (p. 368)

1. In 1868 Myra Bradwell founded the *Chicago Legal News*.
2. Although she had qualified, Bradwell was later denied admission to the Illinois Bar Association.
3. In an attempt finally to gain admission to the bar, she carried the case to the Supreme Court, but the justices decided against her.
4. Bradwell was determined that no other woman would be denied entrance to a profession if she were qualified.

5. In response to Bradwell's persuasion, the Illinois legislature finally passed a bill ensuring that no one would be restricted from a profession on the basis of gender.

21f Arrange adjectives appropriately.

CLASSROOM IDEAS

CULTURE LANGUAGE Modifications of modification rules ESL students may make errors with modifiers because of insufficient knowledge of adjective order and agreement. For instance, in many languages (Spanish, Korean, Vietnamese, Armenian, and others) adjectives follow the nouns they modify ("the sky blue" instead of "the blue sky"). Spanish speakers may make adjectives agree in number with the nouns they modify ("the greys clouds" instead of "the grey clouds"). To help your ESL students remember the English rules and to give your native English-speaking students some exposure to other languages' rules, have your ESL students teach the rest of the class how modifier word order and agreement works in their native language.

ANSWERS

EXERCISE 21.5 Revising: Placement of adverbs and adjectives (p. 370)

1. Some years ago Detroit cars were often praised.
2. Large luxury cars were especially prized.
3. Sentence correct.
4. When ample gasoline supplies returned, consumers again bought large American cars.
5. However, the large cars were not luxury sedans but vans and sport-utility vehicles.

21g Relate dangling modifiers to their sentences.

INSTRUCTOR RESOURCES

The following Presentation Aids are available for download on this book's companion Web site at *http://www.ablongman.com/littlebrown.*

PRESENTATION AID 21.1: Identifying and revising dangling modifiers (p. 372)

PRESENTATION AID 21.2: Exercise 21.6. Revising: Dangling modifiers (p. 372)

CLASSROOM IDEAS

COLLABORATIVE LEARNING Collecting howlers An amusing exercise is to have students collect examples of misplaced and dangling modifiers to share; reward the team that collects the most examples with a prize like a day's extension on the next assignment. The "finds" may include some particularly funny ones like this:

> Stitched on 14-count canvas, your daughter will enjoy learning to cross-stitch.

COLLABORATIVE LEARNING Exercises 21.6 and 21.7 Have students work in small groups to discuss their responses to Exercises 21.6 and 21.7. Then ask each group to complete Exercise 8 together and present part of the revised paragraph to the class. As each group gives its presentation, encourage other groups to contribute their differing revisions of the same sentences. This helps students to become more aware of the numerous possibilities for revision.

Sentence combining Exercise 21.7 requires students to combine pairs of sentences whose content and structure make them likely causes of misplaced or dangling modifiers. Extend this activity by having students create their own sentences that would be easy to miscombine. Choose the best pairs, copy them, and have the class do them for an exercise. This activity leads to considerable discussion and some imaginative and amusing results when the students work in groups.

ANSWERS

EXERCISE 21.6 Revising: Dangling modifiers (p. 372)

Possible answers

1. After Andrew Jackson had accomplished many deeds of valor, his fame led to his election to the presidency in 1828 and 1832.
2. By the time Jackson was fourteen, both of his parents had died.
3. To aid the American Revolution, Jackson chose service as a mounted courier.
4. Though not well educated, Jackson proved his ability in a successful career as a lawyer and judge.
5. Because Jackson won many military battles, the American public believed in his leadership.

EXERCISE 21.7 Sentence combining: Placing modifiers (p. 373)

Possible answers

1. As evening falls in the Central American rain forests, the tungara frogs begin their croaking chorus.
2. Croaking loudly at night, male tungara frogs sing "songs" designed to attract female frogs.
3. But predators, also hearing the croaking, gather to feast on the frogs.
4. Lured by their croaking dinners, the predators include bullfrogs, snakes, bats, and opossums.
5. Although the frogs hope to mate, their nightly chorus can result in death instead.

EXERCISE 21.8 Revising: Misplaced and dangling modifiers (p. 373)

Possible revision

<u>Several nights a week</u>, Central American tungara frogs silence their mating croaks. When not croaking, <u>they</u> reduce the chance that they will be eaten by predators. The frogs seem <u>to believe fully</u> in "safety in numbers." <u>More than likely</u>, they will croak along with a large group rather than by themselves. By forgoing croaking on some nights, <u>the frogs</u> prevent the species from "croaking."

RESOURCES AND IDEAS

Chaika, Elaine. "Grammars and Teaching." *College English* 39 (1978): 770–83. Chaika offers fresh explanations from a linguistic perspective for a number of standard errors, including dangling modifiers.

Pixton, William H. "The Dangling Gerund: A Working Definition." *College Composition and Communication* 24 (1973): 193–99. Pixton reviews discussions of dangling modifiers and, using a variety of sample sentences, formulates a definition of the dangling gerund.

22

Mixed and Incomplete Sentences

CHAPTER HIGHLIGHTS

The first two sections of Chapter 22 treat sentences whose subjects and predicates are incompatible. The tangled sentences in some student writing have more complex causes than this brief discussion of mixed sentences can address. But the two most common problems do seem to be subjects and predicates that are incompatible in grammar and in meaning.

The third section deals with compound constructions that are grammatically or idiomatically incomplete. Ill-prepared students seem to encounter this problem less often than better-prepared students do, perhaps because only the latter use such constructions. On the other hand, incomplete comparisons (22d) are common, and you may wish to call particular attention to them.

The final section, covering omission of needed words, is designed primarily as an aid to grading papers. Instructors who notice words missing in a student essay can call attention to the problem by using the number-and-letter code to refer students to this section.

MEDIA RESOURCES FOR CHAPTER 22

mycomplab⒇ Please visit MyCompLab at *www.mycomplab.com* for more on the writing process.

http://www.ablongman.com/littlebrown ▶ See page 73 of this manual for companion Web site content description.

22a Untangle sentences that are mixed in grammar.

CLASSROOM IDEA

Using student writing Because the mixed and incomplete sentences in student writing have complicated causes and because the problems in one student's essay are likely to differ widely from those in another student's paper, most instructors choose simply to discuss the chapter and use some of the exercises rather than elaborate with classroom activities and assignments. In working with individual students, however, most instructors are able to devise activities that suit individual needs. Instructors who wish to alert students to the problem of incomplete compound constructions, incomplete comparisons, and omission of needed words can draw from a student paper or write a passage containing these problems and then ask students to work with the passage, perhaps in small groups, proofreading it and correcting the errors. Students' journals and error logs are excellent sources of material as well as good places to practice revision strategies. Encourage students to keep a log of the patterns of error that tend to recur in their work, along with corrected examples. That log can provide a good resource for future revision and editing sessions.

RESOURCES AND IDEAS

Krishna, Valerie. "The Syntax of Error." *Journal of Basic Writing* 1 (1975): 43–9. The author views problems like mixed constructions and shifts as the result of a weak sentence core, and she encourages teachers to pay attention to this underlying problem in helping students avoid such errors.

Shuman, R. Baird. "Grammar for Writers: How Much Is Enough." The *Place of Grammar in Writing Instruction: Past, Present, Future*. Ed. Susan Hunter and Ray Wallace. Portsmouth: Boynton, 1995. 114–28. Shuman offers simplified strategies for presenting sentence structure as a meaningful concept in an effort to prevent some student errors.

22b Match subjects and predicates in meaning.

CLASSROOM IDEA

COLLABORATIVE LEARNING Exercise 22.1 Students can work together to create or to compare their responses to Exercise 22.1. Encourage each group to explore various possible answers.

ANSWERS

EXERCISE 22.1 Revising: Sentences mixed in grammar or meaning (p. 377)

Possible answers

1. A hurricane <u>occurs</u> when the winds in a tropical depression rotate counterclockwise at more than seventy-four miles per hour.
2. Because hurricanes can destroy so many lives and much property, people fear them.
3. Through high winds, storm surge, floods, and tornadoes, a hurricane can kill thousands of people.
4. Many scientists observe that hurricanes in recent years have become more ferocious and destructive.

5. However, in the last half-century, improved communications systems and weather satellites have made hurricanes less deadly.

EXERCISE 22.2 Revising: Repeated sentence parts (p. 377)

1. Global warming is caused by the gradual erosion of the ozone layer that protects the earth from the sun.
2. Scientists who study this problem say that the primary causes of erosion are the use of fossil fuels and the reduction of forests.
3. Many nonscientists mistakenly believe that aerosol spray cans are the primary cause of erosion.
4. One scientist whom others respect argues that Americans have effectively reduced their use of aerosol sprays.
5. He argues that we will stop global warming only when the public learns the real causes.

22e Include all needed prepositions, articles, and other words.

CLASSROOM IDEA

COLLABORATIVE LEARNING Exercises 22.3 and 22.4 Exercises 22.3 and 22.4 work well as an extended group project. Encourage groups to experiment with alternate responses, and ask each group to present any problem points they encountered as well as their successful responses to one or more sections.

ANSWERS

EXERCISE 22.3 Revising: Incomplete sentences (p. 380)

1. The first ice cream, eaten in China in about 2000 BC, was more lumpy than ice cream in [*or* that in] the modern era.
2. The Chinese made their ice cream of milk, spices, and overcooked rice and packed it in snow to solidify.
3. In the fourteenth century ice milk and fruit ices appeared in Italy and on the tables of the wealthy.
4. At her wedding in 1533 to the King of France, Catherine de Médicis offered more flavors of fruit ices than any other hostess offered.
5. Modern sherbets resemble her ices; modern ice cream resembles her soft dessert of thick, sweetened cream.

EXERCISE 22.4 Revising: Mixed and incomplete sentences (p. 381)

Possible revision

The Hancock Tower in Boston is a thin mirror-glass slab that rises almost eight hundred feet. When it was being constructed, its windows began cracking, and some fell crashing to the ground. In order to minimize risks, the architects and owners replaced over a third of the huge windows with plywood until the problem could be found and solved. With its plywood sheath, the building was homelier than any other skyscraper, the butt of many jokes. Eventually, however, it was discovered that the windows cracked because the joint between the double panes of glass was too rigid. Thicker single-pane windows were installed, and the silly plywood building crystallized into a reflective jewel.

EXERCISE ON CHAPTERS 17-22 Revising: Clear sentences (p. 381)

Possible answers

Many people who are physically challenged have accomplished much, which proves that they are not "handicapped." Confined to wheelchairs, Bob Sampson and Stephen Hawking have forged successful careers. Despite his muscular dystrophy, Sampson has earned a law degree. He has also worked for United Airlines for more than thirty years. Stephen Hawking is most famous for his book *A Brief History of Time*. Hawking is unable to speak, but his voice synthesizer allows him to dictate his books, conduct public lectures, and teach mathematics classes at Cambridge University.

Franklin D. Roosevelt, Ann Adams, and Itzhak Perlman all refused to let polio destroy their lives. Indeed, as President, Roosevelt led the United States during two of the worst periods of its history: the Great Depression and World War II. Roosevelt inspired hope and determination in the American people, reassuring them with his strong, clear voice. Ann Adams, who was talented in art before polio paralyzed her, knew she had to continue to be an artist. Having retrained herself to draw with a pencil grasped in her teeth, she produced sketches of children and pets. These drawings were turned into greeting cards whose profits sustained her. Roosevelt and Adams were stricken with polio when they were adults; Itzhak Perlman was stricken when he was a child. He was unable to play sports; instead, he studied the violin. Now many think he is greater than any other violinist in the world.

Like Perlman, many physically challenged individuals turn to the arts. Perhaps they do so because [*or:* the reason is that] the joy of artistic achievement compensates for other pleasures they cannot experience. Stevie Wonder, José Feliciano, and Andrea Bocelli all express their souls through their music. Although they are unable to see physically, their music reveals how well they truly see. Hearing impairment struck Ludwig van Beethoven and Marlee Matlin, but it did not stop them from developing their talents. Already a successful composer, Beethoven wrote many of his most powerful pieces after he became deaf. Similarly, Matlin has had excellent acting roles in movies, plays, and television programs; indeed, she won an Oscar for *Children of a Lesser God*. She encourages others to develop their abilities, and she has inspired many hearing-impaired actors.

PART 5

Effective Sentences

CHAPTER 23
Emphasizing Ideas

CHAPTER 24
Using Coordination and Subordination

CHAPTER 25
Using Parallelism

CHAPTER 26
Achieving Variety

Emphasizing Ideas

CHAPTER HIGHLIGHTS

This chapter looks at two ways to achieve emphasis within sentences: by the distribution of information and by the choice of strategies to create specific effects. The opening sections consider subjects and verbs as the heart of sentences and the importance of beginnings and endings. Additional special features of the chapter include its treatment of cumulative and periodic sentences and discussions that stress the rhetorical effect of each sentence pattern. The exercises are designed to help students feel comfortable using these patterns in their writing. Most students benefit from some work with these basic ways of controlling emphasis as well as from discussion of conciseness (23f). Students who have problems with sentence structure, however, may have more difficulty with the effective uses of repetition (23d) and separation (23e) for emphasis.

MEDIA RESOURCES FOR CHAPTER 23

mycomplab Please visit MyCompLab at *www.mycomplab.com* for more on the writing process.

http://www.ablongman.com/littlebrown ▶ See page 73 of this manual for companion Web site content description.

INSTRUCTOR RESOURCE

The following Presentation Aid is available for download on this book's companion Web site at *http://www.ablongman.com/littlebrown*.

PRESENTATION AID 23.1: Ways to emphasize ideas (p. 384)

23a Using subjects and verbs effectively

RESOURCES AND IDEAS

An understanding of the roles of topics and comments and of the possible relationships of old and new information can be very useful for writers seeking greater clarity and more effective emphasis in their writing. To supplement the discussion in this section of the handbook you may wish to turn to three excellent texts:

Lanham, Richard. *Revising Prose*. 4th ed. New York: Longman, 1999. Lanham offers extensive advice on revising for stylistic effect.

Vande Koppel, William J. *Clear and Coherent Prose*. Glenview: Scott Foresman, 1989.

Williams, Joseph M. Style: *Ten Lessons in Clarity and Grace*. 6th ed. New York: Longman, 1999.

ANSWERS

Exercise 23.1 Revising: Emphasis on subjects and verbs (p. 386)

Possible answers

1. Many heroes helped to emancipate the slaves.
2. Harriet Tubman, an escaped slave herself, guided hundreds of other slaves to freedom on the Underground Railroad.
3. Tubman risked a return to slavery or possible death.
4. During the Civil War she also carried information from the South to the North.
5. After the war Tubman helped needy former slaves by raising money for refuges.

23b Using sentence beginnings and endings

CLASSROOM IDEAS

Memory Aid: Thinking about cumulative and periodic sentences The following examples may help students remember how to formulate and how to distinguish between cumulative and periodic sentences:

1. *Cumulative sentences*: A cumulative sentence is created much like a portrait, detail by detail. The diver (for example) paused at the end of the board, gazing down at the smooth, greenish-blue water meters below, his arms stretched out in front, his legs trembling slightly with anticipation and tension, drops of water falling from his fingertips into the swirling wind filled with murmurs from the crowd below and behind his solitary figure.

2. *Periodic sentences*: In a form that parallels the dramatic movement of a tragedy, the meaning of a periodic sentence is built from words and phrases preceding the main clause. In Shakespeare's play *Othello*, step by step, with slowly gathering force and filled with increasing tension and foreboding, the opening scenes create a situation that makes the tragic events inevitable.

COLLABORATIVE LEARNING Exercise 23.2 Ask students to complete Exercise 23.2 individually and then to compare and revise their responses in groups. Have each group present one of their responses to the class, and encourage the other groups to call attention to places where they created an alternative response.

RESOURCES AND IDEAS

Christensen, Francis. "A Generative Rhetoric of the Sentence." *Notes Toward a New Rhetoric: Nine Essays for Teachers*. Ed. Francis Christensen and Bonniejean Christensen. 2nd ed. New York: HarperCollins, 1978. 23–44. Christensen demonstrates how to analyze the levels of generality in sentences and discusses and illustrates the structure of the cumulative sentence.

ANSWERS

Exercise 23.2 Sentence combining: Beginnings and endings (p. 388)

Possible answers

1. Pat Taylor strode into the packed room, greeting students called "Taylor's Kids" and nodding to their parents and teachers.
2. This wealthy Louisiana oilman had promised his "Kids" free college educations because he was determined to make higher education available to all qualified but disadvantaged students.
3. The students welcomed Taylor, their voices singing "You Are the Wind Beneath My Wings," their faces flashing with self-confidence.
4. They had thought a college education was beyond their dreams, seeming too costly and too demanding.
5. To help ease the costs and demands of getting to college, Taylor created a bold plan of scholarships, tutoring, and counseling.

23c Arranging parallel elements effectively

CLASSROOM IDEAS

COLLABORATIVE LEARNING More combining Give students a list of information about a topic and ask them to combine the information to emphasize certain features or to achieve a particular rhetorical purpose. They can do the combining in groups or meet together to discuss and revise the results.

COLLABORATIVE LEARNING Exercise 23.3 Ask students to work in pairs or small groups on Exercise 23.3 and present their responses to the class. You might also ask each group to create two additional sentences, one with elements in a series and one with balanced elements.

ANSWERS

Exercise 23.3 Revising: Series and balanced elements (p. 390)

Possible answers

1. Remembering her days as a "conductor" on the Underground Railroad made Harriet Tubman proud, but remembering her years as a slave made her angry.

2. Tubman wanted freedom regardless of personal danger, whereas <u>her</u> husband, John, wanted personal safety regardless of freedom.
3. Tubman proved her fearlessness in many ways: she <u>disobeyed John's order not to run away</u>, she <u>was a spy for the North during the Civil War</u>, and she <u>led hundreds of other slaves to freedom.</u>
4. To conduct slaves north to freedom, Tubman risked <u>being caught by Southern patrollers</u>, <u>being returned to slavery</u>, and <u>being hanged for a huge reward.</u>
5. After the war Tubman worked tirelessly for civil rights and women's suffrage; <u>she also raised money for homes for needy former slaves.</u>

23d Separating ideas

CLASSROOM IDEAS

COLLABORATIVE LEARNING Rewrite Take a passage from a student essay or a professional essay and ask students to rewrite it, using different sentence patterns that give different emphasis to the content of the sentences. Split the class into groups and have them compare their versions with the original, trying to identify a new version that is in some ways clearer than the original and that contains more appropriate emphasis on the main ideas. Since students may well have decided to emphasize different ideas from those emphasized by the original writer, their analysis of the versions may involve matters of content as well as style.

COLLABORATIVE LEARNING Exercise 23.4 Have students work on Exercise 23.4 in pairs or small groups. Encourage each group to come up with more than one possible answer and ask them to present their most effective responses to the class.

ANSWERS

Exercise 23.4 Emphasizing with repetition or separation (pp. 391–92)

Possible answers

1. One of the few worthwhile habits is daily reading: <u>reading for</u> information, <u>reading for</u> entertainment, <u>reading for</u> a broader view of the world.
2. Reading introduces new words and <u>new styles of expression.</u>
3. Students who read a great deal will <u>more likely write vividly, coherently, and grammatically. They will have learned from other authors.</u>
4. Reading gives <u>knowledge about</u> other cultures, <u>knowledge about</u> history and current events, and <u>knowledge about</u> human nature.
5. As a result of reading, writers have more resources and more flexibility. <u>Thus reading creates better writers.</u>

23e Being concise

CLASSROOM IDEAS

COMPUTER ACTIVITY Clear the confusion Choose a particularly confusing or unemphatic passage from a student essay, give it to student groups, and ask them to decide what devices covered in the chapter could be used to improve the passage. Ask them to make the changes as a group, and have a representative of each group write the revised passage on the board so that the class as a whole can compare the various revisions. This exercise works well in a networked classroom where responses can be posted for general discussion.

COLLABORATIVE LEARNING Exercise 23.5 Ask students to compare Exercise 23.5 in small groups and to present their most effective responses to the class.

COLLABORATIVE LEARNING Exercise 23.6 Have students work in groups to revise the paragraph in Exercise 23.6. Encourage each group to discuss various possible responses and to make a case for the effectiveness of their revision. Then have each group present their revised paragraph to the class either by writing on the blackboard to by photocopying it for a subsequent class meeting. This exercise works well in a networked classroom where each group's response can be posted for general discussion.

ANSWERS

Exercise 23.5 Revising: Conciseness (p. 392)

Possible answers
1. Customers in restaurants must be wary of suggestive selling.
2. In suggestive selling, the waiter asks diners to buy menu selections besides what they ordered.
3. For each item on the menu, another food will naturally complement it.
4. For example, customers will be asked whether they want french fries with a sandwich or a salad with a steak dinner.
5. Customers who give in to suggestive selling often find that their restaurant meals cost more than they had intended to pay.

Exercise 23.6 Revising: Emphasizing ideas (p. 393)

Possible revision

Preparing pasta requires common sense and imagination rather than complicated recipes. The key to success is fresh ingredients for the sauce and perfectly cooked pasta. The sauce may contain just about any fresh fish, meat, cheese, herb, or vegetable. The pasta itself may be dried or fresh, although many experienced cooks find fresh pasta more delicate and flavorful. Dried pasta is fine with zesty sauces; fresh pasta is best with light oil and cream sauces. Dried pasta takes longer to cook than fresh pasta does. The cook should follow the package directions and should test the pasta before the cooking time is up. According to the Italians, who ought to know, the pasta is done when the texture is neither tough nor mushy but *al dente*, or "firm to the bite."

CHAPTER 24

Using Coordination and Subordination

CHAPTER HIGHLIGHTS

The material in this chapter emphasizes how writers can use coordination and subordination to relate ideas and distinguish central ideas from less important material. The opening section illustrates how coordination relates facts and ideas and then goes on to address the problems of excessive and faulty coordination. The second section follows a parallel pattern in discussing subordination, focusing on subordinate clauses. But since effective writing depends on a writer's ability to work with the whole range of subordinate structures, the uses of single words, appositives, and prepositional, verbal, and absolute phrases are also illustrated. The final section cautions briefly against the often unclear and misused connectors *like, while,* and *as.*

Included in this chapter are subsections on punctuating coordinated and subordinated elements, designed to help students not only punctuate correctly but also see punctuation as an instrument and extension of effective sentence structure. Coordination and subordination are strategies that can be enhanced by practicing sentence-combining techniques. Such practices work best if students are encouraged to work on them over the course of a semester, as this handbook recommends, rather than just in one unit or lesson. The exercises in this chapter ask students to revise sentences and longer passages and to combine sentences in ways that implement the range of strategies introduced in the chapter.

MEDIA RESOURCES FOR CHAPTER 24

mycomplab Please visit MyCompLab at *www.mycomplab.com* for more on the writing process.

http://www.ablongman.com/littlebrown ▶ See page 73 of this manual for companion Web site content description.

24a Coordinating to relate equal ideas

INSTRUCTOR RESOURCE

The following Presentation Aid is available for download on this book's companion Web site at *http://www.ablongman.com/littlebrown.*

PRESENTATION AID 24.1: Ways to coordinate information in sentences (p. 395)

CLASSROOM IDEAS

COMPUTER ACTIVITY I've got a little list You may wish to remind students that section 12d of the handbook contains a detailed discussion of coordinating conjunctions. If students make a simple list of the conjunctions and keep it on their computer where it is handy, they may find themselves becoming more aware of the words and their functions as they read and write:

and	or
but	for
nor	so
yet	

Section 12d of the handbook also contains a detailed discussion of conjunctive adverbs. You can help create awareness of conjunctive adverbs by asking students to make a list of the words and keep it in a convenient place on their computer. As they read and write later, students may pay greater attention to the conjunctive adverbs and their functions:

also	namely	anyway
next	besides	now
certainly	otherwise	finally
similarly	further	still
however	then	indeed
therefore	likewise	thus
meanwhile	undoubtedly	

COLLABORATIVE LEARNING Coordinating for fun Have each small group write a paragraph or two made up of short declarative sentences. (Students often enjoy the opportunity to create humorously short sentences on a topic of their choice.) Groups then trade exercises and revise them using the sentence-combining techniques they have learned in this section.

COMPUTER ACTIVITY Macro punctuation Many people (not just students) do not know that they must in some instances precede "however" with a semicolon rather than a comma. If your students make this mistake frequently, they can create a "macro" command in their word processor containing the keystrokes "; however" and press the macro function key instead of typing out the word "however." They will still need to check to see whether or not their sentence is properly punctuated.

Missing information Have each student create a sentence using coordination. The sentence should have one piece of necessary information omitted so that the resulting coordination is illogical. Ask the student to send it around by e-mail or post it; the rest of the class can try to guess what information needs to be filled in.

Conjunctive Mad Libs Give one student in each group a short piece of writing from which all the conjunctive adverbs have been removed and replaced by blanks. That student asks other group members to supply conjunctive adverbs. As in the game "Mad Libs," the other students do not look at the page, so their choices are made randomly. After all the blanks have been filled, the first student reads the resulting, faulty essay aloud, and students collapse with laughter.

COLLABORATIVE LEARNING Exercises 24.1 and 24.2 Ask students to complete Exercises 24.1 and 24.2 individually and then to compare and revise their responses in small groups. You might ask each group to present a successful combination to the class and to discuss why it seems more effective.

ANSWERS

Exercise 24.1 Sentence combining: coordination (p. 397)

1. Many chronic misspellers do not have the time or motivation to master spelling rules. They may rely on dictionaries to catch misspellings, but most dictionaries list words under their correct spellings. One kind of dictionary is designed for chronic misspellers. It lists each word under its common *mis*spellings and then provides the correct spelling and definition.
2. Henry Hudson was an English explorer, but he captained ships for the Dutch East India Company. On a voyage in 1610 he passed Greenland and sailed into a great bay in today's northern Canada. He thought he and his sailors could winter there, but the cold was terrible and food ran out. The sailors mutinied and cast Hudson and eight others adrift in a small boat. Hudson and his companions perished.

Exercise 24.2 Revising: Excessive or faulty coordination (p. 398)

1. Because soldiers admired their commanding officers, they often gave them nicknames containing the word "old," even though not all of the commanders were old.
2. General Thomas "Stonewall" Jackson was also called "Old Jack," although he was not yet forty years old.
3. Another Southern general, whose full name was James Longstreet, was called "Old Pete."
4. The Union General Henry W. Halleck had a reputation as a good military strategist, and he was an expert on the work of a French military authority, Henri Jomini. Therefore, Halleck was called "Old Brains."
5. After General William Henry Harrison won a victory at the Battle of Tippecanoe, he received the nickname "Old Tippecanoe." He used the name in his presidential campaign slogan "Tippecanoe and Tyler, Too." Although he won the election in 1840, he died of pneumonia a month after taking office.

24b Subordinating to distinguish main ideas

INSTRUCTOR RESOURCE

The following Presentation Aid is available for download on this book's companion Web site at *http://www.ablongman.com/littlebrown*.

PRESENTATION AID 24.2: Ways to subordinate information into sentences (p. 399)

CLASSROOM IDEAS

COLLABORATIVE LEARNING Using student writing Ask students to share a paragraph or two from their drafts with the other members of their group. Group members should comment on the use of coordination and subordination and suggest places where more or less of either might aid the writer in achieving her or his purpose.

Avoiding excessive subordination Choose paragraphs from student essays that demonstrate overuse or faulty use of subordination, and distribute them to the class. Have students rewrite the paragraphs and then compare their versions in small groups to determine which are the most clear and effective revisions.

COMPUTER ACTIVITY Scavenger hunt Ask students to hunt around on the Web for one example of each kind of subordinating structure (space or time, cause or effect, condition, concession, purpose, and identification.) If your classroom is networked, you can do this exercise as a race during a class period, and have students post their examples (and the links to where they found them) to the rest of the class.

COLLABORATIVE LEARNING Reducing To help students practice subordination, create several groups and give each group a different passage. Ask the groups to first reduce sentences to clauses and then to identify the subordinate clauses in each passage. At the end of the activity, the groups can exchange passages and repeat the process, comparing their work at the end with the work of the prior group.

COMPUTER ACTIVITY The coordination/subordination police Have your students seek out examples of faulty coordination or subordination on their favorite Web sites. You can keep an archive of them on your class Web site and students can add links as they discover them.

Getting a fresh look Give students a fresh look at their own writing by asking them to revise a portion of a graded essay following specific directions, such as "Add subordination" or "Use more imaginative subordinating words." To maximize the freshness of the viewing process, tell students who have been composing on the computer screen to perform this revision on a printout copy of their draft; students who have been working on printouts can try performing the revision onscreen.

CULTURE LANGUAGE **Distinctions between subordinating words** Some ESL students may understand the conceptual differences among words that subordinate according to space or time, cause or effect, condition, concession, purpose, and identification (see the list on pp. 399–400). However, within each category, they may have a harder time knowing which word to use; so, for instance, they may use *although, as if, even though, though, despite, except for,* and *in spite of* interchangeably. Ask them to collect examples of proper use of each of these terms from their reading, and then discuss why each one works in its particular context.

COLLABORATIVE LEARNING Exercises 24.3 and 24.4 Ask students to complete Exercise 24.3 individually and compare their responses in small groups. Then have each group create a response to Exercise 24.4 and present their resulting paragraph to the class. This assignment works well in a networked classroom where the resulting paragraphs in Exercise 24.4 can be posted so that the class as a whole can discuss the effectiveness of various subordinating strategies.

ANSWERS

Exercise 24.3 Sentence combining: Subordination (p. 402)

Possible answers

1. When the bombardier beetle sees an enemy, it shoots out a jet of chemicals to protect itself.

   Seeing an enemy, the bombardier beetle shoots out a jet of chemicals to protect itself.

2. Consisting of hot and irritating chemicals, the beetle's spray is very potent.

   The beetle's spray of hot and irritating chemicals is very potent.

3. Stored separately in the beetle's body and mixed in the spraying gland, the spray's two chemicals resemble a nerve-gas weapon.

   The spray's two chemicals, which are stored separately in the beetle's body and mixed in the spraying gland, resemble a nerve-gas weapon.

4. Revolving like a turret on a World War II bomber, the tip of the beetle's abdomen sprays the chemicals.

   Spraying the chemicals, the tip of the beetle's abdomen revolves like a turret on a World War II bomber.

5. Although the beetle defeats most of its enemies, it is still eaten by spiders and birds.

   The beetle defeats most of its enemies except spiders and birds.

Exercise 24.4 Revising: Subordination (p. 403)

Possible revision

Fewer students today are majoring in the liberal arts—that is, in such subjects as history, English, and the social sciences. Although students think a liberal arts degree will not help them get jobs, they are wrong. They may not get practical, job-related experience from the liberal arts, but they will get a broad education that will never again be available to them. Many employers look for more than a technical, professional education because they think such an education can make an employee's views too narrow. Instead, they want open-minded employees who can think about problems from many angles. Such flexibility—vital to the health of our society—is just what the liberal arts curriculum instills.

Exercise 24.5 Revising: Faulty or excessive subordination (p. 403)

Possible answers

1. Because Genaro González is blessed with great writing talent, his novel *Rainbow's End* and his story collection *Only Sons* have been published.
2. Although he loves to write, he has also earned a doctorate in psychology.
3. His first story, which is entitled "Un Hijo del Sol," reflects his consciousness of his Aztec heritage and place in the world.
4. González writes equally well in English and Spanish. He received a large fellowship enabling him to take a leave of absence from the University of Texas–Pan American, where he teaches psychology. He could write without worrying about an income.
5. González wrote the first version of "Un Hijo del Sol" while he was a sophomore at Pan American. The university is in the Rio Grande valley of southern Texas, which González calls "el Valle" in the story.

RESOURCES AND IDEAS

On improving sentence style

Angell, David, and Brent Heslop. *The Elements of E-Mail Style.* Boston: Addison, 1994. This account of the particular conventions of e-mail style makes clear how the context and medium shape writers' stylistic choices and effects.

Lanham, Richard. *Analyzing Prose.* New York: Scribner, 1983. Lanham offers extensive advice on revising for stylistic effect.

Soles, Derek. "An Analyis of the Style of Exemplary Freshman Writing." *Teaching English in the Two-Year College* 33 (September 2005): 38–49. Using Corbett's prose style matrix, Soles analyzes the style of exemplary freshman essays and concludes that there is an identifiable, hence teachable style valued by freshman writing instructors.

Williams, Joseph. Style: *Ten Lessons in Clarity and Grace*. 6th ed. New York: Longman, 1999. Williams's how-to manual for improving style at the sentence and word level is especially strong in discussing coordination and subordination.

On sentence combining

Crowhurst, Marion. "Sentence Combining: Maintaining Realistic Expectations." *College Composition and Communication* 34 (1983): 62–72. Crowhurst offers pragmatic suggestions about what teachers should and should not expect when introducing sentence combining into their classrooms.

Daiker, Donald, Andrew Kerek, and Max Morenberg. *Sentence Combining: A Rhetorical Perspective*. Carbondale: Southern Illinois UP, 1985.

Melamed, Evelyn B., and Harvey Minkoff. "Transitions: A Key to Mature Reading and Writing." *Teaching the Basics—Really!* Ed. Ouida Clapp. Urbana: NCTE, 1977, 17–21. The authors describe exercises to help students make logical links between sentences and parts of sentences with transitions.

O'Hare, Frank. *Sentence-Combining: Improving Student Writing without Formal Grammar Instruction*. Urbana: NCTE, 1973. O'Hare demonstrates the improvements that can be effected when students practice sentence combining.

Strong, William. "Creative Approaches to Sentence Combining." ERIC, 1986. ED 274 985. Strong offers a number of examples and classroom activities to help teach sentence-combining techniques.

Williams, James D. *Preparing to Teach Writing*. Mahwah: Lawrence Erlbaum Associates, 1996. See the section on "Style and Sentence Combining," which explores the connections between syntactic and developmental maturity in teaching sentence combining (124–30).

24c Choosing clear connectors

INSTRUCTOR RESOURCE

The following Presentation Aid is available for download on this book's companion Web site at *http://www.ablongman.com/littlebrown*.

PRESENTATION AID 24.3: Exercise 24.6. Revising: Coordination and subordination (p. 405)

CLASSROOM IDEAS

Rewriting an essay Give students a passage from a student or professional essay (posted to your class Web site or sent as an e-mail attachment) and ask them to rewrite it following a specified strategy: adding subordination, using different subordinators, or adding coordination. They can use one color script for subordination revisions, and another color script for coordination revisions. This exercise can be extended by having students rewrite the passage to change its emphasis.

COLLABORATIVE LEARNING Identifying connectors Have students work in groups to identify the connectors (subordinating and coordinating conjunctions) in several essays: an essay from a reader, a news item in a newspaper, or a student essay. If the uses of subordination and coordination and the kinds of connectors differ in each kind of essay, ask students to try to account for the differences.

COMPUTER ACTIVITY Lyrical liberties Lyricists often take liberties with language use. If your students listen to music on the Web, ask them to keep an ear out for incorrect uses of *as, while,* and *like.* If they find any such uses, they can post a link to the Web site so that you and the rest of the class can tune in.

"Like, you know" The word *like* peppers the speech of many college students (and others, of course). When you are teaching your students to use *as* and *like* correctly, you can sensitize them to the overuse and misuse of the word *like* by asking them to observe the conversation of others. Send them to the student union or another gathering place, and tell them to record as many instances of the word *like* as they hear in 10–30 minutes. They can bring their records to class and work in small groups to determine whether any of the examples they collected followed correct usage.

COLLABORATIVE LEARNING Exercise 24.6 Ask students to complete Exercise 24.6 in small groups. Encourage the groups to explore various possibilities for coordination and subordination and to discuss the effects those changes have on the meaning of the paragraph.

ANSWERS

Exercise 24.6 Revising: Coordination and subordination (p. 405)

Possible revision

Sir Walter Raleigh personified the Elizabethan Age, the period of Elizabeth I's rule of England, in the last half of the sixteenth century. Raleigh was a courtier, a poet, an explorer, and an entrepreneur. Supposedly, he gained Queen Elizabeth's favor by throwing his cloak beneath her feet at the right moment, just as she was about to step over a puddle. Although there is no evidence for this story, it illustrates Raleigh's dramatic and dynamic personality. His energy drew others to him, and he was one of Elizabeth's favorites. She supported him and dispensed favors to him. However, he lost his queen's goodwill when without her permission he seduced and eventually married one of her maids of honor. After Elizabeth died, her successor, James I, imprisoned Raleigh in the Tower of London on false charges of treason. Raleigh was released after thirteen years but arrested again two years later on the old treason charges. At the age of sixty-six he was beheaded.

CHAPTER 25

Using Parallelism

CHAPTER HIGHLIGHTS

This discussion of parallelism is divided into two sections, and it moves from correctness to effective style. The opening section addresses the obligatory use of parallelism in coordinate constructions—those linked by coordinating conjunctions and correlative conjunctions; those in comparisons and contrasts; and those in lists, outlines, and the like.

The second section examines how parallelism can be used within and among sentences to increase coherence, emphasize meaning, and heighten the effect. For some students you may wish to emphasize the items in the opening section. But students who have no trouble maintaining obligatory parallelism can often profit by working more creatively with parallelism to tighten and clarify their writing. Exercise 25.3, a sentence-combining exercise, is designed to give students a chance to explore the options for expression that parallelism provides. The exercise is likely to be most effective when students are given a chance to (1) discuss with one another the impact of various combinations or (2) work collaboratively in exploring various sentence-combining options.

MEDIA RESOURCES FOR CHAPTER 25

mycomplab Please visit MyCompLab at *www.mycomplab.com* for more on the writing process.

http://www.ablongman.com/littlebrown ▶ See page 73 of this manual for companion Web site content description.

25a Using parallelism for coordinate elements

INSTRUCTOR RESOURCES

The following Presentation Aids are available for download on this book's companion Web site at *http://www.ablongman.com/littlebrown*.

PRESENTATION AID 25.1: Patterns of parallelism (p. 407)

PRESENTATION AID 25.2 Exercise 25.1: Identifying parallel elements (p. 409)

CLASSROOM IDEAS

Sample essays Journal entries and student drafts, along with essays from a reader or a similar source, provide a gold mine of material on which to practice. Ask students to look for parallelism in essays from a reader or a similar source. If the students are working in groups, ask them not only to reach consensus on which elements are parallel but also to decide what functions the parallelism performs.

Adding parallelism Take a loose-jointed student essay or a professional essay and distribute it to students (working individually or in groups), asking them to make the sentences denser by adding parallelism wherever possible. Ask them also to decide when the parallelism adds to the essay and when it detracts.

COLLABORATIVE LEARNING Patterns for parallelism Working on their own, students might find it difficult to write many sentences containing correlative conjunctions, lists, and coordinate structures that require parallelism; but if you ask them to do this in groups, they can probably generate quite a few. As part of the assignment, ask students to vary the sentences as much as they can in content and in use of parallelism. Then ask the groups to judge each other's work for originality, clarity, and effectiveness.

COLLABORATIVE LEARNING Exercise 25.1 Students can complete Exercise 25.1 individually or in groups and then compare responses. This gives students who are confused about the concept of parallelism the opportunity to practice identifying parallel structures in a nonintimidating environment. Ask each group to create one or two sentences that demonstrate parallelism, using the models provided by this exercise. Each group might then present their most creative response to the class as a whole.

COLLABORATIVE LEARNING Exercise 25.2 Ask students to complete Exercise 25.2 individually and then to compare and revise their responses in small groups. Ask each group to present one or two of the most effective revisions to the class.

ANSWERS

Exercise 25.1 Identifying parallel elements (p. 409)

1. The two sets of parallel phrases (*an automatic or an everyday affair; on solemn occasions and for a special treat*) and the parallel main clauses (*. . . has not always been . . . has tended to be*) emphasize the differences between then and now.
2. The parallel verbs (*rolled out . . . cooked . . . tended . . . marked*) stress the number and variety of the women's responsibilities.
3. Supporting *pleasantest* is a wealth of detail expressed in five parallel absolute phrases: *exhaustion . . . in; the sated mosquitoes . . . off; the room . . . garments; the vines . . . day;* and *the air conditioner . . . mosquitoes.* The phrases convey no action, emphasizing the stillness of the scene.
4. The limiting effects of aging are emphasized by the increasingly narrow parallel verbs—*paints, lies, imprisons*—and the parallel objects—*every action, every movement, every thought.*

Exercise 25.2 Revising: Parallelism (p. 410)

Possible answers

1. The ancient Greeks celebrated four athletic contests: the Olympic Games at Olympia, the Isthmian Games near Corinth, the Pythian Games at Delphi, and the Nemean Games at Cleonae.
2. Each day of the games consisted of either athletic events or ceremonies and sacrifices to the gods.
3. In the years between the games, competitors were taught wrestling, javelin throwing, and boxing.
4. Competitors ran sprints, participated in spectacular chariot and horse races, and ran long distances while wearing full armor.
5. The purpose of such events was developing physical strength, demonstrating skill and endurance, and sharpening the skills needed for war.
6. Events were held both for men and for boys.
7. At the Olympic Games the spectators cheered their favorites to victory, attended sacrifices to the gods, and feasted on the meat not burned in offerings.
8. The athletes competed less to achieve great wealth than to gain honor for both themselves and their cities.
9. Of course, exceptional athletes received financial support from patrons, poems and statues by admiring artists, and even lavish living quarters from their sponsoring cities.
10. With the medal counts and flag ceremonies, today's Olympians sometimes seem to be proving their countries' superiority more than demonstrating individual talent.

RESOURCES AND IDEAS

Brooks, Phyllis. "Mimesis: Grammar and the Echoing Voice." *College English* 35 (1973): 161–68. Brooks suggests the writing of paragraphs that imitate the style of a writer but use different content. She indicates that the practice helps students learn to use a variety of structures, including parenthetical expressions, appositives and modifiers, and parallelism plus reference.

Graves, Richard L. "Symmetrical Form and the Rhetoric of the Sentence." Rhetoric *and Composition: A Sourcebook for Teachers*. Upper Montclair: Boynton/Cook, 1984. 119–27. Graves argues that since comparison is a natural way for humans to organize information, parallelism is an effective way of helping readers acquire and interpret information.

Walker, Robert L. "The Common Writer: A Case for Parallel Structure." *College Composition and Communication* 21 (1970): 373–79. Walker believes that students should be encouraged to use a variety of sentence structures and parallelism, which he considers important features of mature sentences.

Williams, Joseph M. "The Phenomenology of Error." *College Composition and Communication* 32 (1981): 152–68. Williams describes parallelism problems from the point of view of a writer's stylistic choices.

25b Using parallelism to increase coherence

CLASSROOM IDEA

COLLABORATIVE LEARNING Exercise 25.3 Ask students to complete Exercise 25.3 individually and work together to compare and revise their responses. Then have each group create a response to Exercise 25.4 and present it to the class. In a networked classroom you might ask groups to post their revised paragraphs for the class to compare and discuss.

ANSWERS

Exercise 25.3 Sentence combining: Parallelism (p. 411)

Possible answers

1. People can develop post-traumatic stress disorder (PTSD) after experiencing a dangerous situation and fearing for their survival.
2. The disorder can be triggered by a wide variety of events, such as combat, a natural disaster, or a hostage situation.
3. PTSD can occur immediately after the stressful incident or not until many years later.
4. Sometimes people with PTSD will act irrationally and angrily.
5. Other symptoms include dreaming that one is reliving the experience, hallucinating that one is back in the terrifying place, and imagining that strangers are actually one's former torturers.

Exercise 25.4 Revising: Parallelism (p. 412)

Possible revision

The great white shark has an undeserved bad reputation. Many people consider the great white not only swift and powerful but also a cunning and cruel predator on humans. However, scientists claim that the great white attacks humans not by choice but by chance. To a shark, our behavior in the water is similar to that of porpoises, seals, and sea lions—the shark's favorite foods. These sea mammals are both agile enough and fast enough to evade the shark. Thus the shark must attack swiftly and noiselessly to surprise the prey and give it little chance to escape. Humans become the shark's victims not because the shark has any preference for or hatred of humans but because humans can neither outswim nor outmaneuver the shark. If the fish were truly a cruel human-eater, it would prolong the terror of its attacks, perhaps by circling or bumping into its intended victims before attacking them.

CHAPTER 26

Achieving Variety

CHAPTER HIGHLIGHTS

This chapter asks students to think of sentences not as single units but as a sequence of ideas working together. Emphasis, coordination, subordination, and parallelism—topics covered in the preceding chapters—all come into play in the examples in this chapter. You will probably want to direct attention to the introduction to this chapter and to the first two sections, covering strategies for varying the length and structure of sentences and for varying sentence beginnings. You may have to decide, though, how much time to devote to the last two sections, which cover the occasional uses of inverted sentence order and of minor sentence types such as questions and commands.

MEDIA RESOURCES FOR CHAPTER 26

mycomplab Please visit MyCompLab at *www.mycomplab.com* for more on the writing process.

`http://www.ablongman.com/littlebrown` ▶ See page 73 of this manual for companion Web site content description.

INSTRUCTOR RESOURCE

The following Presentation Aid is available for download on this book's companion Web site at *http://www.ablongman.com/littlebrown*.

PRESENTATION AID 26.1: Ways to achieve variety among sentences (p. 412)

CLASSROOM IDEAS

Additional activities Many of the student activities described for Chapter 23 and 24 can be easily adapted for this chapter.

COMPUTER ACTIVITY Using style checkers Computerized style checkers are now widely available; however, the quality of the advice they offer varies considerably. These programs are based on standardized readability tests and are not particularly sensitive to writers' purposes or the levels of sophistication of their audiences. (Try feeding the *Gettysburg Address* or *A Letter from Birmingham Jail* into such a program; the advice the style checkers provide for "improving" these essays will shock and amuse you and your students.)

RESOURCES AND IDEAS

Barrett, Edward. "Collaboration in the Electronic Classroom." *Technology Review* (February/ March 1993): 51–55. This article suggests strategies for structuring group work using computers.

Lanham, Richard. *Analyzing Prose.* New York: Scribner, 1983. Lanham offers extensive advice on revising for stylistic effect.

Rubin, Donald, and Kathryn Greene. "Gender-Typical Style in Written Language." *Research in the Teaching of English* 26 (1992): 7–40. The authors catalog stylistic and syntactic variations that fall along gender lines.

26a Varying sentence length and structure

CLASSROOM IDEAS

COLLABORATIVE LEARNING Simple sentences Take a professional or student essay, reduce it to simple sentences, and ask students to rewrite it, adding variety. Then ask them to work in groups to compare their versions with the original, analyze the differences, and decide as a group which versions are more effective and why.

Visual analysis Students may wish to make bar charts showing sentence lengths to see the average lengths of sentences they use and to target the variations in length they might want to consider.

COLLABORATIVE LEARNING Exercise 26.1 Have students work in groups to create responses to Exercise 26.1. Encourage each group to discuss various possible revisions and ask them to present their responses to the class. This exercise works well in a networked classroom where each group's responses can be posted for comparison and general discussion.

RESOURCES AND IDEAS

Walpole, Jane R. "The Vigorous Pursuit of Grace and Style." *The Writing Instructor* 1 (1982): 163–69. Walpole describes six ways students can manipulate a good but not great passage (improving their own prose in the process), along with an example to show how the procedure works.

Williams, Joseph. Style: *Ten Lessons in Clarity and Grace.* 6th ed. New York: Longman, 1999. Williams provides an excellent how-to manual for improving style at the sentence and word level.

ANSWERS

Exercise 26.1 Revising: Varied sentence structures (p. 415)
Possible revision

Charlotte Perkins Gilman was a leading intellectual in the women's movement during the first decades of the twentieth century. Her book

Women and Economics challenged Victorian assumptions about the differences between the sexes and explored the economic roots of women's oppression. Gilman wrote little about gaining the vote for women, the issue that then preoccupied feminists and that historians have since focused their analyses on. As a result, Gilman's contribution to today's women's movement has often been overlooked.

26b   Varying sentence beginnings

CLASSROOM IDEAS

CULTURE LANGUAGE **Sentence length and variety** ESL students may replicate the sentence length and sentence variety conventions of their first language when creating sentences in English. It may require considerable practice before they develop an ear for the rhythm and variety of sentences according to English conventions. The same may hold true for native English speakers if they are unfamiliar with the conventions of a particular genre of English writing. The first two paragraphs of Jane Austen's *Pride and Prejudice* are a good example of long sentences used effectively:

> It is a truth universally acknowledged, that a single man in possession of a good fortune, must be in want of a wife.
>
> However little known the feelings or views of such a man may be on his first entering a neighbourhood, this truth is so well fixed in the minds of the surrounding families, that he is considered as the rightful property of some one or other of their daughters.

Contrast these paragraphs with an excerpt from Ralph Ellison's *Invisible Man*, in which Ellison uses both short and long sentences to accentuate the content of the story he is telling:

> Once I saw a prizefighter boxing a yokel. The fighter was swift and amazingly scientific. His body was one violent flow of rapid rhythmic action. He hit the yokel a hundred times while the yokel held up his arms in stunned surprise. But suddenly the yokel, rolling about in the gale of boxing gloves, struck one blow and knocked science, speed and footwork as cold as a well-digger's posterior. The smart money hit the canvas. The long shot got the nod.

Invite your students to become attuned to sentence variety in their reading. Reading assignments for your course or their other courses can be plumbed for examples, and your class can make a collection of examples from various genres and forms of writing. This exercise may be especially helpful to students who are just beginning to develop an ear for rhythm and variety in sentence patterns.

COLLABORATIVE LEARNING Exercise 26.2 Have students complete Exercise 26.2 in small groups and present one or two of their responses to the class. During the group presentations, encourage a general discussion of the relative effectiveness of various responses. This may help students to focus on the connection between stylistic changes and sentence content.

COLLABORATIVE LEARNING Exercise 26.3 Have students work in pairs or in small groups to create responses to Exercise 3. This exercise works well in a networked classroom where groups can post their responses for general discussion.

ANSWERS

Exercise 26.2 Revising: Varied sentence beginnings (p. 417)

Possible answers

1. Some people are champion procrastinators. Consequently, they seldom complete their work on time.
2. If procrastinators fear criticism or rejection, they will delay completing an assignment.
3. Procrastinators often desire to please a boss or a teacher. Yet they fear failure so much that they cannot do the work.
4. Although procrastination seems a hopeless habit, it is conquerable.
5. Helpfully encouraging procrastinators, teachers or employers can give them the confidence to do good work on time.

Exercise 26.3 Revising: Varied sentence beginnings (p. 418)

Possible revision

When scientists in Egypt dug up 40-million-year-old fossil bones, they had evidence of primitive whales. Called mesonychids, the whale ancestors were small, furry land mammals with four legs. These limbs were complete with kneecaps, ankles, and little toes. In contrast, gigantic modern whales have tiny hind legs inside their bodies and flippers instead of front legs. But scientists are certain that these two very different creatures share the same family tree.

26c Inverting the normal word order

CLASSROOM IDEA

Using forms Tell students to write a paragraph making use of the strategies suggested in this chapter. Leave the content of the paragraph up to them; they will discover how form can help suggest content. Then have them work in groups to compare paragraphs written with these strategies in mind to paragraphs taken from previous papers. This kind of comparison can encourage students to become more aware of their stylistic strengths and weaknesses.

26d Mixing types of sentences

CLASSROOM IDEAS

COLLABORATIVE LEARNING Exercise 26.4 Have students create individual responses to Exercise 26.4, then ask them to discuss their responses in small groups and create revisions. In a computer classroom, students might trade seats in order to read and comment on each other's work (in each case the commentator can add revision suggestions using a different font). Students can print out and share responses, or post them—in a networked classroom.

COLLABORATIVE LEARNING Exercise 26.5 Have students complete Exercise 26.5 individually and then discuss their responses in small groups. Encourage students to debate the effects of sentence variety in the passage and to use detailed evidence from the passage to support their claims. You might follow up this group activity by leading a general discussion in which you invite groups to report back on the debates they have generated.

COLLABORATIVE LEARNING Exercise 26.6 Ask students to complete Exercise 26.6 individually and then discuss their responses in groups in preparation for revising them. You might choose several of the revised responses to photocopy and hand out in order to generate discussion of the effects of variety. In a networked classroom, you might ask several student volunteers to post their revised responses in order to provide the basis for discussion.

ANSWERS

Exercise 26.4 Writing varied sentences (p. 419)

Possible answers

1. How many cars are registered on this campus?
2. Try to find a parking space on this campus any weekday morning after nine o'clock.
3. What an unexpected pleasure to find a parking space within two blocks of the library!
4. Can the frustration caused by the parking problem be healthy for students? They drive round and round the campus, the minutes of lost study or class time ticking away. Tension builds. As they pass filled row upon filled row in one lot after another, drivers begin to tremble, sweat, and swear. And the anger and panic, instead of abating when finally the car is safely stowed, stays with the students throughout the day.

Exercise 26.5 Analyzing variety (pp. 419–20)

Possible answers

The shortest sentence is one word: *No.* The longest is sentence 5, *I pictured the man as. . . .* The opening periodic sentence sets the scene before coming to the point. The longest sentence gains its length and power from the six modifying verbal phrases that convey Wright's first impression of Mencken. Wright relies on questions interspersed with tentative answers to show his own incremental awakening on discovering Mencken. Repetition—*fighting, fighting; using . . . using; maybe, perhaps*—

also shows Wright wrestling with what he has found. The last question leads to the conclusion of the final three sentences, which gradually increase in length and complexity.

Exercise 26.6 Revising: Variety (p. 420)
Possible revision

After being dormant for many years, the Italian volcano Vesuvius exploded on August 24 in the year AD 79. The ash, pumice, and mud from the volcano buried two towns—Herculaneum and the more famous Pompeii—which lay undiscovered until 1709 and 1748, respectively. The excavation of Pompeii was the more systematic, the occasion for initiating modern methods of conservation and restoration. Whereas Herculaneum was simply looted of its most valuable finds and then left to disintegrate, Pompeii appears much as it did during the eruption. A luxurious house opens onto a lush central garden. An election poster decorates a wall. And a dining table is set for breakfast.

Exercise on Chapters 23-26 Revising: Effective Sentences (p. 421)
Possible revision

Modern Americans owe many debts to Native Americans, including several pleasures. Native Americans originated two fine junk foods: popcorn and potato chips.

Native Americans introduced popcorn to the European settlers, Massasoit providing popcorn at the first Thanksgiving feast and the Aztecs offering popcorn to the Spanish explorer Hernando Cortés. The Aztecs and natives of the West Indies wore popcorn necklaces. Native Americans popped the corn in three ways. First, they roasted an ear skewered on a stick over fire and ate the corn that fell outside the flames. Second, they scraped the corn off the cob, threw the kernels into a low fire, and ate the popped kernels that did not fall into the fire. Third and most sophisticated, they heated a shallow pottery vessel containing sand, stirred corn kernels into the hot sand, and ate what popped up to the surface.

A Native American chef named George Crum devised the crunchy potato chip. In 1853 Crum was cooking at Moon Lake Lodge in Saratoga Springs, New York. A customer complained that Crum's french-fried potatoes were too thick. Crum tried a thinner batch, but these were also unsuitable. Frustrated, Crum deliberately made the potatoes so thin and crisp that they could not be cut with a knife and fork. Crum's joke backfired, for the customer raved about the potato chips. Soon these Saratoga Chips appeared on the lodge's menu and throughout New England. Crum later opened his own restaurant, of course offering potato chips.

Now all Americans munch popcorn in movies, crunch potato chips at parties, and gorge on both when alone and bored. They can be grateful to Native Americans for these guilty pleasures.

PART 6

Punctuation

CHAPTER 27
End Punctuation

CHAPTER 28
The Comma

CHAPTER 29
The Semicolon

CHAPTER 30
The Apostrophe

CHAPTER 31
Quotation Marks

CHAPTER 32
Other Punctuation Marks

End Punctuation

CHAPTER HIGHLIGHTS

This chapter discusses the three marks of punctuation used to end sentences: periods, question marks, and exclamation points. Encourage students to see that these are not just physical boundaries but important parts of the meaning of sentences—and that they therefore deserve careful consideration.

MEDIA RESOURCES FOR CHAPTER 27

mycomplab Please visit MyCompLab at *www.mycomplab.com* for more on the writing process.

http://www.ablongman.com/littlebrown ▶ See page 73 of this manual for companion Web site content description.

27a Use periods after most sentences and with some abbreviations.

CLASSROOM IDEA

Polite demands Students often question the punctuation of polite demands, such as "Would you please send me your catalog." These sentences are used frequently for requests that the writer expects to be granted. In business use they are punctuated with periods; however, it's never wrong to use a question mark if the writer is in doubt.

ANSWERS

EXERCISE 27.1 Revising: Periods (p. 427)

1. The instructor asked when Plato wrote *The Republic*.
2. Give the date within one century.
3. The exact date is not known, but it is estimated at 370 BC.
4. Dr. Arn will lecture on Plato at 7:30 p.m.
5. The lecture hall is only 1600 sq. ft.

RESOURCES AND IDEAS

Dawkins, John. "Teaching Punctuation as a Rhetorical Tool." *College Composition and Communication* 46 (1995): 533–48. Dawkins makes a case for teaching the rhetorical thinking processes that accompany decisions about punctuation marks.

27b Use question marks after direct questions and some times to indicate doubt.

ANSWERS

EXERCISE 27.2 Revising: Question marks (p. 428)

1. In Homer's *Odyssey*, Odysseus took seven years to travel from Troy to Ithaca. Or was it eight years? Or more?
2. Odysseus must have wondered whether he would ever make it home.
3. "What man are you and whence?" asks Odysseus's wife, Penelope.
4. Why does Penelope ask, "Where is your city? Your family?"
5. Penelope does not recognize Odysseus and asks who this stranger is.

27c Use an exclamation point after an emphatic statement, interjection, or command.

CLASSROOM IDEAS

COLLABORATIVE LEARNING Exclamation points and advertising Have students scan advertisements in newspapers, magazines, and junk mail for exclamation points. Individually or in groups, ask them to decide whether the exclamation points are used effectively or overused. Encourage them to rewrite these advertising sentences to convey the emphasis without using exclamation points for spice.

COLLABORATIVE LEARNING End punctuation Have students complete Exercise 4 individually and compare their responses in small groups. Then ask each group to review the punctuation of paragraphs from their own work and help each other to locate and revise punctuation errors. Ask each student to keep a list of the errors that commonly recur in his or her work (along with revised examples) and to use that list in future proofreading tasks.

ANSWERS

EXERCISE 27.3 Revising: Exclamation points (p. 429)

1. As the firefighters moved their equipment into place, the police shouted, "Move back!"
2. A child's cries could be heard from above: "Help me! Help!"
3. When the child was rescued, the crowd called, "Hooray!"
4. The rescue was the most exciting event of the day.
5. Sentence correct.

EXERCISE 27.4 Revising: End punctuation (p. 429)

When visitors first arrive in Hawaii, they often encounter an unexpected language barrier. Standard English is the language of business and government, but many of the people speak Pidgin English. Instead of an excited "Aloha!" the visitors may be greeted with an excited Pidgin "Howzit!" or asked if they know "how fo' find one good hotel." Many Hawaiians question whether Pidgin will hold children back because it prevents communication with the *haoles,* or Caucasians, who run businesses. Yet many others feel that Pidgin is a last defense of ethnic diversity on the islands. To those who want to make standard English the official language of the state, these Hawaiians may respond, "Just 'cause I speak Pidgin no mean I dumb." They may ask, "Why you no listen?" or, in standard English, "Why don't you listen?"

CHAPTER 28

The Comma

A WRITER'S PERSPECTIVE _____

> *It is highly important to put [commas] in place as you go along. If you try to come back after doing a paragraph and stick them in the various spots that tempt you you will discover that they tend to swarm like minnows into all sorts of crevices whose existence you hadn't realized and before you know it the whole long sentence becomes immobilized and lashed up squirming in commas. Better to use them sparingly, and with affection, precisely when the need for one arises, nicely, by itself.*
>
> —LEWIS THOMAS, "NOTES ON PUNCTUATION"

CHAPTER HIGHLIGHTS

The comma probably causes more anguish for apprentice writers than any other punctuation mark. There's no magic formula for accurate use of the comma. Most uses are conventional, but a few require judgment calls—and writers can develop the necessary judgment only through lots of reading and writing. For example, the problem of whether to use commas with essential and nonessential modifiers is probably not a punctuation problem but a matter of understanding what these modifiers do. Commas, or their absence, are just a graphic way of reinforcing the meaning of the modifier. The text's discussion of how context determines a modifier's role in a sentence can help students see this point.

Forcing students to memorize these rules may not make them more accurate writers. Students need to learn how to take the generalizations conveyed by these rules and apply them to specific situations; that means helping them understand the rules, not just getting them to memorize.

MEDIA RESOURCES FOR CHAPTER 28

mycomplab📘 Please visit MyCompLab at *www.mycomplab.com* for more on the writing process.

http://www.ablongman.com/littlebrown ▶ See page 73 of this manual for companion Web site content description.

INSTRUCTOR RESOURCE

The following Presentation Aid is available for download on this book's companion Web site at *http://www.ablongman.com/littlebrown*.

PRESENTATION AID 28.1: Principal uses of the comma (p. 431)

RESOURCES AND IDEAS

Punctuation

Dawkins, John. "Teaching Punctuation as a Rhetorical Tool." *College Composition and Communication* 46 (1995): 533–48. Dawkins makes a case for teaching the rhetorical thinking processes that accompany decisions about punctuation marks.

Meyer, Emily, and Louise Z. Smith, "Punctuation." *The Practical Tutor.* New York: Oxford UP, 1987. The authors offer detailed advice for the often frustrating task of helping students develop effective punctuation skills.

Commas

Meyer, Charles F. "Teaching Punctuation to Advanced Writers." *Journal of Advanced Composition* 6 (1985–86): 117–29. Meyer offers a number of strategies that can be used in any classroom.

Shaughnessy, Mina P. *Errors and Expectations: A Guide for the Teacher of Basic Writing.* New York: Oxford UP, 1977. 14–43. Shaughnessy explains teaching punctuation in the context of understanding students' hypotheses about their texts.

Thomas, Lewis. "Notes on Punctuation." *New England Journal of Medicine* 296 (1977): 1103–05. Reprinted in The Medusa and the Snail: More Notes of a Biology Watcher. New York: Viking, 1979. An experienced scientist and writer explores how punctuation use can affect the meaning of texts.

28a Use a comma before *and, but,* or another coordinating conjunction linking main clauses.

CLASSROOM IDEAS

Comma power Though writing instructors often treat commas and other marks of punctuation as if they were primarily cues to grammatical structures, these marks also function legitimately as stylistic cues, as indicators of the writer's voice—or so argues Wallace Chafe in "What Good Is Punctuation?" (*The Quarterly of the National Writing Project and the Center for the Study of Writing* 10 [1988]: 8–11). Chafe supports his argument with examples from the work of Herman Melville and James Agee and concludes with some useful advice for teaching:

Students, in addition to being sensitized to their inner voices, will benefit from knowing the range of punctuating options that are available, and
from being shown, through examples, what is most appropriate to one style
and another. They can learn from practice in writing advertising copy as
well as the more academic kinds of exposition, and from experimenting with
fiction that mimics the very different punctuation styles of, say, Melville and
Agee. At the same time, developing writers need to know that there are certain specific rules for punctuating that violate the prosody of their inner
voices and that simply have to be learned. These arbitrary rules are few in
number and well defined, and to learn them need be no burden . . . The bot-
tom line is that punctuation contributes substantially to the effectiveness of
a piece of writing, and that its successful use calls for an awareness of something that is, for this and other reasons, essential to good writing; a sensitivity to the sound of written language.

"In Praise of the Humble Comma," a short and amusing paean to the
power of punctuation to affect meaning, might also be handed out to students as a useful reminder of the connections between grammar and content. (Pico Iyer, *Time*, June 13, 1988: 348).

COLLABORATIVE LEARNING Exercise 28.2 Ask students to complete Exercise
28.2 individually and then discuss their responses in small groups. Have
each group discuss the effect of alternative answers and then present one
or two of the most successful responses.

ANSWERS

EXERCISE 28.1 Punctuating linked main clauses (p. 432)

1. Parents once automatically gave their children the father's surname,
   but some no longer do.
2. Instead, they bestow the mother's name, for they believe that the
   mother's importance should be recognized.
3. The child's surname may be just the mother's, or it may link the
   mother's and the father's with a hyphen.
4. Sometimes the first and third children will have the mother's surname, and the second child will have the father's.
5. Occasionally the mother and father combine parts of their names,
   and a new hybrid surname is born.

EXERCISE 28.2 Sentence combining: Linked main clauses (p. 433)

Possible answers

1. Parents were once legally required to bestow the father's surname on
   their children, but these laws have been contested in court and found
   invalid.

2. Parents may now give their children any surname they choose, and the arguments for bestowing the mother's surname are often strong and convincing.
3. Critics sometimes question the effects of unusual surnames on children, or they wonder how confusing or fleeting the new surnames will be.
4. Children with surnames different from their parents' may suffer embarrassment or identity problems, for giving children their father's surname is still very much the norm.
5. Hyphenated names are awkward and difficult to pass on, so some observers think they will die out in the next generation or before.

28b Use a comma to set off most introductory elements.

CLASSROOM IDEAS

COLLABORATIVE LEARNING Court reporter To help students understand how commas affect understanding, have them play "court reporter." Ask one or two students to read a passage from their papers or some reading for the class while the other students try to write what they say. Then have the reporters prepare a transcript of what they heard, inserting punctuation where they think it is needed. Each group should compare the reporters' versions with the originals and solve any disputes over comma use by referring to the appropriate sections of this chapter.

COLLABORATIVE LEARNING Exercise 28.3 Have students complete Exercise 28.3 individually and then compare their responses in small groups. This allows students to debate different kinds of comma usage in a nonintimidating setting.

COLLABORATIVE LEARNING Exercise 28.4 Ask students to complete Exercise 28.4 individually and then compare responses in small groups. You might then have each group create one or two sentences of their own involving introductory clauses set off by commas.

ANSWERS

EXERCISE 28.3 Punctuating introductory elements (p. 434)

1. Sentence correct.
2. Because it is sudden and apparently well coordinated, the movement of flocks and schools has seemed to be directed by a leader.
3. However, new studies have discovered that flocks and schools are leaderless.
4. When each bird or fish senses a predator, it follows individual rules for fleeing.
5. Multiplied over hundreds of individuals, these responses look as if they have been choreographed.

EXERCISE 28.4 Sentence combining: Introductory elements (p. 435)

Possible answers

1. In an effort to explain the mysteries of flocks and schools, scientists have proposed bizarre magnetic fields and telepathy.
2. Since scientists developed computer models, they have abandoned earlier explanations.
3. Starting with each individual, the movement of a flock or school is rapidly and perhaps automatically coordinated among individuals.
4. Observing that human beings seek coherent patterns, one zoologist suggests that investigators saw purpose in the movement of flocks and schools where none existed.
5. To study the movement of flocks or schools, one must abandon a search for purpose or design.

28c Use a comma or commas to set off nonessential elements.

INSTRUCTOR RESOURCE

The following Presentation Aid is available for download on this book's companion Web site at *http://www.ablongman.com/littlebrown*.

PRESENTATION AID 28.2: A test for essential and nonessential elements (p. 436)

CLASSROOM IDEAS

Essential vs. nonessential modifiers The difference between essential and nonessential elements is one of the most difficult concepts for students to grasp. Try using these two examples as a way of illustrating the difference:

Bring me the books that are on the desk.

Bring me the books, which are on the desk.

In the first example, the essential modifier *that are on the desk* selects a specific group of books: only those that are on the desk, as opposed to others in the room. In the second sentence, the nonessential modifier *which are on the desk* tells us that the location of the books is not a restricting factor; the requester wants all the books, and they just happen to be on the desk. Ask students to make up other pairs of examples to show the difference between essential and nonessential modifiers, and stress that only the nonessential (nonselecting) modifier is set off by a comma.

Recognizing nonessential elements For students who are still uncertain about whether elements are nonessential or essential, emphasize that nonessential elements *require* punctuation and *follow* these types of items:

1. One of a kind (including proper nouns):
   Secretariat, a beautiful chestnut colt, won the Triple Crown in 1973.

2. All of a kind:
   United States senators, who serve six-year terms, face constant pressure to raise campaign funds.
3. Previously mentioned:
   Animal rights activists have been known to stage outrageous demonstrations. The activists, who seek media attention, are prepared to risk criticism to promote their cause.

COLLABORATIVE LEARNING Word puzzles Divide the class into small groups and give them word puzzles like the following. Each of these puzzles can be solved only if the reader knows how essential and nonessential phrases are punctuated.

1. You are a CIA agent whose job is to keep track of all the Russian spies in Melopolia. One day you receive this telegram from Washington: "All the Russian spies, formerly residing in the Russian embassy, have been sent home."
   Is there anyone left for you to watch?

2. After a long and successful season the university basketball team played its cross-state rival for the conference championship. Pandemonium broke out when a long shot dropped in at the buzzer to give the university the victory. Parties were held all over campus.
   When Professor Kean arrived at class the next morning, the students, who had celebrated long into the night, were fast asleep at their desks.
   Can you tell what portion of the class was asleep?

3. A severe electrical storm swept through town just after noon. Lightning struck several buildings, including the computer center. Technicians repairing damage there found that the microcomputers which were not equipped with electrical surge protectors needed to have their circuit boards replaced.
   Are any of the microcomputers still usable?

Commas and parentheses Students who know math will appreciate that the commas around parenthetical expressions are like the parentheses in a mathematical equation; if you use one to open the expression, you must have one to close it, or it can't be "solved" properly.

COLLABORATIVE LEARNING Exercise 28.5 Have students complete Exercise 28.5 individually and then compare their responses in small groups. This allows students the opportunity to discuss the differences between essential and nonessential elements in a supportive setting. You might then ask each group to present one or two of their corrected responses on the blackboard or on transparencies while explaining how they reached their conclusions.

COLLABORATIVE LEARNING Exercise 28.6 Ask students to complete Exercise 28.6 individually and then compare their responses in small groups. Encourage the groups to focus on the places where individuals reached alternative conclusions and to discuss the effects of those differences on the meaning of the sentence.

ANSWERS

EXERCISE 28.5 Punctuating essential and nonessential elements (p. 439)

1. Italians insist that Marco Polo, the thirteenth-century explorer, did not import pasta from China.
2. Pasta, which consists of flour and water and often egg, existed in Italy long before Marco Polo left for his travels.
3. Sentence correct.
4. Most Italians dispute this account, although their evidence is shaky.
5. Wherever pasta originated, the Italians are now the undisputed masters in making and cooking it.
6. Sentence correct.
7. Most cooks must buy dried pasta, lacking the time to make their own.
8. Sentence correct.
9. Pasta manufacturers choose hard durum wheat because it makes firmer cooked pasta than common wheat does.
10. Pasta made from common wheat tends to get soggy in boiling water.

EXERCISE 28.6 Sentence combining: Essential and nonessential elements (p. 440)

Possible answers

1. American colonists first imported pasta from the English, who discovered it as tourists in Italy.
2. The English returning from their grand tours of Italy were called *macaronis* because of their fancy airs.
3. A hair style with elaborate curls was also called *macaroni*.
4. The song "Yankee Doodle" refers to this hairdo when it reports that Yankee Doodle "stuck a feather in his cap and called it macaroni."
5. The song, a creation of the English, was actually intended to poke fun at unrefined American colonists.

RESOURCES AND IDEAS

Christensen, Francis. "Restrictive and Nonrestrictive Modifiers Again." In *Notes Toward a New Rhetoric: Nine Essays for Teachers.* 2nd ed. Ed. Francis Christensen and Bonniejean Christensen. New York: Harper-Collins, 1978. 117–32. Christensen discusses and illustrates uses of the comma with a variety of modifying elements.

22d Use a comma or commas to set off absolute phrases.

ANSWERS

EXERCISE 28.7 Punctuating absolute phrases and phrases of contrast (p. 441)

1. Prices having risen rapidly, the government debated a price freeze.
2. A price freeze, unlike a rise in interest rates, seemed a sure solution.

3. The President would have to persuade businesses to accept a price freeze, his methods depending on their resistance.
4. No doubt the President, his advisers having urged it, would first try a patriotic appeal.
5. The President, not his advisers, insisted on negotiations with businesses.

28f Use commas between items on a series and between coordinate adjectives.

INSTRUCTOR RESOURCE

The following Presentation Aid is available for download on this book's companion Web site at *http://www.ablongman.com/littlebrown*.

PRESENTATION AID 28.3: Punctuating two or more adjectives (p. 442)

CLASSROOM IDEA

COLLABORATIVE LEARNING When handbooks disagree Often, the advice on using commas in a series varies from handbook to handbook and style guide to style guide. Ask students as teams to compare the comma rules given in this handbook with the advice in some other usage manual (for instance, *The Associated Press Stylebook*, or *The New York Times Manual of Style and Usage*. These and other newspaper guides are available in the writing reference section of their library or bookstore.) They can then report back to the class on where these guides agree and disagree. The rules in this handbook are based on the style of reference common to the humanities; the advice in other handbooks may be based on styles appropriate to other disciplines.

ANSWERS

EXERCISE 28.8 Punctuation series and coordinate adjectives (p. 443)

1. Shoes with high heels originated to protect feet from the mud, garbage, and animal waste in the streets.
2. Sentence correct.
3. The heels were worn by men and made of colorful silk brocades, soft suedes, or smooth leathers.
4. High-heeled shoes received a boost when the short, powerful King Louis XIV of France began wearing them.
5. Eventually only wealthy, fashionable French women wore high heels.

28g Use a commas according to convention in dates, addresses, place names, and long numbers.

CLASSROOM IDEA

COMPUTER ACTIVITY US Postal Regulations In addresses on envelopes, the United States Postal Service now asks that the city name be written in block capitals with no comma, followed by the state abbreviation, one space, and the zip code, as in the following example: BERKELEY CA 94720. This format enables their automatic sorting devices to process mail more effectively.

Students using word-processing or mail-merge programs may find that the computer automatically puts addresses into this format. However, writers still use the format shown in these examples when writing town and state names in the body of their texts. (See 55a for a sample envelope that illustrates the format recommended by the Postal Service.)

ANSWERS

EXERCISE 28.9 Punctuating dates, addresses, place names, numbers (p. 444)

1. The festival will hold a benefit dinner and performance on March 10, 2006, in Asheville.
2. The organizers hope to raise more than $100,000 from donations and ticket sales.
3. Performers are expected from as far away as Milan, Italy, and Kyoto, Japan.
4. All inquiries sent to Mozart Festival, PO Box 725, Asheville, North Carolina 28803, will receive a quick response.
5. The deadline for ordering tickets by mail is Monday, December 3, 2005.

28h Use commas with quotations according to standard practice.

CLASSROOM IDEA

Audience expectations Discuss the notion of audience expectations when students say, "My biology teacher says to do this," and remind students that being consistent within a document and meeting the expectations of one's readers are the most important considerations in deciding how to use particular punctuation marks. Part X lists style guides for various disciplines, which offer students additional information in making the punctuation decisions expected by various communities of readers.

ANSWERS

EXERCISE 28.10 Punctuating quotations (p. 446)

1. Sentence correct.
2. "I think of the open-ended writing process as a voyage in two stages," Elbow says.
3. "The sea voyage is a process of divergence, branching, proliferation, and confusion," Elbow continues; "the coming to land is a process of convergence, pruning, centralizing, and clarifying."

4. "Keep up one session of writing long enough to get loosened up and tired," advises Elbow, "long enough in fact to make a bit of a voyage."
5. "In coming to new land," Elbow says, "you develop a new conception of what you are writing about."

28i Use commas to prevent misreading.

CLASSROOM IDEA

COLLABORATIVE LEARNING Exercise 28.11 Ask students to complete Exercise 28.11 individually and then have them compare their responses in small groups. Encourage the groups to consider the effect of varied comma placement on the meaning of each sentence. As a follow-up exercise you might ask each student to bring in a sentence taken from a magazine or newspaper in which the removal or addition of a comma creates a noticeable change in meaning.

ANSWERS

EXERCISE 28.11 Punctuating to prevent misreading (p. 447)

1. Though happy, people still have moments of self-doubt.
2. In research, subjects have reported themselves to be generally happy people.
3. Among those who have, life has included sufferings as well as joys.
4. Of fifty, eight subjects reported bouts of serious depression.
5. For half, the preceding year had included at least one personal crisis.

28j Use commas only where required.

INSTRUCTOR RESOURCES

The following Presentation Aids are available for download on this book's companion Web site at *http://www.ablongman.com/littlebrown*.

PRESENTATION AID 28.4: Principal misuses of the commas (p. 449)

PRESENTATION AID 28.5: Exercise 28.12 Revising: Needless or misused commas (p. 451)

CLASSROOM IDEAS

COMPUTER ACTIVITY Grammar checkers If students are using grammar and style checkers, they may find that the computer challenges punctuation that follows the rules in this book. (Commas in a series are particular targets.) Warn students that such programs may follow slightly different rules, and tell them which rules you want them to follow if such conflicts arise. As a useful case in point you might choose a paragraph of student work with errors and have students run it through various grammar checkers and then display the results for general discussion. While such a display of contradictory "rules" of grammar might seem unnecessarily confusing, it's important to keep in mind that students will be able to use punctuation more effectively when they understand the various reasons behind the rules.

COLLABORATIVE LEARNING Repunctuating Take an essay from a reader or a similar source, remove the punctuation you wish to emphasize, make copies of the essay, and ask students to work in groups in order to reach consensus about how it should be punctuated. Tell them not to look at the handbook but to decide on their own the best way to serve the reader's needs through punctuation. When the students have finished, they can compare their work with the original and, using the handbook as a reference, decide which punctuation they think best serves the needs of the essay and the reader. If they decide to disagree with the advice given in the handbook, ask them to write out their own punctuation rules.

Have students practice proofreading, first on articles taken from local newspapers or papers written by members of other classes, and then on their own papers. Discuss why it is more difficult to find mistakes in their own papers than in the writings of others. For many, the difficulty arises because they are looking for what they wanted to write, or thought they wrote, not what they actually put on the page. Advise students to wait several hours between writing and proofreading so that their short-term memories clear and they can see what they've actually written instead of what they wanted to write.

COLLABORATIVE LEARNING Exercises 28.12 and 28.13 Ask students to complete Exercise 28.12 individually and to compare their responses in small groups. Then have each group complete Exercise 28.13 as a collaborative project, encouraging each group to debate the placement and elimination of commas.

ANSWERS

EXERCISE 28.12 Revising: Needless or misused commas (p. 451)

1. Nearly 32 million US residents speak a first language other than English.
2. After English the languages most commonly spoken in the United States are Spanish, French, and German.
3. Almost 75 percent of the people who speak foreign languages used the words "good" or "very good" when judging their proficiency in English.
4. Sentence correct.
5. The states with the highest proportion of foreign language speakers are New Mexico and California.

EXERCISE 28.13 Revising: Commas (p. 452)

Ellis Island, New York, reopened for business in 1990, but now the customers are tourists, not immigrants. This spot, which lies in New York Harbor, was the first American soil seen or touched by many of the nation's immigrants. Though other places also served as ports of entry for foreigners, none has the symbolic power of Ellis Island. Between its opening in 1892 and its closing in 1954, over 20 million people, about two-thirds of all immigrants, were detained there before taking up their new lives in the United States. Ellis Island processed over 2000 [*or* 2,000] newcomers a day when immigration was at its peak between 1900 and 1920.

As the end of a long voyage and the introduction to the New World, Ellis Island must have left something to be desired. The "huddled masses," as the Statue of Liberty calls them, indeed were huddled. New arrivals were herded about, kept standing in lines for hours or days, yelled at, and abused. Assigned numbers, they submitted their bodies to the pokings and proddings of the silent nurses and doctors who were charged with ferreting out the slightest sign of sickness, disability, or insanity. That test having been passed, the immigrants faced interrogation by an official through an interpreter. Those with names deemed inconveniently long or difficult to pronounce often found themselves permanently labeled with abbreviations of their names or with the names of their hometowns. But millions survived the examination, humiliation, and confusion to take the last short boat ride to New York City. For many of them and especially for their descendants, Ellis Island eventually became, not a nightmare, but the place where life began.

RESOURCES AND IDEAS

Benson, S. Kenneth. "Profitable Proofreading." *Teaching the Basics—Really!* Ed. Ouida Clapp. Urbana: NCTE, 1977. 80–81. Benson describes exercises in proofreading and in getting students to pay attention to correction symbols.

CHAPTER 29

The Semicolon

CHAPTER HIGHLIGHTS

Many inexperienced writers are hesitant to use the semicolon. They may be unfamiliar with the purposes of the mark and therefore reluctant to use it. This chapter should help students understand the four main uses of the semicolon: to separate main clauses not joined by a coordinating conjunction; to separate main clauses joined by a conjunctive adverb; to separate main clauses if they are very long and complex, even when they are joined by a coordinating conjunction; and to separate items in a series if they are long or contain commas.

The chapter also covers the places where the semicolon can be misused. When students take risks in using the semicolon, positive reinforcement from you will help encourage them to add this useful punctuation mark to their repertoire.

MEDIA RESOURCES FOR CHAPTER 29

mycomplab Please visit MyCompLab at *www.mycomplab.com* for more on the writing process.

http://www.ablongman.com/littlebrown ▶ See page 73 of this manual for companion Web site content description.

29a **Use a semicolon between main clauses not joined by *and, but,* or another coordinating conjunction.**

INSTRUCTOR RESOURCE

The following Presentation Aid is available for download on this book's companion Web site at *http://www.ablongman.com/littlebrown*.

PRESENTATION AID 29.1: Distinguishing the comma, the semicolon, and the colon (p. 454)

CLASSROOM IDEA

COLLABORATIVE LEARNING Exercise 29.2 Ask students to complete Exercise 29.2 individually and then to compare their responses in small groups. Encourage group members to discuss their varying responses and to consider the effects of those differences on the meaning of each sentence. Then have each group present one of their responses to the class and explain the reasons for their sentence-combining choices.

ANSWERS

EXERCISE 29.1 Punctuating between main clauses (p. 453)

1. More and more musicians are playing computerized instruments; more and more listeners are worrying about the future of acoustic instruments.
2. The computer is not the first new technology in music; the pipe organ and saxophone were also technological breakthroughs in their day.
3. Musicians have always experimented with new technology; audiences have always resisted the experiments.
4. Most computer musicians are not merely following the latest fad; they are discovering new sounds and new ways to manipulate sound.
5. Few musicians have abandoned acoustic instruments; most value acoustic sounds as much as electronic sounds.

EXERCISE 29.2 Sentence combining: Related main clauses (p. 455)

Possible answers

1. Electronic instruments are prevalent in jazz and rock music; they are less common in classical music.
2. Jazz and rock change rapidly; they nourish experimentation and improvisation.
3. Traditional classical music does not change; its notes and instrumentation were established by a composer writing decades or centuries ago.
4. Contemporary classical music not only can draw on tradition; it also can respond to innovations such as jazz rhythms and electronic sounds.
5. Much contemporary electronic music is more than just jazz, rock, or classical; it is a fusion of all three.

29b Use a semicolon between main clauses related by *however, for example,* and so on.

CLASSROOM IDEA

COLLABORATIVE LEARNING Exercises 29.3 and 29.4 Ask students to complete Exercise 29.3 individually and then to compare their responses in small groups. Have each group complete Exercise 29.4 as a collaborative project, and encourage group members to debate various possible answers to each question. Then have each group present one of their responses to the class and explain the reasons for their choices.

ANSWERS

EXERCISE 29.3 Punctuating main clauses related by conjunctive adverbs or transitional expressions (p. 456)

1. Music is a form of communication like language; the basic elements, however, are not letters but notes.
2. Computers can process any information that can be represented numerically; as a result, they can process musical information.
3. A computer's ability to process music depends on what software it can run; it must, moreover, be connected to a system that converts electrical vibration into sound.
4. Computers and their sound systems can produce many different sounds; indeed, the number of possible sounds is infinite.
5. The powerful music computers are very expensive; therefore, they are used only by professional musicians.

EXERCISE 29.4 Sentence combining: Main clauses related by conjunctive adverbs or transitional expressions (p. 456)

1. Most music computers are too expensive for the average consumer; however, digital keyboard instruments can be inexpensive and are widely available.
2. Inside the keyboard is a small computer that controls a sound synthesizer; consequently, the instrument can both process and produce music.
3. The person playing the keyboard presses keys or other controls; immediately, the computer and synthesizer convert these signals into vibrations and sounds.
4. The inexpensive keyboards can perform only a few functions; still, to the novice computer musician the range of drum rhythms and simulated instruments is exciting.
5. Would-be musicians can orchestrate whole songs from just the melody lines; thus [or thus,] they need never again play "Chopsticks."

RESOURCES AND IDEAS

Petit, Angela. "Stylish Semicolon: Teaching Punctuation as Rhetorical Choice." *English Journal* 92 (January 2003): 66–72. Using the semicolon as her example, Petit argues that punctuation is best taught in the context of lessons on style.

29c Use a semicolon to separate main clauses if they are complicated or contain commas, even, with a coordinating conjunction.

CLASSROOM IDEA

COMPUTER ACTIVITY Style checkers Often, style checkers may reject uses of semicolons like the ones shown here, since they are apparent exceptions to semicolon rules. When such conflicts arise, have students check to see that their sentences are well constructed and that the semicolons are needed. As a case in point, you might have students run a passage from a published writer (such as Thoreau or O'Connor) through their grammar checkers and present the results to the class. Encourage students to discuss the effects of semicolon placement on the meaning of each passage.

ANSWERS

EXERCISE 29.5 Punctuating long main clauses and series items (p. 458)

1. The Indian subcontinent is separated from the rest of the world by clear barriers: the Bay of Bengal and the Arabian Sea to the east and west, respectively; the Indian Ocean to the south; and 1600 miles of mountain ranges to the north.
2. In the north of India are the world's highest mountains, the Himalayas; and farther south are fertile farmlands, unpopulated deserts, and rain forests.
3. India is a nation of ethnic and linguistic diversity, with numerous religions, including Hinduism, Islam, and Christianity; with distinct castes and ethnic groups; and with sixteen languages, including the official Hindi and the "associate official" English.
4. Between the seventeenth and nineteenth centuries, the British colonized most of India, taking control of government, the bureaucracy, and industry; and they assumed a social position above all Indians.
5. During British rule the Indians' own unresolved differences and their frustrations with the British erupted in violent incidents such as the Sepoy Mutiny, which began on February 26, 1857, and lasted two years; the Amritsar Massacre on April 13, 1919; and violence between Hindus and Muslims during World War II that resulted in the separation of Pakistan from India.

29d Use a semicolon only where required.

CLASSROOM IDEAS

Memory aid Introduce students to this brief list of ways not to use the semicolon.

> Do not use a semicolon to separate a subordinate clause from a main clause.
> Do not use a semicolon to introduce a series.
> Do not overuse a semicolon.

COLLABORATIVE LEARNING Exercises 29.6 and 29.7 Ask students to complete Exercise 29.6 individually and to compare their responses in small groups. Then ask each group to work collaboratively on Exercise 29.7, encouraging them to debate the effectiveness of each change in punctuation.

ANSWERS

EXERCISE 29.6 Revising: Misused or overused semicolons (p. 460)

1. The main religion in India is Hinduism, a way of life as well as a theology and philosophy.
2. Unlike Christianity and Judaism, Hinduism is a polytheistic religion, with deities numbering in the hundreds.
3. *Possible revision:* Unlike many other religions, Hinduism allows its creeds and practices to vary widely from place to place and person to person. Whereas other religions have churches and principal prophets and holy books, Hinduism does not. And whereas other religions center on specially trained priests or other leaders, Hinduism promotes the individual as his or her own priest.
4. In Hindu belief there are four types of people: reflective, emotional, active, and experimental.
5. Each type of person has a different technique for realizing the true, immortal self, which has infinite existence, infinite knowledge, and infinite joy.

EXERCISE 29.7 Revising: Semicolons (p. 460)

The set, sounds, and actors in the movie captured the essence of horror films. The set was ideal: dark, deserted streets; trees dipping their branches over the sidewalks; mist hugging the ground and creeping up to meet the trees; looming shadows of unlighted, turreted houses. The sounds, too, were appropriate; especially terrifying was the hard, hollow sound of footsteps echoing throughout the film. But the best feature of the movie was its actors, all of them tall, pale, and thin to the point of emaciation. With one exception, they were dressed uniformly in gray and had gray hair. The exception was an actress who dressed only in black, as if to set off her pale yellow, nearly white, long hair, the only color in the film. The glinting black eyes of another actor stole almost every scene; indeed, they were the source of all the film's mischief.

Apostrophe

CHAPTER HIGHLIGHTS

This chapter deals with the three reasons to use an apostrophe: to show possession; to indicate a contraction; or to form the plural of letters, numbers, and words named as words. It also explains when the apostrophe should not be used. The chapter focuses on the trouble spots writers are most likely to face and on the strategies they can use to avoid such problems.

MEDIA RESOURCES FOR CHAPTER 30

mycomplab Please visit MyCompLab at *www.mycomplab.com* for more on the writing process.

`http://www.ablongman.com/littlebrown` ▶ See page 73 of this manual for companion Web site content description.

30a Use the apostrophe to indicate the possessive case for nouns and indefinite pronouns.

INSTRUCTOR RESOURCE

The following Presentation Aid is available for download on this book's companion Web site at *http://www.ablongman.com/littlebrown*.

PRESENTATION AID 30.1: Uses and misuses of the apostrophe (p. 463)

CLASSROOM IDEAS

COMPUTER ACTIVITY Spelling checkers Spelling checkers vary; some require both an apostrophe and an *s* after words ending in *s*, while others don't.

COLLABORATIVE LEARNING Yellow pages The apostrophe is a messy punctuation mark and is frequently misused. Help students see how popular use is changing the perception of apostrophes by asking students in groups to examine sections of the Yellow Pages or the advertisements in the local newspaper to find examples where expected apostrophes are missing (for instance, "Karins Kurtains" or "Farmers Market"). Encourage them to notice such misuses and bring them to the class's attention.

RESOURCES AND IDEAS

Hashimoto, Irvin. "Pain and Suffering: Apostrophes and Academic Life." *Journal of Basic Writing* 7(2) (1988): 91–98. Hashimoto reviews, in often humorous fashion, some of the problems students have with apostrophe use.

Wiener, Harvey S. *The Writing Room: A Resource Book for Teachers of English.* New York: Oxford UP, 1981. 175–80. Wiener offers advice on explaining possession to students and describes several exercises designed to help them master the possessive forms of words.

ANSWERS

EXERCISE 30.1 Forming possessives (p. 464)

1. In the myths of the ancient Greeks, the goddesses' roles vary widely.
2. Demeter's responsibility is the fruitfulness of the earth.
3. Athena's role is to guard the city of Athens.
4. Artemis's function is to care for wild animals and small children.
5. Athena and Artemis's father, Zeus, is the king of the gods.
6. Even a single goddess's responsibilities are often varied.
7. Over several centuries' time, Athena changes from a mariner's goddess to the patron of crafts.
8. Athena is also concerned with fertility and with children's well-being, since Athens's strength depended on a large and healthy population.
9. Athena often changes into birds' forms.
10. In Homer's *Odyssey* she assumes a sea eagle's form.
11. In ancient Athens the myths of Athena were part of everyone's knowledge and life.
12. A cherished myth tells how Athena fights to retain possession of her people's land when the god Poseidon wants it.
13. Athena's and Poseidon's skills are different, and each promises a special gift to the Athenians.
14. At the contest's conclusion, Poseidon has given water and Athena has given an olive tree, for sustenance.
15. The other gods decide that the Athenians' lives depend more on Athena than on Poseidon.

30b　Delete or replace any apostrophe in a plural noun, a singular verb, or a possessive personal pronoun.

INSTRUCTOR RESOURCE

The following Presentation Aid is available for download on this book's companion Web site at *http://www.ablongman.com/littlebrown*.

PRESENTATION AID 30.2: Exercise 30.2. Distinguishing between plurals and possessives (p. 465)

CLASSROOM IDEA

It's **hunting** The most troublesome possessive is *its*, which many students confuse with the contraction *it's*. Ask students to keep a list in their journals of places where they see these words confused, including published work and other students' writing. *It's* hunting makes students learn the *its/it's* rule and become more aware of how they use these words in their own writing.

ANSWERS

EXERCISE 30.2 Distinguishig between plurals and possessives (p. 465)

1. Demeter may be the oldest of the Greek gods, older than Zeus.
2. Many prehistoric cultures had earth goddesses like Demeter.
3. In myth she is the earth mother, which means that the responsibility for the fertility of both animals and plants is hers.
4. The goddess's festival came at harvest time, with its celebration of bounty.
5. The people's prayers to Demeter thanked her for grain and other gifts.

30c Use an apostrophe to indicate the omission in a standard contraction.

CLASSROOM IDEA

Contractions Some students may have been prohibited from using contractions in high school writing and remain unwilling to use such forms, for any audiences. Discuss with your classes the appropriate places for using contracted words.

ANSWERS

EXERCISE 30.3 Forming contractions (p. 466)

Possible answers

1. She'd rather be dancing.
2. He couldn't see her in the crowd.
3. They're at the front door now.
4. He's my brother.
5. We don't like the beach.
6. She'll speak her mind.
7. The recent storm was nearly as bad as the hurricane of '62.
8. Isn't that your cousin?
9. It's a fact.
10. The door won't budge.

EXERCISE 30.4 Revising: Contractions and personal pronouns (p. 466)

1. In Greek myth the goddess Demeter has a special fondness for Eleusis, near Athens, and its people.

2. Sentence correct.
3. Demeter rewards the Eleusians with the secret for making their land fruitful.
4. The Eleusians begin a cult in honor of Demeter, who's worshipped in secret ceremonies.
5. It's unknown what happened in the ceremonies, for no participant ever revealed their [correct] rituals.

30d Increasingly, the apostrophe does not mark plural abbreviations, dates, and words or characters named as words.

CLASSROOM IDEA

COLLABORATIVE LEARNING Exercise 30.5 Have students complete Exercise 30.5 individually and then compare their responses in groups. Then ask the groups to review paragraphs from each student's work in order to check apostrophe usage. It's important that students make the connection between the handbook exercises and correct apostrophe usage in their own work.

ANSWERS

EXERCISE 30.5 Revising: Apostrophes (p. 467)

Landlocked Chad is among the world's most troubled countries. The peoples of Chad are poor: their average per capita income equals $1000 a year. Less than half of Chad's population is literate, and every five hundred people must share only two teachers. The natural resources of the nation have never been plentiful, and now, as it's [correct] slowly being absorbed into the growing Sahara Desert, even water is scarce. Chad's political conflicts go back to the nineteenth century, when the French colonized the land by brutally subduing its people. The rule of the French—whose inept government of the colony did nothing to ease tensions among racial, tribal, and religious groups—ended with independence in 1960. But since then the Chadians' experience has been one of civil war and oppression, and now they're also threatened with invasions from their neighbors.

Quotation Marks

CHAPTER HIGHLIGHTS

The two most common problems students have with quotation marks are failing to close the quotation (see the special cautionary note in the chapter's introduction) and misplacing other punctuation marks inside or outside quotation marks. Take time to review these rules and encourage students to double-check their use of quotation marks. Both practices may save you a great deal of time in marking papers, especially when the students are preparing papers that require the use of cited material.

MEDIA RESOURCES FOR CHAPTER 31

mycomplab Please visit MyCompLab at *www.mycomplab.com* for more on the writing process.

http://www.ablongman.com/littlebrown ► See page 73 of this manual for companion Web site content description.

INSTRUCTOR RESOURCE

The following Presentation Aid is available for download on this book's companion Web site at *http://www.ablongman.com/littlebrown*.

PRESENTATION AID 31.1: Handling quotations from speech or writing (p. 469)

CLASSROOM IDEA

Indented quotations and poetry MLA style for double-spacing indented quotations of poetry or prose is new to some students, who may have been taught to single-space such quotes in high school. If you are conducting draft-review workshops, ask students to check the spacing of such quotes in their drafts. If they are preparing papers on word processors, they may be able to take advantage of automatic indentation and spacing features to format such quotations.

31a Use double quotation marks to enclose direct quotations.

CLASSROOM IDEA

COLLABORATIVE LEARNING Using quotations Hand out a page from the class readings or from another printed source. Have students work in pairs to quote and respond to short passages from the reading. This exercise will help to remind students of the uses of quotation in their own work.

31b Use single quotation marks to enclose a quotation within a quotation.

ANSWERS

EXERCISE 31. 1 Using double and single quotation marks (p. 471)

1. "Why," the lecturer asked, "do we say 'Bless you!' or something else when people sneeze but not acknowledge coughs, hiccups, and other eruptions?"
2. Sentence correct.
3. "Sneezes feel more uncontrollable than some other eruptions," she said.
4. "Unlike coughs and hiccups," she explained, "sneezes feel as if they come from inside the head."
5. She concluded, "People thus wish to recognize a sneeze, if only with a 'Gosh.'"

31c Put quotation marks around the titles of works that are parts of other works.

INSTRUCTOR RESOURCE

The following Presentation Aid is available for download on this book's companion Web site at *http://www.ablongman.com/littlebrown*.

PRESENTATION AID 31.2: Titles to be enclosed in quotation marks (p. 472)

ANSWERS

EXERCISE 31.2 Quoting titles (p. 473)

1. In Chapter 8, titled "How to Be Interesting," the author explains the art of conversation.
2. The Beatles' song "Let It Be" reminds Martin of his uncle.
3. The article that appeared in Mental Health [correct] was titled "Children of Divorce Ask, 'Why?'"
4. In the encyclopedia the discussion under "Modern Art" fills less than a column.
5. One prizewinning essay, "Cowgirls on Wall Street," first appeared in Entrepreneur [correct] magazine.

31d Place other punctuation marks inside or outside quotation marks according to standard practice.

INSTRUCTOR RESOURCE

The following Presentation Aid is available for download on this book's companion Web site at *http://www.ablongman.com/littlebrown*.

PRESENTATION AID 31.3: Exercise 31.3 Revising: Quotation marks (p. 475)

CLASSROOM IDEA

Note Students should note that this rule applies even when closing quotation marks are both single and double. Example: *"The author of the article pointed out that the rock group the Police coined the word 'synchronocity.'"*

COLLABORATIVE LEARNING Exercises 31.3 and 31.4 Ask students to complete Exercise 31.3 individually and to compare their responses in small groups. Then have the groups work through Exercise 31.4 as a collaborative project and present their conclusions to the class.

Disciplines do vary in their formats for long quotations. When in doubt, students should be encouraged to consult the discipline formatting guidelines cross-referenced in the chapter introduction or to consult their instructor practice.

ANSWERS

EXERCISE 31.3 Revising: Quotation marks (p. 475)

1. In the title essay of her book "The Death of the Moth" and Other Essays, Virginia Woolf describes the last moments of a "frail and diminutive body." [Underlining correct for book title, but essay title within it is quoted.]
2. An insect's death may seem insignificant, but the moth is, in Woolf's words, "life, a pure bead."
3. The moth's struggle against death, "indifferent, impersonal," is heroic.
4. Where else but in such a bit of life could one see a protest so "superb"?
5. At the end Woolf sees the moth lying "most decently and uncomplainingly composed"; in death it finds dignity.

EXERCISE 31.4 Revising: Quotation marks (p. 476)

In one class we talked about a passage from "I Have a Dream," the speech delivered by Martin Luther King, Jr., on the steps of the Lincoln Memorial on August 28, 1963:

> When the architects of our republic wrote the magnificent words of the Constitution and the Declaration of Independence, they were signing a promissory note to which every American was to fall heir. This note was a promise that all men would be guaranteed the unalienable rights of life, liberty, and the pursuit of happiness.

"What did Dr. King mean by this statement?" the teacher asked. "Perhaps we should define 'promissory note' first." Then she explained that a person who signs such a note agrees to pay a specific sum of money on a particular date or on demand by the holder of the note. One student suggested, "Maybe Dr. King meant that the writers of the Constitution and Declaration promised that all people in America should be equal." "He and over 200,000 people had gathered in Washington, DC," added another student. "Maybe their purpose was to demand payment, to demand those rights for African Americans." The whole discussion was an eye opener for those of us (including me) who had never considered that those documents make promises that we should expect our country to fulfill.

32

Other Punctuation Marks

> Q. What is the purpose of the colon?
> A. The colon forms a barrier alerting the reader not to go any
> farther in the sentence.
>
> —DAVE BARRY

CHAPTER HIGHLIGHTS

Chapter 32 covers the marks of punctuation not treated in the preceding chapters (27–31): the colon, the dash, parentheses, brackets, the ellipsis mark, and the slash. In addition to exercises for these marks of punctuation, an exercise at the end of the part (p. 488) asks students to practice using most of the punctuation marks covered in Chapters 27–32.

MEDIA RESOURCES FOR CHAPTER 32

mycomplab Please visit MyCompLab at *www.mycomplab.com* for more on the writing process.

`http://www.ablongman.com/littlebrown` ▶ See page 73 of this manual for companion Web site content description.

32a Use the colon to introduce and to separate.

INSTRUCTOR RESOURCE

The following Presentation Aid is available for download on this book's companion Web site at *http://www.ablongman.com/littlebrown*.

PRESENTATION AID 32.1: Distinguishing the colon and the semicolon (p. 478)

CLASSROOM IDEA

COLONS Colons with lists In business and professional writing, colons often end phrases or subordinate clauses that precede lists formatted vertically:

The system requires:
Pentium 60 MHz processor
64 MB of RAM
SVGA video
Microsoft Windows XP

ANSWERS

EXERCISE 32.1 Revising: Colons (p. 479)

1. In remote areas of many developing countries, simple signs mark human habitation: a dirt path, a few huts, smoke from a campfire.
2. In the built-up sections of industrialized countries, nature is all but obliterated by signs of human life, such as houses, factories, sky-scrapers, and highways.
3. The spectacle makes many question the words of Ecclesiastes 1.4: "One generation passeth away, and another generation cometh; but the earth abideth forever."
4. Yet many scientists see the future differently: they hold that human beings have all the technology necessary to clean up the earth and restore the cycles of nature.
5. All that is needed is a change in the attitudes of those who use technology.

32b Use a dash to indicate shifts in tone or thought and to set off some sentence elements.

INSTRUCTOR RESOURCE

The following Presentation Aid is available for download on this book's companion Web site at *http://www.ablongman.com/littlebrown*.

PRESENTATION AID 32.2: Distinguishing dashes, commas, and parentheses (p. 481)

CLASSROOM IDEA

THE DASH Adding the dash For many students, using dashes is a way of avoiding a decision about which punctuation mark to use. Dashes can be used this way in informal writing, but in more formal situations, students should use dashes only in the accepted ways discussed in the text.

ANSWERS

EXERCISE 32.2 Revising: Dashes (p. 481)

1. The movie-theater business is undergoing dramatic changes—changes that may affect what movies are made and shown.

2. The closing of independent theaters, the control of theaters by fewer and fewer owners, and the increasing ownership of theaters by movie studios and distributors—these changes may reduce the availability of noncommercial films.

3. Yet at the same time the number of movie screens is increasing—primarily in multiscreen complexes—so that smaller films may find more outlets.

4. The number of active movie screens—that is, screens showing films or booked to do so—is higher now than at any time since World War II.

5. The biggest theater complexes seem to be something else as well—art galleries, amusement arcades, restaurants, spectacles.

32c Use parentheses to enclose parenthetical expressions and labels for lists within sentences.

CLASSROOM IDEA

PARENTHESES Alternative example When you are enclosing a complete sentence within another complete sentence, you need not start the sentence in parentheses with a capital letter nor end it with a punctuation mark. For example:

> I spent the weekend buried in books (this is my usual practice) and emerged on Monday in time to go to the library.

ANSWERS

EXERCISE 32.3 Revising: Parentheses (p. 483)

1. Many of those involved in the movie business agree that multiscreen complexes are good for two reasons: (1) they cut the costs of exhibitors, and (2) they offer more choices to audiences.

2. Those who produce and distribute films (and not just the big studios) argue that the multiscreen theaters give exhibitors too much power.

3. The major studios are buying movie theaters to gain control over important parts of the distribution process (what gets shown and for how much money).

4. For twelve years (1938–50) the federal government forced the studios to sell all their movie theaters.

5. But because they now have more competition (television and videocassette recorders), the studios are permitted to own theaters.

RESOURCES AND IDEAS

Arthur L. Palacas. "Parenthetics and Personal Voice." *Written Communication* 6 (1989): 506–28. Palacas argues that the use of parenthetical expressions (including those punctuated by parentheses, commas, and dashes) is an important factor in developing a personal style.

32d Use brackets within quotations to indicate your own comments or changes.

CLASSROOM IDEA

BRACKETS Additional uses of brackets Brackets may also be used to supply missing letters to complete names that are given partly in initials in a quotation: E[lwyn] B[rooks] White.

32e Use the ellipsis mark to indicate omissions from quotations and pauses in speeches.

ANSWERS

EXERCISE 32.4 Using ellipsis marks (p. 486)

1. "To be able to read the Bible in the vernacular was a liberating experience. . . ."
2. "To be able to read the Bible in the vernacular . . . freed the reader from hearing only the set passages read in the church and interpreted by the church."
3. "Women in the sixteenth and seventeenth centuries were educated in the home and, in some cases, in boarding schools. . . . A Protestant woman was expected to read the scriptures daily, to meditate on them, and to memorize portions of them."

RESOURCES AND IDEAS

Keith Grant-Davie. "Functional Redundancy: Ellipsis as Strategies in Reading and Writing." *Journal of Advanced Composition* 15:3 (1995): 455–69. Grant-Davie looks at the differences between functional and needless redundancy in relation to the use of ellipses, particularly in the field of technical writing.

32f Use the slash between options, between lines of poetry, and in electronic addresses.

CLASSROOM IDEAS

THE SLASH Slashing The rules governing when to put spaces around the slash confuse many students; it's worth a moment's time to review them. In addition, warn students that many word-processing programs that justify (align) the right margins of text may add or remove spaces around slashes.

COLLABORATIVE LEARNING Exercise 32.5 Ask students to work individually or in pairs to complete Exercise 32.5, then have them work in small groups to compare and discuss their responses. In asking the groups to report on their findings, encourage students to debate the effect of each punctuation mark.

COLLABORATIVE LEARNING Revising punctuation Have students work in small groups to complete the punctuation exercise on page 488. Encourage group members to debate the effect of each punctuation mark, and ask them to present some portion of the passage for class discussion.

ANSWERS

EXERCISE 32.5 Revising: Colons, dashes, parentheses, brackets, ellipsis marks, slashes (p. 488)

"Let all the learned say what they can, / 'Tis ready money makes the man." These two lines of poetry by the Englishman William Somerville (1645–1742) may apply to a current American economic problem. Non-American investors with "ready money" pour some of it—as much as $1.3 trillion in recent years—into the United States. The investments of foreigners are varied: stocks and bonds, savings deposits, service companies, factories, art works, even the campaigns of political candidates. Proponents of foreign investment argue that it revives industry, strengthens the economy, creates jobs (more than 3 million, they say), and encourages free trade among nations. Opponents discuss the risks of heavy foreign investment: it makes the American economy vulnerable to outsiders, sucks profits from the country, and gives foreigners an influence in governmental decision making. On both sides, it seems, "the learned say . . . / 'Tis ready money makes the man [or country]." The question is, whose money?

EXERCISE ON CHAPTERS 27-32 Revising: Punctuation (p. 488)

Brewed coffee is the most widely consumed beverage in the world. The trade in coffee beans alone amounts to well over $6,000,000,000 a year, and the total volume of beans traded exceeds 4,250,000 tons a year. It's believed that the beverage was introduced into Arabia in the fifteenth century AD [correct; *or* A.D.], probably by Ethiopians. By the middle or late sixteenth century, the Arabs had introduced the beverage to the Europeans, who at first resisted it because of its strong flavor and effect as a mild stimulant. The French, Italians, and other Europeans incorporated coffee into their diets by the seventeenth century; the English, however, preferred tea, which they were then importing from India. Since America was colonized primarily by the English, Americans also preferred tea. Only after the Boston Tea Party (1773) did Americans begin drinking coffee in large quantities. Now, though, the US [correct; *or* U.S.] is one of the top coffee-consuming countries, consumption having been spurred on by familiar advertising claims: "Good till the last drop"; "Rich, hearty aroma"; "Always rich, never bitter."

Produced from the fruit of an evergreen tree, coffee is grown primarily in Latin America, southern Asia, and Africa. Coffee trees require a hot climate, high humidity, rich soil with good drainage, and partial shade; consequently, they thrive on the east or west slopes of tropical volcanic mountains, where the soil is laced with potash and drains easily. The coffee beans—actually seeds—grow inside bright red berries. The berries are picked by hand, and the beans are extracted by machine, leaving a pulpy fruit residue that can be used for fertilizer. The beans are usually roasted in ovens, a chemical process that releases the beans' essential oil (caffeol), which gives coffee its distinctive aroma. Over a hundred different varieties of beans are produced in the world, each with a different flavor attributable to three factors: the species of plant (*Coffea arabica* and *Coffea robusta* are the most common) and the soil and climate where the variety was grown.

PART 7

Mechanics

CHAPTER 33
Capitals

CHAPTER 34
Underlining or Italics

CHAPTER 35
Abbreviations

CHAPTER 36
Numbers

Capitals

CHAPTER HIGHLIGHTS

Capitalization at the beginning of sentences will probably not trouble most native speakers of English; however, capitalization within sentences, and in acronyms, can be a challenge for all writers. If your campus has a writing center, check to see if it has special instructional modules that students who have problems with capitalization can use for review.

MEDIA RESOURCES FOR CHAPTER 33

mycomplab²⁰ Please visit MyCompLab at *www.mycomplab.com* for more on the writing process.

http://www.ablongman.com/littlebrown ▶ See page 73 of this manual for companion Web site content description.

33a Capitalize the first word of every sentence.

CLASSROOM IDEA

COMPUTER ACTIVITY Spelling checkers Sometimes computer spelling checkers will not distinguish between capitalized and noncapitalized words; as a result, students using these devices will not be alerted to misplaced or missing capitalizations. Have students check their capitalization visually as well as electronically to make sure they haven't made mistakes.

RESOURCES AND IDEAS

Relatively little has been written about the teaching of capitalization, and most teachers probably assume that rules and drills are the only available instructional strategies. In *The Writing Room: A Resource Book for Teachers of English* (New York: Oxford UP, 1981, 172–74), however, Harvey S. Wiener looks at the sources of capitalization problems for many basic writers—particularly problems of misunderstanding the rules governing sentence boundaries, of confusion over the capitalization of *I* and other personal pronouns, and of difficulty with the sometimes inexact categories of words that are to be treated as proper nouns. Wiener suggests looking for patterns of error in a student's writing, creating groups of words illustrating a particular rule, and asking a student to prepare sentences that demonstrate his or her grasp of a particular convention. These strategies can be used for more skilled writers as well.

33b   Capitalize most words in titles and subtitles of works.

CLASSROOM IDEA

CULTURE LANGUAGE **Capitalization problems** Nonnative students sometimes have trouble with the use of capitals; they need to become more familiar with English practice. Have such students review the rules in this chapter, then analyze the capitalization in some written document (for instance, a newsmagazine or textbook) to see how the rules are applied. ESL students may find that using the writing center's resources can also be very helpful.

33d   Capitalize proper nouns, proper adjectives, and words used as essential parts of proper nouns.

INSTRUCTOR RESOURCE

The following Presentation Aid is available for download on this book's companion Web site at *http://www.ablongman.com/littlebrown*.

PRESENTATION AID 33.1: Proper nouns and adjectives to be capitalized (p. 492)

CLASSROOM IDEAS

CULTURE LANGUAGE **Proper nouns in other languages** Not all languages capitalize proper adjectives and proper nouns used as adjectives. Remind students that in English such words are always capitalized: Swahili culture, not swahili culture.

Extra examples Capitalizing compound words:

un-American
post-Victorian

Note You may wish to point out that when a generic term occurs with a proper name, the generic term is capitalized (the Congo *River*), but when the generic term occurs with two or more proper names, it is usually capitalized when it precedes the proper names but lowercased when it succeeds them (*Lakes* Superior and Ontario; the Congo and Amazon *rivers*).

33e   Capitalize most titles of persons only when they precede proper names.

CLASSROOM IDEAS

Note You may wish to remind students not to capitalize *doctor, madame, sir,* or similar forms of address unless they occur directly before a name.

When styles conflict Students may notice that newspapers and some magazines sometimes capitalize more words than the handbook advises them to capitalize. The trend is toward less rather than more capitalization, but popular periodicals often have their own style guides and use capitals to reflect local interests, punch up their copy, or call attention to important distinctions (like Federal and State governments).

33f Avoid common misuses of capital letters.

INSTRUCTOR RESOURCE

The following Presentation Aid is available for download on this book's companion Web site at *http://www.ablongman.com/littlebrown*.

PRESENTATION AID 33.2: Exercise 33.1. Revising: Capitals (p. 495)

ANSWERS

EXERCISE 33.1 Revising: Capitals (p. 495)

1. San Antonio, Texas, is a thriving city in the Southwest.
2. The city has always offered much to tourists interested in the roots of Spanish settlement of the New World.
3. The Alamo is one of five Catholic missions built by priests to convert Native Americans and to maintain Spain's claims in the area.
4. But the Alamo is more famous for being the site of an 1836 battle that helped to create the Republic of Texas.
5. Many of the nearby streets, such as Crockett Street, are named for men who gave their lives in that battle.
6. The Hemisfair Plaza and the San Antonio River link new tourist and convention facilities developed during Mayor Cisneros's terms.
7. Restaurants, hotels, and shops line the river. The haunting melodies of "Una Paloma Blanca" and "Malagueña" lure passing tourists into Casa Rio and other excellent Mexican restaurants.
8. The University of Texas at San Antonio has expanded, and a medical center has been developed in the northwest part of the city.
9. Sentence correct.
10. The city has attracted high-tech industry, creating a corridor of economic growth between San Antonio and Austin and contributing to the Texas economy.

CHAPTER 34

Underlining or Italics

A WRITER'S PERSPECTIVE

*Her letters to Kitty, though rather longer, were much too full
of lines under the words to be made public.*
—JANE AUSTEN, *Pride and Prejudice*

CHAPTER HIGHLIGHTS

Of all the chapters on mechanics, this chapter, on the uses of underlining
or italics, most frequently needs to be reviewed, particularly by students
writing essays or research papers that require incorporating material from
outside the classroom. The chapter includes the rules for underlining or
italicizing titles; the names of various craft; foreign words and phrases that
have not yet become part of the English language; and words, oro characters named as words. It also gives the rules for underlining or italicizing
for emphasis.

MEDIA RESOURCES FOR CHAPTER 34

mycomplab Please visit MyCompLab at *www.mycomplab.com* for more
on the writing process.

http://www.ablongman.com/littlebrown ▶ See page 73 of this manual for companion
Web site content description.

34b Underline or italicize the titles of works that appear independently.

INSTRUCTOR RESOURCE

The following Presentation Aid is available for download on this book's
companion Web site at *http://www.ablongman.com/littlebrown*.

PRESENTATION AID 34.1: Titles to be underlined or italicized (p. 497)

CLASSROOM IDEA

COMPUTER ACTIVITY Underlining the spaces Students preparing papers on
word processors have the option of underlining the spaces between words;

make sure your students understand what option (to underline or not to underline) you recommend. This handbook, like most other style guides, shows spaces underlined, a style that is less distracting and also easier for students who aren't using word processors.

34e Underline or italicize words or characters named as words.

CLASSROOM IDEAS

Note You may wish to remind students that when sounds (e.g., kerplunk, oof) are represented in writing, they are usually underlined or italicized.

COLLABORATIVE LEARNING Add the mechanics If you have assigned one or more of Chapters 33–36, this activity may be useful and interesting. Take an essay, either student or professional; remove capitals, italics, and the like; and ask students to work in groups reaching consensus on how to correct the mechanics in the "new" essay. Tell them not to look at the handbook but to decide on their own the best way to serve the readers' needs through mechanics. When the students have finished, they can compare their work with the original and, using the handbook as a reference, decide which choices in mechanics they think best serve the needs of the essay and the readers. If they decide to disagree with the advice given in the handbook, ask them to write out their own rules.

34g In online communication, use alternatives for underlining or italics.

ANSWERS

EXERCISE 34.1 Revising: Underlining or italics (p. 499)

1. Of the many Vietnam veterans who are writers, Oliver Stone is perhaps the most famous for writing and directing the films <u>Platoon</u> and <u>Born on the Fourth of July</u>.
2. Tim O'Brien has written short stories for <u>Esquire</u>, <u>GQ</u>, and <u>Massachusetts Review</u>.
3. <u>Going After Cacciato</u> is O'Brien's dreamlike novel about the horrors of combat.
4. The word <u>Vietnam</u> is technically two words (<u>Viet</u> and <u>Nam</u>), but most American writers spell it as one word. [Viet and Nam were correctly underlined.]
5. American writers use words or phrases borrowed from Vietnamese, such as <u>di di mau</u> ("go quickly") or <u>dinky dau</u> ("crazy").

6. Philip Caputo's (gripping) account of his service in Vietnam appears in the book <u>A Rumor of War</u>.

7. Sentence correct.

8. David Rabe's plays—including <u>The Basic Training of Pavlo Hummel</u>, <u>Streamers</u>, and <u>Sticks and Bones</u>—depict the effects of the war (not only) on the soldiers (but) on their families.

9. Called ("the poet laureate of the Vietnam war,") Steve Mason has published two collections of poems: <u>Johnny's Song</u> and <u>Warrior for Peace</u>.

10. <u>The Washington Post</u> published (rave) reviews of <u>Veteran's Day</u>, an autobiography by Rod Kane.

Abbreviations

CHAPTER HIGHLIGHTS

The discussion in this chapter covers the rules for using abbreviations in general writing. The first four sections cover the use of standard abbreviations for titles, the appropriate use of familiar abbreviations and acronyms, the abbreviations that accompany dates and numbers to show time and amount, and the use of common Latin abbreviations. The last two sections deal with the misuse of abbreviations.

MEDIA RESOURCES FOR CHAPTER 35

mycomplab Please visit MyCompLab at *www.mycomplab.com* for more on the writing process.

`http://www.ablongman.com/littlebrown` ▶ See page 73 of this manual for companion Web site content description.

35a Use standard abbreviations for titles immediately before and after proper names.

INSTRUCTOR RESOURCE

The following Presentation Aid is available for download on this book's companion Web site at *http://www.ablongman.com/littlebrown*.

PRESENTATION AID 35.1: Abbreviations for nontechnical writing (p. 501)

CLASSROOM IDEA

Additional rules Civil and military titles are abbreviated only when used before a full name, not before the last name only.

Scholarly degrees are abbreviated when the degree follows a name. When a name is followed by an abbreviated title, no other title goes before the name.

35b Familiar abbreviations and acronyms are acceptable in most writing.

CLASSROOM IDEAS

CULTURE LANGUAGE **Abbreviations and articles** Abbreviations can be particularly challenging for nonnative writers; for instance, when do we use words like *a, an,* or *the* (*the FBI* but *NATO*)? Encourage ESL students to build a word list of abbreviations and acronyms and sort them by the use (or nonuse) of such markers.

Ibid. and *op. cit.* Many students are unsure about how to use scholarly abbreviations like *ibid.* ("in the same place") or *op. cit.* ("in the work cited"). These Latin abbreviations are no longer used in the citation styles of the Modern Language Association, American Psychological Association, or Council of Science Editors. The *Chicago Manual of Style* still sanctions the use of *ibid.* in some circumstances; see Chapter 51.

35f Spell out most units of measurement and names of places, calendar designations, people, and courses.

INSTRUCTOR RESOURCE

The following Presentation Aid is available for download on this book's companion Web site at *http://www.ablongman.com/littlebrown*.

PRESENTATION AID 35.2: Exercise 35.1. Revising: Abbreviations (p. 503)

CLASSROOM IDEA

When to abbreviate Many writers use abbreviations like *in.* or *yr.* in their drafts. However, in all but informal or technical writing situations, the audience expects such abbreviations to be spelled out. Writers who don't want to confuse their readers will make sure that their final drafts meet these expectations.

ANSWERS

EXERCISE 35.1 Revising: Abbreviations (p. 503)

1. In the September 17, 2003, issue of *Science* magazine, Virgil L. Sharpton discusses a theory that could help explain the extinction of dinosaurs.
2. About 65 million years ago, a comet or asteroid crashed into the earth.
3. The result was a huge crater about 10 kilometers (6.2 miles) deep in the Gulf of Mexico.
4. Sharpton's new measurements suggest that the crater is 50 percent larger than scientists previously believed.
5. Indeed, 20-year-old drilling cores reveal that the crater is about 186 miles wide, roughly the size of Connecticut.
6. Sentence correct.
7. On impact, 200,000 cubic kilometers of rock and soil were vaporized or thrown into the air.
8. That's the equivalent of 2.34 billion cubic feet of matter.
9. The impact would have created 400-foot tidal waves across the Atlantic Ocean, temperatures higher than 20,000 degrees, and powerful earthquakes.
10. Sharpton theorizes that the dust, vapor, and smoke from this impact blocked the sun's rays for months, cooled the earth, and thus resulted in the death of the dinosaurs.

Numbers

CHAPTER HIGHLIGHTS

The representation of numbers in general writing is the subject of this chapter. The rules for when to use figures for numbers and when to write out numbers are few and easily memorized.

MEDIA RESOURCES FOR CHAPTER 36

mycomplab Please visit MyCompLab at *www.mycomplab.com* for more on the writing process.

http://www.ablongman.com/littlebrown ▶ See page 73 of this manual for companion Web site content description.

INSTRUCTOR RESOURCE

The following Presentation Aid is available for download on this book's companion Web site at *http://www.ablongman.com/littlebrown*.

PRESENTATION AID 36.1: Numbers (pp. 504–06)

36a Use numerals according to standard practice in the field you are writing in.

CLASSROOM IDEA

Using numbers Audience expectations dictate whether or not numbers are spelled out. As the text notes, audiences that routinely use numerical data, like engineers or accountants, generally prefer figures. Other audiences, including other academic readers and general readers, follow the guidelines discussed here.

36b Use numerals according to convention for dates, addresses, and other information.

CLASSROOM IDEAS

Additional references

Biblical reference
II Kings 3.6

Measurements
    55 miles per hour
    2 liters
    1 tablespoon

Dramatic references The MLA recommends Arabic numerals alone, separated by periods, for acts, scenes, and lines: Hamlet 5.1.35.

36c Always spell out numbers that begin sentences.

INSTRUCTOR RESOURCE

The following Presentation Aid is available for download on this book's companion Web site at *http://www.ablongman.com/littlebrown.*

PRESENTATION AID 36.2: Exercise 36.1. Revising: Numbers (p. 506)

ANSWERS

EXERCISE 36.1 Revising: Numbers (p. 506)

1. The planet Saturn is 900 million miles, or nearly 1.5 billion kilometers, from the sun.
2. Sentence correct.
3. Thus, Saturn orbits the sun only 2.4 times during the average human life span.
4. It travels in its orbit at about 21,600 miles per hour.
5. Fifteen to twenty times denser than Earth's core, Saturn's core measures seventeen thousand miles across.
6. The temperature at Saturn's cloud tops is –170 degrees Fahrenheit.
7. In 1933, astronomers found on Saturn's surface a huge white spot two times the size of Earth and seven times the size of Mercury.
8. Saturn's famous rings reflect almost 70 percent of the sunlight that approaches the planet.
9. The ring system is almost 40,000 miles wide, beginning 8800 miles from the planet's visible surface and ending 47,000 miles from that surface.
10. Saturn generates about 130 trillion kilowatts of electricity.

EXERCISE ON CHAPTERS 33–36 (pp. 507–08)

According to many sources—for example, the Cambridge Ancient History and Gardiner's Egypt of the Pharaohs [titles underlined]—the ancient Egyptians devoted much attention to making life more convenient and pleasurable for themselves.

Our word pharaoh [defined word underlined] for the ancient Egyptian rulers comes from the Egyptian word pr'o [foreign word underlined], meaning "great house." Indeed, the Egyptians placed great emphasis on family residences, adding small bedrooms as early as 3500 BCE. By 3000 BCE, the

Egyptians made ice through evaporation of water at night and then used it to cool their homes. About the same time they used fans made of palm fronds or papyrus to cool themselves in the day. To light their homes, the Egyptians abandoned the animal-fat lamps humans had used for fifty thousand years. Instead, around 1300 BCE the people of Egypt devised the first oil lamps.

Egyptians found great pleasure in playing games. Around 4300 years ago they created one of the oldest board games known. The game involved racing ivory or stone pieces across a papyrus playing board. By 3000 BCE, Egyptian children played marbles with semiprecious stones, some of which have been found in gravesites at Nagada, Egypt. Around 1360 BCE, small children played with clay rattles covered in silk and shaped like animals.

To play the game of love, Egyptian men and women experimented with cosmetics applied to skin and eyelids. Kohl, history's first eyeliner, was used by both sexes to ward off evil. Five thousand years ago Egyptians wore wigs made of vegetable fibers or human hair. In 900 BCE, Queen Isimkheb wore a wig so heavy that she needed assistance in walking. To adjust their make-up and wigs, Egyptians adapted the simple metal mirrors devised by the Sumerians in the Bronze Age, ornamenting them with carved handles of ivory, gold, or wood. Feeling that only those who smelled sweet could be attractive, the Egyptians made deodorants from perfumed oils, for example, cinnamon and citrus.

PART 8

Effective Words

CHAPTER **37**
Using Appropriate Language

CHAPTER **38**
Using Exact Language

CHAPTER **39**
Writing Concisely

CHAPTER **40**
Using Dictionaries

CHAPTER **41**
Spelling and the Hyphen

Using Appropriate Language

A WRITER'S PERSPECTIVE

> *Proper words in proper places make the true definition of a style.*
> —JONATHAN SWIFT, *"Letter to a Clergyman"*

CHAPTER HIGHLIGHTS

There's no substitute for experience when it comes to choosing the right words, and students with limited experience in reading and writing, or whose first language is not English, may find learning to use proper diction a formidable hurdle. Time, encouragement, and careful explanations can help them gain confidence. If your campus has a writing center, check to see if it offers drills or instructional materials to help students improve their resources in language.

This chapter covers types of diction to be avoided or used with care in formal standard American English: dialect, regionalisms, slang, colloquialisms, archaic terms, neologisms, technical language, pretentious language, sexist or biased language, and labels. The chart on "Eliminating sexist language" (pp. 515–16) should be particularly helpful for students who have had little or spotty exposure to standards of inclusive, nonsexist language.

MEDIA RESOURCES FOR CHAPTER 37

mycomplab Please visit MyCompLab at *www.mycomplab.com* for more on the writing process.

http://www.ablongman.com/littlebrown ▶ See page 73 of this manual for companion Web site content description.

INSTRUCTOR RESOURCE

The following Presentation Aid is available for download on this book's companion Web site at *http://www.ablongman.com/littlebrown*.

PRESENTATION AID 37.1: Language in academic and public writing (p. 511)

RESOURCES AND IDEAS

On vocabulary building

Harklau, Linda. "From the 'Good Kids' to the 'Worst': Representation of English Language Learners across Educational Settings." *TESOL Quarterly* 34 (Spring 2000) 35–67. Harklau shows how the institutional image of language minority students changes in negative ways as these students transition from nurturing high school to indifferent college.

Simpson, Mary Scott. "Teaching Writing: Beginning with the Word." *College English* 39 (1978): 934–39. The author describes class activities and readings designed to develop sensitivity to words and build vocabulary.

On sexism in language

Goueffic, Louise. *Breaking the Patriarchal Code: The Linguistic Basis of Sexual Bias*. Manchester, CT: Knowledge, Ideas and Trends, 1996. Goueffic argues for the relationship between biased language and discriminatory social practices.

Maggio, Rosalie. *The Bias-Free Word Finder*. Boston: Beacon, 1992. Originally published as *The Dictionary of Bias-Free Usage: A Guide to Nondiscriminatory Language*. Phoenix: Oryx, 1991. Maggio provides a thesaurus of bias-free synonyms for gendered terms.

Miller, Casey, and Kate Swift. *The Handbook of Nonsexist Writing for Writers, Editors, and Speakers*. 2nd ed. New York: HarperCollins, 1988. Miller and Swift's book is the standard handbook for people concerned with avoiding linguistic sexism.

Penelope, Julia. *Speaking Freely: Unlearning the Lies of the Fathers' Tongues*. New York: Pergamon, 1990. The author provides a scathing but illuminating critique of the effects of using biased language.

37a Revising nonstandard dialect

INSTRUCTOR RESOURCE

The following Presentation Aid is available for download on this book's companion Web site at *http://www.ablongman.com/littlebrown*.

PRESENTATION AID 37.2: Eliminating sexist language (p. 505)

CLASSROOM IDEA

Pundits' perspectives Students may have heard of popular usage commentators like William Safire, John Simon, or James Kilpatrick; ask students to review books or articles by these commentators in the library, see what diction issues they consider most important, and consider whether they agree. A good counterpoint to such commentators is Harvey A. *Daniels's Famous Last Words: The American Language Crisis Reconsidered* (Urbana: NCTE,

1983). See also, Bill Bryson's *Made in America: An Informal History of the English Language in the United States* (New York: Morrow, 1994) for an appealing historical overview of shifts in usage.

37b   Using regionalisms only when appropriate

CLASSROOM IDEA

Huck Finn You may wish to make the following examples the subject of class discussion. Students usually find them quite interesting.

In his explanatory note at the beginning of *The Adventures of Huckleberry Finn*, Mark Twain explains one of the difficulties with using nonstandard language:

> In this book a number of dialects are used, to wit: the Missouri negro dialect; the extremist form of the backwoods Southwestern dialect; the ordinary "Pike County" dialect; and four modified varieties of this last. The shadings have not been done in a haphazard fashion, or by guesswork; but painstakingly, and with the trustworthy guidance and support of personal familiarity with these several forms of speech. I make this explanation for the reason that without it many readers would suppose that all these characters were trying to talk alike and not succeeding.
>
> —THE AUTHOR

From the opening lines of *The Adventures of Huckleberry Finn*:

> You don't know about me without you have read a book by the name of *The Adventures of Tom Sawyer*; but that ain't no matter. That book was made by Mr. Mark Twain, and he told the truth, mainly. There was things which he stretched; but mainly he told the truth. That is nothing. I never seen anybody but lied one time or another, without it was Aunt Polly, or the widow, or maybe Mary. Aunt Polly—Tom's Aunt Polly, she is—and Mary, and the widow Douglas is all told about in that book, which is mostly a true book, with some stretchers, as I said before.

37c   Using slang only when appropriate

CLASSROOM IDEA

COLLABORATIVE LEARNING Field research Have students work in teams as "anthropologists" to collect examples of college slang on your campus. They can compare their research with the collection published in *A Concise Collection of College Students' Slang* by Xin-An Lu and David W. Graf, Jr. (Lincoln: iUniverse, 2004). Other topics for research reports might be the languages of rap or rock music, of some activity (skateboarding or football), or of some social group (fraternities, volunteer firefighters).

37d Using colloquial language only when appropriate

CLASSROOM IDEA

CULTURE LANGUAGE **Theoretical perspective on dialect** If your students are interested in the matter of what ought to be done about language variation, you could share a theoretical perspective from linguistics. Linguists have identified three different philosophies about how to resolve the problem of language variation. One philosophy is that of eradication, which holds that language variations should be completely eliminated. A second philosophy is that of appreciation, which holds that dialects ought to be celebrated as reflections of our diverse cultural traditions. A third philosophy is that of biloquialism or bidialectalism, which holds that people should learn more than one language variety so that they can express themselves in multiple situations without giving up their ways of relating in the multiple communities to which they belong. A class discussion on the relative merits of these three approaches might be a lively one.

37f Using technical words with care

CLASSROOM IDEA

Technical jargon Using technical language is appropriate when both writers and readers understand the specialized body of knowledge to which the technical language refers. Have students practice translating between technical and nontechnical language to gain experience in deciding what level of language might be appropriate for particular situations. For a study of the sources of academic and newspaper jargon see Walter Nash's *Jargon: Its Uses and Abuses* (Oxford: Blackwell, 1993).

37g Revising indirect or pretentious writing

CLASSROOM IDEAS

COLLABORATIVE LEARNING Euphemistically speaking Have small groups of students find examples of pretentious or euphemistic language in political or other public speeches. Groups can compare notes in class and decide which examples are the most silly and which are the most duplicitous.

COMPUTER ACTIVITY Overblown language A good way to help students understand how pretentious language gets in the way of understanding is to give them "fancied-up" versions of common expressions and ask them to translate them. You might start with "Permit me to express my heartfelt felicitations on the celebration of your natal anniversary" for "Happy birthday" or "Scintillate, scintillate, asteroidal nimific" for "Twinkle, twinkle, little star," and work from there.

384 Chapter 37: Using appropriate language

Next, ask students to use their computer thesaurus programs to "translate" a professional or student-written paragraph into overly embellished language. This exercise can provide the basis for a useful discussion of appropriate uses of the thesaurus.

37h Revising sexist and other biased language

INSTRUCTOR RESOURCES

The following Presentation Aids are available for download on this book's companion Web site at *http://www.ablongman.com/littlebrown*.

PRESENTATION AID 37.2: Eliminating sexist language (pp. 515–16)

PRESENTATION AID 37.3: Exercise 37.1. Revising: Appropriate words (p. 517)

CLASSROOM IDEAS

Correct language? Some students may see the insistence on bias-free writing as an instance of "political correctness" and reject it; however, if you emphasize the need to win readers' goodwill, and help students see that offensive language usually diminishes that goodwill, you may be able to show them that avoiding biased language is normally to their advantage. In the end, if a writer deliberately uses nonstandard or biased language, he or she should have considered its probable effect. Anne Matthews's satiric article "Brave, New 'Cruelty-Free' World" (*New York Times*, 7 July 1991, E11) might be a good model for students to discuss and imitate, since she offers many examples of "politically correct" terms for apparently innocuous phrases.

COMPUTER ACTIVITY Bias online Web chat rooms and discussion lists are sometimes monitored by a list coordinator and/or by participants, but there are plenty of sites where biased language can be found. Tell your students to explore some such sites. Their explorations can prompt a class discussion about why bias seems to flourish in such discussion groups—whether, for instance, the anonymity the Web provides encourages participants to use stronger or more biased language than they otherwise would.

COLLABORATIVE LEARNING Exercise 37.1 Ask students to complete Exercise 37.1 individually, with the aid of their own dictionaries. Then have students work in small groups to compare their responses and debate the appropriateness of each member's substitutions. This exercise can often provide the basis for a class-wide discussion on the correlation between word choice and context.

ANSWERS

EXERCISE 37.1 Revising: Appropriate words (p. 517)

1. Acquired immune deficiency syndrome (AIDS) is a <u>serious threat</u> all over the world.

2. The disease is transmitted primarily by sexual intercourse, exchange of bodily fluids, shared needles, and blood transfusions.
3. Those who think the disease is limited to homosexuals, drug users, and foreigners are quite mistaken.
4. Statistics suggest that in the United States one in every five hundred college students carries the virus.
5. People with AIDS do not deserve others' exclusion or callousness. Instead, they need all the compassion, medical care, and financial assistance due the seriously ill.
6. A person with AIDS often sees a team of doctors or a single doctor with a specialized practice.
7. The doctor may help patients by obtaining social services for them as well as providing medical care.
8. The person with AIDS who loses his or her job may need public assistance.
9. For someone who is very ill, a full-time nurse may be necessary. The nurse can administer medications and make the sick person as comfortable as possible.
10. Some people with AIDS have insurance, but others lack the money for premiums.

Using Exact Language

A WRITER'S PERSPECTIVE

*Whenever we come upon one of those intensely right words . . .
the resulting effect is physical as well as spiritual, and electrically
prompt.* —MARK TWAIN, *"William Dean Howells"*

CHAPTER HIGHLIGHTS

Chapter 38 helps students understand the value of precision in word
choice. It begins with a discussion of the difference between denotative
and connotative meanings and the necessity of knowing both kinds of
meanings when choosing a word. The second section explains why maintaining balance between abstract and concrete terms, and between general
and specific terms, is an important element of good writing. Next, the
chapter treats idiomatic language. This section contains a useful chart listing idioms and the prepositions they take, which will be helpful for ESL
students and native speakers alike. The chapter closes with sections on figurative language and clichés. The exercises in this chapter will be easier to
complete if students use a dictionary.

MEDIA RESOURCES FOR CHAPTER 38

mycomplab Please visit MyCompLab at *www.mycomplab.com* for more
on the writing process.

http://www.ablongman.com/littlebrown ▶ See page 73 of this manual for companion
Web site content description.

38a Using the right word for your meaning

CLASSROOM IDEAS

COLLABORATIVE LEARNING Synonymy To help students develop their sensitivity to denotation and connotation, give them a group of words and
phrases like *overweight*, *out of money*, and *failing the class* and ask them to

come up with as many different ways of expressing the term as possible. Then, either alone or in groups, have them decide what connotations each synonym has, and for what audiences and situations each might be appropriate. (Some synonyms for *overweight*, for instance, might be *plump* [neutral], *tubby* [probably negative], *porky* [negative], and so on.)

COLLABORATIVE LEARNING Exercises 38.1 and 38.2 When students have completed Exercises 38.1 and 38.2 individually, have them compare their answers in small groups. Encourage group members to discuss the connotation and denotation of each of the choices, and to consider the effect on the sentence when an inappropriate word is used.

ANSWERS

EXERCISE 38.1 Revising: Denotation (p. 520)

1. Maxine Hong Kingston was awarded many prizes for her first two books, *The Woman Warrior* and *China Men*.
2. Kingston cites her mother's tales about ancestors and ancient Chinese customs as the sources of these memoirs.
3. In her childhood Kingston was greatly affected by her mother's tale about a pregnant aunt who was ostracized by villagers. [*Ostracized* correct.]
4. The aunt gained vengeance by drowning herself in the village's water supply.
5. Kingston decided to make her nameless relative famous by giving her immortality in *The Woman Warrior*. [*Immortality* correct.]

EXERCISE 38.2 Considering the connotations of words (p. 521)

1. AIDS is a serious health problem.
2. Once the virus has entered the blood system, it destroys T-cells.
3. The function of T-cells is to combat infections.
4. Without enough T-cells, the body is nearly defenseless against infections.
5. To prevent exposure to the disease, one should be especially cautious in sexual relationships.

RESOURCES AND IDEAS

Ammirati, Theresa, and Ellen Strenski. "Using Astrology to Teach Connotation and Bias." *Exercise Exchange* 25 (1980): 9–11. The authors tell how to use the language in astrology books as a source of examples of connotation and bias.

Nilsen, Don L. F. "Clichés, Trite Sayings, Dead Metaphors, and Stale Figures of Speech in Composition Instruction." *College Composition and Communication* 27 (1976): 278–82. Nilsen points out that reviving dead metaphors and clichés in class discussion can create an awareness of figurative language.

Sossaman, Stephen. "Detroit Designers: A Game to Teach Metaphors." *Exercise Exchange* 21 (1976): 2–3. Sossaman points out that car names provide good examples of metaphoric language.

Williams, Joseph M. *Style: Ten Lessons in Clarity and Grace,* 7th ed. Boston: Longman, 2002. Williams' book is full of practical and relevant advice students can heed to improve their writing style.

38b Balancing the abstract and concrete, the general and specific

CLASSROOM IDEAS

COLLABORATIVE LEARNING Filler words Asking students to come up with more descriptive synonyms for adjectives like nice or good in a draft is an easy way to begin class (or small group) discussion of the distinctions between abstract and concrete or general and specific words.

COMPUTER ACTIVITY Human versus computer Have your students run their grammar/style checker on a draft of their papers to see what inexact usages the computer can identify. Then have the students see if they can beat the computer at the task by identifying any additional inexact usages.

COLLABORATIVE LEARNING Exercises 38.3 and 38.4 When students have completed Exercises 38.3 and 38.4 individually, have them discuss their responses in small groups. Encourage groups to discuss the impact of members' various concrete substitutions, and have each group present its most creative solutions to the class.

ANSWERS

EXERCISE 38.3 Revising: Concrete and specific words (p. 522)

Possible revision

I remember as if it were last week how frightened I felt the first time I crossed the threshold of Mrs. Murphy's second-grade class. Just three days before, I had moved from a rural one-street town in Missouri to a suburb of Chicago where the houses and the people were jammed together. My new school looked monstrous from the outside and seemed forbiddingly dim inside as I walked haltingly down the endless corridor toward the classroom. The class was clamorous as I neared the door; but when I slipped inside, twenty faces became still and gawked at me. I felt terrified and longed for a place to hide. However, in a booming voice Mrs. Murphy ordered me to the front of the room to introduce myself.

EXERCISE 38.4 Using concrete and specific words (p. 523)

Possible answers

1. fabric, upholstery fabric, velvet
   She chose a wine-colored velvet for backing the pillow.

2. delicious, tart, lemony
   He made a meringue pie, lemony and delicately brown.

3. car, foreign car, Volvo station wagon
   He bought a 1973 Volvo station wagon.

4. narrow-minded, prejudiced, sexist
   My uncle's sexist attitudes cause many arguments in our family.

5. reach, stretch, lunge
   Each child lunged for the prize thrown by the clown.

6. green, dark green, bilious green
   The algae covered the surface with a bilious green scum.

7. walk, march, goose-step
   The soldiers goose-stepped menacingly.

8. flower, daisy, ox-eyed daisy
   Some people call the ox-eyed daisy a "brown-eyed Susan."

9. serious, solemn, grim
   His grim expression frightened us.

10. pretty; with small, regular features; with a button nose and a tiny, smiling mouth
    The infant, with a button nose and a tiny, smiling mouth, was a perfect model for baby products.

11. teacher, history teacher, American history teacher
    My American history teacher requires three research papers.

12. nice, considerate, sympathetic
    I need a sympathetic friend.

13. virtue, honesty, frankness
    His frankness was refreshing after I had heard so much flattery.

14. angry, furious, raging
    Raging uncontrollably, Andy insulted everyone around him.

15. crime, theft, armed robbery
    Drug addicts sometimes commit armed robbery to pay for their habits.

38c Using idioms

INSTRUCTOR RESOURCE

The following Presentation Aid is available for download on this book's companion Web site at *http://www.ablongman.com/littlebrown*.

PRESENTATION AID 38.1: Idioms with prepositions (p. 523)

CLASSROOM IDEAS

COMPUTER ACTIVITY Rare specimens Establish a "gallery" of interesting idioms on your class shareware/Web site. As students come across interesting or unusual examples of idioms they can post them to the site. They should check a dictionary of idioms and report on what they find about their specimen.

CULTURE LANGUAGE Idioms Idioms are particularly challenging for nonnative speakers of English, and even native speakers may find some idioms impenetrable. Asking students to add to the lists in this chapter, or to examine dictionaries of idioms, may yield interesting discussions and paper topics.

CULTURE LANGUAGE Prepositions As the text notes, prepositions follow few specific rules, and, because of idiomatic usage, they often cannot be translated directly into students' first languages. As a result, even advanced ESL students find prepositions difficult. In addition to consulting an ESL dictionary, as recommended in the text, students who need additional help with prepositions might refer to Unit 6 of Len Fox, *Focus on Editing: A Grammar Workbook for Advanced Writers* (White Plains: Longman, 1992), and Appendix C of Alan Meyers, *Writing with Confidence*, 8th ed. (New York: Longman, 2006).

ANSWERS

EXERCISE 38.5 Using prepositions in idioms (p. 525)

1. As Mark and Lana waited for the justice of the peace, they seemed oblivious to [or of] the other people in the lobby.
2. But Mark inferred from Lana's glance at a handsome man that she was no longer occupied by him alone.
3. Angry with Lana, Mark charged her with not loving him enough to get married.
4. Impatient at Mark's childish behavior, Lana disagreed with his interpretation of her glance.
5. They decided that if they could differ so violently over a minor incident, they should part from each other.

38d Using figurative language

CLASSROOM IDEAS

COLLABORATIVE LEARNING Figurative clichés Have students brainstorm commonplace figures of speech like those listed in the text (others might include "I was sick as a dog," "you lie like a rug," "he eats like a horse") and list them on the board. Ask students to work in small groups to identify the figurative connection implied in each saying, and then to substitute a fresher or more accurate image to convey a similar idea.

COLLABORATIVE LEARNING Naming cars Stephen Sossaman's article on car names (see "Resources and Ideas," under 38a) could be the inspiration for a good group activity. Ask your small groups to expand on Sossaman's ideas by brainstorming lists of car names and sorting them into categories (e.g., animals, natural forces, and so on). Students then can decide what kind of attributes each category of names suggests and speculate why car manufacturers might want to emphasize these attributes.

COMPUTER ACTIVITY Hyperbolic ads Advertising is full of hyperbole. Ask students to collect good examples and post them to your Web site's "hyperbole gallery."

COLLABORATIVE LEARNING Exercise 38.6 Have students work in small groups to complete Exercise 38.6. Encourage groups to be imaginative in playing out the implications of each figure, and ask each group to report several of their responses to the class.

COLLABORATIVE LEARNING Exercise 38.7 When students have completed Exercise 38.7 individually, have them discuss their responses in small groups. Encourage groups to discuss the implications of various responses, and ask each group to present their most creative findings to the class.

ANSWERS

EXERCISE 38.6 Analyzing figurative language (p. 527)

1. *A delta wing out of nightmare* is a metaphor. *Like a stingray crossing upstream* is a simile. Both convey the menace of an airplane and its shadow.
2. *Her roots ran deep into the earth* and *from those roots she drew strength* are both metaphors establishing the person's indomitability.
3. *Outdistanced unpleasant sensations* and *headed for the freedom of open fields* are both metaphors equating Angelou's sense of release with the runner's freedom.
4. *Lash of adverse criticism* is a metaphor that makes clear the words' power to hurt.
5. The judge is like a *chickadee* and the roomful of writers is like a *caucus of crows*—two similes that convey the judge's powerlessness in the face of the writers' bombast.

EXERCISE 38.7 Using figurative language (p. 527)

Individual response.

38e Using fresh, not trite, expressions

INSTRUCTOR RESOURCES

The following Presentation Aids are available for download on this book's companion Web site at *http://www.ablongman.com/littlebrown.*

PRESENTATION AID 38.2: Using fresh, not trite, expressions (p. 527)

PRESENTATION AID 38.3: Exercise 38.8. Revising: Trite expressions (p. 528)

CLASSROOM IDEAS

COLLABORATIVE LEARNING Cliché hunting Have students work in small groups to scan each other's drafts for trite expressions or clichés. (For this exercise, students might work in groups of three or four to scan each paper, circle possible clichés, and then hand the paper to the next person in the group.) Each group should then consider the circled expressions and decide if they are appropriate to the context or could be replaced by fresher or more accurate expressions.

COLLABORATIVE LEARNING Exercise 38.8 Have students complete Exercise 38.8 individually and then discuss their responses in small groups. Encourage groups to discuss the effects of the substitutions on the meaning of each sentence, and have them report their findings to the class. You might have each group follow up on this exercise by scanning samples of their own work for trite expressions in preparation for revision.

ANSWERS

EXERCISE 38.8 Revising: Trite expressions (p. 528)

Possible answers

1. These disasters of the war have shaken the small nation severely.
2. Prices for food have risen markedly, and citizens suspect that others are profiting on the black market.
3. Medical supplies are so scarce that even very sick civilians cannot get treatment.
4. With most men fighting or injured or killed, women have had to take the men's places in farming and manufacturing.
5. Finally, the war's high cost has destroyed the nation's economy.

CHAPTER 39

Writing Concisely

A WRITER'S PERSPECTIVE

A good word is like a good tree whose roots are firmly fixed and whose top is in the sky. —THE KORAN 14.24

CHAPTER HIGHLIGHTS

Eliminating unnecessary words is a task almost as difficult as choosing the right word. Students often revert to very simple sentence structures when they begin to cut flab from their sentences. You'll have to help them see that lean sentences can still be complex sentences. This chapter can help show your students techniques to achieve conciseness: strengthening subjects and verbs; cutting empty words; cutting excess repetition; reducing or combining sentences, clauses, and phrases; eliminating expletives; and rewriting jargon.

MEDIA RESOURCES FOR CHAPTER 39

mycomplab Please visit MyCompLab at *www.mycomplab.com* for more on the writing process.

http://www.ablongman.com/littlebrown ▶ See page 73 of this manual for companion Web site content description.

RESOURCES AND IDEAS

Connors, Robert J. "The Erasure of the Sentence." *College Composition and Communication* 52:1 (2001): 96–128. Argues for the efficacy of pedagogy that uses sentence-based rhetorics.

39a Focusing on the subject and verb

INSTRUCTOR RESOURCE

The following Presentation Aid is available for download on this book's companion Web site at *http://www.ablongman.com/littlebrown*.

PRESENTATION AID 39.1: Ways to achieve conciseness

CLASSROOM IDEAS

COLLABORATIVE LEARNING Cutting words Before your students hand in their essays, ask them to cut a specific number of words (ten to fifteen for a start) without harming the meaning. This approach can work with paragraphs as well and makes a good small-group activity.

COMPUTER ACTIVITY The lard factor Richard Lanham in *Revising Prose* (4th ed., New York: Longman, 1999) uses this equation to calculate the "lard factor" of unnecessary words in any piece of writing:

> \# of words cut from original ÷
> \# of words in original =
> % of lard in original

Lanham argues that as much as 40 percent of any piece of writing may be lard; this estimate emphasizes the need to revise for unnecessary words. Ask students to revise sample passages of published writing or one another's work and calculate the lard factor to test this argument. Students working on computers can use the Word Count function of their word processor to estimate the "lard factor" in a longer piece.

Using the active voice Not all passives are undesirable. For instance, "I was born" is usually preferable to "My mother bore me." Encourage students to see that it's not the passive itself but its unnecessary use that weakens their writing.

39b Cutting or shortening empty words and phrases

CLASSROOM IDEAS

COLLABORATIVE LEARNING Deliberate wordiness To show students the effect of wordiness, give each small group of students a simple sentence and ask them to fatten it up. One group began with the sentence "I failed the test" and ended with "Due to mitigating circumstances involving the completion of specified educational objectives, the subject in question achieved a negative outcome in the completion of a standardized measuring instrument application."

COLLABORATIVE LEARNING Exercise 39.1 Have students complete Exercise 39.1 individually and then work in small groups to compare their responses. As a follow-up exercise, ask each group to create an overly wordy paragraph. Have groups exchange paragraphs and revise them.

ANSWER

EXERCISE 39.1 Revising: Subjects and verbs; empty words and phrases (p. 532)
Possible answers

1. *Gerrymandering* means redrawing the lines of a voting district to benefit a particular party or ethnic group.

2. The name refers to Elbridge Gerry, who as governor of Massachusetts in 1812 redrew voting districts in Essex County.
3. On the map one new district looked like a salamander.
4. Upon seeing the map, a critic of Governor Gerry's administration cried out, "Gerrymander!"
5. Now a political group may try to change a district's voting pattern by gerrymandering to exclude rival groups' supporters.

39c Cutting unnecessary repetition

CLASSROOM IDEAS

Legal bilingualism Sometimes, particularly in legal language, phrases contain paired synonyms like last will and testament. These go back to the time immediately after the Norman Conquest of England in 1066, when English law proceedings were conducted in both French and English, and the words had to be clear to speakers of either language.

CULTURE LANGUAGE Discursive versus concise styles ESL students may have difficulty being concise if their native language is more discursive, or if repetition is encouraged in their native language. Reinforce with these students that English is an extremely compact language compared to many. Remind them as well that as their English vocabulary increases, they will have more words at their disposal to use in place of longer, more descriptive phrases.

COLLABORATIVE LEARNING Exercise 39.2 When students have completed Exercise 39.2 individually, have them compare their responses in small groups and discuss the effects of their varying strategies.

ANSWERS

EXERCISE 39.2 Revising: Unnecessary repetition (pp. 533–34)

Possible answers

1. After their tours of duty, some Vietnam veterans had problems readjusting to life in America.
2. Afflicted with post-traumatic stress disorder, some veterans had trouble holding jobs and maintaining relationships.
3. Some who used drugs in Vietnam could not break their habits after they returned to the United States.
4. The few veterans who committed crimes and violent acts gained so much notoriety that many Americans thought all veterans were crazy.
5. As a result of such stereotyping, Vietnam-era veterans are protected by antidiscrimination laws.

39e Eliminating *there is* and *it is* constructions

CLASSROOM IDEA

COMPUTER ACTIVITY "But it says in the catalog . . ." Members of educational institutions often resort to windy prose, especially when describing their goals and objectives or policies and procedures. Ask students to download a section from your college catalog or a similar document and rewrite it in "plain" English.

39f Combining sentences

CLASSROOM IDEAS

Revising student paragraphs As a revision exercise, ask students to work in groups to identify paragraphs from their own work that seem jargon laden or that simply "don't sound right." You might display several of these sample paragraphs (using an overhead projector or networked computers and screen-sharing applications) to provide the basis for a class discussion on effective condensing strategies. Some teachers ask for paragraphs from student volunteers or only use examples from other classes because they fear that in-class attention to weaker paragraphs may discourage the students whose work is selected. However, if such discussions of student work are presented constructively, and if all students take a turn, students seem to benefit most from working on their own texts.

COLLABORATIVE LEARNING Exercise 39.3 When students have completed Exercise 39.3 individually, have them discuss their responses in pairs, noting places where they used different strategies to achieve conciseness. As a follow-up to this exercise you might use several student revisions as the basis for a general discussion of the point at which a productive revision for conciseness might become reductive of the meaning of the passage.

ANSWERS

EXERCISE 39.3 Revising: Conciseness (p. 535)

Possible answers

1. The Mexican general Antonio López de Santa Anna introduced chewing gum to the United States.
2. After defeat by the Texans in 1845, the exiled general chose to settle in New York.
3. In his baggage the general had stashed a piece of chicle, the dried milky sap of the Mexican sapodilla tree.
4. Santa Anna's friend Thomas Adams brought more of this resin into the country, planning to make rubber.

5. When the plan failed, Adams got a much more successful idea from the way General Santa Anna used the resin, as a gum for chewing.

EXERCISE 39.4 Revising: Conciseness (p. 536)

Possible answers

After much thought, he concluded that carcinogens could be treated like automobiles. Instead of giving in to a fear of cancer, we should balance the benefits we receive from potential carcinogens (such as plastic and pesticides) against the damage they do. Similarly, instead of responding irrationally to the pollution caused by automobiles, we have decided to live with them and enjoy their benefits while simultaneously working to improve them.

39g Rewriting jargon

INSTRUCTOR RESOURCE

The following Presentation Aid is available for download on this book's companion Web site at *http://www.ablongman.com/littlebrown.*

PRESENTATION AID 39.2: Exercise 39.4. Revising: Conciseness (p. 536)

Using
Dictionaries

"When I use a word," Humpty Dumpty said, "it means just what I choose it to mean—neither more nor less."
"The question is," said Alice, "whether you can make words mean so many different things."
"The question is," said Humpty Dumpty, "which is to be master—that's all."
—LEWIS CARROLL, *Through the Looking-Glass*

CHAPTER HIGHLIGHTS

Chapter 40 describes the information provided in a good dictionary, summarizes briefly the characteristics of several widely used desk dictionaries (in print and electronic form) and some unabridged and specialized dictionaries, and explains a typical entry from an abridged dictionary to help students find information. Although the unavoidable accumulation of detail in such a brief chapter makes dense reading in places, the chapter is organized for easy reference so that you and your students can single out the most useful sections. Throughout the handbook, students are urged to consult a dictionary for answers to particular questions—the right preposition to use in an idiom, the usage status of a word, the forms of an irregular verb, and the like. No other supplementary reference will serve students as well as a good desk dictionary, as long as they know how to use it and do so. Students should be required, whenever practicable, to purchase one of the standard desk dictionaries.

MEDIA RESOURCES FOR CHAPTER 40

mycomplab Please visit MyCompLab at *www.mycomplab.com* for more on the writing process.

http://www.ablongman.com/littlebrown ▶ See page 73 of this manual for companion Web site content description.

40a Choosing a dictionary

CLASSROOM IDEAS

CULTURE LANGUAGE Idiomatic usage For ESL students, the most difficult part of learning English is learning idiomatic usage. In addition to the dictionaries cited in the student text, the following sourcebooks may be particularly helpful to these students:

Cowie, A. P., and R. Mackin. *The Oxford Dictionary of Current Idiomatic English*. 2 vols. London: Oxford UP, 1975.

Freeman, William. *A Concise Dictionary of English Idioms*. Boston: Writer, 1976.

Whitford, Harold C., and Robert J. Dixson. *Handbook of American Idioms and Idiomatic Usage*. New York: Regents, 1973.

A brief history of dictionaries

> 1721—Nathaniel Bailey's *Universal Etymological Dictionary of the English Language*, the first dictionary to resemble the dictionaries we have at present.
> 1755—Samuel Johnson's two-volume *Dictionary*.
> 1828—Noah Webster's *American Dictionary of the English Language*.
> 1857–1928—The compilation of the most comprehensive dictionary, the twelve-volume (now sixteen-volume) *Oxford English Dictionary*.

Dictionary variations Dictionaries come in many varieties, and students should be encouraged to examine the different kinds. For instance, the inexpensive dictionaries found in grocery store racks are probably less comprehensive than collegiate work demands. Dictionaries published more than a decade ago may lack up-to-date words or usage information.

Choosing a dictionary To unify the answers that students give to the exercises in this chapter, select a dictionary suitable to your class's needs and make it a required text for your course. Some teachers allow students to bring in any one from a selected list of dictionaries, and then make their varied answers to exercises part of the ongoing class discussion.

40b Working with a dictionary's contents

CLASSROOM IDEAS

Usage experts Some dictionary publishers ask panels of usage experts about the acceptability of certain terms. Though the recommendations are usually helpful, students should understand that these are still opinions, and they may not apply to the situations in the student's own writing. Some dictionaries also censor the terms they include, omitting vulgar words or other offensive terms.

Judging style Some good references on usage judgments are found in Harvey A. Daniels, *Famous Last Words: The American Language Crisis Reconsidered* (Urbana: NCTE, 1983) and Dennis Baron, *Grammar and Good Taste* (New Haven: Yale UP, 1982). See also, Walter Nash's *An Uncommon Tongue: The Uses and Resources of English* (New York: Routledge, 1992) for a broader study of usage, including dictionaries, punctuation, paraphrase, and parody.

Misspeller's dictionary Frequently, students complain that they cannot spell words correctly because they do not know how to find them in the dictionary without being able to spell them. Using a thesaurus is one solution to this problem. A second solution is to have students create a misspeller's dictionary based on the words incorrectly spelled in their papers. This dictionary would include all the variant spellings as well as the correct spellings for the misspelled words. The activity will use the efforts of both the good and the fair spellers and can be "published" for future use in classes that involve writing. The misspeller's dictionary can also be placed online so that students can add material to it each semester.

COMPUTER ACTIVITY Electronic spelling aids Some students use handheld spelling aids to check their spelling. Because such machines have limited memories, they may not include all the words students use in their writing. Students need to understand the limits of such machines (and the need to keep extra batteries on hand). Since more and more students rely on spell-checking computer software, you might also remind students that spelling checkers are not context sensitive and are not usually case sensitive. However, students can add words to customize and enlarge their electronic dictionaries.

Reading the whole entry Remind students to read the entire entry, not just the spelling, when they look up a word. Many dictionaries include the word *alot*, for instance, defining it as "a common misspelling for *a lot*." Students who see *alot* in the list of entries may assume it's correct if they don't actually read the definition. In addition, careful reading of all the meanings of a word often reveals symbolism and intentions frequently missed by an assumed understanding of a word's usage.

Analogous forms Students often invent new forms for words by analogy; thus, from *drink, drank, drunk* they create *think, thank, thunk*. Such irregular forms exist in a few verbs surviving from Anglo-Saxon times. However, since the time of the Norman Conquest of England in 1066, every new verb that has entered the English language has followed the regular verb pattern of *-d* or *-ed* ending for the past tense and the past participle.

A dictionary with plenty of synonyms Of the many dictionaries that include synonyms with their definitions of words, the *Funk & Wagnall's New Standard College Dictionary* gives more extensive coverage than most. The *Funk & Wagnall's* includes paragraphs on synonyms that define the various shades of meaning.

Additional sample entry From *Webster's New Universal Unabridged Dictionary*, 1983.

reck'ŏn, *v.t.*; reckoned, *pt., pp.;* reckoning, *ppr.* (ME. *rekenen, reknen,* from AS, *gerecenian,* to explain. A derivative verb allied to AS, *gereccan,* to rule, direct, order, explain, tell; D. *rekenen:* Ice. *reikna,* to reckon.)

1. to count; to figure up; to compute; to calculate. I *reckoned* above two hundred and fifty on the outside of the church. —Addison

2. to consider as; to regard as being. He was *reckoned* among the transgressors. —Luke XXII.37

3. to make account or reckoning of. (Obs.) Faith was *reckoned* to Abraham for righteousness. —Rom. IV. 9

4. to judge; to consider; to estimate.

5. to suppose, think, or believe; as, *I reckon* it will rain. (Colloq. or Dial.)

reck'ŏn, *v.i.,*

1. to count up; to figure

2. to depend; to rely (with *on*)

3. to settle an account

4. to pay a penalty; to be answerable (Obs.) If they fail in their bounden duty, they shall reckon for it one day. —Sanderson

to reckon for: to be answerable or responsible for.

to reckon with: (a) to balance accounts and make a settlement with; (b) to take into consideration.

to reckon without one's host: to ignore, in a transaction, one whose cooperation is essential; hence, to reckon without considering some important factor. or factors.

Additional examples of dictionary labels

Slang—novel and colorful expressions that reflect a group's special experiences and set it off from others. Examples: *cool, into, funky, awesome.*

Colloquial—words and expressions appropriate to everyday spoken language and to informal writing. Example: Housework often takes a *bite* out of my weekend.

Regional—words and expressions used only in some geographical locations. For example, one kind of sandwich may be called a *hero*, a *hoagie*, a *submarine*, a *torpedo*, or a *grinder,* depending upon which region you are in. Nonstandard—words and grammatical forms frequently used in speech but never acceptable in standard written English. Examples: *nowheres, hisself, throwed, could of, and hadn't ought*.

Obsolete or archaic—words or meanings of words that we never or rarely use but that appear in older documents and literature still read today. Examples: *enwheel* ("to encircle") and *belike* ("perhaps").

RESOURCES AND IDEAS

Further reading

For more synonyms and antonyms, students can consult Norman Lewis, *The New Roget's Thesaurus of the English Language in Dictionary Form* (New York: Putnam, 1978).

ANSWERS

EXERCISE 40.1 Using a dictionary (p. 541)

The answers to this exercise will depend on the dictionary being consulted. Each one uses a different notation system, and in some cases they disagree over syllable divisions. Thus, no answers are provided.

CHAPTER 41

Spelling and the Hyphen

WRITERS' PERSPECTIVES

*Everyone misspells occasionally, usually because of careless-
ness or simple failure to observe closely. Good spelling
requires an eye for detail.* —WILLIAM F. IRMSHER

*It's a poor imagination that can only think of one way to
spell a word.* —ATTRIBUTED TO MARK TWAIN

CHAPTER HIGHLIGHTS

No quick formula exists for turning poor spellers into good ones. Students with serious spelling problems may need systematic instruction in
spelling, which, like systematic instruction in vocabulary, is rarely allowed
by course time. You may want to refer such students to a skills center on
campus or, if there are no such services, to a good spelling workbook. There
are, however, activities and assignments that can help. Most students can
improve their spelling markedly by learning and actually applying the limited number of standard rules, by maintaining a record of words that
repeatedly cause them trouble, and by faithfully practicing brief groups of
words from a spelling list. Such advice, though uninspired and unoriginal,
does produce real improvement if a student can be persuaded to follow it,
perhaps with the added reminder that lack of confidence in spelling distracts the student from more important matters in writing.

MEDIA RESOURCES FOR CHAPTER 41

mycomplab Please visit MyCompLab at *www.mycomplab.com* for more
on the writing process.

http://www.ablongman.com/littlebrown ▶ See page 73 of this manual for companion
Web site content description.

41a Recognizing typical spelling problems

INSTRUCTOR RESOURCE

The following Presentation Aid is available for download on this book's companion Web site at *http://www.ablongman.com/littlebrown.*

PRESENTATION AID 41.1: Words commonly confused (p. 543)

CLASSROOM IDEAS

COLLABORATIVE LEARNING Homonym homework Sometimes the quickest way to learn distinctions in spelling between words that sound the same is to memorize the words and their definitions. The context in which the word is encountered can also become a kind of mnemonic (in addition to deliberately constructed mnemonics such as "the principal is a pal"). Divide the text's list of homonyms among the class and have students work in groups to create exercise questions by posing one-sentence contexts for several of the words on this list, as for example: "I [*accept/except*] the package from the UPS driver." The compiled exercise questions might be assigned as a quiz either in a subsequent class or on the network.

Extra examples In addition to the words listed in the text, words that can be expressed by different forms, depending on the intended meaning, might also give students trouble. For example, *a while* is often written *awhile.* The two most frequently miswritten expressions, however, are *a lot* (commonly written *alot*) and *all right* (commonly written *alright*).

Spelling patriotically The confusion between British and American spellings can be blamed on American patriots at the time of the Revolutionary War. Led by Noah Webster, a group of linguistic patriots set out to make America linguistically independent of Britain and invented the American spellings of these common words.

RESOURCES AND IDEAS

Some good references on teaching spelling

Brown, Alan S. "Encountering Misspellings and Spelling Performance: Why Wrong Isn't Right." *Journal of Educational Psychology* 80 (1988): 488–94. Brown analyzes the psychology of student misspellings.

Chomsky, Carol. "Reading, Writing, and Phonology." *Harvard Educational Review* 40 (1970): 287–309. Chomsky ties problems with spelling and word recognition to problems with hearing and distinguishing certain morphemes.

Clapp, Ouida, ed. *Teaching the Basics—Really!* Urbana: NCTE, 1977. The book includes several chapters on teaching spelling.

Clark, Roger, and I. Y. Hashimoto. "A Spelling Program for College Students." *Teaching English in the Two-Year College* 11 (1984): 34–38. The authors describe activities to help students improve spelling over the course of a semester.

Dobie, Ann R. "Orthographical Theory and Practice; or, How to Teach Spelling." *Journal of Basic Writing* 5 (1986): 41–48. Responses to this article appear in both the 1987 and 1988 volumes of this journal.

Irmscher, William F. *The Holt Guide to English.* 3rd ed. New York: Holt, 1981. Ch. 12. Irmscher offers concrete diagnostics and remedies for common spelling problems.

Sensenbaugh, Roger. "Spelling Instruction and the Use of Word Lists." *Composition Chronicle* 6.3 (April 1993): 8–9. The author describes techniques for helping students become better spellers.

Taylor, Karl, and Ede Kidder. "The Development of Spelling Skills from First Grade through Eighth Grade." *Written Communication* 5 (April 1988): 222–44. The authors tie spelling development to cognitive development and show instructors how to diagnose and help correct spelling problems.

41b Following spelling rules

INSTRUCTOR RESOURCE

The following Presentation Aid is available for download on this book's companion Web site at *http://www.ablongman.com/littlebrown*.

PRESENTATION AID 41.2: Exercise 41.1. Distinguishing between *ie* and *ei* (p.546)

CLASSROOM IDEAS

Learning the rules Most spelling rules have only a few exceptions, so it's often easier for students to memorize the short list of exceptions and assume that any other word follows the normal pattern. An excellent list of these deviations appears in the *National Labor Relations Board Style Manual* (Washington, DC: Government Printing Office, 1984).

Irregular plurals There are a few irregular plurals in English; most survive from Anglo-Saxon (for example, *child/children*) or are borrowed from other languages (*alumnus/alumni*). All native English nouns added since the Norman Conquest of England in 1066 have been regular, using the *-s* or *-es* suffixes to form the plural.

ANSWERS

EXERCISE 41.1 Distinguishing between *ie* and *ei* (p. 546)

1. brief
2. deceive
3. receipt
4. seize
5. foreign
6. priest
7. grievance
8. fiend
9. leisurely
10. achieve
11. patience
12. pierce
13. height
14. freight
15. feint
16. sieve

EXERCISE 41.2 Keeping or dropping a final *e* (p. 547)

1. malicious
2. lovable *or* loveable
3. serviceable
4. retirement
5. suing
6. virtuous
7. notable
8. battling
9. suspension

EXERCISE 41.3 Keeping or dropping a final *y* (p. 547)

1. implies
2. messier
3. applying
4. delaying
5. defiance
6. says
7. solidifies
8. Murphys
9. supplied

EXERCISE 41.4 Doubling consonants (p. 548)

1. repairing
2. admittance
3. benefited
4. shopped
5. concealed
6. allotted
7. dripping
8. declaimed
9. paralleling

EXERCISE 41.5 Forming plurals (p. 549)

1. piles
2. donkeys
3. beaches
4. summaries
5. miles per hour
6. boxes
7. switches
8. sisters-in-law
9. Baleses
10. cupfuls
11. librettos *or* libretti
12. videos
13. thieves
14. geese
15. hisses
16. appendixes *or* appendices

41c Developing spelling skills

CLASSROOM IDEAS

Careful proofreading Many of the errors made with spelling can be avoided through careful proofreading. Two proofreading techniques that force the writer to read more slowly and carefully are (1) reading the essay aloud and (2) reading the essay backward, from the last sentence to the first.

Making words your own One way to help students remember words they look up in a dictionary is to have them highlight the word, jot it down on an ongoing list, and then use it in a sentence of their own. At a later date, students should go back to their "dictionary list" and try to use each word in a one-sentence context. If students keep up this practice throughout a semester they will have added those words to their working vocabularies.

COMPUTER ACTIVITY Spelling logs Most students benefit from keeping lists, or logbooks, of their spelling problems. After a few weeks of recording data, they may be able to see patterns of difficulty emerge. Students should add misspelled words found using a computer spelling checker to their spelling logs for those times when they are away from their machines or the computer is down. Some good examples of pattern recognition are found in Kristene F. Anderson, "Using a Spelling Survey to Develop Basic Writers' Linguistic Awareness," *Journal of Basic Writing* 6 (1987): 72–78.

Separating the *-sedes* Students may learn to distinguish whether *-sede*, *-ceed*, or *-cede* should be planted at the end of a word by memorizing the words *proceed, exceed, succeed*, and *supersede*. *Proceed, exceed*, and *succeed* are the only words ending in *-ceed*. *Supersede* is the only word ending in *-sede*. All the remaining *-cede* words end in *-cede*.

COLLABORATIVE LEARNING Spelling bee Ask students to submit lists of words they have trouble with. Circulate all the lists to give student teams time to memorize them; then hold an old-fashioned spelling bee in class.

RESOURCES AND IDEAS

Gere, Anne Ruggles. "Alternatives to Tradition in Teaching Spelling." *Teaching the Basics—Really!* Ed. Ouida H. Clapp. Urbana: NCTE, 1977. 100–03. Gere proposes the use of individualized word lists and classroom games and also the teaching of phoneme-grapheme correspondences and word division.

Harris, Muriel. "The Big Five: Individualizing Improvement in Spelling." *Teaching the Basics—Really!* Ed. Ouida H. Clapp. Urbana: NCTE, 1977. 104–07. Harris suggests making students aware of their habitual problems deriving from homophones, pronunciation, doubled consonants, word roots, and the schwa.

McClellan, Jane. "A Clinic for Misspellers." *College English* 40 (1978): 324–29.
  McClellan suggests using several kinds of word lists and frequent drills to
  bring about improvement.

41d   Using the hyphen to form compound words

CLASSROOM IDEA

The a-b-c rule A useful rule for determining whether an adjective before a
noun is compound and should be hyphenated is the *a-b-c* rule. For example, in the phrase *record-setting pace*, the first word, *record*, is term *a*. The
second word, *setting*, is term *b*, and the noun being modified, *pace*, is term
c. According to the *a-b-c* rule, if the writer can make the statement "The *c*
was *a* and *b*," no hyphen is needed. If that statement is impossible, *a* and *b*
must be hyphenated. Since the writer can't say "The pace was record and
setting," *record-setting pace* needs to be hyphenated. The test here is similar to the one for coordinate adjectives in 28f-2.

ANSWERS

EXERCISE 41.6 Using hyphens in compound words (p. 556)

1. Correct
2. de-escalate
3. forty-odd soldiers
4. little-known bar
5. seven-eighths
6. seventy-eight
7. happy-go-lucky
8. pre-existing
9. senator-elect
10. Correct
11. two- and six-person cars
12. ex-songwriter
13. V-shaped
14. re-educate

Research Writing

CHAPTER 42
Planning a Research Project

CHAPTER 43
Finding Sources

CHAPTER 44
Working with Sources

CHAPTER 45
Avoiding Plagiarism and Documenting Sources

CHAPTER 46
Writing the Paper

CHAPTER 47
Using MLA Documentation and Format

CHAPTER 48
Two Research Papers in MLA Style

Planning a Research Project

A WRITER'S PERSPECTIVE

Not the least part of discovery is asking the right questions.
—St. Augustine

CHAPTER HIGHLIGHTS

Many students actively dislike or fear writing research papers—either because of misconceptions about the purpose of such assignments or because of previous unpleasant or purely mechanistic experiences with research writing. As a result, you may find that some students resist this type of writing. The chapters in Part 9 show students not only how valuable and interesting research writing can be, but that it is an extension of the critical thinking, reading, and writing skills stressed in the handbook.

Part 9 offers a detailed overview of research writing, from finding information (using both electronic and print resources) to shaping it, documenting it, and presenting it according to a consistent set of standards. New to this edition of the handbook are an updated discussion of computer-aided research and standard reference sources and an expanded chapter-length treatment of plagiarism.

A special feature of Part 9 is its use of the research and writing process of two students (Edward Begay and Vanessa Haley) as examples. Following Begay's and Haley's progress from beginning to end of their research process will give your students a better sense of how the strategies discussed in the handbook might be applied in actual first-year college writing projects.

Chapter 42 presents research gathering as a strategic task and offers a series of descriptions and suggestions to help students move through a research project effectively.

This edition includes a new section (42d3) on annotating a working bibliography.

MEDIA RESOURCES FOR CHAPTER 42

mycomplab²⁹ Please visit MyCompLab at *www.mycomplab.com* for more on the writing process.

http://www.ablongman.com/littlebrown ▶ See page 73 of this manual for companion Web site content description.

42a Starting out

INSTRUCTOR RESOURCE

The following Presentation Aid is available for download on this book's companion Web site at *http://www.ablongman.com/littlebrown*.

PRESENTATION AID 42.1: Scheduling steps in research writing (p. 560)

CLASSROOM IDEAS

COLLABORATIVE LEARNING Support for the research-phobic Some students, especially those who have never done a research project before, may have significant anxiety about their ability to undertake a research project, manage all the phases, and end up with a decent final product. It may be helpful for students to share anxieties in small groups as a way of overcoming them. Such discussions work only if there is mutual trust among members of the group, so this activity would work best with a group that has been working together regularly for a while and has had a chance to build trust.

Smart scheduling Beginning college students need help in establishing a realistic schedule. Emphasize strongly that each of the four segments in the "Scheduling steps" chart (p. 560) truly will take about a quarter of the time. Share with them the schedule for a writing project you've recently completed, and point out the kinds of places where delays are likely to occur.

COMPUTER ACTIVITY Put it on the calendar If students have calendar or scheduling software, they can put their research schedule in calendar format and keep it handy for easy reference. Revising the schedule becomes a matter of a few keystrokes.

Notekeeping Note cards or notebooks are fairly easy tools for inexperienced writers to use. However, some students just aren't comfortable with cards, and their research actually may suffer if they are forced to use them. If students have great trouble keeping cards, suggest that they keep their notes in their journal; the greater space may give them more freedom to compose effectively.

Trading schedules After students have drafted schedules for their research projects individually, have them show their schedule to a partner, who can help to evaluate the feasibility of the project and how to adjust the schedule if necessary.

RESOURCE AND IDEAS

Ford, James E., ed. *Teaching the Research Paper: From Theory to Practice, From Research to Writing*. Metuchen: Scarecrow Press, 1995. These essays address the value of teaching research papers in composition classes; models of research units and practical suggestions are included.

Lutzker, Marilyn. *Research Projects for College Students: What to Write Across the Curriculum*. Westport: Greenwood, 1988. Lutzker provides a librarian's guide to intellectually challenging projects from all disciplines.

Moulton, Margaret and Vicki Homes. "The Research Paper: A Historical Perspective." *Teaching English in the Two-Year College* 35 (May 2003): 365–73. The authors present a fascinating historical account, from the 1870s to the present, of the value and relevance of the research paper assignment.

Nelson, Jennie. "The Research Paper: A 'Rhetoric of Doing' or a 'Rhetoric of the Finished Word'?" *Composition Studies* 22 (Fall 1994): 65–75. Nelson argues that the research paper does not serve any useful educational purpose unless students understand it as a learning process.

Pelham, Fran O'Byrne. "The Research Journal: Integrating Reading, Writing, and Research." *Composition Chronicle* 6.3 (April 1993): 4–5. Pelham recommends using a journal to supplement typical research activities and to allow students to "research, reflect, write, and then attend recursively to these events."

Quantic, Diane. "Insights into the Research Process from Student Logs." *Journal of Teaching Writing* 6 (1986): 211–25. Quantic analyzes aspects of research projects that may cause writing anxiety or blocks and suggests ways to overcome these problems.

Strickland, James. "The Research Sequence: What to Do Before the Term Paper." *College Composition and Communication* 37 (1986): 233–36. Strickland presents a sequence moving students from opinion papers to documented research projects.

Wilson, Matthew. "Research, Expressivism and Silence." *Journal of Advanced Composition* 15 (1995): 241–60. A thought-provoking analysis of the challenges that teachers face in defining the research paper, and that students face in writing them.

42b Finding a researchable subject and question

INSTRUCTOR RESOURCE

The following Presentation Aid is available for download on this book's companion Web site at *http://www.ablongman.com/littlebrown*.

PRESENTATION AID 42.2: Checklist for a good research subject (p. 561)

CLASSROOM IDEAS

Librarians as allies It's useful to work with the research librarians at your school throughout the process of planning and implementing a research course. In particular, you might consult with the librarians before students begin to generate subjects for their research papers. The librarians can tell you which subjects may have limited resources available or describe new materials they've recently acquired. This will help you guide your students in selecting workable subjects.

COMPUTER ACTIVITY Computer journal The advantage to keeping a hard copy journal is that the student can write in it anywhere at any time. However, some students may find it easier to keep an electronic journal, particularly if they are doing a lot of their searching and source consultation on computers. Students can carry a floppy disk with their journal file and load the file whenever they want to make a journal entry.

COMPUTER ACTIVITY Scope assessment Beginning researchers often have difficulty assessing the scope of the subject they have chosen. Ask all students to post their subject ideas to the class Web site. Then, have an online class discussion in which everyone helps to evaluate the scope of each student's subject.

Doubling up If students have been assigned research projects in other courses, and the instructors of those other courses don't object, permit students to work on those papers in your class or to write a separate paper for you based on the same research materials. Such dual assignments help students transfer writing skills from your classroom to other courses, and your colleagues may appreciate your helping students to write better papers in their disciplines.

COLLABORATIVE LEARNING Research about research Assign teams of students to interview researchers—professors in other departments, employees of local businesses, salespeople looking for new leads, and so on. Have them ask how these researchers go about looking for and limiting subjects, what kinds of "tricks" or strategies they use, why they value research, and what rewards they get from it. In this way, students will see that research is a valued activity outside the writing classroom as well as in it. Each team should report its findings to the entire class.

COMPUTER ACTIVITY E-mail buddies E-mail can be an extremely productive forum, particularly in freeing students from the anxiety of formal writing. You can promote ongoing e-mail conversations by asking students to designate one or two e-mail partners in the class and encouraging them to write to each other once a week about their progress with the research project. You might occasionally assign an exercise that the e-mail partners should also copy to you, such as "Tell your e-mail partners exactly what you want to argue in your paper," or "Describe one of the sources you've found to your e-mail partners in a way that makes them understand how interesting and important the source is to your project." You can also have students prepare for their revision groups by e-mailing and reading drafts before the class meeting.

COLLABORATIVE LEARNING Creating question lists If students have trouble formulating questions on the basis of discovery techniques, you can have them work in groups to come up with question lists for each group member's subject.

COLLABORATIVE LEARNING Exercise 42.1 In Exercise 42.1 (as with all the exercises in this chapter) students should complete the assigned task individually in order to focus their research interests and develop their own projects. However, you can greatly enhance this process of individual learning by creating ongoing collaborative workshops in which students share their findings from each exercise and keep up on the progress of each other's research projects. When students have completed Exercise 42.1, for example, you might divide them into groups according to the subjects they have chosen so that they have the opportunity to learn how other students narrowed particular subjects in different directions. You might also invite students to propose other areas of interest that could be added to the list in Exercise 42.1 and then narrowed.

ANSWERS

EXERCISE 42.1 Finding a topic and question (p. 563)

Individual response.

RESOURCES AND IDEAS

Brent, Doug. *Reading as Rhetorical Invention: Knowledge, Persuasion, and the Teaching of Research-Based Writing.* Urbana: NCTE, 1992. Brent shows how students can use sources to generate researched essays including directed reading projects that help students to develop individualized subjects.

Capossela, Toni-Lee. "Students as Sociolinguists: Getting Real Research from Freshman Writers." *College Composition and Communication* 42 (1991): 75–79. Capossela uses students' command of their own language to engage in real-world issues and write research papers.

Davis, Robert and Mark Shadle. "Building a Mystery": Alternative Research Writing and the Academic Art of Seeking." *College Composition and Communication* 52 (February 2000): 417–66. The authors urge us to expand our definition of the research paper and allow students to write personal research papers and compose multi-genre/media/disciplinary/cultural research papers.

Dellinger, Dixie G. "Alternatives to Clip-and-Stitch: Real Research and Writing in the Classroom." *English Journal* 78 (1989): 31–38. Dellinger claims that engaging students in primary research helps them generate material and enthusiasm for writing.

Nelson, Jennie. "The Library Revisited: Exploring Students' Research Processes." In *Hearing Ourselves Think: Cognitive Research in the College Writing Classroom.* Ed. Ann M. Penrose and Barbara M. Sitko. New York: Oxford UP, 1993. 102–24. Includes case studies of students' composing processes throughout the research paper project, including assembling sources and developing subjects.

42c Developing a research strategy

CLASSROOM IDEAS

COLLABORATIVE LEARNING Reviewing sources Have students bring several likely sources to class and work in pairs to review them, using the strategies for evaluating sources provided by the text.

As a follow-up exercise, you might have students present one of their sources verbally, identify it as primary or secondary, scholarly or popular, old or new, impartial or biased, describe useful features such as bibliographies and indexes, and suggest how its content might function in their research paper.

It is important for students to understand that this process of evaluating and synthesizing their sources will help them to generate a critical argument as well as the information for their paper. Discussing the different purposes and audiences for college writing will also help students who may have written successful research papers in high school using only an entry or two from a general encyclopedia.

COMPUTER ACTIVITY Let your fingers do the walking Students who are inexperienced in Web navigation and searching may avoid doing any searching online. On the other hand, some students are so comfortable Web surfing that they would just as soon research their papers without ever setting foot in the library to look at a print source. In both cases, students may end up with bibliographies that are limited. To make sure that they explore all the avenues of research available to them you may want to require that your students use both print and some online sources in their papers.

COMPUTER ACTIVITY Scholarly versus popular sources Post some examples of sources on your class Web site or courseware, and ask students to evaluate whether they are scholarly or popular sources. Students should cite the evidence upon which they base their judgments.

ANSWERS

EXERCISE 42.2 Developing a research strategy (p. 567)
Individual response.

42d Making a working, annotated bibliography

INSTRUCTOR RESOURCE

The following Presentation Aid is available for download on this book's companion Web site at *http://www.ablongman.com/littlebrown.*

PRESENTATION AID 42.3: Information for a working bibliography (p. 569)

CLASSROOM IDEAS

How many sources? Students always ask, "How many sources do I need in my working bibliography?" A good rule of thumb is two sources per antici- pated page of paper: if students are writing a five-page paper, they should try to find at least ten sources. This rule of thumb should give them ample mate- rial from which to choose while preventing them from becoming obsessed with finding sources at the expense of getting on with their writing.

Keep an eye on your materials A student's research project can be ruined when unattended notes are lost or stolen in the library. Remind students to keep an eye on their materials while they work.

COMPUTER ACTIVITY Shuffling the deck If students have access to biblio- graphic software, they can use it to record and keep track of their working bibliographies. One of the advantages of using bibliographic software is that students can quickly produce lists of citations arranged alphabetically, chronologically, or by subject. This way, they can quickly evaluate whether they rely too much on works by one particular author; how many sources they have on a particular aspect of their subject; and whether their sources are mostly outdated or whether they have sufficient recent titles.

COLLABORATIVE LEARNING Bibliography contest Recording bibliographic information completely and in the proper format is a task that some peo- ple enjoy and some people despise but one that everyone must learn how to do properly. Assign students to two teams and let them check each team member's working bibliography. Whichever team's set of bibliographies has the fewest errors and omissions wins the contest.

COMPUTER ACTIVITY Printing from an e-catalog Students may be able to move source information directly from the library's online catalog to a sep- arate file or a printer. It will save them time to amass bibliographic sources this way; they can format source information later.

COMPUTER ACTIVITY Web page printouts When a Web page is relatively short and includes all necessary source information, students may find it easier to print the page than to copy the bibliographic information by hand. Most Web browsers automatically print some of this information (including the URL). Remind your students to make a note of any informa- tion that doesn't appear on the printout before they leave the Web page.

COLLABORATIVE LEARNING/COMPUTER ACTIVITY Collective annotations As a class, create an online annotated bibliography on a subject of interest to students on campus. Each student can be responsible for finding and annotating a certain number of sources.

COLLABORATIVE LEARNING Exercise 42.3 Have students complete Exercise 42.3 individually; then ask them to work in small groups to review one another's bibliographies. Working together, students can often catch typos and misunderstandings of bibliographic form that they might miss individually.

EXERCISE 42.3 Compiling an annotated working bibliography (p. 571)
Individual response.

RESOURCES AND IDEAS

Chappell, Virginia A., Randall Hensley, and Elizabeth Simmons-O'Neill. "Beyond Information Retrieval: Transforming Research Assignments into Genuine Inquiry." *Journal of Teaching Writing* 13:2 (1994): 209–24. Describes techniques for teaching students to evaluate sources, develop research questions, and analyze data within a range of disciplinary contexts.

Horning, Alice. "Advising Undecided Students Through Research Writing." *College Composition and Communication* 42 (1991): 80–84. Horning provides a sequence of assignments encouraging students to explore various career options, incorporating a number of research strategies.

Macrorie, Ken. *Searching Writing*. Upper Montclair: Boynton/Cook, 1986. Macrorie teaches students to conduct "I-search," personally motivated and inspired research using primary sources as well as library work.

Randall, Sally N. "Information Charts: A Strategy for Organizing Student Research." *Journal of Adolescent and Adult Literacy* 39 (April 1996): 536–43. Randall suggests methods for helping students to organize information and plan further research strategies.

Schwegler, Robert A., and Linda K. Shamoon. "The Aims and Processes of the Research Paper." *College English* 44 (1982): 812–24. The authors contend that all academic research begins with a review of the literature, followed by either examination of a theory, clarification or amplification of previous research, or contesting a hypothesis.

CHAPTER 43

Finding Sources

A WRITER'S PERSPECTIVE

Magazines all too frequently lead to books. —Fran Lebowitz

CHAPTER HIGHLIGHTS

Students may feel overwhelmed by the number of sources available in the library or on the Web and may not know where to begin. This chapter breaks down the steps involved in locating sources and guides students through each one. Section 43a begins with a review of the kinds of electronic sources that may be available at or through the library and explains how to use keywords in searching those sources. The next two sections cover reference works, books, and catalog searching. Section 43d has expanded coverage of periodicals and periodical indexes; how to search periodical databases; how to make use of full text databases and abstracts; and finally, how to locate articles in periodicals. This section stresses the use of library subscription services.

A special feature of this chapter is an in-depth and up-to-date discussion (in sections 43e and 43f) of how to access online sources using Web search engines, e-mail, discussion groups, and synchronous communication. Students are told how to use a search engine effectively, and a sample search is provided for them to follow. A list of the most popular search engines is also provided.

The final sections of this chapter cover pamphlets and government publications, as well as how to conduct original research through interviewing. Woven throughout the chapter are examples drawn from Edward Begay's search for sources.

MEDIA RESOURCES FOR CHAPTER 43

mycomplab Please visit MyCompLab at *www.mycomplab.com* for more on the writing process.

http://www.ablongman.com/littlebrown | ▶ See page 73 of this manual for companion Web site content description

43a Searching electronically

INSTRUCTOR RESOURCE

The following Presentation Aid is available for download on this book's companion Web site at *http://www.ablongman.com/littlebrown*.

PRESENTATION AID 43.1: Ways to refine keywords (p. 574)

CLASSROOM IDEAS

COMPUTER ACTIVITY Getting the best sources If your students are going to have a library instruction session covering online searching you might reconnoiter with the reference librarian before your class meets. Give the librarian a list of your students' research questions, so that when class meets, the librarian can help point your students to the most useful sources and search tools.

COMPUTER ACTIVITY Comparing searches Ask students to enter the same search phrase into *Google* and one or more other search engines. Then ask them to compare the source links each search yields.

The library as office If space and library regulations permit, consider holding office hours in the library while students are conducting their research there. Your presence will encourage more consultation between you and your students. This practice is especially useful in conjunction with whatever library orientation programs your school offers first-year students.

Making the library accessible Students are often confused when the library provides both an electronic catalog of its own books and access to online subscription services. They may think that every source they find on a subscription service is in the library, or that searching the library catalog is the same as searching the other databases. Make sure that students understand what kind of information is available from each source.

Also keep in mind that learning to use a new cataloging system (electronic or print) can be frustrating and slow and may involve a series of baffling dead ends. To help students through this process, you might implement a combination of the following:

Plan frequent trips to the library (or allow for ongoing work with research databases in your own electronic classroom).

Assign students to ongoing research teams, partnering students who are more skilled with computers in mentoring relationships with those who are tackling the electronic medium for the first time.

Demonstrate (or ask your research librarian to demonstrate) common dead ends, such as keyword searches that generate plentiful sources in one database and no sources in another.

Frequently direct the class to bring their research journals to class and to report their progress and their setbacks, so that students understand that they are sharing a learning process.

Remind students to vary electronic information with material found in print sources (for example, the bibliography of one good article can often yield several more productive sources and start the student off on a new set of electronic searches).

COLLABORATIVE LEARNING Keyword brainstorming Have students work together to brainstorm keywords that might work for each student's subject.

COLLABORATIVE LEARNING Hands-on learning The barrage of information about various types of sources available through the library can be overwhelming to your students, and they may not retain it unless they have a chance to use the databases, search engines, and catalogs themselves. If you have time, consider an experiential approach rather than a long lecture about sources and how to use them. Create a worksheet of questions for students to answer, working in groups. The students will be the detectives, and will have to discover sources and figure out how to use them in order to complete the worksheet. You can give strategic hints along the way, and at the end of the exercise ask them to report on what they have discovered.

COMPUTER ACTIVITY To Works Cited If your students have bibliographic software, they may be able to e-mail source citations to themselves in a compatible format, so that they can get the information into their bibliographies without retyping.

COMPUTER ACTIVITY Keyword lists Have students meet you in the library or the electronic classroom with individual lists of keywords in their areas of interest. Have students try their keywords in several databases, noting subheadings of interest and revising the keywords in places where a database or search engine works from a different system of subject headings. The goal of the exercise is not only to generate the variations on keywords that may be needed for different databases but also to narrow and define their topics further.

RESOURCES AND IDEAS

Anderson, Daniel, Bret Benjamin, Christopher Busiel, and Bill Paredes-Holt. *Teaching Online: Internet Research, Conversation, and Composition.* New York: Longman, 1998. A useful and practical guide to electronic research; in particular, see Chapter 5, "The Electronic Library."

Gavin, Christy. "Guiding Students Along the Information Highway: Librarians Collaborating with Composition Instructors." *Journal of Teaching Writing* 13:2 (1994): 225–35. Gavin explores the possibilities of cooperative instruction between reference librarians and writing teachers. Given the rapidly transforming nature of bibliographic instruction, this kind of collaborative work seems crucial.

Mark, Beth L., and Trudi E. Jacobson. "Teaching Anxious Students Skills for the Electronic Library." *College Teaching* 43.1 (Fall 1995): 28–31. Suggests do's and don't's when introducing students to electronic library databases.

Selfe, Cynthia L., and Richard J. Selfe, Jr. "The Politics of the Interface: Power and Its Exercise in Electronic Contact Zones." *College Composition and Communication* 45:4 (1994): 480–504. The authors probe some of the larger cultural issues surrounding technological innovations such as the World Wide Web, including their political and ideological ramifications for education.

43b   Finding reference works

INSTRUCTOR RESOURCE

The following Presentation Aid is available for download on this book's companion Web site at *http://www.ablongman.com/littlebrown.*

PRESENTATION AID 43.2: Guide to research sources (p. 576)

CLASSROOM IDEAS

COLLABORATIVE LEARNING Reference reviews Assign a small group of students to each category of reference works. Have the group find which of these sources their library holds and what kind(s) of information these works contain. Ask them to report to the class either orally or in writing. If students have begun to work on topics, have them shape their reports around the usefulness of the resource for those particular topics.

COLLABORATIVE LEARNING Comparing encyclopedias Working with a partner, students can look up a subject in both a general encyclopedia and a specialized encyclopedia. They will quickly discover differences in scope and depth of coverage.

COMPUTER ACTIVITY Quick access dictionaries Some dictionaries can be accessed online for free, or your library may hold a subscription. Your students may find it helpful to bookmark a dictionary web site and use it when they need to look up a word.

COMPUTER ACTIVITY Check publication dates Reference books are expensive, and few college libraries can afford to update all the references in their collections all the time. Remind students to check the editions and publication dates of the reference sources they use; the information in older works may need to be updated or supplemented. Online versions of reference works may be updated more frequently.

43c   Finding books

CLASSROOM IDEAS

COMPUTER ACTIVITY Browsing nearby books Once your students have located a book relevant to their topics, they might try browsing the nearby shelves for additional titles. Some library e-catalogs will allow you to do this onscreen.

COLLABORATIVE LEARNING Reviewing reviews Students who are new to research may not be used to the idea of reading review literature. To get them started, you might give a preliminary assignment in which pairs of students locate several reviews of a particular book, summarize them, and present oral summaries to the class.

43d Finding periodicals

CLASSROOM IDEAS

COLLABORATIVE LEARNING Citation reports Have teams of students look up a book or article of your choosing in a citation index. Have each team review a different work that reviews or cites the original source. When all groups summarize what they found, your class will have a fairly good sense of how the original source has been received by peers.

COLLABORATIVE LEARNING Periodical jungle Students will sometimes rely on books rather than periodical articles in an attempt to avoid the complications of periodical indexes. You can help them get started by planning a library visit in which students work in pairs to find and photocopy or download periodical articles on their topics.

COMPUTER ACTIVITY Abstract reports Have students locate several articles in a database that provides abstracts. After upon reading the abstracts, students should report back to you about which articles seem most relevant and why.

43e Finding sources on the Web

INSTRUCTOR RESOURCE

The following Presentation Aid is available for download on this book's companion Web site at *http://www.ablongman.com/littlebrown*.

PRESENTATION AID 43.3: Web search engines (p. 589)

CLASSROOM IDEAS

COLLABORATIVE LEARNING Web source evaluation Since sources found on the Web are sometimes difficult to evaluate, you might devote class time to helping students analyze sample sources. Begin by reviewing a sample item in class: What clues are there about whether the material is primary or secondary, scholarly or popular? Is it dated? Did the material come from an individual's home page, an institutional archive? Is the author named? Has that author published additional work found in print? Is the material referenced in a scholarly bibliography? Does the author cite other sources; does the piece include a bibliography of its own sources? Then have each student bring in a printout of material gleaned from the Web along with a record of the search procedures he or she used to find it (in an electronic classroom you might have students work directly from the screen). Ask students to work in small groups to evaluate their sources and to report their findings on one source to the class.

COMPUTER ACTIVITY Reviewing the search engines Pick one subject for all your students to search. Have students use different search engines to conduct their searches and then report their findings to the class.

COMPUTER ACTIVITY All roads lead to Rome Hold a contest to see which of your students can find the greatest number of different paths to your school's Web site by using different search engines, different search terms, and different links. Have them make notes of the paths they follow by using the History features of their browser.

COMPUTER ACTIVITY Finding good search terms Have your students conduct a search on their own research topics. They might begin by brainstorming some search terms. Like Edward Begay, they may find it necessary to modify their search strategies, so remind them to try different search engines and to look for likely search terms as they go. The assignment ends with a report to you on how they conducted the search and what they found.

RESOURCES AND IDEAS

Crump, Eric, and Nick Carbone. *The English Student's Guide to the Internet*. New York: Houghton, 1996. A useful guide for narrowing the Web's vast search capabilities toward directed areas.

Davis, Chris. "The I-Search Paper Goes Global: Using the Internet as a Research Tool." *English Journal* 84:6 (1995): 27–33. Davis shows how the Internet enhances students' abilities to develop and follow through on their own research interests.

43f Finding other online sources

CLASSROOM IDEAS

COLLABORATIVE LEARNING Levels of discourse To help students learn to differentiate between the more scholarly discussions found on discussion lists and the less scholarly ones found on Web forums and newsgroups, assign pairs of students to explore one example of each kind of conversation on a single topic. For instance, a discussion list about World War II will probably have historians as participants, discussing approaches to interpretation, primary and secondary data, or historiography. In contrast, a Web forum about World War II would be more likely to attract war buffs and veterans as participants, discussing their own experiences and opinions. Each kind of conversation has its usefulness for research, but they should not be granted equal authority.

COMPUTER ACTIVITY Online lurking Ask your students to join one discussion list, Web log, or newsgroup relevant to their topic and read postings for one week. Then ask them to write a brief evaluation of the list, forum, or newsgroup and e-mail it to the other members of your class.

COMPUTER ACTIVITY Breaking the ice After your students have spent a little time lurking on a discussion list, Web log, or newsgroup relevant to their topic, tell them to submit a posting asking for information on their topic and then report to you about the responses they receive.

43g Finding government publications

CLASSROOM IDEA

COMPUTER ACTIVITY Online vs. print catalogs Some online catalogs cover material dating only from the years since online databases and the Web became popularized, so for older data your students may have to consult a print version of the catalog. For instance, the online *Catalog of United States Government Publications* (which is updated daily) goes back to 1994. Information predating 1994 can be found in the print version, the *Monthly Catalog of United States Government Publications*.

43h Finding images

CLASSROOM IDEAS

COMPUTER ACTIVITY Finding new research pathways Public image databases often have guides to their collections that include relevant information about historical periods, publications in which images appeared, and related works. Students might find these resources helpful in their search process.

COMPUTER ACTIVITY Unusual images Students might be surprised at some of the categories of images that can be found online. Some collections of images are arranged by medium, such as book jackets, Yiddish theater placards, American song sheet covers. Other collections are arranged by subject, such as ablution fountains, national emblems, or washtubs. Esoteric groupings of images might be suggestive for students in shaping their research projects.

43i Generating your own sources

CLASSROOM IDEAS

COLLABORATIVE LEARNING Ethnography and research Many instructors require students to begin their research projects with an interview so that they get a human perspective on their topic before they begin locating secondary sources. You can have students practice by interviewing a partner in class.

COMPUTER ACTIVITY Synchronous interviewing To help students understand the value of in-person interviews, have them conduct a brief practice interview with a classmate using email or synchronous communication and then compare the results with a practice in-person interview (using the same questions but a different subject). Ask them to record their impressions of the interviewee's tone, gestures, and expressions and then report back to you about how those factors influenced the content of what the interviewee said.

COLLABORATIVE LEARNING Exercise 43.1 Have students complete Exercise 43.1 in teams. Hold a contest to see which team can find answers to all five sets of questions in the shortest amount of time.

COLLABORATIVE LEARNING Exercises 43.2 and 43.3 Have students complete Exercises 43.2 and 43.3 individually and bring three of the sources to class. Then ask students to work in small groups to write a very brief summary of each source. Students can use the summaries as annotations in their working bibliographies.

ANSWERS

EXERCISE 43.1 Using the library (p. 597)

Individual response.

EXERCISE 43.2 Finding library sources (p. 598)

Individual response.

EXERCISE 43.3 Finding Web sources (p. 598)

Individual response.

RESOURCES AND IDEAS

Heath, Shirley Brice. *Ways with Words: Language, Life, and Work in Communities*. New York: Cambridge UP, 1983. Heath provides a thorough and accessible demonstration of how to conduct ethnographic research, illustrated by her study of the communities of Roadville and Trackton.

Tryzna, Thomas N. "Research Outside the Library: Learning a Field." *College Composition and Communication* 37 (1986): 217–23. Tryzna shows how to begin a research project outside the library and find valuable primary sources.

CHAPTER 44

Working with Sources

CHAPTER HIGHLIGHTS

This chapter tackles one of the most difficult aspects of research writing. Students unskilled in research or with comparatively undeveloped critical thinking skills may not know what to do with the sources they find. Students will follow Edward Begay's and Vanessa Haley's research in progress and observe how these students work with sources. New to this edition of the handbook is an expanded discussion (44a) of how to evaluate Web sites and online discussions, including a new section on Web logs.

Subsequent sections focus on how students may respond to and interact with the sources they find, including detailed coverage of methods of gathering and organizing information. Section 44d, which covers summary, paraphrase, and quotation, includes new detailed examples of summary and paraphrase that students should find helpful. The final section covers methods of introducing source material into the text of a research paper. The chapter's exercises provide practice in all aspects of handling sources.

MEDIA RESOURCES FOR CHAPTER 44

mycomplab Please visit MyCompLab at *www.mycomplab.com* for more on the writing process.

http://www.ablongman.com/littlebrown ▶ See page 73 of this manual for companion Web site content description.

44a Evaluating sources

INSTRUCTOR RESOURCES

The following Presentation Aids are available for download on this book's companion Web site at *http://www.ablongman.com/littlebrown*.

PRESENTATION AID 44.1: Questions for evaluating sources (p. 601)

PRESENTATION AID 44.2: Questions for evaluating Web sites (p. 602)

PRESENTATION AID 44.3: Questions for evaluating Web logs and online discussions (p. 608)

CLASSROOM IDEAS

COLLABORATIVE LEARNING Getting a clue Because students are often unfamiliar with the clues provided by the publication context, bibliographic and indexing apparatus, and tone of a source, they may find the task of scanning sources difficult and confusing. Pose a sample paper topic that is related to the material found in a source you distribute, and ask students to work in small groups to evaluate the source for relevance and reliability. Then lead a discussion in which you help students to identify the kinds of clues they used to help them decide whether the source was appropriate to the topic, whether it was too specialized or too simplistic, too out-of-date, or too biased.

COLLABORATIVE LEARNING Group evaluation As a follow-up to the "Getting a Clue" exercise, ask students to bring to class one or two sources they are considering using in their own research papers. Have them work with their groups to evaluate the sources and then present their findings to the rest of the class.

COLLABORATIVE LEARNING Annotation assignment Ask students to submit an annotated bibliography of sources as a mini-assignment. This assignment can be one phase of a larger research assignment; by breaking the assignment into min-assignments, you can help ensure that students pay adequate attention to all parts of the research process.

COMPUTER ACTIVITY Web clues Since electronic sources pose special problems, particularly for determining reliability, it will be helpful to conduct additional in-class evaluations of such sources. In a networked classroom, you might run through a short Web search and then ask students to help you evaluate the reliability of the sources you find, using the criteria provided by the handbook. Then ask students to work in pairs to evaluate one or two of their Web site sources and to report their findings to the class. In each case, encourage students to recount (and to keep journal records of) the methods they used to determine a source's reliability and relevance.

COMPUTER ACTIVITY Disingenuous sites Some Web sites, particularly those sponsored by some kinds of activist organizations, attempt to appear non-biased when in fact they have a very strong bias. They may post pseudo-scholarship on their sites in an attempt to look research-based and academic. If you come across such sites, they can be excellent teaching tools. Students will be eager to develop the savvy to uncover the true bias underlying a Web site, and you can point out to them that intelligent readers use the same methods of analysis to evaluate all texts, including student research papers.

COMPUTER ACTIVITY Trying out sites Ask students to provide you with an example of these five types of sites (scholarly, informational, advocacy, commercial, and personal) on their research topic. Then ask them to outline a research paragraph based on each site to get a better understanding of how useful (or useless) each kind of site is for their purposes.

COLLABORATIVE LEARNING/COMPUTER ACTIVITY Blog hall of fame As a class, compile a collection of memorable blogs. Give awards for the most boring, the most redundant, the most entertaining, the most self-indulgent, the one with the most grammatical errors, and the most heartfelt; or ask students to make up their own award categories.

COLLABORATIVE LEARNING Exercise 44.1 Exercise 44.1 works well as a group project, particularly since the library may contain limited copies of Packard's book. You might consider putting this book on reserve so that each group can examine it for a limited amount of time. Have each group present its findings to the class, paying particular attention to the methods the students used to evaluate the book. As the groups give their presentations, you might have students keep a running list of those methods on the blackboard, on the overhead, or on the computer network.

As a variation on Exercise 44.1 (or a follow-up to it) you might have one group work with Packard and other groups work with additional authors who have varying approaches to advertising (such as Michael Schudson, Mark Crispin Miller, or Stuart Ewen). This task will encourage students to identify differences in arguments and approaches.

COLLABORATIVE LEARNING Exercise 44.3 In a networked classroom, you could do Exercise 44.3 and 44.4 as a class. Look at the postings together and discuss them, using the chart for evaluating online discussions and blogs on page 608. Or have students e-mail their evaluation paragraphs to the rest of the class or post them on your class Web site. As a class, you can develop your own annotated list of newsgroups,Web forums, and blogs.

ANSWERS

EXERCISE 44.1 Evaluating a source (p. 609)

Responses will vary. Packard's book is famously critical of advertising methods. Students should recognize Packard's bias while also valuing his expertise and evidence.

EXERCISE 44.2 Evaluating Web sites (p. 609)

Individual response.

EXERCISE 44.3 Evaluating a Web log (p. 610)

Individual response.

EXERCISE 44.4 Evaluating an online discussion (p. 610)

Individual response.

RESOURCES AND IDEAS

Higgens, Lorraine. "Reading to Argue: Helping Students Transform Source Texts." *Hearing Ourselves Think: Cognitive Research in the College Writing Classroom.* Ed. Ann M. Penrose and Barbara M. Sitko. New York,

Oxford: Oxford UP, 1993. 70–101. Higgens explores strategies through which students learn to use their sources, and debates between their sources, as the basis for developing their own arguments.

Spivey, Nancy Nelson. "The Shaping of Meaning: Options in Writing the Comparison." *Research in the Teaching of English* 25 (1991): 390–418. Spivey shows that the use of sources can affect students' processes of invention, arrangement, and style.

44b Synthesizing sources

CLASSROOM IDEAS

COLLABORATIVE LEARNING Understanding the debates Students often experience some difficulty in identifying connections among their sources. To help them develop a better sense of the debates surrounding their topic and the major authors involved in these debates, ask your students to look through the bibliographies and footnotes (or endnotes) of their principal sources for additional sources to read. Likely prospects include titles or authors that are more frequently cited than others. As a follow-up exercise, you might have students work in groups to give oral presentations about the connections and debates as developed among three of their sources. You might also have students turn in a one-page analysis of the crucial connections among those three sources.

COLLABORATIVE LEARNING Exercise 44.5 As a preliminary activity to Exercise 44.5, have students work in groups to debate the similarities and differences among the three authors and their approaches. Encourage students to support their views with evidence from the three passages. Then have each student create the paragraph specified by Exercise 44.4 and share it with his or her group. The collaborative approach will enrich students' interpretive responses to the passages, and will help make them aware that their own views on the topic are not self-evident but must be argued on the basis of evidence.

COMPUTER ACTIVITY Sounding boards If you are teaching a distance education course, your students may miss out on the opportunity to have a sounding board for their impressions of a source. Let pairs or small groups read the same source and then have an open-ended discussion about the source online, using e-mail, your courseware, or synchronous communication.

RESOURCES AND IDEAS

Kantz, Margaret. "Helping Students Use Textual Sources Persuasively." *College English* 52 (1990): 74–91. Kantz suggests using analysis of the rhetorical situation and lists of questions to help students meet the demands of research essays.

Pelham, Fran O'Byrne. "The Research Journal: Integrating Reading, Writing, and Research." *Composition Chronicle* 6.3 (April 1993): 4–5. Pelham advocates using a journal to supplement typical research activities and to allow students to "research, reflect, write, and then attend recursively to these events."

44c Mining and interacting with sources

CLASSROOM IDEAS

COLLABORATIVE LEARNING Skimming together Give your students a medium-length article and tell them to skim it with a pertinent research question (of your choosing) in mind. Give them a time limit for skimming, plus a few more minutes to reread key passages. Then, working in small groups, they can discuss what they gleaned from the article in relation to the research question.

COLLABORATIVE LEARNING Partners for gathering Students can show a partner the results of their efforts to gather and organize information. The partner should evaluate the researcher's material, checking for accuracy in the recording of source information and advising the researcher on efficient methods of information gathering.

COMPUTER ACTIVITY Source accessibility Students working on popular topics or on topics for which little information is available may find that they do better accessing sources online than in the library stacks. Popular books and articles in the library sometimes have a way of disappearing from the shelves, and students often aren't able to consult them again if they need to. Encourage students working on such topics to use full-text databases and download where possible.

Reading and thinking while gathering To combat the problem of indiscriminate downloading or printing of information that interferes with the researcher's interaction with sources, encourage your students to skim and summarize sources they find online as they print them out or download them. This will help them make sure that the information they are gathering is truly relevant to their subject and may give them ideas for next steps in their research.

RESOURCES AND IDEAS

Kennedy, Mary Lynch. "The Composing Process of College Students Writing from Sources." *Written Communication* 2 (1985): 434–56. Kennedy's research shows that "fluent" readers and writers take more notes, do more planning, and reread more frequently than do less effective readers.

McGinley, William. "The Role of Reading and Writing while Composing from Sources." *Reading Research Quarterly* 27 (1992): 227–48. McGinley demonstrates that students writing from sources use highly recursive nonlinear as well as linear reading, writing, and reasoning processes.

ANSWERS

EXERCISE 44.5 Synthesizing sources (p. 611)

The key similarities and differences are these:

Similarities: Nadelmann and Posey agree that crackdowns or penalties do not stop the drug trade. Nadelmann and Runkle agree that the drug trade affects the young, who are most impressionable.

Differences: Nadelmann maintains that the illegal drug trade does more to entice youths to drugs than do the drugs themselves, whereas Runkle maintains that the illegality discourages youths from using prohibited drugs. Posey, in contrast to Runkle, claims that penalties do nothing to discourage drug abusers.

Students' paragraphs will depend on their views, but here is a sample response:

Posey seems to invalidate the whole debate over drug legalization: nothing, he says from experience, will stop drug abuse. But such a futile view, whatever its truth, cannot stop the search for a solution. We have tried the prohibition favored by Runkle. Even if, as she claims, students are using fewer illegal drugs, prohibition has not worked. It may be time to try the admittedly risky approach proposed by Nadelmann, legalizing drugs to "drive the drug-dealing business off the streets."

EXERCISE 44.6 Evaluating and synthesizing sources (p. 613)

Individual response.

44d Using summary, paraphrase, and quotation

INSTRUCTOR RESOURCE

The following Presentation Aid is available for download on this book's companion Web site at *http://www.ablongman.com/littlebrown*.

PRESENTATION AID 44.4: Tests for direct quotations from secondary sources (p. 620)

CLASSROOM IDEAS

COLLABORATIVE LEARNING Skills drill Pick an essay or article to use in class, and practice taking notes from it with your students. If they all summarize, paraphrase, and quote from the same article and discuss their results in groups, they may gain confidence when moving on to their own research materials.

COLLABORATIVE LEARNING Summaries and ADD Students who have attention deficit disorder (ADD or ADHD) often have difficulty summarizing texts. They may benefit from working on summarizing assignments with their learning specialist.

CLASSROOM IDEA Begay's example The trickiest aspect of paraphrasing is changing the language without changing the meaning. Note for your students that Begay's paraphrase uses very few words from the original (you might want to have your students count them). Note that he does not merely replace words with synonyms, but changes sentence structure as well.

CLASSROOM IDEA A mnemonic for paraphrasing A useful mnemonic that helps students remember how to paraphrase effectively is "New words and new word order." The emphasis on syntactic change in the mnemonic helps prevent mere synonym substitution.

CULTURE LANGUAGE **Paraphrase and sentence structure** While ESL students may be comfortable using synonyms to express the content of a source, they may feel insecure about using other sentence structures. Emphasize to students that they must change the sentence structure as well as the vocabulary of the original in writing paraphrases. Collaborative work on paraphrasing helps students develop their vocabularies and find alternative ways to express ideas. In addition, more advanced ESL students (and native speakers) can reinforce their own writing skills by helping less advanced students.

Key quotations Students often have trouble identifying the key passages or parts of passages that will become effective quotations. Remind students that the quotation should represent the author's position fairly and that quoting provides an occasion for the student to speak directly back to that author. It can also help to conduct workshops in which students practice choosing key quotations from a shared text and write one-paragraph responses to one of their chosen quotations.

COLLABORATIVE LEARNING Quotation evaluation Have students work in small groups to review every quotation in one another's drafts-in-progress. Is each quotation necessary and appropriate? Is the writer integrating the quotation smoothly into the paper? Is the writer making effective use of the quotation, supplying an interpretation of it, and making it work toward some larger purpose in his or her own argument? This discussion can often help student writers rethink their uses of quotation and elaborate on their interpretive responses, thus helping them to create effective revisions of their drafts.

COMPUTER ACTIVITY Responsible use Students can learn a great deal about the ethics of responsible summary, paraphrase, and quotation by practicing on each other. Have each student e-mail an abstract of his or her paper-in-progress to a partner in the class. Ask the partner to quote directly from the abstract, to paraphrase part of the abstract, and then to summarize the other person's project. Have each student check the accuracy of his or her partner's quotation, paraphrase, and summary.

COMPUTER ACTIVITY Irresponsible use As a follow-up to the previous exercise you might ask each student's partner to misquote deliberately or to paraphrase or summarize in a way that misrepresents the project. Then ask the student authors to identify the particular ways in which their work has been misrepresented.

COLLABORATIVE LEARNING Exercise 44.7 Have students complete Exercise 44.7 individually and then discuss and revise their responses in small groups. Students will learn a great deal by seeing the alternative strategies that other group members employed in completing the exercise. Encourage the groups to discuss the effectiveness of various strategies and to consider how fairly Eisinger's views have been represented in each student's response.

COLLABORATIVE LEARNING Exercise 44.8 Have students complete Exercise 44.8 individually and then discuss and revise their responses in small groups. Ask each group to report any strategies for condensing and organizing material that they discover in the process.

ANSWERS

EXERCISE 44.7 Summarizing and paraphrasing (p. 622)

Possible summary

Eisinger et al. 44

Federalism, unlike a unitary system, allows the states autonomy. Its strength and its weakness—which are in balance—lie in the regional differences it permits.

Possible paraphrase

Eisinger et al. 44

Under federalism, each state can devise its own ways of handling problems and its own laws. The system's advantage is that a state can operate according to its people's culture, morals, and wealth. A unitary system like that in France does not permit such diversity.

EXERCISE 44.8 Combining summary, paraphrase, and direct quotation (p. 623)

Possible summary

Farb 107

Speakers at parties often "unconsciously duel" in conversations in order to assert "dominance" over others. A speaker may mumble, thus preventing a listener from understanding what is said. Or he or she may continue talking after the listener has moved away, a "challenge to the listener to return and acknowledge the dominance of the speaker."

EXERCISE 44.9 Gathering information from sources (p. 623)

Individual response.

RESOURCES AND IDEAS

Sherrard, Carol. "Summary Writing: A Topographical Study." *Written Communication* 3 (1986): 324–43. Sherrard discusses both common and effective summary-writing techniques of college students.

44e Integrating sources into your text

INSTRUCTOR RESOURCE

The following Presentation Aid is available for download on this book's companion Web site at *http://www.ablongman.com/littlebrown*.

PRESENTATION AID 44.5: Verbs for signal phrases (p. 626)

CLASSROOM IDEAS

COLLABORATIVE LEARNING Link highlights Give each group a research-based essay (student or professional). Ask students to highlight all of the links used to integrate quotations and to discuss the effectiveness of each link.

COLLABORATIVE LEARNING Signal phrases Assign students to work as partners to practice using signal phrases. Students can trade drafts of their papers, and each reader can write a short summary of the writer's paper, using signal phrases as appropriate.

COMPUTER ACTIVITY Tense examples Students unfamiliar with the humanities convention of using present tense in signal phrases may have difficulty applying this principle to their own writing. Ask them to collect examples of present-tense signal phrases in published works and post them to the class Web site.

COMPUTER ACTIVITY Exercise 44.10 Have students circulate their responses to Exercise 44.10 to the rest of the class via e-mail or Web posting. Students will see that there are multiple ways of using the source material and integrating it into a paragraph of one's own.

ANSWERS

EXERCISE 44.10 Introducing and interpreting borrowed material (p. 629)

Sample paragraph

Why does a woman who is otherwise happy regularly suffer anxiety attacks at the first sign of spring? Why does a man who is otherwise a competent, relaxed driver feel panic whenever he approaches a traffic rotary? According to Willard Gaylin, a professor of psychiatry and a practicing psychoanalyst, such feelings of anxiety are attributable to the uniquely human capacities for remembering, imagining, and forming "symbolic and often unconscious representations" of experiences (23). The feeling of anxiety, Gaylin says, "is . . . compounded by its seemingly irrational quality": it may appear despite the absence of an immediate source of worry or pain (23). The anxious woman is not aware of it, but her father's death twenty years before in April has caused her to equate spring with death. Similarly, the man has forgotten that a terrible accident he witnessed as a child occurred at a rotary. For both people, the anxious feelings are not reduced but heightened because they seem to be unfounded.

Avoiding Plagiarism and Documenting Sources

A WRITER'S PERSPECTIVE

If you copy from one author, it's plagiarism; if you copy from two, it's research.
—Wislon Minzner

CHAPTER HIGHLIGHTS

Chapter 45 focuses exclusively on plagiarism and documentation. As students increasingly conduct research online, they have more opportunities for both accidental and deliberate plagiarism. Inculcating good habits of documentation in your students is an essential task of the writing and research educator. Section 45a introduces the subject of plagiarism on the Internet and features a checklist for avoiding plagiarism. Students may want to keep a copy of the checklist handy in their research journals. Sections 45b and 45c discuss how students can determine what they do and do not need to acknowledge, section 45d focuses on acknowledgment of online sources, and section 45e explains and points students to documentation formats in the various disciplines.

MEDIA RESOURCES FOR CHAPTER 45

mycomplab Please visit MyCompLab at *www.mycomplab.com* for more on the writing process.

http://www.ablongman.com/littlebrown ▶ See page 73 of this manual for companion Web site content description.

INSTRUCTOR RESOURCE

The following Presentation Aid is available for download on this book's companion Web site at *http://www.ablongman.com/littlebrown*.

PRESENTATION AID 45.1: Checklist for avoiding plagiarism (p. 630)

CLASSROOM IDEAS

COMPUTER ACTIVITY Thwarting plagiarism To impress upon your students how easy it is for you to catch deliberate plagiarism, have the whole class visit a site that sells term papers and see how easy it is to find papers and key passages on the site. You can also guard against plagiarism by requiring drafts and research reports and holding workshops to show work in progress.

COLLABORATIVE LEARNING Learn by doing One way to teach students how not to plagiarize is to require deliberate plagiarism. Have students practice deliberately plagiarizing from an online source. Then have them exchange their plagiarized passages with fellow group members, who must locate and correct the plagiarism.

RESOURCES AND IDEAS

Fulkerson, Richard. "Oh, What a Cite! A Teaching Tip to Help Students Document Researched Papers Accurately." *The Writing Instructor* 7 (1988): 167–72. Fulkerson suggests giving students a sample research paper with documentation removed to help them determine where and what kind(s) of citation must be used.

Kroll, Barry M. "How College Freshmen View Plagiarism." *Written Communication* 5 (1988): 203–21. A survey of 150 students shows the five most popular reasons they think plagiarism is wrong and discusses effective means to teach students the seriousness and possible consequences of plagiarism.

Whitaker, Elaine E. "A Pedagogy to Address Plagiarism." *College Composition and Communication* 44 (1993): 509–14. Whitaker describes classroom activities designed to help students understand and avoid plagiarism.

45a Committing and detecting plagiarism on the Internet

CLASSROOM IDEA

CULTURE LANGUAGE **Intellectual property and culture** Ideas about ownership of intellectual property vary among cultures. In some cultures scholarly research consists of finding expert sources and copying information without attribution. ESL students who copy without attribution or too closely paraphrase sources may be following the procedures they have been taught. In their countries plagiarism may be considered less objectionable than in the United States, or perhaps in their culture students are encouraged to use classic works in their own writing. See "Teaching Writing to ESL Students" (p. 101 of this manual) for further discussion of ESL students' attitudes toward plagiarism. Discuss the issue of intellectual ownership with your students, emphasizing that in the United States research and writing are valued for their originality.

45b Knowing what you need not acknowledge

CLASSROOM IDEAS

COLLABORATIVE LEARNING Common-knowledge evaluation Give students a worksheet with examples of statements that may or may not qualify as common knowledge. In small groups, students can work together to evaluate the statements and discuss the basis for their decisions.

COMPUTER ACTIVITY Common-knowledge archive When your students find material that they are unsure about, have them post it to a common-knowledge query page of your class Web site. Other members of the class can give opinions about whether the material is, in fact, common knowledge, and you can maintain an archive of all the submissions that qualify.

45c Knowing what you *must* acknowledge

CLASSROOM IDEAS

COLLABORATIVE LEARNING Cited material and originality Students who are new to research writing may fail to document their sources properly out of the fear that their papers will look insufficiently original if they are full of in-text citations. Reassure students that research papers are meant to be full of documented material and that the originality in their papers resides in their approach to the subject, their thesis, the choice of sources and the way they present them, and the conclusions they draw. Students who have been successful in writing good research papers for other courses can volunteer to bring those papers in and pass them around, so that their classmates can see how much of the material in their papers is from outside sources.

COMPUTER ACTIVITY Highlighting nonoriginal material To help students avoid plagiarism, have each one use the Highlight function on a word processor to mark all passages in his or her paper that are not original. Then you or a classmate can review the draft to ensure that the writer quoted, paraphrased, and cited properly and to ensure that the writer did not neglect to highlight a borrowed passage.

COLLABORATIVE LEARNING Exercise 45.1 Have students complete Exercise 45.1 individually and then discuss their responses in small groups. Encourage groups to debate the accuracy of each attempted quotation or paraphrase, paying particular attention to items on which group members have differing responses. Students learn a great deal from the task of identifying the particular way in which a passage has been plagiarized or accurately represented.

ANSWERS

EXERCISE 45. 1 Recognizing plagiarism (p. 435)

1. Plagiarized: takes phrases directly from the original without quotation marks.
2. Acceptable.
3. Inaccurate and plagiarized: the passage uses phrases from the original without quotation marks and distorts its meaning.
4. Acceptable: puts the original into the author's own words and correctly conveys its meaning.

5. Inaccurate and plagiarized: fails to acknowledge the source and fails to convey accurately the concepts of "discrimination" and "confusing" outlined in the original.
6. Inaccurate: ellipses are needed to indicate that material was omitted, and brackets must be placed around lowercase *s* to indicate revision.

45d Acknowledging online sources

CLASSROOM IDEAS

COLLABORATIVE LEARNING Fair-use jury When students are unsure whether they have violated principles of fair use for their online sources, have them submit the material in question to the rest of the class, who can render opinions. This exercise will help to impress upon students that the principles of fair use are ones that reasonable people would agree to.

COMPUTER ACTIVITY Permission letters Ask your students to create a template for an e-mail letter requesting permission to use an author's material. Keep the template on your class Web site, or have your students store it on their own computers. When they need to request an author's permission, they will be able to do so expediently.

45e Documenting sources

CLASSROOM IDEAS

COLLABORATIVE LEARNING Documentation tutorials Students in your class who are familiar with one of the discipline's documentation styles may want to volunteer to give the rest of your class a short lecture/tutorial about that style.

COMPUTER ACTIVITY Documentation practice Your students may need to become familiar with more than one documentation style in the course of their college educations. Post a paper in MLA format to your class Web site (or send it around by e-mail), and ask your students to convert it to one of the other styles. Even without bibliographic software, students should be able to make the conversions quickly, especially if they use the Find and Replace functions of a word processor.

Writing the Paper.

CHAPTER HIGHLIGHTS

Some students can read and conduct research indefinitely but have trouble getting down to writing the paper. Chapter 46 helps students move from the preliminary stages of research to the paper-writing stage. It begins with the tentative thesis statements of student writers Edward Begay and Vanessa Haley and shows how each student revised the thesis in a later phase of research. Next come discussions of how to use formal and informal outlines to create a structure for the paper. The second half of the chapter covers drafting, revising, and proofreading, with special attention given to the necessity of tracking and completing source citations. The exercises ask students to apply the strategies discussed in the chapter to their own research essays.

MEDIA RESOURCES FOR CHAPTER 46

mycomplab Please visit MyCompLab at *www.mycomplab.com* for more on the writing process.

http://www.ablongman.com/littlebrown ▶ See page 73 of this manual for companion Web site content description.

46a Developing a thesis statement

CLASSROOM IDEAS

Stated intentions Have students complete this sentence in their journals or on a stick-on note they can post at their workplaces: "In this paper I intend to [statement of purpose], so that my audience, [describe intended readers], will [desired result]." This sentence reminds students to consider purpose, audience, and desired results as they write, and it should lead to clearer thesis statements.

COLLABORATIVE LEARNING Thesis statement Have students write their thesis statements on large sheets of paper. Exchange thesis lists among groups, and have each group analyze and suggest revisions for the theses on their lists. The revising group should be prepared to explain its suggestions to the original writers.

In the later stages of their projects have students repeat this exercise as they read one another's drafts. In this case, groups should check to make sure that each student's thesis accurately represents the crucial project of his or her paper.

The evolving thesis Remind students that the thesis of a research paper can change. As they conduct their research and write their papers, they may find that their purpose, opinion, or conception of their audience has shifted. In such circumstances, revising the thesis is not only desirable but necessary to compose an effective paper.

ANSWERS

EXERCISE 46.1 Developing a thesis statement (p. 640)
Individual response.

46b Creating a structure

CLASSROOM IDEAS

A dozen hats unused Reassure students that they're not the only researchers who find interesting information that just doesn't fit in their final work. Historian Barbara Tuchman reports that while researching *The Guns of August*, she discovered that Emperor Franz Joseph gave his wife the same birthday present each year: a dozen hats, which he required her to wear. Tuchman says that she moved the note card from stack to stack, trying to fit it in her 500-plus-page book; however, she finally had to relegate it to the stack marked "unused." Tuchman told this story in an essay she wrote a decade after *The Guns of August* was published—it took that long for her to find a place to use it. You might also encourage students to use a word processor's Footnote function to store information that doesn't seem immediately to fit into a draft in progress. When that draft gets printed out complete with footnotes or endnotes, the student has another opportunity to review the material and decide whether it should become a formal footnote or endnote, should be added in, or should be deleted.

COMPUTER ACTIVITY Outlining The informal outline will probably be less intimidating than the formal one for students who find outlining paralyzing. As an alternative, reluctant outliners who are using word-processing programs may be able to use automatic outlining features to create effective formal outlines.

ANSWERS

EXERCISE 46.2 Creating a structure (p. 643)
Individual response

46c Drafting the paper

INSTRUCTOR RESOURCE

The following Presentation Aid is available for download on this book's companion Web site at *http://www.ablongman.com/littlebrown*.

PRESENTATION AID 46.1: Tips for drafting a research paper (p. 643)

CLASSROOM IDEAS

The five-minute overview A variation on the short summary suggested in the text is the five-minute overview. Students (perhaps in their journals) try, in five minutes, to give readers as full an overview of the paper they intend to write as they can. This five-minute overview might then serve as a road map for creating a draft of the paper itself.

To avoid the initial anxiety of beginning a draft, have students bring in their notes and outlines and write for a full class period. Then ask students to go home and rework this initial piece of writing into a typed rough draft that they can share with their revision groups.

COLLABORATIVE LEARNING Rough drafts Let students work in groups to assess each paper draft and help the author find opportunities for new ideas, associations, or arrangements.

ANSWERS

EXERCISE 46.3 Drafting your paper (p. 644)
Individual response

46d Revising and editing the paper

A WRITER'S PERSPECTIVE

> *Intelligent, even fastidious revision . . . is, or certainly should be, an art in itself.* —JOYCE CAROL OATES

INSTRUCTOR RESOURCE

The following Presentation Aid is available for download on this book's companion Web site at *http://www.ablongman.com/littlebrown*.

PRESENTATION AID 46.2: Checklist for revising a research paper (p. 645)

CLASSROOM IDEAS

COLLABORATIVE LEARNING Revision outlines Some students will profit by using outlining as a revision strategy. Once students have written one or two drafts, have them work in pairs or small groups to outline their drafts, paying particular attention to connections between paragraphs and the presentation of major points.

COLLABORATIVE LEARNING Eleventh-hour theses Students can panic when it becomes clear in the final revision stages that the paper still lacks a crucial source or a strong thesis. You can prepare students for these moments by helping them to understand that papers often develop beyond the scope or direction of writers' original research, outlines, and planned theses. Taking advantage of these developments by finding an additional source or writing a new thesis statement is often the key to a successful revision.

COLLABORATIVE LEARNING   Exercises 46.4 and 46.5 Group work can be invaluable in the final stages covered by Exercises 46.4 and 46.5 by as students help one another revise, edit, and proofread. They can fine-tune thesis statements, hone arguments, and read drafts aloud to catch errors.

ANSWERS

EXERCISE 46.4 Revising and editing your paper (p. 646)

Individual response.

EXERCISE 46.5 Preparing and proofreading your final draft (p. 647)

Individual response.

46e Preparing and proofreading the final draft

RESOURCES AND IDEAS

Gallagher, Chris W. *Radical Departures: Composition and Progressive Pedagogy.* Urbana: NCTE, 2002. Gallagher advocates a composition pedagogy based upon shared knowledge building, collective action, and reflective inquiry, a pedagogy that includes community outreach.

Walvoord, B. E., V. J. Anderson, J. R. Breihan, L. P. McCarthy, S. M. Robinson, and A. K. Sherman. "Functions of Outlining Among College Students in Four Disciplines." *Research in the Teaching of English* 29 (1995): 390–421. This statistical study of the functions of outlining shows that students who produce successful papers tend to outline at several points in the drafting process.

CHAPTER 47

Using MLA Documentation and Format

CHAPTER HIGHLIGHTS

This chapter explains the procedure for documenting sources as stipulated by the Modern Language Association (MLA), conforming to the latest guidelines as specified by the *MLA Handbook for Writers of Research Papers*, 6th ed. (2003). Students are shown both how to document sources within the text using parenthetical citations and how to prepare a works-cited list for the end of the paper; indexes on pp. 649 and 658–59 provide quick reference to the models.

New graphic representations of book and article title and copyright pages, along with screenshots of online sources, show students exactly where to look for the information they need for citations. New models have been added for citing a variety of images as well as web log and web forum entries.

The following chapter provides two sample research papers in their entirety, with annotations showing correct application of MLA citation rules.

MEDIA RESOURCES FOR CHAPTER 47

mycomplab Please visit MyCompLab at *www.mycomplab.com* for more on the writing process.

http://www.ablongman.com/littlebrown ▶ See page 73 of this manual for companion Web site content description.

47a Using MLA in-text citations

CLASSROOM IDEAS

Basketball analogy Students frequently ask why there are so many different styles for them to learn. Use the analogy of basketball: while some rules are the same in all games (regular field goals count as two points, free throws one), others differ depending on the court and players. For instance, the three-point line is farther from the basket in professional basketball than it is in college. These different rules are designed to suit the abilities and expectations of players at each level. Likewise, different documentation systems are designed for the needs of each audience. The social sciences value the timeliness of information, so the date of publication is included in in-text citations and emphasized in references. The humanities value titles and authors' names, so humanities citations emphasize those elements.

COLLABORATIVE LEARNING Punctuation practice Give students the following sentences, but omit the citation punctuation. Ask them to work in small groups to punctuate them properly.

> In his biography of his father, Aram Saroyan notes that William Saroyan turned down a Pulitzer Prize, which "created far more publicity than the award itself had" (44).

> "The realization dawns simultaneously on the hero and the reader of the story alike", comments Aram Saroyan, "that the young man . . . is on the verge of a fatal swing, that he is working without a net" (31).

> Saroyan's outlook on life may have been shaped by his experience as a member of an ethnic minority:

>> Saroyan had known prejudice against Armenians at firsthand in his childhood: "For Sale" signs posted in front of houses with "No Armenians" written beneath in smaller letters; a grammar school teacher who complained to the class of the odor of spicy food on the Armenian children's breath. (72)

COMPUTER ACTIVITY Highlight the citations It is always a good practice to keep citation information together with cited content, but occasionally your students may find as they write that they want to use a quotation for which they have forgotten to find a page reference or are unsure of the spelling of the author's name. To avoid derailing their drafting process, they can put in a parenthetical in-text citation with as much information as they do have, highlight it in their word processor, and then go on drafting their paper. They can go back and find the missing information later.

47b Preparing the MLA list of works cited

INSTRUCTOR RESOURCES

The following Presentation Aids are available for download on this book's companion Web site at *http://www.ablongman.com/littlebrown*.

PRESENTATION AID 47.1: MLA works-cited page (p. 657)

PRESENTATION AID 47.2: Sample of MLA works cited: Book (p. 659)

PRESENTATION AID 47.3: Sample of MLA works cited: Article (p. 666)

PRESENTATION AID 47.4: Sample of MLA works cited: Electronic Sources (p. 671)

CLASSROOM IDEAS

A handy list Students might want to keep a copy of the list of possible elements of an online source handy when they are researching, so that as they record information about the source they have a quick checklist of what to look for.

COMPUTER ACTIVITY The importance of dates To get your students to understand the critical importance of including the posting and access dates for an online source, remind them that Web pages and other electronic documents can be changed easily. A reader trying to locate an electronic text cited in a research paper may find that the text has changed since the author of the paper visited that site. Ask students to keep an eye out for examples of this phenomenon as they conduct their research, and to bring those examples to the attention of the rest of the class.

COMPUTER ACTIVITY Citation as evaluation In a networked classroom, you can easily give students practice in getting citation information from online sources by displaying them on-screen. You can point out to students that the information they gather for citations helps them to evaluate the source. (For more on evaluating sources for research papers, see 42c.)

COLLABORATIVE LEARNING Preparing citations Divide students into teams of three. Have the first student take five entries from the second student's working bibliography and make up correct MLA citations for them. Ask the third student to check the first student's work. This activity allows students to confer on citations that puzzle them and to get help learning the fine points (such as where the periods and quotation marks go).

COLLABORATIVE LEARNING Exercise 47.1 Have students work through Exercise 47.1 individually, and then give them the opportunity to discuss and revise their entries in small groups. This process will allow students to develop specific questions about correct bibliographic form and then address them in a supportive setting.

As a follow-up, have students list their own sources in correct bibliographic form, making note of entries that pose unusual classification or citation challenges. Ask them to send those entries to the rest of the class by e-mail, so that their classmates can see how they resolved the challenge.

ANSWERS

EXERCISE 47.1 Writing works-cited entries (pp. 686–87)
The citations below are in MLA style and are alphabetized.

Eggert, Wayne G. "State and Local Sales/Use Tax Simplification." The Sales Tax in the Twenty-First Century. Ed. Matthew N. Murray and William F. Fox. Westport: Praeger, 2004. 67-80.

Granfield, Anne. "Taxing the Internet." Forbes 17 Dec. 2003: 56-68.

The Internet Tax Freedom Home Page. 3 June 2005. 2 Nov. 2002 <http://cox.house.gov/nettax/frmain.htm>.

James, Nora. E-mail interview. 1 Nov. 2005.

Osborne, Sally G. All's Fair in Internet Commerce, or Is It? New York: Random, 2004.

United States. Advisory Commission on Electronic Commerce. Report to Congress. Apr. 2005. 12 Nov. 2005 <http://www.ecommercecommission.org/report.htm>.

Zimmerman, Malai, and Kent Hoover. "Use of Third Parties to Collect State and Local Taxes on Internet Sales." Pacific Business Journal 5.2 (2004): 45-48.

47c Using MLA document format

CLASSROOM IDEAS

COLLABORATIVE LEARNING Document check Have students check one another's papers to make sure they conform to MLA document format. They can check papers on computer, but it is also a good idea to have them check a print copy.

COMPUTER ACTIVITY MLA templates Create a template for an MLA document for your students, and put it online where they can easily access it whenever they need to. Alternatively, have students create the template and keep it on the hard drive of their computers.

RESOURCES AND IDEAS

National Council of Writing Program Administrators. "Defining and Avoiding Plagiarism: The WPA Statement on Best Practices." 2003 <http://www.wpacouncil.org>. A clear statement from an authoritative professional body on what plagiarism is and is not.

Price, Margaret. "Beyong 'Gotcha!': Situating Plagiarism in Policy and Pedagogy." *College Compositions and Communication* 54 (September 2002): 85–115. Price reviews current scholarship on plagiarism and offers practical advice on helping students understand and hence forestall the growing tendency to plagiarize.

CHAPTER 48

Two Research Papers in MLA Style

CHAPTER HIGHLIGHTS

This chapter contains annotated versions of Edward Begay's and Vanessa Haley's final research papers for students to examine and discuss. Even if your students are not yet able to produce papers as strong as the ones in this chapter, they may find it helpful to have concrete examples to emulate. Both papers are presented as papers-in-progress throughout the chapters in Part 9; if your students have read Chapters 42-47, they will be able to trace the processes by which Begay and Haley arrived at their final papers. You can also discuss the papers in terms of the rhetorical features and mechanical requirements of good research writing.

You might want to begin by asking your students to respond to either or both of the papers in their journals and to discuss their responses in small groups. Students may have strong opinions about these final drafts. Both papers are effective, but neither is perfect, so you can ask your students to reflect upon any aspect of the final drafts that surprised them, how they themselves would have written the paper differently, or what, as readers, they would like to see added, omitted, or changed.

MEDIA RESOURCES FOR CHAPTER 48

mycomplab[20] Please visit MyCompLab at *www.mycomplab.com* for more on the writing process.

MODEL OF STUDENT WRITING

"Closing the Digital Divide" Edward Begay's paper is an example of a successful student effort at research writing. One of its best features, and one which you may want to discuss at some length with your students, is the balance between argument and presentation of evidence. Students who are new to research may have trouble determining how much of the research paper is meant to be reportage. Some may get so caught up in reporting evidence that they lose track of their argument; others may produce an argument paper based upon insufficient research. You can emphasize for your students that Begay's outline sketches the argument, not the evidence, and that using an outline is one of the best ways to make sure that a research paper is more than a mere report. You can also point out that Begay's argument arose and evolved out of his research and that he worked hard to shape his paper and make it argument-driven.

Another strength of this paper is the deftness of its transitions. Begay connects chunks of his research logically and astutely. The first major pivot occurs on page 3 of his paper (see comment 13) where he begins to make his argument for improved Internet access in public libraries. The second pivot occurs on page 4 of his paper (see comment 20). Here, Begay turns his attention to schools, arguing that they need not only improved Internet access but also improved quality of use from a pedagogical perspective. The third pivot, occurring on page 9 of his paper (see comment 39) begins the final section of the paper, in which Begay discusses the role of government and business in bridging the digital divide.

You can also use this paper to discuss the mechanical issues associated with research writing, from the introduction of quoted material to citation style to page layout. The annotations provide detailed comments on all these features, and a variety of electronic sources for the paper gives students examples of proper citation of such sources.

COLLABORATIVE LEARNING Using the commentary technique The commentary on Begay's paper is very comprehensive and addresses content, structure, and mechanics. Your students may benefit from practicing this holistic method. Give them a short research-based article of your choice and have them work as partners or in small groups to evaluate the essay using the commentary method demonstrated in this chapter. In earlier chapters of the handbook, commentary focuses on discrete elements of writing one at a time. But as student writers become more experienced, it will be helpful for them to be able to expand their focus. Try having them make one pass for content, one for structure, one for grammar and mechanics, and one for citations.

MODEL OF STUDENT WRITING

"Annie Dillard's Healing Vision" Vanessa Haley's paper is a good example of a short essay with limited outside research. Students who are new to critical writing often have difficulty establishing their own position in contradistinction to those of other critics. In her paper, Haley has accomplished the delicate task of drawing upon the perspectives of critics while articulating her own unique perspective, and you may want to spend some time discussing this with your students. You could even ask them to read the same outside sources Haley read and then to evaluate how successful she was in distinguishing her own point of view from those of the other critics.

This paper also features a sophisticated introduction, in which Haley identifies two reductive and mutually opposed points of view about nature and rejects them both in favor of a third alternative. You can use this paragraph as an example of writing that goes beyond binary thinking. You may also find that your students want to talk about Haley's contention that human civilization is a part of nature—it's an interesting, debatable claim, one that Haley wields well but that may be controversial in your classroom.

COLLABORATIVE LEARNING Analyzing the papers Break students into four groups and have each group compare one of the following aspects of Begay's and Haley's papers: rhetorical strategy, structure, appropriateness of sources, and introduction of borrowed material.

COMPUTER ACTIVITY Hypertext commentary The numbered comments that go with Begay's paper and the marginal comments on Haley's paper can provide your students with a model of how readers (including you) evaluate papers. They can practice this sort of holistic critique and commentary on one another's papers. Have them trade computer files of their papers with a partner. Have each partner provide commentary on the other's paper, using the commentary in this chapter as a model. They can either insert comments (highlighted or in a different color) directly into the text, or they can use the Comment function of their word processor.

RESOURCES AND IDEAS

Soles, Derek. "Grading as a Teaching Strategy." *Teaching English in the Two-Year College* 29 (December 2001): 122–34. Grading supports process instruction when teachers grade drafts, grade with colleagues, comment in a positive and encouraging voice, and share with students their evaluative criteria.

PART 10

Writing in the Disciplines

CHAPTER 49
Working with the Goals and Requirements of the Disciplines

CHAPTER 50
Reading and Writing About Literature

CHAPTER 51
Writing in Other Humanities

CHAPTER 52
Writing in the Social Sciences

CHAPTER 53
Writing in the Natural and Applied Sciences

Working with the Goals and Requirements of the Disciplines

A WRITER'S PERSPECTIVE

If no one knows what you have done, then you have done nothing. —ATTRIBUTED TO MICHEL DE MONTAIGNE

CHAPTER HIGHLIGHTS

Students in their first semester of college are already learning that they will have to write in most of their classes, not just in their English classes. This new pressure can be overwhelming because students most likely will be required to use writing to show their professors what they know. Chapter 49 introduces Part 10 by reminding students that writing can be a powerful tool for learning in all disciplines. While each discipline has its own conventions and expectations, students should see that the foundations of each lie in critical thinking, reading, and writing and in the process of communicating what has been learned. Chapters 50-53 discuss conventions for writing and documentation in specific disciplines and present sample student papers as illustrations.

MEDIA RESOURCES FOR CHAPTER 49

mycomplab Please visit MyCompLab at *www.mycomplab.com* for more on the writing process.

http://www.ablongman.com/littlebrown ▶ See page 73 of this manual for companion Web site content description.

INSTRUCTOR RESOURCE

The following Presentation Aid is available for download on this book's companion Web site at *http://www.ablongman.com/littlebrown*.

PRESENTATION AID 49.1: Guidelines for academic writers (p. 733)

RESOURCES AND IDEAS

Bartholomae, David. "Inventing the University." *When a Writer Can't Write*. Ed. Mike Rose. New York: Guilford, 1985. 134–65. For Bartholomae, mastering the various specialized discourses of the academic community is an essential part of being a college student but is also a gradual process that is likely to pass through several stages, each more closely approximating the work of thinking and writing that characterizes a discipline.

Fulwiler, Toby, and Art Young, eds. *Programs That Work: Models and Methods for Writing Across the Curriculum*. Upper Montclair: Boynton/Cook, 1990. Teachers describe how writing has been incorporated throughout the disciplines at their fourteen institutions nationwide.

Herrington, Anne, and Charles Moran, eds. *Writing, Teaching, and Learning in the Disciplines*. New York: MLA, 1992. The essays in this collection examine the "history, theory, practice, and prospects" of writing across the curriculum.

Kerr, Nancy H., and Madeleine Picciotto. "Linked Composition Courses: Effects on Student Performance." *Journal of Teaching Writing* 11.1 (1992): 105–28. The authors use a case study at Oglethorpe University to show the pros and cons of linking writing courses to introductory courses in the disciplines—a currently popular WAC approach.

Walvoord, Barbara E. "The Future of WAC." *College English* 58.1 (1996): 58–79. Walvoord, a long-time WAC program administrator, examines the challenges facing this "movement," including its relationship to other programs and institutions and its role in assessment.

Wiley, Mark. "The Popularity of Formulaic Writing (and Why We Need to Resist)." *English Journal* 62 (September 2000): 61–67. Wiley argues that some instruction in formulaic writing is appropriate because many standardized tests require the extemporaneous writing of an essay.

49b Understanding writing assignments

CLASSROOM IDEA

COLLABORATIVE LEARNING Clarifying assignments Many students have trouble identifying the primary expectations of some assignments. It is important for students to learn to read assignments carefully and to learn to ask teachers for more information when the assignment is unclear. Have students bring in paper assignments from previous and current courses. Choose a selection of assignments from various disciplines and photocopy them for the class. Then ask students to work in small groups to highlight the primary expectations of each assignment, consider the goal implied by the assignment, and make lists of additional questions that might help clarify each assignment further. As groups present their findings, you might also generate a discussion of the similarities and differences in expectations across the disciplines.

49c   Using tools and language

A WRITER'S PERSPECTIVE _____

Has not every one of us struggled for words, although the connection between "things" was already clear?

—ALBERT EINSTEIN

CLASSROOM IDEA

Discipline styles Divide students into groups according to their intended majors (humanities majors, business majors, and so on). Send them to the library to survey professional journals in their intended fields and discover what style(s) of documentation these journals require. (The style is often found in an "Instructions to Authors" section, usually located somewhere near the table of contents.) Ask groups to report their discoveries to the class.

49d   Following styles for source citations and document format

RESOURCES AND IDEAS

Anderson, Worth, et al. "Cross-Curricular Underlife: A Collaborative Report on Ways with Academic Words." *College Composition and Communication* 41 (1990): 11–36. A research project by faculty and students revealed that the content of a typical first-year composition course had little in common with the type of writing expected in introductory courses within the disciplines.

Astin, Alexander. *What Matters in College?* San Francisco: Jossey-Bass, 1993. Astin argues that both the number of writing courses students take and the number of courses that require writing strongly affect students' general knowledge, skills, and success in college.

McCleod, Susan, and Elaine Maimon. "Clearing the Air: WAC Myths and Realities." *College English* 62 (May 2000): 573–83. The authors provide an excellent summary of why WAC programs fail and discuss model programs.

Palmquist, Mike. "A Brief History of Commputer Support for Writing Centers and Writing-Across-the Curriculum Programs." *Computers and Composition* 20.4 (2003): 395–413. Palmquist reviews the literature on the efficacy or lack thereof of the use of computers in writing centers and WAC programs.

CHAPTER 50

Reading and Writing About Literature

CHAPTER HIGHLIGHTS

In classes where literature is studied, there's a temptation to spend more time talking about literature and less time writing about it, which can be counterproductive to the goals of a writing class. To keep students developing positively, this chapter stresses using the processes of critical reading, thinking, and writing skills as a way of analyzing imaginative writing. It also focuses on helping students to transfer the skills they have worked on throughout their writing course to other courses and purposes. The chapter covers different kinds of writing assignments about literature and points students to a wide variety of library and online resources for research. It also takes students through the process of researching and drafting essays about literature and includes sample student essays on works of fiction, poetry, and drama.

MEDIA RESOURCES FOR CHAPTER 50

mycomplab Please visit MyCompLab at *www.mycomplab.com* for more on the writing process.

http://www.ablongman.com/littlebrown ▶ See page 73 of this manual for companion Web site content description.

RESOURCES AND IDEAS

Bawarshi, Aris. "The Genre Function." *College English* 62 (2000): 335–60. Bawarshi explores genre as constitutive of texts, authors, readers, and social identity and argues against the privileging of literary texts by teachers.

Gould, Christopher. "Literature in the Basic Writing Course: A Bibliographic Survey." *College English* 49 (1987): 558–74. Gould provides a survey of "easily accessible materials that relate to the use of literature" in introductory courses.

Hayes, John R., Jill A. Hatch, and Christine M. Silk. "Does Holistic Assessment Predict Writing Performance? Estimating the Consistency of Student Performance on Holistically Scored Writing Assignments." *Written Communication* 17 (January 2000): 3–26. The authors report on their study that indicates considerable divergence in the grades of some 800 student essays, holistically graded by experts.

Lindemann, Erika. "Freshman Composition: No Place for Literature." *College English* 55 (1993): 311–16. Lindemann warns that using literature in composition classes may lead to a deemphasis on student writing; she includes useful advice for class design.

Lynn, Steven. *Texts and Contexts: Writing About Literature with Critical Theory*. New York: HarperCollins, 1994. Lynn introduces a number of critical approaches from New Criticism through deconstruction to feminist studies, and he brings all methods to bear on a selected group of texts to demonstrate how they might "open up" texts for students.

Reilly, Jill M., et al. "The Effects of Prewriting on Literary Interpretation." ERIC, 1986. ED 276 058. Reilly shows how focused prewriting exercises can lead students to write more effectively about literature.

Tate, Gary. "A Place for Literature in Freshman Composition." *College English* 55 (1993): 317–21. Tate argues that using literature makes student writers more aware of the resources implicit in language.

50a Using the methods and evidence of literary analysis

CLASSROOM IDEAS

No "right" or "wrong" Students tend to have tunnel vision about literary interpretation, believing there's only one "right way" to read a work. In guiding their reading and response, encourage them to see the multiple possibilities implicit in literary works. You might ask them to compose point-counterpoint readings of texts or to use a text like Steven Lynn's *Texts and Contexts* (reference above) to construct a spectrum of responses to the literature they are reading. A consistent use of group workshops in which students discuss their varying responses to a literary text can also help students to recognize the multiplicity of possible responses.

Looking back Remind students of the reasons they have been keeping journals throughout your course. You may want to encourage them to review 2a-1 as they begin keeping a reading journal.

COLLABORATIVE LEARNING Analyzing passages Have students work in small groups to analyze a key passage from Kate Chopin's "The Story of an Hour." Ask each group to consider the appropriate questions provided by the handbook: Does the passage reveal a significant move in the plot? Does it explore a key development for one of the characters? What evidence of point of view and tone are available in the passage? Does it contain imagery or symbolism? Then have each group give their analysis of the passage. Where student readings differ markedly, encourage those groups to find additional evidence for their readings.

COLLABORATIVE LEARNING Finding themes Divide the class into several groups and have each group brainstorm about the many themes that occur in a particular work. Choose Kate Chopin's "The Story of an Hour" or another short work from an anthology. Have each group explain its three favorite themes to the rest of the class, supplying evidence for each theme with one or two explicated passages from the piece.

COMPUTER ACTIVITY Continuations Post the opening paragraph of a published short story on the class network and ask students to continue of the story, keeping in mind the expectations about plot, character, setting, and tone that have been set up by that opening paragraph. Have students "publish" the resulting stories on the network, and lead a discussion about the different choices that various students made in their continuations, the elements in the original paragraph that they picked up on or discarded, and the extent to which the tone of the original was maintained or parodied. Encourage students to talk about the elements that they noticed in the original paragraph as they created their continuations.

Incorporating evidence Students are often confused about how to incorporate source material into a literary analysis. Duplicate a short passage from a literary analysis, but remove the documentation. Have students decide where documentation is needed. You might also duplicate or contrive a passage with awkwardly long quotations and ask the class how to trim or paraphrase them to make the passage more effective.

RESOURCES AND IDEAS

Biddle, Arthur W., and Toby Fulwiler, eds. *Reading, Writing, and the Study of Literature*. New York: McGraw, 1989. This collection of essays details many ways of introducing students to various methods of literary interpretation; the authors provide extensive bibliographies.

Lentricchia, Frank, and Thomas McLaughlin. *Critical Terms for Literary Study*. Chicago: U of Chicago P, 1989. The authors have compiled twenty-two cogent essays defining key terms in light of contemporary theory.

Rockas, Leo. *Ways In: Analyzing and Responding to Literature*. Upper Montclair: Boynton/Cook, 1984. Rockas offers students a number of ways of beginning the work of literary analysis, providing numerous examples and exercises.

50b Understanding writing assignments in literature

CLASSROOM IDEA

COLLABORATIVE LEARNING First steps If your students are not used to writing about literature, you might start them off by assigning a personal response paper, followed by a book review. You might also ask them to see a play on campus and then work together in small groups to outline a theater review.

50c Using the tools and language of literary analysis

CLASSROOM IDEAS

The mystique of literature Most students will need to be convinced that critical thinking, reading, and writing skills can be transferred to literature. Students sometimes acquire the attitude that literature is somehow "untouchable," that it is "special," different from other works they read. Work through Janet Vong's critical strategies (pp. 739–40) with your students to help them understand how the skills they've developed will enable them to read and write about literature.

COLLABORATIVE LEARNING Tenses Students sometimes have trouble making their prose conform to the conventions of tense usage in critical writing about literature. To get them used to these conventions, have students review each other's drafts and make suggestions for revision of tense usage.

COLLABORATIVE LEARNING Sources To help students become familiar with the literary research sources listed in the text (pp. 744–45), have each student look up one source (either a library source or a Web source) and make a brief presentation on it in class.

50e Drafting and revising a literary analysis

CLASSROOM IDEAS

COLLABORATIVE LEARNING Developing a thesis Ask each student to develop a thesis about Kate Chopin's "The Story of an Hour" or another short work from an anthology, and to compile evidence for that thesis. Then have students work in small groups to debate their various theses and the validity of the evidence.

COLLABORATIVE LEARNING Plot summaries Give your students a short story to read, and ask them to work in small groups to write a brief plot summary. See which group can come up with the most economical summary.

MODEL OF STUDENT WRITING

"Ironies of Life in Kate Chopin's 'The Story of an Hour'" The final draft of Janet Vong's paper on Kate Chopin's "The Story of an Hour" is a fine model of the short literary analysis, and you may wish to spend some time discussing it with students. It features a creative thesis and a tightly organized, economical development. Students who have little experience writing about literature sometimes organize their papers to match the progression of the text they are analyzing instead of around the development of their thesis statements. If your students have this difficulty, they may find it particularly helpful to see that Vong's paper moves from the least important to the most important of her arguments and that in presenting evidence she moves back and forth from the beginning to the end of Chopin's story.

You might also want to use Chopin's story to talk about irony, a literary device students sometimes have difficulty identifying. Vong does a particularly nice job of discussing how readers may come to a deeper understanding of Chopin's story as its ironic implications sink in.

COLLABORATIVE LEARNING Opening paragraph Students can learn a great deal about the choices a writer makes in creating a piece of fiction by writing fiction of their own. Ask each student to create a one-paragraph opening for a short story; then have students work in small groups to analyze their fictional paragraphs. What does each opening paragraph reveal about the kind of story being told—will it be comic, tragic, realistic, supernatural? What expectations does the opening set up about the characters and events that will follow? What questions does it raise?

As a follow-up to this exercise, ask each group to turn back to the Kate Chopin story and analyze its one-sentence opening with some of the same questions in mind. Having read the story, students may be surprised to find how much they can deduce from that seemingly simple statement.

50f Writing about fiction, poetry, and drama

A WRITER'S PERSPECTIVE

> *A poem is a perhaps.*   —IVOR WILLIAMS
>
> *You can tear a poem apart to see what makes it technically tick . . . but you come back to the mystery of having been moved by words.*   —DYLAN THOMAS

INSTRUCTOR RESOURCES

The following Presentation Aids are available for download on this book's companion Web site at *http://www.ablongman.com/littlebrown*.

PRESENTATION AID 50.1: Questions for analyzing fiction (p. 751)

PRESENTATION AID 50.2: Questions for analyzing poetry (p. 753)

PRESENTATION AID 50.3: Questions for analyzing drama (p. 755)

CLASSROOM IDEAS

MODEL OF STUDENT WRITING

"Marking Time Versus Enduring in Gwendolyn Brooks's 'The Bean Eaters'"
Gwendolyn Brooks's "The Bean Eaters" may strike students as being so

quotidian in its language and subject as to defy interpretation. Particularly if they are new to literary interpretation, students may not be sensitive to the nuances a single word or phrase can carry and may think that critics like Kenneth Scheff and those he quotes read too much into poetry. If your students feel this way, try having several of them read the poem aloud in class to see if their readings come across in different ways. Ask them to try to see how much they can affect the meaning of the poem by reading it aloud in as many different ways as possible.

You can also use Scheff's paper to talk about how to incorporate the perspectives of other critics in one's own interpretations. Scheff's paper is strong overall, but you might ask your students if they think he has differentiated his own perspective sufficiently from those of his critics or whether his interpretation is too derivative of those he cites. Ask them to suggest ways Scheff could strengthen his argument.

Drama onstage Many students have only read dramas in literature classes and have never seen them acted. If your campus or local library has videotapes of the dramas you are studying, arrange to show scenes (or even the entire work) to the class. Many students are genuinely shocked to see and hear how performers interpret (i.e., analyze) dramatic works, and their resulting papers often benefit from the insights they gain by watching performances.

COLLABORATIVE LEARNING Performing a scene Break the class into small groups and ask each group to perform a scene from a play for their classmates. You can allow students to bring in props or encourage them to make their interpretations through voice and gesture. Then ask the rest of the class to analyze the group's interpretation. What aspects did the group emphasize, and why?

MODEL OF STUDENT WRITING

"Macbeth as Hero" Michael Spinter's paper on *Macbeth* is strong in both argumentation and organization. Spinter makes an excellent case for his claim that Macbeth is heroic. Your students may wish to discuss this claim, and you can ask them whether they find Spinter's arguments persuasive. If they don't think Spinter is persuasive, ask them what he could have done to make his case stronger, or how they would suggest he modify his thesis.

You may also want to use this paper to talk about matters of structure. It takes a skillful writer to make a paper work with a thesis positioned at the end. Ask your students whether they think it works in Michael Spinter's paper or whether he would have been better off putting the thesis at the beginning, and ask them to justify their opinions.

Finally, you might ask students to reflect upon all three sample papers in this chapter (Janet Vong's, Kenneth Scheff's, and Michael Spinter's) and to compare and contrast their respective strengths and weaknesses.

RESOURCES AND IDEAS

Barnet, Sylvan, and William Cain. *A Short Guide to Writing About Literature*. 10th ed. New York: Longman, 2006.

Bizzaro, Patrick. *Responding to Student Poems: Applications of Critical Theory*. Urbana: NCTE, 1993. See Chapter 7 in particular for a discussion of having students read and produce poetry as complementary activities (159–91).

Hollander, John. *Rhyme's Reason: A Guide to English Verse*. 3rd ed. New Haven: Yale UP, 2001. Hollander offers a brief guide to poetry analysis, with amusing examples and some innovative analysis strategies.

Rockas, Leo. *Ways In: Analyzing and Responding to Literature*. Upper Montclair: Boynton/Cook, 1984. Chapters 4–6 offers examples of and exercises for writing about fiction, poetry, and drama.

Suchet, David. "Caliban in The Tempest." *Players of Shakespeare*. Ed. Philip Brockbank. Cambridge: Cambridge UP, 1985. 167–79. Suchet, an experienced Shakespearean actor, shows how he reads and rereads a drama to find the clues that lead him to create a character.

Writing in
Other Humanities

CHAPTER HIGHLIGHTS

Chapter 51 gives students some of the essentials they need to know about writing in history and the other humanities. The opening discussions define the operations of explanation, analysis, interpretation, synthesis, and evaluation and explain writing tools and language conventions. Next, students are told about a wide variety of library and online resources for research. The chapter also includes sections on how to cite sources and format documents in the humanities according to *The Chicago Manual of Style*.

MEDIA RESOURCES FOR CHAPTER 51

mycomplab²⁰ Please visit MyCompLab at *www.mycomplab.com* for more on the writing process.

http://www.ablongman.com/littlebrown ▶ See page 73 of this manual for companion Web site content description.

51a Using the methods and evidence of the humanities

CLASSROOM IDEA

Not just the facts Students may need to be persuaded that writing history is an interpretive endeavor and not merely a matter of recording facts. To help students understand that historians construct the past as they write about it, bring to class two brief accounts of a single historical incident written by two different writers. Let your students evaluate how the inclusion or exclusion of data, the organization, and the narrative style used by the writer influence the reader's understanding of the "facts."

RESOURCES AND IDEAS

Anson, Chris, M. "Response and the Social Construction of Error." *Assessing Writing* 7 (2000): 5–21. Anson suggests teachers reflect upon the significance of their response to errors students make in their writing, because the rules that govern language use change as social contexts evolve.

Bawarshi, Anis. "The Genre Function." *College English* 62.3 (2000): 335–60. Bawarshi shows how the genre in which a text is written influences the composing process and shapes ways readers responds to the text.

Beyer, Barry K. "Using Writing to Learn in History." *The History Teacher* 13 (1980): 167–78. Beyer suggests using writing not only to seek and report information but to help students understand the ways of thinking characteristic of historians.

MacNealy, Mary Sue. *Strategies for Empirical Research in Writing.* Needham Heights, MA: Allyn & Bacon, 1999. An introduction to research methods in the humanities, geared for students but useful to teachers as well.

Thelin, William H. "Understanding Problems in Critical Classrooms." *College Composition and Communication* 57 (September 2005): 114–41. The author offers a defense of critical pedagogy in the face of mounting criticism against it.

Tuchman, Barbara. *Practicing History: Selected Essays.* New York: Knopf, 1981. Tuchman demonstrates and gives practical recommendations for analytic writing in history.

Weisser, Christian. *Moving Beyond Academic Discourse: Composition Studies and the Public Sphere.* Carbondale: Southern Illinois UP, 2002. Weisser argues that student writing will improve if students do more nonacademic writing for specific audiences.

51b Understanding writing assignments in the humanities

RESOURCES AND IDEAS

Additional resources for students

If your students need more help in writing for the humanities, you might refer them to the following:

Barnet, Sylvan. *A Short Guide to Writing About Art.* 6th ed. New York: Longman, 1999.

Bellman, Jonathon. *A Short Guide to Writing About Music.* New York, Longman, 2000.

Corrigan, Timothy. *A Short Guide to Writing About Film.* 5th ed. New York: Longman, 2004.

Marius, Richard. *A Short Guide to Writing About History.* 5th ed. New York: Longman, 2005.

Steffens, Henry, and MaryJane Dickerson. *Writer's Guide: History.* Boston: Heath, 1987.

51c Using the tools and language of the humanities

CLASSROOM IDEAS

COLLABORATIVE LEARNING Writing assignments Ask students to bring in examples of writing assignments from their other humanities courses and to classify them according to the list on page 760. Which are most and least frequently used? Students might also interview professors from their other courses, individually or in teams, to learn which writing strategies are most important for success in those courses

COLLABORATIVE LEARNING Tenses Students sometimes have trouble making judgments about which tense to use in historical writing. To get them used to conventions of tense usage, have students review each other's drafts and suggest revisions.

Sources To help students become familiar with the humanities research sources listed in the text (pp. 761–64), have each student look up one source (either a library source or a Web source) and make a brief presentation on it in class.

51d Citing sources in Chicago style

CLASSROOM IDEAS

COLLABORATIVE LEARNING Preparing citations Divide students into teams of three. Have the first student take five entries from the second student's working bibliography and make up correct Chicago citations for them. Ask the third student to check the first student's work. This activity allows students to confer on citations that puzzle them and to get help learning the fine points (such as where the periods and quotation marks go).

COMPUTER ACTIVITY Numbering and formatting notes Students who write on computers will be able to number and format footnotes and endnotes automatically. Remind these students that such word-processing programs usually have a Setup or Options menu that they can adjust to make the footnote or endnote print out with proper spacing, note numbers, and so forth.

51e Formatting documents in Chicago style

CLASSROOM IDEA

COLLABORATIVE LEARNING Document check Have students format a draft of a paper in Chicago style, print it out, and bring it to class. Have partners check each other's papers and make recommendations for any necessary revisions in format.

Writing in the Social Sciences

CHAPTER HIGHLIGHTS

Chapter 52 begins by introducing students to research methods in the social sciences, including observation, interviewing, survey conducting, and experimentation. It also covers the distinction between quantitative and qualitative data, types of social science assignments, writing tools, and language conventions. Updated resources for research in the various disciplines, including both print and online resources, are listed in 52c. Section 52d explains to students how to cite sources in the social sciences according to American Psychological Association (APA) standards. This section includes expanded coverage of how to document online and media sources. Section 52e shows students how to format documents using APA style. The chapter concludes with excerpts from a sample student paper for a sociology course.

MEDIA RESOURCES FOR CHAPTER 52

mycomplab Please visit MyCompLab at *www.mycomplab.com* for more on the writing process.

http://www.ablongman.com/littlebrown ▶ See page 73 of this manual for companion Web site content description.

52a Using the methods and evidence of the social sciences

INSTRUCTOR RESOURCE

The following Presentation Aid is available for download on this book's companion Web site at *http://www.ablongman.com/littlebrown*.

PRESENTATION AID 52.1: Conducting a survey (p. 779)

CLASSROOM IDEAS

COMPUTER ACTIVITY Qualitative and quantitative data To help your students become more familiar with the two kinds of data, have them conduct a brief study of a topical conversation while lurking on an online discussion (but not a synchronous one). Ask them to choose a collection of postings from the discussion (a day's worth, perhaps) and to gather some statistical data about the conversation (for instance, the number of participants, the number of times a word or phrase is mentioned, or the number of participants adhering to each opinion stated). After amassing the data, they can graph it and post the graph to your class Web site. Then ask them to go back over the same collection of postings and write a qualitative description of them in the style of one of the social science disciplines.

COMPUTER ACTIVITY Links to examples Go online to locate good published examples of each of the kinds of papers listed in 50b: a research summary, a case analysis, a problem-solving analysis, a research paper, and a research report. Download them or post links on your class Web site so that students can have models easily available to them.

RESOURCES AND IDEAS

Bazerman, Charles. *The Informed Writer: Using Sources in the Disciplines*. 5th ed. Boston: Houghton, 1995. Bazerman offers a number of examples and exercises to help students learn the discourse conventions of various academic disciplines.

College Composition and Communication 36 (1985). All four numbers of this volume are devoted to the role(s) writing plays in professional and academic disciplines; numbers 2 and 4 are particularly rich.

Daemmrich, Ingrid. "A Bridge to Academic Discourse: Social Science Research Strategies in the Freshman Composition Course." *College Composition and Communication* 40 (1989): 343–48. Daemmrich argues for use of social-science writing as a way to help students move from personal to academic writing.

Hemmeter, Thomas, and David Conners. "Research Papers in Economics: A Collaborative Approach." *Journal of Advanced Composition* 7 (1987): 81–91. The authors describe a course taught collaboratively by an economist and a writing specialist, focusing on activities leading to the term-ending research paper.

Shamoon, Linda K., and Robert A. Schwegler. "Sociologists Reading Student Texts: Expectations and Perceptions." *The Writing Instructor* 7 (1988): 71–81. The authors argue that the way sociologists perceive the features of a student paper differ considerably from the way composition instructors often perceive the features. Sociologists look first of all for a line of sociological reasoning carried through-out a paper, supported by evidence acceptable to sociologists and made clear by indicators such as topic sentences.

Further reading for your students

If your students need more help in writing for the social sciences, you might refer them to some of the following:

Becker, Howard S., et al. *Writing for Social Scientists: How to Start and Finish Your Thesis, Book, or Article*. Chicago: U of Chicago P, 1986.

Cuba, Lee. *A Short Guide to Writing About Social Science*. 4th ed. New York: Longman, 2002.

Dunn, Dana. *A Short Guide to Writing About Psychology*. New York: Longman, 2004.

Holland, Kenneth, and Arthur W. Biddle. *Writer's Guide: Political Science*. Lexington: Heath, 1987.

McCloskey, Donald. *The Writing of Economics*. New York: Macmillan, 1987.

Richlin-Klonsky, Judith, and Ellen Strenski, eds. *A Guide to Writing Sociology Papers*. 4th ed. New York: Worth, 1997.

52c Using the tools and language of the social sciences

CLASSROOM IDEAS

COLLABORATIVE LEARNING Smart questions Framing questions is one of the most important aspects of good social-science research, and students will need to apply their skills in critical thinking and in writing to the task of composing research questions and survey questions. Have your students practice question writing by conceiving a research question and then carrying out a small survey among the members of the class. Then have them work in small groups to look at survey results and evaluate each student's research and survey questions.

Research logs Encourage any student considering a career in research to keep a research log. Almost every company that employs researchers will require those workers to document each day's activities in a log in order to record and protect potentially patent-worthy research.

COLLABORATIVE LEARNING Classifying samples Ask students to bring in examples of writing assignments from their social-science courses and to classify them according to the list on page 780. They might also work in teams to interview professors from their other courses about which writing strategies are most important for success in those courses.

COLLABORATIVE LEARNING Language check Have students work in small groups to check each other's drafts for biased language and make suggestions for revision.

COLLABORATIVE LEARNING Sources To help students become familiar with the social-science research sources listed on pages 81–84, have each student look up one source and make a brief presentation on it in class.

COMPUTER ACTIVITY Reusable sources Students may want to bookmark one or more of the general Web sources listed on page 783, if those sources are ones students will reuse. You can also ask students to write a brief annotation of any source they find especially helpful. Annotations can be posted to your class Web site and your class can create its own annotated list of sources.

52d Citing sources in APA style

CLASSROOM IDEAS

The importance of research dates Remind students that since the social sciences prize the timeliness of research as much as the author's name, APA text citations combine name and date while references place the date just after the author's name. If students understand why a documentation system looks the way it does, they are more likely to learn how to use it correctly.

COLLABORATIVE LEARNING Preparing citations Divide students into teams of three. Have the first student take five entries from the second student's working bibliography and make up correct citations for them according to APA standards. Ask the third student to check the first student's work. This activity allows students to confer on citations that puzzle them and to get help learning the fine points (such as where the periods and quotation marks go).

COMPUTER ACTIVITY Online documentation clinic While your students are working on their own social-science research papers, you can hold an ongoing documentation clinic online. Students can post questions or citations they are unsure about to your class Web site or send them by group e-mail, and either you or other members of the class can respond with suggestions for proper citation.

52e Formatting documents in APA style

CLASSROOM IDEAS

COLLABORATIVE LEARNING Document check Have students format a draft of a paper in APA style, print it out, and bring it to class. Have partners check each other's papers and make recommendations for any necessary revisions in format.

COMPUTER ACTIVITY Templates for shortcuts If your students know that they will be producing a lot of social-science documents, they might want to create a document template on their word processor, including a title page, abstract page, body (including headings for method, results, illustrations, and discussion), and references. They can adapt the template as needed for individual papers, but if they include basic structural elements and formatting, they will not have to reproduce those for every paper.

52f Examining a sample social science paper

CLASSROOM IDEAS

MODEL OF STUDENT WRITING

"An Assessment of Dating Violence on Campus" Karen Tarczyk's paper may give your students a better idea of what their social-science professors will expect from their writing. Her report is well organized, and she uses unbiased language throughout. You may want to discuss the conciseness and clarity of her abstract, the way she sets up the central problem and reviews the relevant research, her presentation of methodology and results, and the cogency of her discussion and interpretation of results.

COLLABORATIVE LEARNING Approaching the topic The topic of Karen Tarczyk's paper and its findings about dating violence may be interesting to your students. They may have a lot to say about James Makepeace's contention that violence in dating relationships potentially leads to violence in later domestic relationships. If you have received other papers on the subject, you might bring them in to give students a sense of approaches to the topic. Then, have them work in groups to brainstorm ideas and questions for further research.

COMPUTER ACTIVITY Hypertext commentary Post a copy of Tarczyk's paper online, and have your students use the Comment function of their word processors to evaluate it section by section. You can also ask them to use this method on a partner's draft.

Writing in the Natural and Applied Sciences

CHAPTER HIGHLIGHTS

Chapter 53 introduces students to the essentials of writing in the natural and applied sciences. A brief discussion of the scientific method and empirical evidence begins the chapter, followed by discussions of types of science assignments (summaries, critiques, lab reports, research reports, and research proposals), writing tools, and language conventions. Library and online resources for research are listed, and there are sections on how to cite sources and format documents in the natural and applied sciences according to the style of the Council of Science Editors (CSE). The chapter concludes with excerpts from a sample student lab report for a biology course.

MEDIA RESOURCES FOR CHAPTER 53

mycomplab Please visit MyCompLab at *www.mycomplab.com* for more on the writing process.

http://www.ablongman.com/littlebrown ▶ See page 73 of this manual for companion Web site content description.

53a Using the methods and evidence of the sciences

RESOURCES AND IDEAS

Greenway, William. "Imaginary Gardens with Real Toads: Nature Writing in the Curriculum." *Teaching English in the Two-Year College* 17 (1990): 189–92. Greenway demonstrates that nature writing, such as Annie Dillard's personal essays and Wordsworth's poetry, can help prepare students to write scientific research papers.

Hamilton, David. "Writing Science." *College English* 40 (1978): 32–40. Hamilton argues that instruction in science writing should emphasize writing not simply as a tool for scientists but as an essential and creative part of the scientific act.

Vargas, Marjorie Fink. "Writing Skills for Science Labs." *The Science Teacher* 53.8 (1986): 29–33. The author describes a fifty-minute class activity that helps students understand choices of person and voice dictated by the stylistic conventions of lab reports.

Winsor, Dorothy A. "Engineering Writing/Writing Engineering." *College Composition and Communication* 41 (1990): 58–70. Winsor uses "contemporary views about the textual shaping of knowledge" to examine engineers' writing and their "domain-specific" knowledge.

Further reading for students

If your students need more help in writing about the sciences, you might refer them to these student texts:

Beall, Herbert, and John Trimbur. *A Short Guide to Writing About Chemistry.* 2nd ed. New York: Longman, 2001.

Day, Robert. *How to Write and Publish a Scientific Paper.* 5th ed. Phoenix: Oryx, 1995.

Pechenik, Jan. *A Short Guide to Writing About Biology.* 5th ed. New York: Longman, 2004.

Porush, David. *A Short Guide to Writing About Science.* New York: Longman, 1994.

53b Understanding writing assignments in the sciences

CLASSROOM IDEAS

Scientists as writers Students might think that good writing is not all that important in science. You can dispel this myth by pointing out that scientists need to be good critical thinkers and to wield language with power and accuracy in order to articulate their ideas and present their research.

COLLABORATIVE LEARNING Ask students to bring in examples of writing assignments from their science courses and to classify them according to the list on p. 808. Which assignments are most and least frequently used? They might also interview professors from their science courses, individually or in teams, to learn which writing strategies are most important for success in those courses.

53c Using the tools and language of the sciences

CLASSROOM IDEAS

COLLABORATIVE LEARNING Objective language Have students practice using objective language by observing some natural phenomenon out of doors and writing a paragraph based on their observations. Then let them work in small groups to check each other's drafts and make suggestions for revision.

COLLABORATIVE LEARNING Sources To help students become familiar with the science research sources listed on pp. 810–12, have each student look up one source (either a library source or a Web source) and make a brief presentation on it in class.

RESOURCES AND IDEAS

Ambron, Joanna. "Writing to Improve Learning in Biology." *Journal of College Science Teaching* 16 (1987): 263–66. Ambron shows how using journal entries, freewriting, and short ungraded essays contribute to improved analytical skills.

American Chemical Society. *ACS Style Guide: A Manual for Authors and Editors.* 2nd ed. Washington: ACS, 1997.

Dorroh, John. "Reflections on Expressive Writing in the Science Class." *The Quarterly of the National Writing Project and the Center for the Study of Writing and Literacy* 15.3 (1993): 28–30. Dorroh describes use of an "expressive mode" notebook, portfolio grading, and writing-based instruction to improve student performance.

Goodman, W. Daniel, and John C. Bean. "A Chemistry Laboratory Project to Develop Thinking and Writing Skills." *Journal of Chemical Education* 60 (1983): 483–84. The authors outline "a method for conducting an undergraduate chemistry laboratory, in this case sophomore organic chemistry, that integrates a project laboratory with a writing task involving peer group interaction." The method requires "students to carry out an independent investigation of the synthesis of one or more aliphatic esters and to present their research in the form of professional papers."

Johnstone, Anne C., et al. *Uses for Journal-Keeping: An Ethnography of Writing in a University Science Class.* Norwood: Ablex, 1994. Johnstone offers an ethnographic study of the uses of different writing activities in learning science.

Killingsworth, M. Jimmie, and Michael K. Gilbertson. *Signs, Genres, and Communities in Technical Communication.* Amityville: Baywood, 1992. An examination of reports, manuals, and proposals characterizes them as "crystals of social action" within particular discourse communities.

Olmsted, John III. "Teaching Varied Technical Writing Styles in the Upper Division Laboratory." *Journal of Chemical Education* 61 (1984): 798–800. Olmsted describes a course that asks students to prepare reports in a variety of styles on experiments they have conducted. He describes in detail the twelve different kinds of reports students must submit during the course.

Wilkinson, A. M. "Jargon and the Passive Voice: Prescriptions and Proscriptions for Scientific Writing." *Journal of Technical Writing and Communication* 22 (1992): 319–25. The author reviews circumstances under which scientific writers should use the passive and warns against sweeping prohibitions of this strategy.

Young, Art, and Toby Fulwiler. Writing *Across the Disciplines: Research into Practice*. Upper Montclair: Boynton/Cook, 1986. This collection contains a number of essays demonstrating writing assignments in the sciences.

53d Citing sources in CSE style

CLASSROOM IDEAS

COLLABORATIVE LEARNING Preparing citations Divide students into teams of three. Have the first student take five entries from the second student's working bibliography and make up correct citations for them according to CSE standards. Ask the third student to check the first student's work. This activity allows students to confer on citations that puzzle them and to get help learning the fine points (such as where the periods and quotation marks go).

COLLABORATIVE LEARNING Quick access to references Remind students that in mathematics and the natural and applied sciences, the hallmark of documentation is retrievability. Readers need to find references as easily as possible, since they may have to consider older work to interpret newer developments. The CSE's numerical system allows researchers to retrieve information quickly and easily. If students understand *why* the documentation works as it does, they will be better able to learn *how* to use it.

53f Examining a sample science paper

CLASSROOM IDEA

MODEL OF STUDENT WRITING

"Exercise and Blood Pressure" Liz Garson's paper on the effects of exercise on blood pressure is a properly documented and clearly written lab report, appropriately organized into sections (abstract, introduction, method, results, discussion, and references). Garson correctly uses the present tense when talking about established facts and the past tense when talking about her own research. She uses objective language and specialized vocabulary, properly conforming to the conventions of writing in biology. Students who have to write lab reports for their science courses may find Garson's paper helpful as a model of how to structure, write, and document their own reports.

PART 11

Special Writing Situations

CHAPTER **54**
Writing Online

CHAPTER **55**
Public Writing

CHAPTER **56**
Oral Presentations

Writing Online

CHAPTER HIGHLIGHTS

Chapter 54 provides up-to-date information about online writing from e-mail and online discussion to composing documents and Web sites. The degree of familiarity with online writing technology is likely to vary widely amongst your students. Some students may already have their own personal Web pages or blogs, while to others the process of creating Web pages may seem arcane and mysterious. For all students, this chapter covers essential skills needed to utilize online writing and collaboration tools and to participate appropriately online.

Students are first introduced to e-mail composition, netiquette, and methods of handling file attachments. Next, they are taught about two methods of online collaboration they are likely to use in their courses: online discussions and peer review of document drafts.

The second half of the chapter discusses how to create an original Web site. Topics covered include structure and content development, how to achieve good flow and ease of navigation, and the use of images, video, and sound on Web sites.

MEDIA RESOURCES FOR CHAPTER 54

mycomplab Please visit MyCompLab at *www.mycomplab.com* for more on the writing process.

`http://www.ablongman.com/littlebrown` ▶ See page 73 of this manual for companion Web site content description.

54a Writing effective electronic mail

CLASSROOM IDEAS

COMPUTER ACTIVITY Strategies for novices Students new to e-mail and/or the Web may find it difficult to master the technology, focus on a project, and fine-tune their etiquette all at once. You might want to give them a purely social topic the first time they send e-mail or chat messages, so that they can focus on getting comfortable with the software. Then they can begin working on group dynamics and writing collaboration.

COMPUTER ACTIVITY Filing mail Most e-mail programs allow you to make folders or mailboxes in which to store messages. Students might want to set up e-mail folders in which to keep incoming and outgoing mail on different topics or regarding different class projects.

COMPUTER ACTIVITY/COLLABORATIVE LEARNING E-mail and community Some teachers find that e-mail is an excellent tool for developing a sense of community and fostering dialogue among the members of their classes. Each small group can function as a study group and can stay in touch by e-mail. Larger conversations might include all the members of one class, or even members of different class sections.

COMPUTER ACTIVITY Composed messages If your students are using e-mail to request access to information from outside sources (institutions, archives, individuals, etc.) you may want to have them draft a polite e-mail request and circulate it to the class for comment before sending it out.

COMPUTER ACTIVITY Discretion and the group address It can be helpful to create a nickname the group members can all use to send mail to one another, with the complete list of email addresses linked to the nickname in each students electronic address book. But if groups use this shortcut method, they should be reminded to keep their electronic address books up to date: if a student drops out of the group, all other members should delete that student's address from the nickname list. New members of the group must be added to each other member's electronic address book to ensure they receive all group mailings.

COMPUTER ACTIVITY E-mail and courtesy It might be interesting for your students to think about why people incline to discourtesy online, either in their e-mail or when posting to electronic discussion groups. This topic might be especially useful when you teach audience, tone, or rhetorical stance. Ask students to bring in examples of discourteous discussion postings and suggest revisions that would change the tone of those postings.

RESOURCES AND IDEAS

Hawisher, Gail E., and Paul LeBlanc, eds. *Reimagining Computers and Composition: Teaching and Research in the Virtual Age*. Portsmouth: Boynton/Cook, 1992. This collection of essays explores the implications of using computers in the classroom, from electronic conferencing to hypermedia. Teachers who are new to computer technology might benefit from Chapter 12, "What Are They Talking About? Computer Terms That English Teachers May Need to Know," by Richard J. Selfe (207–18).

Hawisher, Gail E., and Charles Moran. "Electronic Mail and the Writing Instructor." *College English* 55 (1993): 627–43. The authors discuss the use of e-mail in teaching, with extensive bibliography.

Monroe, Rick. *Writing and Thinking with Computers: A Practical and Progressive Approach*. Urbana: NCTE, 1993. Monroe models hands-on practice in the computer classroom, including assignments and exercises such as "Electronic Read-Arounds" and "the business letter."

Reiss, Donna, at al., eds. *Electronic Communication Across the Curriculum.* Urbana, IL: NCTE, 1998. Written from a range of disciplinary perspectives, these essays discuss how teachers have used electronic communication to create communities within and across disciplines.

Tornow, Joan. *Link/Age: Composing in the Online Classroom.* Logan: Utah State UP, 1997. An ethnographical study of how students use language online and the implications for teaching composition.

54b Collaborating online

CLASSROOM IDEAS

COLLABORATIVE LEARNING Keep it small Students can experience shyness online just as they do in person, and you may find some voices dominating while others are always silent. Working in very small groups can help reticent students feel more comfortable about adding their voices to the conversation.

COLLABORATIVE LEARNING/COMPUTER ACTIVITY Backup class plan If you have to cancel a class, you can still hold class discussion if you have *Blackboard* or *WebCT* software for your course. Create a discussion topic and start several discussion threads. If you wish to have a live chat, you can set it up for the time your class would normally meet. Alternatively, you can have a delayed discussion and ask students to contribute to at least one thread before class meets again.

COMPUTER ACTIVITY/COLLABORATIVE LEARNING Online community I Ask students to have an online chat in which they brainstorm ideas for a study of community, anonymity, and identity online. Give them a time limit for their session (try 10 minutes), and have them save the transcript and then review later when they meet in person. Ask them to pick the best ideas from the transcript and present them to the class.

COMPUTER ACTIVITY/COLLABORATIVE LEARNING Online community II As a follow up to the first "Online community" exercise, have students participate in one or more Web forums with national or international membership in order to conduct their own research on the topic of anonymity, identity, and community online.

COMPUTER ACTIVITY/COLLABORATIVE LEARNING Naming conventions As a class, come up with a set of conventions for naming shared files that will work well for class assignments throughout the semester.

COMPUTER ACTIVITY/COLLABORATIVE LEARNING Comment requests In peer review, requests from the author about what the group should pay attention to in review are often helpful. Tell your students to use the Comment function of their word processor to insert questions they would like their peer group to respond to on their draft. This can help focus the critique so that it is as helpful as possible.

54c Creating effective Web compositions

CLASSROOM IDEAS

COMPUTER ACTIVITY Saving all the versions Tell students to keep each draft of their paper, including those that include the comments of their peer groups, in a separate file so that they can have a record of the progression of their own writing process. Later, they can look back over the drafts and discuss their writing process with you.

Hard copy hypertext Your students are probably already familiar with hypertext documents. You can point out to them that a hard copy of a paper-in-progress becomes hypertext document when it includes any of the following: peer review comments, instructor's comments, the author's notes for revision, or the next draft of the paper.

COMPUTER ACTIVITY/COLLABORATIVE LEARNING Online community III Ask your students to collect clippings from the Web forum they explored in the "Online community II" exercise on the previous page. Have them share their clipping files with the rest of their small group, and have group members respond with comments.

Spatial learners Some students will excel at creating architectural diagrams of their Web sites like the one shown on page 833. For students with comparatively weak writing skills, the knowledge that they have strengths in visual skills may boost their confidence and suggest how they can best approach prewriting.

Cite the site Students should be reminded that borrowing text from the Web sites of others is a form of plagiarism unless they give attribution. They should use proper quotation, paraphrase, and summary technique, and they may want to include links to the original sites from which they have borrowed material.

COMPUTER ACTIVITY Recommended HTML editors Ask your students to locate some online reviews of different HTML editors. On the basis of what they read, they can compose and send a memo to the rest of the class in which they discuss the various software packages and make a recommendation about which one class members should use.

COMPUTER ACTIVITY Checking the translation Students should remember to look to their papers after saving them as HTML documents but before posting them to your class Web site. They should not assume that their software is a flawless translator. It's always important for human eyes to check the work of the computer.

COMPUTER ACTIVITY Browsing for ideas To help students get started with their site plan sketches, encourage them to look at their favorite Web sites for ideas. They can evaluate the sites for structure, flow, clarity, essential content, ease of navigation, and choice of sound, video, or images; and they may want to adapt ideas they find on those Web sites for their own purposes.

COMPUTER ACTIVITY/COLLABORATIVE LEARNING Teamed Web site design
Point out to students that many Web sites are designed by professionals rather than the Web site owner. Your students could trade Web design consultation and services with a partner in class.

COMPUTER ACTIVITY Design contest   Find a campus or charity group that needs a Web site, and then hold a contest in your class to see which student can come up with the best Web site design, including content, structure, flow, and ease of navigation. This exercise could work especially well in a service learning course.

COMPUTER ACTIVITY/COLLABORATIVE LEARNING Troubleshooting   Have your students maintain an ongoing online discussion in which they can help each other troubleshoot any problems that arise as they work with their Web page files.

COMPUTER ACTIVITY/COLLABORATIVE LEARNING Reflecting on the process
Students can work in groups on creating a Web site on a topic of mutual interest. Then each group can try out the Web sites of the other groups and evaluate the content, structure, flow, and ease of navigation. Allow some time in class for groups to give feedback. Finally, ask each group to discuss how the process of creating a Web site differs from (or resembles) the process of writing a paper. They should consider all the steps along the way, from mapping/prewriting to proofreading.

Captioning photos   Have students bring in photos (not of themselves) that they are considering for inclusion on their Web pages. Collect all the photos, shuffle them, and pass them out to the members of the class. Ask each student to write a caption for the photograph he or she receives. Finally, have students read their captions and ask each photo's owner to identify what it really is. The discrepancies can be hilarious, and this will help students understand the importance of clarity in identifying the images on their Web pages.

COMPUTER ACTIVITY Virtual gallery   To give students practice in the technical side of putting images on their Web sites, establish a gallery page on your class Web site. Ask each student to select or create a photo or drawing on a theme of your choice, scan it, and post it to your class Web site.

COMPUTER ACTIVITY Virtual cinema   To give students practice in the technical side of putting video clips on their Web sites, have a film festival on your class Web site. Each student can find or create a one-minute video on a topic of your choice. If you choose a humorous topic, you can have a lot of fun with this activity.

COMPUTER ACTIVITY Virtual concert hall   To give students practice in the technical side of putting sound recordings on their Web sites, establish a concert hall on your class Web site. Students can post sound recordings. You might want to establish a topical theme, such as "songs about peace," or see how many versions of a single song (John Lennon's "Imagine," for instance) your students can locate.

RESOURCES AND IDEAS

Bass, Randy. "Story and Archive in the Twenty-First Century." *College English* 61 (1999); 659–70. Bass discusses the impact of hypertext and electronic media on English studies.

Myers, Jamie, et al. "Opportunities for Critical Literacy and Pedagogy in Student-Authored Hypermedia." *Handbook of Literacy and Technology: Transformations in a Post-Typographic World.* Ed. David Reinking et al. 63–78. An exploration of how students may develop their powers of critical literacy as they construct hypermedia texts.

CHAPTER 55

Public Writing

CHAPTER HIGHLIGHTS

This chapter focuses on multiple forms of public writing, including business letters and memos, job applications, reports and proposals, and a new section on writing for community work. The proliferation of service learning curricula in colleges and universities means that students may find themselves needing to write on behalf of a community organization. They may also need to write about their experience for their service learning course. Section 55d, "Writing for community work," includes samples of a flyer, a newsletter, and a brochure for a nonprofit organization.

Public writing should be a subject of considerable interest to your students, for almost all of them can imagine a future in which it plays an important role. Although people in business and nonprofit organizations generally write under strict time constraints, they use the same critical thinking, reading, and writing skills presented throughout the handbook to analyzes their audiences, plan their strategies, and compose their work. Professionals who write documents that represent their company or organization need to put a high value on correctness and clarity. Job applicants and laypeople writing business correspondence have similar needs for clarity and accuracy. This chapter emphasizes those virtues in all public writing situations.

MEDIA RESOURCES FOR CHAPTER 55

mycomplab²⁰ Please visit MyCompLab at *www.mycomplab.com* for more on the writing process.

http://www.ablongman.com/littlebrown ▶ See page 73 of this manual for companion Web site content description.

55a Writing business letters and memos

CLASSROOM IDEAS

MODELS OF STUDENT WRITING

"**Dear Ms. Herzog**" Janet Marley's letter of complaint is at once direct, concise, firm, and unemotional, and students may want to discuss exactly how Marley achieves this balance in the tone of her letter. Be prepared for your students to differ in their assessments of Marley's letter: some may think it quite daring while others may think it insufficiently forceful. They probably have their own ideas about how to write a letter of complaint, so you might want to let them revise the letter according to their own predilections. Then pass the revisions around the room and let the class assess the effectiveness of each student's revisions. If students pretend that they are Ann Herzog when they read one another's versions of the letter, they may find it easier to imagine how a circulation supervisor of a magazine would be likely to respond.

Students may find it helpful to use this letter as a model when formatting their own letters.

COLLABORATIVE LEARNING From the mailbox to the classroom Encourage students to bring in copies of professional correspondence they have received (on the job, from the college or university, as junk mail) and discuss the different kinds of formats and rhetorical strategies they find. What similarities and differences do they discover? Can they relate these to the purpose and audience of each communication? Making students aware of such factors helps them realize that business communication employs the same writing strategies as other kinds of writing.

COLLABORATIVE LEARNING Complaint letters Invite students to write letters of complaint about issues (large or small) that have always bothered them but that they have never taken the time to address. Then ask students to work in small groups to critique the letters from the vantage point of the community leaders, legislators, or businesspeople who might receive them. This exercise in role playing may help students to understand the value of discretion and cogency, even in a complaint letter.

COLLABORATIVE LEARNING Memo sharing Encourage students to bring in memos from their current or previous places of business. Photocopy a set of five to ten memos and ask students to work in groups to identify indications of purpose and audience, and to evaluate the clarity and effectiveness of each memo.

COLLABORATIVE LEARNING A strong lead The first paragraph of a memo is the most important one. Have your students practice drafting the first paragraph of a memo, in which they present a solution, make a recommendation, provide an answer, or give an evaluation. They can circulate their drafts in small groups and as a group pick the entry that is clearest and most succinct.

MODEL OF STUDENT WRITING

"2005 sales of Quick Wax in Territory 12" Patricia Phillips's memo is a fine example, one that might prompt a class discussion on how purpose for writing and audience can vary widely in business writing. Each of the other models of writing in this chapter (the letter of complaint on p. 840, the application letter on p. 846, and the résumés on pp. 848 and 849) asks for something significant and is addressed to readers who may be disinclined to do what the writer asks. Those situations demand that the writer pay extra attention to tone. Memo writers, in contrast, usually want to write as quickly and efficiently as possible, and unless they are writing about a very sensitive matter, they do not need to fine-tune their tone or presentation. Ask your students to evaluate Phillips's purpose and audience in order to see why directness is appropriate in her memo.

COMPUTER ACTIVITY Memo templates Your students' word-processing software probably has one or more memo templates that can streamline the process of creating a memo. Your students may wish to use one of these templates or modify one of them to suit their purposes more exactly. Alternatively, your students can create a template entirely of their own devising and store it on their computers. They might want to use the elements listed in 55a3 as a guideline.

COLLABORATIVE LEARNING Evaluating the urgency Give your students a set of memos and have them work in small groups to discuss which memos are urgent enough to be sent by fax and which ought to go by e-mail.

COMPUTER ACTIVITY Electronic wizards Most word-processing programs have wizards, tools that can help students create memos and faxes and then help them send their documents electronically, either as faxes or as e-mail.

RESOURCES AND IDEAS

Drenk, Dean. "Teaching Finance Through Writing." *Teaching Writing in All Disciplines.* Ed. C. Williams Griffith. San Francisco: Jossey-Bass, 1982. 53–58. Drenk discusses the use of writing exercises to improve student handling of business discourse.

Hafer, Gary R. "Computer-Assisted Illustration and Instructional Documents in Technical Writing Classes." *Computers and Composition* 13 (1996): 49–56. Hafer argues for the advantages of teaching technical writing in the electronic classroom and offers practical advice on how to create instructional teams and design assignments.

Keene, Michael L. "Technical Information in the Information Economy." *Perspectives on Research and Scholarship in Composition.* Ed. Ben W. McClelland and Timothy R. Donovan. New York: MLA, 1985. Keene reviews research in technical and business communication.

Lanham, Richard. *Revising Business Prose.* 4th ed. New York: Macmillan, 1999. Lanham offers strategies for recognizing and eliminating "businessese" from professional writing.

Mehaffy, Robert, and Constance Warloe. "Corporate Communications: Next Step for the Community Colleges?" *The Technical Writing Teacher* 16 (1989): 1–11. Mehaffy and Warloe show the curriculum design for a professional writing course taking into account adult learning styles, computer-assisted composition, reader-centered writing, interviewing for information, project management, and team design.

Mendelson, Michael. "Business Prose and the Nature of the Plain Style." *Journal of Business Communication* 24.2 (1987): 3–18. Mendelson demonstrates how various stylistic possibilities afford students different persuasive strategies.

Odell, Lee, and Dixie Goswami, eds. *Writing in Nonacademic Settings.* New York: Guilford, 1985. This essay collection encompasses the theory and practice of writing in the workplace, with heavy emphasis on ethnographic studies of "real" writers at work.

Rogers, Priscilla S. and Jone Rymer. "Analytical Tools to Facilitate Translations into New Writing Contexts: A Communicative Perspective." *Journal of Business Communication* 38.2 (2001): 112–50. The authors studied the writing of business students and developed a matrix for assessing an overcoming deficiencies.

55b Writing a job application

CLASSROOM IDEAS

MODEL OF STUDENT WRITNG

"Dear Mr. Chipault" Students (and job applicants in general) often have a hard time writing reader-based letters of application. Some have difficulty selling their skills strongly enough; some focus on why they need or want the job more than on what they have to offer. Ian Irvine presents his qualifications succinctly and organizes his information well. Your students may disagree, however, about the effectiveness of his letter: some may think it lacks pizzazz; others may like the formality and professionalism of its tone.

Irvine's letter (and the two versions of Irvine's résumé on pp. 848 and 849) may make for a good class discussion. Begin by asking your students to imagine they are Raymond Chipault at the *Dallas News.* Have them read Irvine's letter and decide whether it makes them want to read his résumé. Have them give justifications for their decisions and make any suggestions for revision they deem appropriate. Finally, ask them to read one of the résumés and decide whether they would want to interview Irvine. Again, they should justify their decisions and make suggestions for revision.

COLLABORATIVE LEARNING Job-application clinic Have students work in groups to critique each other's résumés and cover letters. Encourage the groups to ask each candidate about information that seems inconsistent or unclear as well as to check for errors. You might even have the group members pretend to be employers and conduct mock interviews based upon the applicant's materials.

COMPUTER ACTIVITY Standing out in the crowd Students writing with a word processor may be able to take advantage of several commercially prepared résumé-formatting packages. Although these programs are useful, remind students that hiring officers at companies may see literally thousands of these cookie-cutter résumés each year. The time students spend individualizing their own résumés may result in documents that better catch and keep a reader's attention.

Remind students to check each printout or copy of their résumés to be sure it is as clean and sharp as possible. This is especially important if the résumé will be photocopied or electronically scanned.

COMPUTER ACTIVITY/COLLABORATIVE LEARNING E-résumés Ask each student to e-mail an electronic résumé (as an attachment) to a partner in the class. Have the partner read the résumé both onscreen and in printout form and give feedback on design and keywords. The partner should attempt to open the attachment using as many different word-processing programs as possible, in order to verify that the document can be translated with its formatting intact.

MODELS OF STUDENT WRITING

Ian Irvine's résumés These two résumés present the same content in different design formats. In both versions, the content is well arranged and the use of parallelism is precise. You can have your students read these résumés in conjunction with Irvine's application letter on p. 846. Ask students to react to the two different designs—traditional and contemporary—and to discuss what kinds of jobs each design might be best suited for.

55c Writing business reports and proposals

CLASSROOM IDEAS

Other course assignments If your students are taking other courses in which they have report-writing assignments, you could allow them to work on one of those in your course. Contact the instructor of the other course first to discuss whether such an arrangement is feasible and desirable.

COMPUTER ACTIVITY Report gallery Many organizations publish reports online. Have students locate a report from an organization that interests them and create a link to it on your class Web site so other students can view the report.

COLLABORATIVE LEARNING Proposal drafting As an in-class exercise, have students draft a proposal that ice cream should be served in all campus classes daily. Then have them trade papers with a partner and evaluate each other's proposals.

55d Writing for community work

CLASSROOM IDEAS

Presenting documents Ask students to bring in a written document from an organization for which they volunteer or would like to volunteer. Each student can pass the document around and explain what its purpose is, whether they think it is a good example of its kinds, and what they might do to improve it.

Surveying the literature Assign students to attend their student activities fair and observe which flyers or handouts seem to them the most appealing, clear, and effective.

Real-world assignments If your students are in a service learning course and need to write a document for an organization, you could allow them to work on that document as an assignment for your course as well. The principles of good writing and document design which you are teaching will have an immediate and real-world significance to your students.

COMPUTER ACTIVITY AND COLLABORATIVE LEARNING Class newsletter As a class, take on a small service project, such as organizing contributions to World Hunger Day on campus. Have students work together to create two versions of a flyer, a print version to be posted around campus and an electronic version to be sent to students by e-mail.

Oral Presentations

CHAPTER HIGHLIGHTS

Many educators, businesses, and institutions consider the ability to articulate ideas thoughtfully and effectively within a group or in larger public settings to be the most significant and most under-emphasized of educational goals. While writing classes often include an informal speech component, planned oral presentations can help students to develop their critical reading, writing, and *speaking* skills as part of a cohesive process.

Chapter 56 suggests ways to integrate a speechmaking component into the writing curriculum. In particular, it identifies ways in which the handbook's emphasis on critical thinking can be expanded to help students prepare and deliver oral presentations, including identifying the topic, purpose, and audience for the speech; organizing and presenting the material in a way that effectively foregrounds the motivational or informational qualities of the speech; and becoming aware of various strategies for vocal and physical delivery and of ways to cope with presentation anxiety. The chapter also includes a "Checklist for an oral presentation" (p. 856) that students can use in preparing for their speeches and in critiquing each other's presentations. Finally, this edition of the handbook includes a new discussion of how to use PowerPoint effectively in oral presentations.

MEDIA RESOURCES FOR CHAPTER 56

mycomplab Please visit MyCompLab at *www.mycomplab.com* for more on the writing process.

http://www.ablongman.com/littlebrown ▶ See page page 73 of this manual for companion Web site content description.

56b Considering purpose and audience

INSTRUCTOR RESOURCE

The following Presentation Aid is available for download on this book's companion Web site at *http://www.ablongman.com/littlebrown*.

PRESENTATION AID 56.1: Checklist for an oral presentation (p. 856)

CLASSROOM IDEAS

COMPUTER ACTIVITY Global warming presentation I Have your students do a Web search to gather the most current information on the topic of global warming and write up a brief statement of purpose for a presentation they could make on this topic. (Note: This is the first of a series of activities suggested for this chapter. You can do them either individually or as a linked series. You can stick with the topic of global warming or use another topic of your own choosing. If you focus on global warming, you may want to direct students to the case study on evaluating a Web site on pages 604–08.)

COLLABORATIVE LEARNING Checklist interviews Have students break into pairs and work through the checklist for oral presentation. Each partner can take turns asking the checklist questions about the other partner's oral presentation. The "interviewer" can take notes about what the "interviewee" says and then give feedback.

COLLABORATIVE LEARNING Model speeches Watching or listening to speechmakers is a good way to get some experience in how they work. Invite students to gather with classmates outside of class to tune in to speeches on C-Span or network television. They can hold informal discussions about the speeches they hear and then share their findings with the rest of the class.

COLLABORATIVE LEARNING Global warming presentation II To help students get practice in pitching a presentation to a specific audience, ask them to work in groups to outline a presentation on global warming for three different audiences: an elementary-school science class; a campaign fundraiser for a political candidate; and an association of automobile executives. They should aim to keep their central argument the same for each version but decide how they will tailor the presentation appropriately for each audience.

56c Organizing the presentation

CLASSROOM IDEAS

COLLABORATIVE LEARNING Good first impressions on a boring topic In small groups, have students outline an introduction to a presentation on driving etiquette for the campus student body. They can brainstorm different ways of making this potentially boring topic interesting to listeners.

COMPUTER ACTIVITY Global warming presentation III Choose one or more of the outlines created by groups of students in the "Global Warming II" exercise and post it to your class Web site. Then ask students to surf the Web looking for apt quotations, images, or stories to support the presentation. They can post their findings for the rest of the class to review.

56d Delivering the presentation

CLASSROOM IDEAS

COLLABORATIVE LEARNING Global warming presentation IV Having students do a dry run of their global warming presentation with a partner or their small group. Rehearsing is an effective way to reduce anxiety about public speaking and learn to adapt to a live audience.

CULTURE LANGUAGE **Accent, grammar, and credibility** Students who speak English with an accent may fear that they will not be perceived as credible by some members of their audience. Reassure them that as long as an accent doesn't interfere with the audience's ability to understand them, it is not a liability for a public speaker. However, anyone who makes frequent lapses in grammar, whether they be native English speakers or not, may well be perceived as less credible by members of their audience. So remind your students to be rigorous in applying their knowledge of correct grammar to their oral presentations.

COMPUTER ACTIVITY Global warming presentation V Have students prepare a *PowerPoint* presentation to go with their speech on global warming. They might want to put their supporting material (images, statistics, quotations) on *PowerPoint*. They might even choose to display an outline of their main arguments onscreen.

COLLABORATIVE LEARNING *PowerPoint* **tryout** Students can try out different feature options (such as backgrounds, colors, and fonts) in drafts of their presentation. Peer groups can provide quick assessments of the effectiveness of various feature choices to help each writer know what revisions to make.

RESOURCES AND IDEAS

Beason, Larry. "Ethos and Error: How Business People React to Errors." *College Composition and Communication* 53 (2001): 33–64. Beason's study suggests that business leaders see errors in business communication as a sign of carelessness and faulty thinking and would be reluctant to hire applications who commit such errors.

Felske, Claudia Klein. "Beyond the Page: Students as Actor-Readers." *English* 95 (2005): 58–63. The author explains a method she uses to help students understand Shakespeare and develop their oral language skills.

George, Don. "Peer Support in Speech Preparation." *Speech Communication Teacher* 7.3 (1993): 4–5. A brief piece describing exercises for cultivating a team approach to public speaking using debating club strategies.

Hallmark, James R. "Using Your Computer to Evaluate Speeches." And Arnie Madson. "Computer-Assisted Comments for Research Papers and Speeches." Both in *Speech Communication Teacher* 9.3 (1995): 14–15. These two short pieces on computerized narrative evaluations identify the uses and limitations of programs that supply generic evaluations that can be tailored to individual student presentations.

Lucas, Stephen E. *The Art of Public Speaking*. 9th ed. New York: McGraw-Hill, 2001. This is a standard speech communication textbook that can be used to integrate a speechmaking component onto the writing classroom. See also Lucas's videotaped collection, *Speeches for Analysis and Discussion* (New York: Random, 1989).

Menzel, Kent E., and Lori J. Carrell. "The Relationship Between Preparation and Performance in Public Speaking." *Communication Education* 43 (1994): 17–26. Explores the effects of factors like anxiety level, preparation time, and scholastic ability on the quality of oral presentations. The authors show, for example, that time spent on preparing visual aids adds to an effective delivery, partly because of the motivational and anxiety-reducing effects.

Rowan, Katherine E. "A New Pedagogy for Explanatory Public Speaking: Why Arrangement Should Not Substitute for Invention." *Communication Education* 44.3 (1995): 236–50. Rowan makes the case against current speech communication textbooks that focus on the organization of definitions, examples, and visual aids without recognizing the process of critical thinking through which students develop the content of the speech in relation to effective modes of presentation.

Shachtman, Thomas. *The Inarticulate Society: Eloquence and Culture in America*. New York : Free Press, 1995. Shachtman uses an historical overview of the changing value put on eloquence in American society to argue that there is a marked decline in public articulateness, a decline that is rapidly undermining the democratic system.

Sullivan, Gwendolyn F. "Improving Delivery Skills: The Practice Impromptu." *Speech Communication Teacher* 11.2 (1997): 5–6. This short piece describes group activities and preparatory exercises (such as inviting a guest speaker) that help students learn to deliver impromptu speeches.

Whitworth, Randolph H., and Claudia Cochran. "Evaluation of Integrated Versus Unitary Treatment for Reducing Public Speaking Anxiety." *Communication Education* 45 (1996): 306–21. A highly technical case study of the relative merits of using or combining skills training, visualization therapy, and "communication orientation motivation therapy" in overcoming presentation anxiety. The results show the importance of combining skills training with other anxiety-reducing approaches.